MONKS, MIRACLES AND MAGIC

Helen Parish presents an innovative new study of Reformation attitudes to medieval Christianity, revealing the process by which the medieval past was rewritten by Reformation propagandists. This fascinating account sheds light on how the myths and legends of the Middle Ages were reconstructed, reinterpreted and formed into a historical base for the Protestant church in the sixteenth century.

Despite the iconoclastic impulse that underpinned the Reformation in England, this bold new work demonstrates that traditional images of saints, popes, miracles and wonders were not expunged from the religious lexicon but, rather, appropriated, reformed and deployed in the service of religious change.

Crossing the often artificial boundary between medieval and modern history, Parish draws upon a valuable selection of writings on the *lives* of the saints from both periods, and addresses ongoing debates over the relationship between religion and the supernatural in early modern Europe.

Setting key case studies in a broad conceptual framework, *Monks, Miracles and Magic* is essential reading for all those with an interest in the construction of the Protestant church and its medieval past.

Helen L. Parish is Lecturer in History at the University of Reading, author of *Clerical Marriage and the English Reformation* (2000) and co-editor of *Religion and Superstition in Reformation Europe* (2003).

MONKS, MIRACLES AND MAGIC

Reformation representations of the medieval church

Helen L. Parish

Routledge
Taylor & Francis Group

LONDON AND NEW YORK

First published 2005
by Routledge
2 Park Square, Milton Park, Abingdon, Oxon OX14 4RN

Simultaneously published in the USA and Canada
by Routledge
270 Madison Ave, New York, NY 10016

Routledge is an imprint of the Taylor & Francis Group
© 2005 Helen L. Parish

Typeset in Goudy by Bookcraft Ltd, Stroud, Gloucestershire
Printed and bound in Great Britain by TJ International Ltd,
Padstow, Cornwall

British Library Cataloguing in Publication Data
A catalogue record for this book is available from the British Library

Library of Congress Cataloging in Publication Data
1 Church history – Middle Ages, 600–1500   2 Church history –
16th century   3 Reformation   4 Christian saints – Cult – History
of doctrines – Middle Ages, 600–1500   I Title
BR280.P37 2005
270.3'072–dc22
2004016256

ISBN 0-415-31688-X (hbk)
ISBN 0-415-31689-8 (pbk)

CONTENTS

PLATES

ACKNOWLEDGEMENTS

Many debts, professional and personal, have been incurred in researching and writing this book. The project had its origin in work I undertook as a Junior Research Fellow at Wolfson College, Oxford, and I am extremely grateful to the Fellows, staff, and students of the College who provided an environment that was as congenial as it was conducive to study. In recent years I have also benefited greatly from the support of colleagues in the School of History at the University of Reading. Colleagues in early modern history have provided a sympathetic ear, while those in medieval history have tolerated with good humour the ignorant questions of a Reformation specialist. I am particularly grateful to the School and University for a generous period of sabbatical leave, and to the Arts and Humanities Research Board, whose award of a Research Leave Award enabled the completion of the book. I have also benefited from the opportunity to present early drafts of sections of the book to research seminars at the University of Oxford, the University of Reading, University College, Chichester and the University of Birmingham. Participants at the Reformation Studies Colloquium, the Annual Conference of the Tyndale Society and the European Reformation Research Group have been more helpful than they may realise in correcting misconceptions and opening up new avenues for exploration. Readers for the press made helpful and constructive observations, and the advice of editorial staff at Routledge has been consistently prompt and perceptive.

I am grateful to Alison Butler of the University of Bristol for allowing me to read her paper on Pope Silvester II, and to Dr Alexandra Kess of the University of St Andrews for her advice in tracking down references to the works of Johannes Sleidan. I am especially thankful to staff at the British Academy John Foxe project who have provided advice on all things Foxeian, particularly Dr Tom Freeman, who generously allowed me to read his work on Foxe's histories of the medieval papacy prior to its publication on the project website. Sections of Chapter 5 are reproduced with the kind permission of *Sixteenth Century Journal*.

Research for this book has been made all the more enjoyable by the assistance and expertise of the staff of the Bodleian Library in Oxford, the British Library and the University Library in Reading. Gill Cannell at the Parker Library, Corpus Christi College, Cambridge, was particularly helpful and supportive of my efforts to locate texts and documents in the collection. Generous assistance with the illustrations was provided by Allan Soedring, Anne Marshall, Gill Cannell and the staff of the Rare Books Room and Media Production Department of the University of Reading. Plate 1 appears with the permission of Allan Soedring, Plate 2 with the permission of Anne Marshall, Plate 3 with the permission of the Master and Fellows of Corpus Christi College, Cambridge and Plate 4 with the permission of the Library of the University of Reading.

On a more personal note, I have benefited greatly from frequent and timely reminders that there is more to life than medieval saints and Reformation polemicists. Friends and family have been a constant support, and my husband Gavin has treated my ongoing obsessions with a mixture of good humour and penetrating criticism. My father, Peter Parish, tolerated his daughter's reluctance to consider anything after 1800 as 'proper history' with the greatest respect; his death in 2002 was the loss of a parent, friend and inspiration. I am sure he would have been duly critical of what follows.

Stylistic note

In quotations from primary sources, the original spelling has been retained, although Roman numerals in signature references are represented in Arabic form in the notes. The italicisation of *life* and *lives* throughout the text is intended to identify the written biography, or *life* of the saint. Dates are in Old Style, but the year has been taken to begin on January 1.

1

INTRODUCTION

It was in the person of the saint that the many worlds of medieval religion coalesced. The saint existed, both in heaven and on earth, as a spiritual companion whose bodily remains acted as a conduit through which the supernatural intruded into the material world. The saint straddled the boundary of the living and the dead, as a patron and protector whose intercession was vital to the safety and the salvation of the individual. The saint stood at the intersection of Christianity and paganism, in the encounter between a missionary church and its rivals and in the delineation of a Christian supernatural which shaped the relationship between the miracles of the church and the magic of its opponents. The saint personified the common ground between learned theology and popular piety, where local pressures might influence institutional pronouncements and where the didactic purpose of the preacher found expression in familiar words and images. The saint also provided a crucial link between the past and the present, a figure through which models of piety from a previous age could inspire faith and virtue in the present, and through which the faith of the present could shape the record of the past.[1] The role and function of the saint extended from the pastoral to the punitive, from the miraculous to the mundane, and was rehearsed in the liturgy of the church, commemorated in shrines and images, and promoted in print and from the pulpit. It is not surprising, therefore, that the cult of the saints rapidly became a central issue in the debates and controversies of the Reformation. Saints who had dominated the landscape of lay religion became monuments to the presence of false doctrine and superstition in the medieval church. The miracles of the saints, which had acted as signs of their privileged position, were recast as symbols of the magic that was inherent in the faith and traditions of medieval Catholicism. The *lives* of the saints were exploited, not as evidence of piety and virtue among the heroes of the church, but as testimony to the flawed foundations upon which the history of the church was constructed. As the fragmentation of the doctrinal unity of western Christendom gained visible expression in the shattered images of the saints, so the *lives* and legends of the saints were likewise subjected to a process of destruction and reconstruction, and pressed into the service of the nascent reformed church.

The cult of the saints has long been used as a barometer of popular piety in the era of the Reformation. Historians seeking evidence of continued participation in the life of the medieval church, and the enduring popularity of traditional devotional practices, have seen in the cult of the saints a tangible measure of popular enthusiasm for Catholicism.[2] Those looking for evidence of decline and decay have pointed to the existence of a popular refrain of criticism of saints and images, voiced by English Lollards in the fourteenth and fifteenth centuries, and repeated in the debates of the Reformation.[3] By the early sixteenth century, opposition to the cult of images and the veneration of the saints had become a key component in the definition of heterodoxy; as Stephen Gardiner noted, 'in England they are called Lollards, who, denying images, thought therewithal the crafts of painting and graving to be generally superfluous and naught, and against God's law'.[4] Images were condemned as idols, and miracles as superstition and magic. Pilgrimages were satirised as a form of ecclesiastically sponsored tourism, taking in shrines and relics that had been invented or manufactured by money-hungry clerics. However humorous the caricature of the pilgrim, Reformation debates over sanctity and the cult of the saints were far from peripheral, but reached to the heart of doctrinal controversy. Faith in the intercession of the saints provided a testing ground for debates over the authority of Scripture and tradition. Traditional constructs of sanctity embodied characteristics of holiness that were not easily accommodated within the paradigms of piety presented in evangelical polemic. Unmarried clergy and chaste monks presented an unwelcome model of sanctity for those who rejected vows of chastity and argued in favour of a married priesthood. The founders of religious orders, and saints who had chosen and promoted the monastic life, sat uneasily as popular heroes for an English church in which the monasteries had been suppressed. Holy women sustained only by communion wafers, who mortified their flesh and laid claim to insight into the affairs of church and state, set an undesirable example in the England of the 1530s. And saints, most obviously Thomas Becket, whose reputation was erected upon their defence of the liberties of the church from the predations of the monarch, established a pattern of sanctity which provided a dangerous precedent for opposition to the Reformation in the 1530s and 1540s. It is no wonder then that sanctity and the cult of the saints acquired a prominent position in debate, controversy and action in the first decades of the Reformation.

The ease with which the physical and mental images of the saints were removed from the devotional landscape of sixteenth-century England has been the subject of prolonged debate. John Huizinga remarked upon the vigorous attack on the cult of the saints that characterised the Reformation, but concluded that 'nowhere in the whole contested area did it meet with less resistance'.[5] Older histories of the Reformation in England offer some support for this contention, in their emphasis upon the apparent enthusiasm with which the English people participated in the destruction of the great pilgrimage shrines and the suppression of the cult of saints and images.[6] In contrast, much recent scholarship has argued for the enduring popularity of traditional religion on the eve of the Reformation, a popularity reflected in widespread participation in pilgrimage, devotion to the saints and substantial investment in the very images and artefacts that the Reformation sought to destroy. Before the advent of reform, it is suggested, official orthodoxy and local custom had combined to create a system of belief that was broadly based and acted as a cohesive force in the local and national community.[7] The impact of this 'revisionism' has been to remind us that the Reformation was not an event, but a slow process by which Protestantism became established in England over several successive generations. Ronald Hutton has demonstrated that Catholic practices often survived and, indeed, retained their vitality until the very moment that they were proscribed, while Robert Whiting has revealed that reactions to the Reformation could be shaped as much by passivity in the face of government-sponsored reform. This approach has been enhanced by several recent studies of the processes by which the Reformation was negotiated in the parishes and by which the enthusiasms of the early English evangelicals came to be accommodated within the culture that they sought to reform. The people of England, it has been suggested, were weaned, not 'roughly snatched', from traditional religious practices.[8]

Such conclusions have thrown into relief the contrast between the vitality of late-medieval Catholicism, including the cult of the saints, and the apparent vulnerability of the church and its popular devotional practices to evangelical attack in the sixteenth century.[9] George Bernard has argued convincingly that, although the Catholic church had successfully ridden the storm whipped up by its late-medieval critics, the very popularity of late-medieval piety contained the seeds of its own destruction at the hands of English evangelicals. Widespread participation in the cult of saints and relics, for example, left the church exposed to damaging criticisms of the excesses of popular devotion. Once one apparently fraudulent miracle had been identified, it was hard to find a convincing defence against accusations that the church had repeatedly deceived the faithful with false relics and wonders. The apparent discovery of errors and abuses at some of most popular pilgrimage sites in England lent weight to demands for further reform, precisely because these shrines were such a prominent feature of the devotional landscape.[10] The criticisms levelled against the church by English evangelicals were persuasive primarily because they touched upon areas of the devotional life of the church in which there was widespread popular participation.

The popularity of the cult of the saints and pilgrimage on the eve of the Reformation provided English evangelicals with a vast array of recognisable referents upon which to hang their criticisms of medieval piety, with the result that the rhetoric of the reformers continued to be heavily laden with traditional vocabulary. The attack on the physical presence of the saints in shrines and relics facilitated a fundamental assault upon the theology which underpinned faith in the intercession of the saints and encouraged the withdrawal of official support for pivotal devotional practices. However, while destruction of the shrines and images of the saints provided a visible expression of doctrinal change, the material destruction at the hands of the iconoclasts was accompanied by an equally destructive remoulding of images and histories of sainthood and holiness. The communication of the message of the Reformation was accomplished, not only by iconoclasm, but also by the exploitation of enduring images of piety and devotion and the deployment of the past in the service of reform.

The relationship between the reformers and the saints was therefore more complex than the moment of iconoclasm suggests, and the middle decades of the sixteenth century witnessed a debate over saints and images that extended into the realms of miracle, magic, history and politics. Recent years have seen the publication of more detailed investigations into both the impact of the theology of the Reformation upon the cult of the saints and the role that the suppression of the saints played in shaping polemical defences of doctrinal change.[11] The destruction of images, cults and pilgrimages emerged as a priority for the first generation of reformers, and served both as a motivation for religious change and as a justification for such change in the 1530s and 1540s. Evidence that relics, images and miracles had been invented or 'feigned' by the clergy was presented before king and country to vindicate the suppression of the cult, but also facilitated the casting of Henry VIII and his son Edward VI in the role of biblical leaders, delivering their subjects from the yoke of false religion.[12] The Reformation has been represented as the triumph of the printed word over the image of the saint, but the image of the saint clearly survived, albeit in an altered form, in the printed word of evangelical propaganda.[13] English evangelical writers actively engaged with the literature and images contained in traditional hagiographical writing, with the result that the saints of the medieval church were not simply rejected but, rather, recast as players in an unfolding historical and doctrinal drama. The influence of models from the past in the dynamics of Protestant martyrdom in the sixteenth century has been well documented. Those who suffered for their faith in the middle decades of the sixteenth century were represented in evangelical literature as the most recent links in a chain of witnesses to the truth throughout history, a chain that stretched from the early martyrs, through those persecuted by the medieval church, to the fires at Smithfield and beyond.[14] Even in the writings of John Bale, perhaps the most scathing critic of medieval hagiography, there are glimpses of a traditional genre twisted to a new purpose.[15] The miracle-working saints of the medieval church were supplanted by the 'poor persecuted little flock' as the model for pious imitation, and their *lives* remodelled as narratives of superstition, treason and fraud. The convergence of history and hagiography in the literature of the Reformation exposes a multifaceted relationship between English evangelicals and the cult of the saints, and between the sixteenth-century church and the medieval past.

The influence of the medieval past in shaping the Reformation in England has long been recognised. Some 35 years ago, F.J. Levy highlighted the centrality of history and historical anachronism to the debates of the Reformation, while May McKisack identified the many 'enticements' to the study of the past created by religious and political upheaval in sixteenth-century England.[16] The division of Christendom, it has been suggested, served to crystallise a sense of national community which found its roots in history and historical discourse.[17] The search for precedent in the past certainly provided a crucial part of the defence of the Tudor monarchy and more particularly of the Henrician Reformation in the 1530s. An eclectic cast of characters from Constantine to King John afforded both an ancestry for the dynasty and a model for English resistance to the power of the pope in ages past.[18] In a recent study of the reign of Edward VI, Stephen Alford has reminded us of the process by which the mid-sixteenth century kingship was constructed from biblical and historical precedent.[19] For those who fashioned the image of the godly monarch, there was much to be gained from dialogue between the living and the dead, and from the utilisation of press and pulpit in order to bring the present into contact with the past. History was a powerful weapon in religious controversy, and the appeal to *sola scriptura* did not deafen evangelical propagandists to the persuasive voices of figures from the English past.[20] The value inherent in the possession of the past was recognised by sixteenth-century polemicists, churchmen, and monarchs, and was reflected in the peregrinations of John Leland, in John Foxe's construction of a universal history and in Matthew Parker's attempts to reassemble the fragmented records of the national church.[21] History was a malleable resource which could be summoned in the defence of change and as an answer to those who criticised the Reformation as novelty, innovation and schism. The representation of the monarch as heir to a biblical prototype and successor to royal critics of the church in centuries past provided the nascent national church with a useable historical narrative from which the Reformation emerged, not as innovation, but as restoration. Religious division had not only fuelled the appeal to the past in the literature of the Reformation but it also resulted in the construction of a national, Protestant history which itself contributed to the hardening of religious and political identities.

The persuasive power of historical writing in sixteenth-century England lay in the ubiquitous presence of the past in oral and literate culture. D.R.Woolf's investigation of the process which English men and women first became aware of their past argues for the existence of a 'wider historical culture' within which the historical and antiquarian endeavour found fulfilment. The past, he concludes, was constructed via a process of 'social circulation', in which local communities both transmitted factual detail and provided writers with a broad and receptive audience for their labours.[22] Likewise, Adam Fox has highlighted the variety of modes of expression through which the past was communicated in the early modern present, revealing evidence of a well-developed awareness of history and tradition which permeated all levels of English society.[23] The written record of the past, in chronicles, hagiography and romance literature, was widely transmitted by its repetition and elaboration in oral tradition. History was to be found in print, in the spoken word and in the local landscape, which acted as a visual mnemonic in the construction of a popular and familiar narrative of the past. The Reformation shattered the visual link between past and present, but also contributed to the standardisation of new myths and legends, which themselves entered into the canon of popular history through the medium of the printed word.[24] Evangelical writers broke apart traditional histories, myths and legends, which were then reconstructed and rewritten in order to create a history for the English church and its new-found independence from Rome. The same process was at work in the interaction between English evangelicals and the cult of the saints. At the most basic level, the relationship between the reformers and the saints was profoundly hostile, characterised by the denunciation and destruction of shrines and images, and the mockery of the 'monkish fictions' contained in medieval chronicles and hagiography. However, despite the criticisms of evangelical polemicists, the *lives* and legends of the saints were to become crucial building blocks in the construction of a new narrative of the medieval ecclesiastical past. The reformation of the cult of the saints was accompanied by the reformation of their *lives* and legends, not as models of piety and devotion, but as testimony to the presence of false theology and feigned wonders at the heart of the medieval church. The physical and polemical assault on the shrines of the saints was a tangible manifestation of religious change, but the reconstruction of the reputation of the saints at the hands of evangelical writers was itself a highly visible feature of the changing geography of the sacred in Reformation England.

The assumption that the Reformation marked a radical disjuncture with the medieval past has been tempered by a greater awareness of continued presence of images from that past in the transmission of a reformed religious culture. Traditional emphasis upon the success of the Reformation in opening a fracture between the reformed church and the faith and practice of the past has been modified by evidence of syncretism and adaptation in the communication of the message of the Reformation.[25] The saints were a critical part of this process. The figure of St Peter, used by Catholic propagandists in the defence of papal primacy, was first denigrated by English evangelicals in their assault on the authority of Rome, and then transformed into a model of reformed piety in order to create a bridge between past and present.[26] The controversy surrounding the 'Kalendar' of the martyrs presented in Foxe's *Actes and Monumentes* (1583) demonstrates clearly the passions that could be aroused by such exploitation of traditional forms to communicate new content. Damian Nussbaum has argued convincingly that the traditional genre of the calendar was an ideal means by which to define a shape and character for the reformed English church and introduce Foxe's reader to a Protestant narrative of the past, populated by more suitable heroes.[27] Alexandra Walsham's *Providence in Early Modern England* presents a sustained and persuasive account of the creation of a post-Reformation culture which both overlapped with and departed from elements of traditional belief. Despite the efforts of the propagandists, Walsham suggests, the subtle difference between the false wonders of the papists and the special providences enjoyed by the Protestants was one which may well have escaped the understanding of the majority. The doctrine of providence thus blended old and new and 'cut across the invisible iron curtain which contemporary polemic erected between Rome and Geneva'. The result was a conceptual framework in which recourse to an apparently traditional religious supernatural was part of the process of adaptation to new Protestant orthodoxies.[28] If providences provided English Protestantism with a familiar medium for the transmission of new theologies, so it was the rewriting of traditional hagiography that enabled early English evangelicals to transform the saints of the medieval church into a mouthpiece for the Reformation.

The attitude of English evangelical polemicists to the *lives* of the medieval saints illustrates the relationship between history, miracle and magic in the construction of confessional identity in Reformation England. Evangelical writers were reluctant to accord history any normative value in doctrinal controversy, but the records of the past still had a crucial role to play in shaping Reformation debates over the authority of the papacy, the sacraments of the church, and the *lives* and miracles of the saints. Deepening doctrinal division threatened to open an unbridgeable gulf between the past and the present yet, by the end of the sixteenth century, a recognisable narrative of English Protestant history had been constructed which anchored the Reformation in the national past and presented a formidable challenge to traditional assumptions surrounding the history of the church and its saints. Those who defined and defended religious change in England plundered the past for heroes and villains, and provided them with an active role in the conflict between true and false religion throughout Christian history. The Catholic church of the sixteenth century was condemned for using the words and actions of its saints and leaders in the past. Reformation iconoclasm reached beyond the images of the saints and into the very image of sainthood, but here the purpose was not simply destruction but reconstruction and reformation, in order that the *lives* and legends of the saints might be used to give shape to a narrative of ecclesiastical history dominated by manipulation, magic and fraud. Evangelical polemicists created a past that was populated by proto-Protestants who defended the faith of the gospel from the traditions of men, and by Catholic saints and popes whose *lives* and miracles were testimony to doctrinal innovation and corruption in the institutional church. With the origins of the reformed church and its battle with false religion firmly anchored in the events of the past, this same interpretation of the past could be exploited to build a sense of communal identity amid the turmoil of the Reformation. The creation of a useable past by English evangelicals exposes the process by which the Reformation both shaped, and was shaped by, the history of the medieval church.[29]

This process is immediately apparent in evangelical attitudes to those saints whose miracles were cited in defence of the Catholic doctrine, and whose relics had provided a focus for devotion and pilgrimage in the pursuit of curative wonders. The medieval miraculous lay at the heart of Reformation reinterpretations of the *lives* of the saints and provided the staple for evangelical writing against the ecclesiastical supernatural and the magic of the medieval church. Keith Thomas' magisterial work *Religion and the Decline of Magic* has continued to shape the current understanding of attitudes to miracle and magic in early modern England. The medieval church, Thomas suggests, 'appeared as a vast reservoir of magical power' which could be tapped via its rituals, ceremonies and sacraments, and deployed for a variety of pious and practical purposes. Evangelical denunciations of the miracles and magic of the medieval church, Thomas suggests, were reflective of a more general effort to purge traditional religion of its magical elements and place the individual in a direct relationship with the divine.[30] The investigation of the miracles of the medieval saints was a crucial part of the process by which the boundaries of the supernatural were redrawn and religion purged of magical influences. Since the publication of *Religion and the Decline of Magic*, there have been numerous attempts to redefine and reinterpret the relationship between the Reformation and the 'magic' of the medieval church. Such work has served to highlight the complexity of the relationship between the Reformation and the supernatural, and added further colour to the spectrum of beliefs and attitudes that characterised Catholic and Protestant writing on wonders, miracles and demonic illusions. Early modern Europe remained a world of signs and wonders in which the boundaries between miracle, magic, science and religion were vigorously debated.[31]

Reformation criticisms of the miracles of the saints were in no sense a rejection of the possibility that the supernatural might intrude into the material world; indeed the capacity of the devil to work wonders was one of the few areas of common ground among Catholic and Protestant writers. What mattered was the source of the supernatural power behind true miracle and diabolic fraud. If true miracles provided evidence of divine approbation, then evidence of false wonders worked by devilish means facilitated the condemnation of the Roman church as the church of Antichrist. The separation of miracle from magic was firmly defended but poorly defined, with the result that the permeable boundary between truth and falsehood became hotly contested ground. Ongoing debates over the nature of miracle and magic, and the capacity of the devil to deceive even the most vigilant observer, encouraged a re-evaluation of the miracles that were claimed for the saints and sought at their shrines.[32] With medieval miracles recast as demonic fraud, the Catholic church could be represented as an institution headed by papal conjurers and necromancers, preaching doctrines that were shaped by magic and venerating as its heroes saints whose reputation rested on their ability to work false and diabolic wonders.[33] Among the multitude of medieval saints, several were recognised by evangelical polemicists as particularly potent examples. Thomas Becket, whose cult had dominated English pilgrimage in the three centuries before the Reformation, was an irresistible target for evangelical invective: a saint with a reputation that rested upon his defiance of the will of the king, with numerous miracles associated with his shrine and with the proliferation of vials which were claimed to contain his blood. The immediate relevance of St Dunstan to Reformation debates is perhaps less obvious, but as a figure who had promoted monasticism in England, enforced celibacy upon the clergy and worked miracles which involved speaking images, Dunstan rapidly emerged as one of the villains of evangelical history writing.[34] The interest of evangelical writers in the events of the past was far from parochial. The characterisation of the Catholic church as the congregation of Antichrist also ensured a prominent place for the papacy in Protestant narratives of ecclesiastical history. Henry VIII's break with Rome paved the way for the removal of the pope's name from English liturgical books, but the image of the pope was to continue to play a prominent role in polemical debate. The emergence of the papal Antichrist in the pages of Reformation propaganda has been well documented, but the broad rhetoric was accompanied by a more focused engagement with the *lives* of individual popes. Evangelical writers exploited ambiguous, occasionally hostile, commentaries on the character of individual popes in the medieval chronicle tradition in order to represent some of the most influential occupants of the throne of St Peter as magicians and necromancers.[35] The creation of a history for the English national church was made possible by the negative characterisation of its Catholic counterpart in that same history, and central to this characterisation were the popes, saints, legends and miracles of the medieval church.

The transformation of the figure of the saint from hero into villain was made possible by critical tensions within the medieval cult of the saints and the fact that the cult of the saints and their relics was often the embodiment of the very beliefs and practices that the saint had rejected.[36] The exceptional piety that had marked out the saint from the majority in his lifetime became the justification for the veneration of the saint by the community as a whole. The physical body of the saint that had been mortified, or suffered martyrdom, became the object of devotion and veneration. The hermit who had separated himself from the community in life became in death the focal point for the religious life of that same community. The relics of a saint who had rejected material wealth and political power were preserved within a richly decorated shrine and exploited to satisfy the material needs of the community. The position of the written *life* of the saint was equally ambiguous, as a text that both shaped and was shaped by changing perceptions of sanctity. The *lives* of the saints, composed to promote the reputation of the individual, and inculcate interest and enthusiasm among pilgrims, not only marked the intersection of the past and the present, bringing the historical character of the saint to life in the community, but also imposed the values of the present upon the heroes of the past. The image of the saint in the pages of medieval hagiography was that of a historical person, but coloured by myths and legends which linked each saint to his spiritual heirs and ancestors. For this reason, there has been a tendency among historians to dismiss the *lives* of the saints as documents which owe more to fiction than fact, and distort the understanding of the past. Medieval hagiographical writing has been dismissed as 'hopelessly uninteresting', 'fantastical' monkish frauds which demonstrated a 'total disregard for truth and probability', and 'spiritual fables'.[37] Yet it is this very clash between the person and the cult of the saint, the contradictions between history and hagiography, that make the *lives* of the saints so vital to the historian of medieval and early-modern religious culture. In highlighting the common images and *topoi* in the *lives* of the saints as an example of the intrusion of fiction and falsehood into the realm of fact, there is a tendency to overlook the role of the repetition and rearrangement of commonplaces from the past in the construction of religious and cultural identities in the present. By rejecting the *lives* of the saints as texts that are too chronologically and geographically removed from their subject to be useful, historians underestimate the value of such material as a key which unlocks the mentality and culture of the community that produced them.

Hagiographical writing brought the dead to life as their deeds were repeated in the actions of the living, but it also imposed the priorities and personalities of the living upon definitions of sainthood in future generations. New *lives* of the saints drew heavily upon universally recognised characteristics of sainthood, but were themselves woven into the fabric of sanctity and therefore moulded the work of later writers. Models of sanctity had their origins in Scripture, and the *life* of the saint was in many respects a reflection of the life of Christ. Thus the account of the death of the proto-martyr Stephen provided by St Luke attributed to Stephen the repetition of the last words of Christ on the cross, but also helped to establish a pattern for Christian martyrdom in the centuries that followed.[38] Gregory the Great had referred to the *life* (*vita*) rather than *lives* (*vitae*) of the saints, building upon the assumption that each saint shared in this same life of holiness, modelled upon Christ.[39] In the truly hagiographical legend, Delehaye suggests, it is not the figure of the individual saint who appears, but the typical figure of sanctity that they embody. The *life* of St Martin is a representation, not of Martin himself, but of the ideal missionary bishop; in the *life* of St Lawrence, the central figure is less Lawrence than that of the heroic martyr.[40] In the popular imagination, the recorded deeds of the hero were expanded to include actions associated with the archetypal saint and augmented by the achievements of his predecessors. The *lives* of the saints were accorded a key role in the dissemination and propagation of the faith. Gregory the Great claimed that he had composed the *Vitae Patrum* (591), a collection of the *lives* of some 20 Gallic saints, with the intention that his work would 'build up the church' (*ecclesiam aedificare*). Accounts of the life, death and miracles of holy men of the past, Gregory believed, would both inspire the pious reader to emulate their deeds and make the miracles of the saints known to the unbeliever. In the *lives* of the saints, the complex language of doctrinal truth was made plain through miracles, virtue and individual example.[41] Hagiography was therefore both history and propaganda, a discourse in which the past was reconstructed by and for the present in order to inform, inspire, and instil true doctrine and devout practice.

Despite, or perhaps because of, its wide-ranging purposes, medieval hagiography was often conservative and retrospective in its tone. The *lives* of the saints, it has been suggested, were 'characterised by conventionality' and the desire to locate the individual saint within a broader history of sanctity.[42] The form and content of hagiography were not only subject to a concern for the promotion of doctrinal truth, but was also used as a vehicle for the transmission of this model to a wider audience. Medieval hagiographers drew upon and repeated traditional legendary motifs, constructing the *life* of their hero through the repetition and rearrangement of familiar images.[43] However, although the *lives* of the saints contained familiar *topoi*, the production of a legend was also a process by which the mentality of the present was brought to bear upon the events of the past. The perception of holiness in any age reflects the values and morality of the time and, whether the hagiographical narrative was dominated by history, fact or fiction, it still had its roots in the religious and cultural mores of the society that produced it. The didactic purpose of the sacred biographer persisted, but the lessons that were learned by the audience were subject to changing perceptions of the sacred. Saints became saints by and for others, in a complex process of debate, manipulation and negotiation that planted the image of sanctity in the hearts and minds of the faithful. 'One is never a saint except for other people,' Delooz has argued, with the result that the image of the saint is constantly remodelled and reconstructed in the collective imagination.[44] The process by which an individual came to be recognised as a saint was influenced, not only by his actions, but also by the perception of these actions, and the importance and meaning that were attached to them by subsequent generations. Changing typologies, borrowing from familiar legends and transformations in the understanding of sanctity, combined to construct an image of the saint that was in a constant state of movement. The fictions contained in the *lives* of the saint are therefore as instructive as the facts, shedding light upon the values of author and audience, if not upon the historical character of the saint.

The perceptions of sanctity which informed the written *lives* of the saints were far from constant, and the changing image of the medieval saint reflected an ongoing process by which sainthood and holiness were renegotiated and redefined. The cult of the saints had its origins in the commemoration of the holy dead, particularly the martyrs, and the veneration of their relics in the first Christian centuries.[45] The coincidence of miracle, time and place reinforced the association between the holy relics of the dead saint and their function as a locus of supernatural power, and emphasised both the life of the martyr and his continued presence in the community of the living. Relics provided a link between the particular and the eternal, the local church militant and the heavenly church triumphant. Miracles, and especially curative miracles, were experienced in greater numbers in close proximity to the relics of the saint, in which the worlds of the living and the dead, the sacred and the profane, collided.[46] The widespread circulation of stories of miracles enacted at the tombs of the saints was accompanied by a growing demand for both the bodily relics of the saints, and *eulogia* and *brandea*, objects which had been in contact with the saint or his remains. Cloths soaked in the blood of the martyrs were widely revered as relics in their own right, and dust from the tombs of saints was held to have healing properties. The distribution and proliferation of relics across Europe spawned new centres of devotion and pilgrimage, and encouraged the development of new liturgical and paraliturgical practices that placed the saints and their relics at the centre of popular devotion.

However, the expansion of the cult of the saints and the veneration of relics were not without their critics. Writing in the twelfth century, Guibert of Nogent noted that the claims made by rival churches and religious orders to possess the body of a saint were often the result of confusion caused by the fragmentation of the primary relics. Such claims revealed both the potential for conflict around the most valued relics of the church and the difficulties faced in creating an accurate record of objects of cultic veneration. The expansion of Christianity across Europe had created a multitude of new saints and martyrs, and new relics; by the tenth century, Archbishop Dunstan could claim that every step that he took within the church of St Augustine's in Canterbury was planted upon the remains of a saint.[47] The raiding of Constantinople by crusaders in the thirteenth century further increased the available supply of holy remains, many of which were impossible to verify once removed from their immediate context. The emperor Charlemagne attempted to control the spread of unauthenticated relics in the early ninth century, the Fourth Lateran Council condemned the burgeoning relic trade as sacrilege and, in 1299, Boniface VIII prohibited the dismemberment or boiling of bodies in churches.[48]

The response of many churches and communities was to investigate, or simply invent, legends for the relics in their possession. Objects were defended on the basis of a long-standing cult, their role in the inculcation of pious devotion among pilgrims or the miracles that had been worked at the shrine for the benefit of the community. Even where local or popular enthusiasm appeared to be based on misunderstanding, or the confusion of primary and secondary relics, the church was often prepared to tolerate a cult which inspired orthodox, if misdirected, devotion. The medieval cult of the saints had largely accommodated such tensions, but the contrast between ideal and reality, history and legend, became all the more visible as the storm clouds of the Reformation gathered.

The cult of the saints on the eve of the Reformation reflected the ongoing processes by which images of sanctity had been shaped and moulded by the shifting sands of piety, politics and popular culture in the preceding centuries.[49] The martyr saints of the early church had acquired a reputation for holiness through their steadfastness and death, but over subsequent centuries the definition of sainthood was to change in order to accommodate those individuals who had endured more general personal, material or spiritual suffering. By the fourth century, the cult of the martyr had been matched by the cult of the confessor, often a missionary figure or cleric who had committed his life to the dissemination of the faith, or a hermit or monastic who had relinquished the world in order to devote himself to God. Martyrs continued to be made on the frontiers between Christianity and its opponents, but the function of the saints as an inspiration to the faithful required that they embody a morality that was within reach of the majority, even if it was honoured primarily in the breach. Heroic virtue, rather than physical suffering, became the mark of sanctity, as chastity, fasting, humility and solitude emerged as the dominant characteristics of the saint. Such virtues also served to separate the miracle-working saint from the wonder-working magician, both in the official canonisation process and in the popular imagination; the veracity of miracles was underpinned by the virtue of the miracle-worker. These characteristics were not themselves constant, however, and recent studies of the nature of medieval sanctity point to the democracy of the call to sainthood. The saints of the early Middle Ages were often individuals who held positions of authority in the church or wielded temporal power with justice. Until the twelfth century, the ranks of the holy were dominated by members of the clergy, but the male saints of the church were later joined by a burgeoning number of female virgins, who embodied the growing cult of celibacy and chastity in the western church.[50] Female sanctity in the thirteenth century was constructed upon the assumption that the denial of the flesh opened the way to union with Christ, while the battle with heresy opened up new avenues for the pursuit of sanctity through evangelisation and the defence of orthodoxy. The model provided by St Francis restored apostolic poverty to a prime position in the understanding of holiness, while in England the thirteenth century had witnessed the veneration of numerous new saints, including Thomas Becket, whose popularity threatened to undermine that of traditional cults.

The bond between saint, relic and cult was often the fragile construction of written and oral tradition, and even a popular cult might well be undermined by the rise of a new star in the firmament of the *communio sanctorum*. However, for many witnesses, the distinction between saint and ordinary mortal, or between holy relic and the 'pigges bones' of Chaucer's Pardoner, remained one which was culturally induced.[51] As Peter Brown has suggested, the relics of the saints acquired their reputation by acclamation, and the importance attached to them reflected their acceptance by the community or church.[52] Once removed from the tomb, the status of the relic was frequently ambiguous, and the reputation of the holy object was dictated by a written or oral tradition that testified to its authenticity. The *translation* of a relic represented a shift away from the established perception, and set in motion a process by which an alternative meaning was created for the object, informed by the culture and beliefs of its new resting place. The same process can be seen at work in the construction of the saint. The reputation of the saint was established by acclamation, by popular voice and in the decrees of the church. It was as a result of this acclamation that the *life* of the saint entered the liturgy of the church, found a position in the calendar and came to be venerated by the faithful. The cult of the individual saint, like the cult of the relic, reflected and secured his acceptance by the church or community. Pilgrimage to a shrine endured as long as there was widespread acceptance of the miraculous powers of the relics and a sustained belief in the privileged position of the saint. However, the position of a saint as the patron and protector of a community could alter dramatically if the faith and confidence of that community are shaken, a transformation that acquired physical expression in the ritual humiliation of the relics of the saint.[53] Like the status of a relic, the status of a saint was frequently ambiguous and often dependent upon a written or oral tradition that testified to the authenticity of the cult. Just as a period of disaster and division could result in the destruction of the traditions that provided relics with their meaning, so a period of religious conflict could shatter the reputation of the saints and the unity of the hagiographic corpus. The medieval cult of the saints had been flexible enough to accommodate shifts in patterns of sanctity and perceptions of holiness, while upholding the common *spiritus omnium iustorum* which linked the saints with those whom they imitated and those by whom they were imitated. In the turmoil and controversies of the Reformation, this colourful fabric of medieval hagiography began to unravel.

The Reformation critique of the cults and legends of the saints was accompanied by a vigorous assault upon the miracles associated with saints, relics and shrines. Medieval hagiographers and pilgrims had placed the miraculous at the heart of the cult of the saints. Miracles worked in response to the prayers of pilgrims had provided visible testimony to the privileged position of the saint, and pilgrimage to the shrines of the saints had been fuelled by the assumption that the individual saint would be particularly responsive to prayers and petitions made in proximity to his relics. Indeed, as Robert Finucane has noted, it was this belief in the virtues and powers of the saints that distinguished pilgrimage from tourism.[54] Walter Hilton's fourteenth-century *Kalendre of the Newe Legende of Englande*, reprinted in 1516, provided the reader with a list of the names of the English saints, the location of their relics, and 'some lytell thynge of theyr vertues & myracles with some perte of theyr storyes shortlye towched'.[55] The miracles of the saints adorned the pages of the *Golden Legend*, and were proclaimed from the pulpit for the edification and inspiration of the faithful.[56] Miracles worked in life and after death not only implanted the cult of a saint in the popular imagination, but also satisfied the demands of the official canonisation process by testifying to the place of the individual saint in the company of heaven.[57]

The understanding of the miraculous had its origins in the interpretation of Scripture. The vocabulary of the miraculous in the Vulgate was that of *signum* and *prodigium*, and not the *miraculum* of medieval hagiography, but biblical precedent still remained a vital part of the construction of sanctity from the miracles recorded in the *lives* of the saints. The biblical narrative presented a panoply of wondrous events which shed light upon the relationship between creator and created, heaven and earth. New Testament miracles, particularly those contained in Mark's Gospel, provided a pattern of spiritual preaching and physical healing that was to become the model for aspiring saints in the centuries that followed. Biblical language was frequently employed in medieval discussions of the miraculous, biblical images were used to reinforce hagiographic narratives and biblical *topoi* punctuated preaching on saints and their wonders. Themes and patterns emerged which contributed to the continuing construction and reconstruction of models of the saintly miraculous, and provided a critical reference point for the hagiographer and the pilgrim.[58]

As the church proclaimed the miraculous, so it proscribed the magical. At the most basic level, miracles provided a godly antithesis to the false wonders of the magician, and the miracles of the saints, worked through faith and prayer, were contrasted with the demonic theurgy of pagan and demonic magic.[59] The *locus classicus* for this conflict between miracle and magic was the Old Testament account in Exodus 7:8–13 of the clash between the agents of God and the magicians of Pharaoh.[60] A New Testament parallel was provided, in the Acts of the Apostles, in the attempts of Simon Magus to lay claim to the miraculous powers of the Apostles.[61] From the early days of the Christian church, magic was regarded as the concomitant of false religion, the worship of false gods and the work of demons. In the hands of Christian apologists, the example of Simon Magus exemplified the dichotomy between the miracles of the saints and the illusions and deceptions of the devil, and expressed the dualism of religion and magic that was so central to the construction of a culture and identity for the nascent church. The term 'magic' rapidly acquired a pejorative connotation in the literature and canons of the church and a polemical application in religious controversy.[62] Magic was repeatedly condemned in ecclesiastical law, in penitentiaries and in the *lives* of the saints, many of which drew upon biblical texts that upheld the division between true religion and false practice. The distinction between false wonders and Christian miracle was vigorously emphasised in the *lives* of the missionary saints: Bede was careful to assert that Augustine's mission had come to England 'armed with divine not devilish power'.[63] By the twelfth century, magic had become associated, not only with diabolic practices, but with heresy and the deliberate perversion of the rites and sacraments of the church. The claims made for magic continued to be condemned as worthless and illusory, but the representation of magicians as a demonic sect, engaged in sorcery and necromancy, reflected a fear of the very real threat posed by diabolic practices.

However, the same missionary impulse that had led the church to emphasise the fundamental opposition between magic and religion was to test the application of this theoretical dualism at the local level. Accounts of miracles in which those who angered God were struck dead were difficult to separate from maleficent magic, and claims that the capacity of the saint to manipulate the supernatural exceeded that of his pagan opponents encouraged the understanding of miracle as an alternative but proximate form of magic. St Boniface's biographer claimed that his missionary activity in Germany had been built upon the twin pillars of 'sound doctrine and miracles', and Bede's *Life of St Cuthbert* emphasised the miracles worked by Cuthbert to promote his preaching in Northumbria and to overcome pagan magic.[64] Miracles had a vital role to play in the work of conversion, but miracle stories often drew upon non-Christian legend, or relied upon the presence of non-Christian magic to create a battle ground between true and false religion.[65] The cult of the saints also supplied the Christian armoury with what Peter Brown has described as 'weapons of satisfying precision against its superhuman agents', which could be deployed to overwhelm the sorcery of the magician.[66] However, tension between the stark opposition of magic and miracle in Christian apologetics and the interaction of magic and religion at a local level is evinced in images such as the Rothwell cross, in which Christ is represented, wand in hand, restoring sight to the blind. The meaning of godly miracle was imparted in a dialogue between saint and sorcerer in which the distinction between miracle and wonder lay in the eye of the beholder, and in which liturgical words and objects acquired a utility in the realm of magic.[67]

The differentiation between legitimate and illegitimate modes of recourse to the supernatural was also dependent upon an acceptance of the role of the church in determining the boundary between miracle and magic. Magic and miracle, it has been argued, 'provided competing but proximate imageries of power; only something entirely contingent – legitimacy – separated them'.[68] Even this theoretical distinction became more opaque when applied to the particular, including, for example, the judicial ordeal, which acquired a religious character at the hands of the clergy, but was vigorously condemned at the Lateran Council of 1215.[69] As Keith Thomas has famously argued, the imperfect separation of prayer and relic from incantation and charm contributed to a popular belief in the 'magic of the medieval church', manifested in its sacraments and sacramentals. Representations of the miracles of the saints and the rites of the church as an effective form of counter-magic against diabolical deceptions and wonders, Thomas suggests, further undermined the distinction between religious devotion and magic. Religious aspirations within magic, and perceptions of magical elements in religion, point to evidence of practical accommodation alongside the theoretical opposition. Indeed for many, magic and religion were complementary rather than competing systems; David Gentilcore's study of popular beliefs and practices in the *Terra d'Otranto* suggests that therapeutic magic was frequently deployed alongside the sacramental ministry of the priest.[70]

Attitudes to magic and religion did not develop in isolation but were constructed in relation to one another, with the result the distinction between saint and sorcerer often lay within the eye of the beholder.[71] The example of Dorothy of Montau, discussed by Richard Kieckhefer, provides a clear demonstration of the possibility that sanctity and witchcraft might be tightly contested, and the deeds of the aspiring saint condemned as magic. The representation of Dorothy as both heroine and heretic was the consequence of 'empirical indecision'; it was not that her image was painted in shades of grey, but rather that there was simply no consensus as to whether she was a saint or a witch.[72] Similar issues are raised by Gabor Klaniczay's study of Margaret of Hungary. The canonisation process in 1276 revealed both the differences and the parallels between magic and miracle, saint and witch, and high-lighted the multiple interpretations that might be placed upon the actions recorded in the *life* of a saint. The decision as to whether the acts of a saint were *miracula* or *maleficia* was determined by culture and recognised by society. In neither case was the investigation immune from the influence of propaganda, polemic or pastoral concern.[73] Where uncertainty and conflict over miracle and magic were deeply rooted, the reputation of an individual could oscillate between saint and sorcerer over time and space. Yet the notion of miracle remained a central building block in the construction of an identity for the Christian church throughout the Middle Ages. Miracle and magic entered the lexicon of polemical debate, not as mere ornament, but as a central part of the terminology that separated true from false, godly from ungodly. Amid the general consensus that the wonders of the devil were illusions, the rhetoric applied to individuals and groups who were believed to pervert religious practice created a very real fear of diabolic deception. The medieval legacy exerted a powerful influence over Reformation debate, and the contrast between miracle and sorcery remained a potent weapon in the hands of propagandists and polemicists seeking to define the boundary between religion and magic in the past and the present.

Saintly thaumaturgy had extended from the apotropaic to the curative to the punitive, each intimately associated with the culture and society in which they took place. However, the scope of the miraculous was also subject to interpretation and reinterpretation in a changing historical and cultural context. The ontological distinction between the false, preternatural wonders of demons and the real supernatural, intervention of the divine in the world remained contingent upon a perception of visible effect rather than a knowledge of hidden cause. Despite the repeated articulation of the separation of miracle from false wonder, the sheer diversity of medieval miracles, and their interpretation by later generations, created a permeable boundary between miracle and magic. The repositioning of this boundary, especially in a period of religious and cultural upheaval, could have profound consequences for the understanding of the nature of the church and the reputation and authority of its holy men and women. Saints were condemned as sorcerers, miracles were condemned as magic, and uncertainties and ambiguities in medieval histories and hagiographies were exploited in the service of a new histor-ical narrative.[74] At the same time as images of the saints were removed from churches, their *lives* and miracles were re-examined and reinterpreted to accommodate changing assumptions about the nature of miracle and magic.

This re-examination and reinterpretation inverted and exploited key features and foundations of the medieval cult of the saints. The arrival of the relics of the saint at a new shrine, and the rituals that accompanied their elevation, had been an important occasion of community consensus in the early medieval church.[75] In the hands of Reformation controversialists and iconoclasts, the relics of the saints were to become a focus for division and opposition, objects through which religious conflict gained a visible expression in iconoclastic destruction. Medieval hagiographers had linked together examples from the past to construct a position for the saint in a chain of sanctity which stretched back to the Apostles, and reinforced faith in the unity and concord among the community of the saints. The *lives* of the saints acquired their authority by reflecting traditional images of sanctity in the present, and projecting present images of sainthood into the future. Reformation polemicists drew upon this same stock of images, and their repetition in the *lives* of the saints, to promote a theology and practice which was profoundly opposed to the veneration of saints. The polemical, satirical and even political assault upon the cult of the saints acquired its force from the very familiarity of the imagery that it employed.[76] Relics and shrines that were exposed as frauds gained a totemic significance in the writings of English evangelicals, but their polemical utility lay in the fact that they were also popular and prominent features of the devotional landscape. Traditional hagiographical writing had often removed the individual saint from his specific historical and geographical context in order to create an exemplar which was relevant and recognisable to the intended audience. Evangelical writers followed the lead of the sacred biographer, reinterpreting the *life* of the saint in the light of the doctrinal priorities of the Reformation, and constructing a new historical context in which the hero of the past was transformed into the villain of the present. Vowed chastity, monastic solitude and loyalty to the church, which had emerged as the building blocks of medieval sanctity, were profoundly antithetical to the religious culture of the Reformation, but could be transformed into evidence of misplaced faith, moral degeneracy and resistance to the will of the secular power.[77]

The *lives* of the saints, and indeed the polemical literature of the Reformation in which they were reinterpreted, are often treated with a degree of scepticism. Hagiography has been dismissed as the mere collection of spiritual fables, and the writings of English evangelicals rejected as a vitriolic caricature of traditional piety. The polemic and propaganda which form the basis of this study are all too often marginalised in modern studies, and criticised for their partiality, populist tone and base language.[78] Yet such material provides valuable insights into the means by which the message of the Reformation was conceived, communicated and contested in sixteenth-century England. Those who participated in debates over sanctity, miracles and history did not work in a vacuum, but composed tracts and treatises that were very much the product of the context in which they were written. The passage of the Act of Six Articles in 1539, for example, prompted a vigorous response from evangelical writers in England and in exile, while the lifting of restrictions on printing in the first months of the reign of Edward VI opened the floodgates for evangelical writing on the Mass in advance of the publication of the first Prayer Book. Over 30 pamphlets appeared in 1548 alone, and the printing of Luke Shepherd's *John Bon and Mast Person* was clearly timed to coincide with the feast of Corpus Christi and its suppression by the Edwardian regime.[79] The persuasive power of the printed word was recognised by protagonists in polemical debate and by the sixteenth-century church and state. Luther's books were burned in England in the 1520s, and numerous royal proclamations set out the penalties that were to be imposed upon those found in possession of 'seditious and heretical' books and pamphlets.[80] The capacity for cheap printed pamphlets and broadsides to reach a wide audience is now more widely recognised, reflecting a better understanding of levels of literacy and of the public nature of reading in early-modern Britain.[81] The printed pamphlets of the Reformation reflect the priorities and preoccupations of their authors, but also provide a crucial link between doctrinal debate and popular practice in sixteenth-century England. In their use of images and examples culled from chronicles and hagiography, they provide ample testimony to the enduring significance of the medieval past in Reformation England.

The representation of the medieval saints by evangelical history writers in the sixteenth century suggests that saints continued to be created and recognised by and for others. The saint was 'made' by one community and culture, and 'unmade' by another, which reconstructed the image of the saint according to its own perception and imagination. The image of the medieval saint which had been crafted to reflect established models of sanctity in the past was then destroyed and refashioned to fit a different model of the same. Just as the making of the saint was the result of the interaction of doctrine, piety and political authority, so the destruction of the saint was accomplished by a reconsideration of the nature of doctrine, piety and political authority. Medieval hagiography had subjected the past to a continuing process of reinterpretation, and manipulated images of sainthood from the past into models for the present. This same impulse to reconstruct the past, exemplified in the polemical literature of the Reformation, manipulated the same images of sainthood to a dramatically different end. As the *lives* and miracles of the saints were re-examined and reinterpreted by evangelical writers, the boundaries of hagiographical writing were manipulated to accommodate changing assumptions about the nature of sanctity, miracle and magic in the sixteenth century. The historical and polemical writing of the medieval church had done much to establish an association between magic, and heresy, sorcery and doctrinal error. This traditional rendering of ecclesiastical history, refracted through the prism of the evangelical understanding of the miraculous, acquired a dramatically different interpretation in the works of evangelical polemicists. History, hagiography and miracle narrative were to become intertwined in the justification of religious reform and the construction of a plausible past for the Reformation in England.

2

'BROUGHTE OWTE OF DEADLY DARKENES TO LYVELY LIGHTE'

Reconstructing the medieval past in Reformation England

The religious upheavals of the sixteenth century were accompanied by the creation of new traditions, myths and narratives that provided the nascent reformed church with a plausible and polemically useful past. Traditional historical paradigms were dismantled and a new narrative of ecclesiastical history was constructed from legends of monks, miracles and magic in the medieval church. Antiquity and consensus ceased to be the foundation of authority, as religious identities came to be shaped, not by the membership of a visible and historical church, but by a sense of belonging to an invisible spiritual community. In the hands of evangelical polemicists, the universal history of the medieval church became a palimpsest, wiped clean and rewritten until cleansed of the accumulated errors of centuries of monastic history, hagiography and chronicles.[1] History intruded boldly into political and doctrinal discussion as the events and records of the medieval past emerged as a critical battleground in the debates of the Reformation.

For writers on both sides of the confessional divide, history acted as a mirror that reflected the past, the present and the future, and as a record of the unfolding divine plan. Catholic claims to institutional and historical continuity had their foundation in the belief that the visible church was, and had always been, the repository and guardian of religious truth. Evangelical calls for reform were predicated upon the assertion that this same church had demonstrably failed to preserve its early purity and fidelity to the word of God across the course of human history. The past was approached with the intention of demonstrating that the medieval church had betrayed its heritage, abandoned the faith of the Fathers and fallen into error. The challenge that the Reformation posed to the authority of the medieval church was firmly rooted, not only in the biblicism of the early evangelicals, but also in their iconoclastic approach to the history of the church. The reconstruction and reinterpretation of ecclesiastical history were a vital part of evangelical efforts to turn allegations of novelty, error and innovation against their Catholic detractors, and to identify champions of the sixteenth- century reform movement in the events and personalities of the past.

The reinvention of the past, and the invention of traditions that might bind the present to the past, reflected the changing priorities of evangelical polemicists and the depth of the fracture in the universal history of the church that had been opened by the Reformation. It may be true that 'novelty is no less novel for being able to dress up easily as antiquity', but the guising of contentious issues in the clothes of past was a vital part of the defence of the Reformation as restoration rather than innovation.[2] Such invention of tradition is most likely to occur in any age where the social patterns for which 'old' traditions had been devised are weakened or destroyed; 'invented' traditions are a response to change, an attempt to exploit references to familiar situations in order to establish a new understanding of the past and the present.[3] Indeed the scepticism and hostility with which English evangelicals treated the traditional narratives of the medieval past were not without precedent. The turmoil caused by the Norman Conquest had likewise encouraged the production of a revised historical and hagiographical corpus, based upon a close examination of the *lives* and reputations of the Anglo-Saxon saints.[4] Religious upheaval in the sixteenth century spawned an even more determined enthusiasm for the rediscovery and reinterpretation of the past, as history became a quarry for writers on both sides of the opening confessional divide. However, the Reformation concern for the reinvention of the past was not simply a reaction to the rupture of medieval Christendom. The rewriting of the history of the medieval church that took place in the first half of the sixteenth century was as much a part of the process of change as a response to it. The attack on the traditions of the church, and the traditional histories of the church, was an essential part of the evangelical assault on the authority of the institutional church, but the very act of bringing the past to bear upon the present was itself to exert a powerful influence over the development of the Reformation in England.

Evangelical critics of medieval chronicles and hagiography promised a history of the national past that was both accurate and functional, and denuded of the pious accretions of 'monkish' writers. Criticism of the chronicles as 'monkish tales' was a commonplace of Reformation literature, not least because these legends and tales continued to exert a powerful hold over the popular imagination.[5] Writing in the 1530s, Urbanus Rhegius protested that his Catholic opponents brought forth 'old wyues fables for sounde and true thynges', while 60 years later Francis Bacon commented upon the damage that had been done to religion by 'old wives fables' and the 'impostures of the clergy'.[6] Evangelical criticisms of the errors and fables perpetuated in chronicles and hagiography reached to the heart of medieval historical writing. For medieval chroniclers, the distinction between fact and fiction was often less important than the moral and providential lessons that could be drawn from a consideration of individual and collective conduct. The late-fourteenth-century preaching manual, the *Summa Predicantium*, exemplified this functional approach to history in its advice that 'whether it is the truth of history or fiction does not matter, because the example is not supplied for its own sake but for signification'.[7] The intermingling of fact and fiction in the construction of the past was abundantly evident in medieval hagiographical writing in which images taken from the lives of past saints were incorporated into biographies of holy men and women of the present, lending them a veneer of historical authenticity that was at best spurious and often entirely false.[8]

However, despite the criticisms levelled by evangelical polemicists, medieval hagiography and chronicles were to become an encyclopaedia for those who sought to defend and promote religious change in the sixteenth century. The *lives* and legends of the saints were plundered by those who sought models of pious conduct, examples of doctrinal deviation and exaggerated encounters with the miraculous, and by those who recognised the importance of the texts as evidence that could be used to condemn the Catholic church through the words and actions of its members. Traditional narratives of the medieval past were both condemned as frauds and held up as damning evidence of decay and corruption in the institutional church. Iconoclastic attitudes to the medieval past shattered long-standing images and legends, but at the same time contributed to the construction of new myths and histories, new heroes and villains, often on familiar foundations. The building blocks of evangelical histories of the medieval church may not have been fabrications but, as Patrick Collinson has suggested, evangelical authors still 'wove their material into forms that were as fictive as they were factual'.[9]

The form and content of evangelical historical writing differed in one fundamental respect from that of its Catholic opponents. For late-medieval Catholic writers, the importance of the past lay in its capacity to assist in the interpretation and understanding of Scripture. As Y.-M. Congar has suggested, the men of the Middle Ages 'believed that the book of Scripture could be read in the light of what was written in the book of the world and the book of the soul'. The communication of divine truth to mankind was co-extensive with the history of the church, with the result that the writings of the Fathers, and the decrees and determinations of the church throughout history, were all part of the canon of *scriptura sacra*.[10] In the historical writings of evangelical polemicists, the authority of the past was entirely dependent upon its correct interpretation in the light of Scripture. Tradition had no independent or normative value, and the history and authority of the church were to be tested against the words of Scripture. Luther's preface to Robert Barnes' *Vitae Romanorum Pontificum* celebrated the support that history provided for the rejection of papal authority, 'and it gives me the greatest joy and satisfaction to see … that history and Scripture coincide in this respect'.[11] John Bale, one of the most prolific English writers on the history of the church, summed up succinctly the relationship between Scripture and history in his application of the text of Revelation to the medieval past: 'yet is the text a light to ye cronicles and not the cronicles to the texte'.[12] Scripture remained the only touchstone by which the past and present of the church were to be judged, but history contained a narrative of a true church that had become hidden by the accumulation of tradition.

The rejection of the intrinsic value of the traditional church order by evangelical polemicists both liberated them from the medieval past and imposed upon them the necessity of reclaiming and rewriting that same past. The appeal to the authority of Scripture alone privileged the sacred text over the doctrinal formulations and traditions of the church, but did not of itself provide the reformed church with a location in time and space beyond the immediate moment. Tradition was denied the normative authority in the development of doctrine that it had been accorded by the pre-Reformation church, but history was to remain a vital part of evangelical apologetics. In an age where innovation was condemned and novelty treated with circumspection, the reconstruction of the medieval past provided evangelical writers with a necessary riposte to the potentially damaging question posed by their Catholic opponents: where was your church before Luther? The history of medieval Christendom was replete with models of kingship, paradigms of piety and with legends of heroes and villains that could be manipulated to meet the needs of religious controversy.

That history of Christendom was well documented, and the desire to recover the precedent of the past was not the preserve of evangelical writers alone.[13] Chronicles and histories had been among the earliest literature produced by the English printing presses and had played an important role in the development of the book trade under the influence of Caxton and Pynson. The value of an accurate record of the nation's past was impressed upon Henry VIII by the Italian Polydore Vergil, who dedicated his *Anglia Historia* to the king in 1535.[14] By the 1530s, conquering the past had come to be recognised as a vital factor in securing victory in the present, and Henry certainly appreciated the value of the past to the defence of the Tudor monarchy and the Reformation enacted in its name. A preoccupation with the power of the past to inform and validate the present was apparent in the Act in Restraint of Appeals (1533), in which the declaration that 'this realm of England is an empire' was supported by reference to 'diverse sundry and authentic histories and chronicles'.[15] In the same year, John Leland was employed as King's Antiquary and charged to assemble historical corroboration for the claim that the Tudors were indeed the legitimate heirs of the British kings and the restorers of true religion. Leland's search for the records of the past was intended to bring the 'monumentes of auncient writers … owte of deadly darkenes to lyvely lighte' and expose the 'superstition and craftily coloured doctrine' of the Roman bishops.[16] History was a central feature of the construction of the Reformation in England, not only as the political defence for the Tudor dynasty, but also as artillery in the war against superstition and false religion. The death of Leland in 1552 left the project incomplete, but his ambitions influenced the ongoing efforts of English writers to reclaim the national past. In 1549, John Bale completed his edition of Leland's *Laboryouse Journey* and dedicated the work to Edward VI as part of a vigorous defence of the value of history as a weapon in the fight against religious radicalism.[17] The first edition of Edward Hall's *The Union of the Two Noble and Illustre Families of Lancastre and Yorke* (1548) was also dedicated to the young king, with the intention that it should remind Edward of the function and value of history-writing at the point of intersection between the political needs of the present and the precedents provided by the past.

The precedents provided by the past were hotly contested. As Francis Bacon commented at the start of the seventeenth century, Martin Luther had been obliged to 'awake all antiquity and to call former times to his succours … so that the ancient authors both in divinity and humanity which had a long time slept in libraries began generally to be read and resolved'.[18] This 'awakening of antiquity' was already evident in the works of the first generation of English evangelicals. William Tyndale had promised to 'digge again the wells of Abraham' and place Scripture at the centre of doctrine and debate, but he was also quick to appreciate and utilise the polemical potential of the past.[19] Tyndale's writing was shaped by his understanding of the relationship between Scripture and history and his faith in the primacy of the text of the Bible over chronicles and legends. The authority of Scripture lay in its immutability and its status as the written word of God, in sharp contrast to the legends contained in medieval chronicles and hagiography, which Tyndale argued had been deliberately invented and perverted by the clergy. However, it was these very chronicles that were to be exploited and subverted by evangelical writers, including Tyndale, in their reconstruction of the medieval past.

The chronicles, despite their monkish fictions, still contained enough truth, Tyndale claimed, to permit their use as a record of the expansion of error in the institutional church and the extension of the power of the pope over that of the prince. Tyndale trawled the medieval past for ammunition against his opponents and evidence that the clergy had for centuries fabricated the historical record to defend their power and pretensions. Once rescued from the monastic chronicles, history provided compelling testimony to the extent of papal interference in the English church and state, and to the key role that had been played by the clergy in bringing about the downfall of English monarchs. The invasion of the Danes and the victory of William the Conqueror in 1066, Tyndale claimed, were facilitated by papal intervention. The pope and the clergy, he suggested, had conspired to bring about the collapse of the rule of King John, and the English clergy had been implicated in the murder of both John and Richard II.[20] The reinterpretation of the medieval chronicles unfolded a narrative of conflict between truth and falsehood throughout history, a narrative from which the Roman church, popes and clergy emerged as the embodiment of evil.

Evidence of papal interference in the affairs of the English church and monarchy provided the main substance of evangelical history writing in the 1520s and 1530s. Thomas Swinnerton's *Mustre of the Scismatyke Bissopes of Rome* (1534) catalogued the role of successive popes in undermining the authority of English and European monarchs, and Robert Barnes' *Vitae Romanorum Pontificum* (1535) charted the expansion of papal power and the evolution of doctrine over the preceding millennium. Barnes, already an influential preacher, had enjoyed the patronage and protection of Thomas Cromwell in the early 1530s and shared his interest in the construction of historical narratives that justified the break with Rome. In the 1531 edition of *The supplication … vnto the moost gracyous kynge Henrye the eyght*, Barnes had attempted to demonstrate the existence of a treacherous fifth column of clergy within his realm, an argument bolstered in the 1534 edition by the addition of multiple references to clerical misconduct and manipulation in the past.[21] The focus of the 1534 edition was adjusted to make clear the role that the popes had played in subverting the stability of the English crown, and highlighted the reign of King John as a clear example of the price that had been paid by godly monarchs who challenged the power of the bishop of Rome. Barnes' approach echoed Tyndale's exploitation of monastic histories and chronicles in the search for material with which to condemn the institutional church. The account of the pontificate of Gregory VII that appeared in the *Vitae Romanorum Pontificum*, for example, was heavily indebted to information gleaned from the letters of the eleventh-century cardinal Benno, and Barnes also made effective use of Platina's fifteenth-century *Vitae Pontificum* in his account of Paul II.[22] Factual accuracy often mattered less than polemical value; Barnes' narrative of King John's conflict with the pope was less than precise, and references to papal histories in the text were occasionally misleading but still served to support the assertion that Rome's own writers could be used to condemn the medieval Catholic church.

Among English evangelical polemicists in the middle decades of the sixteenth century, it was John Bale who exerted the greatest influence over the exploitation and reconstruction of the medieval past. Bale's interests in ecclesiastical history predated his conversion to the Reformation but were quickly pressed into the service of the evangelical cause. During his career as a Carmelite monk, Bale had travelled widely in England and on the continent, researching the history of the order. Indeed his early writings repeated myths and legends of the kind that were to become the target of his invective in the 1530s and 1540s, including an account of an incident in which the Virgin had appeared in defence of the order in the thirteenth century. However, the interpretative framework that Bale constructed for the Carmelite history also did much to shape his later hostile narratives of the medieval past. Prior to his conversion, Bale had already begun to explore the notion of historical discontinuity that was to become so crucial to the evangelical understanding of the medieval past as a period of decay and superstition during which the faith of the visible church had become corrupted.[23] Incorporated into a developing sense that history, interpreted in the light of scriptural prophecy, described the gradual corruption of the medieval church, this discontinuity became the guiding principle in Bale's acerbic comments upon the medieval ecclesiastical past.[24] In his *Acts of the English Votaries*, Bale expressed his determination to deploy the monastic records of the past in the destruction of the cult of the saints and the religious life, a promise that was to be fulfilled in a series of treatises and pamphlets published in the middle decades of the century.

The interpretation of the ecclesiastical past in the light of the scriptural text dominated Bale's writings. His concern to expose the historical expansion of error within the institutional church encouraged a detailed investigation of the doctrine and discipline of the medieval church. The example of the popes and the clergy in the past was to provide a vehicle for the criticism and condemnation of the Roman church in the present. Bale's prose style and his polemical histories have found few admirers among modern scholars. Andrew Hadfield concludes that Bale's writings were characterised by a 'monolithic consistency imposed upon the reader with an iron determination', while Jesse Harris is less favourable still, suggesting that 'perhaps the less one says about [the non-dramatic writings] the better'.[25] Bale's prose was persuasive rather than polished, and his writings were shaped by his desire to accumulate and present to the reader an incontrovertible mass of evidence that the institutional church had fallen into error. Instances of clerical immorality, doctrinal innovation and traitorous conduct were the building blocks of Bale's new narrative of ecclesiastical history, in which the expansion of ecclesiastical power mirrored the growing influence of Satan within the church. The effectiveness of his polemical writings lay not in their aesthetic appeal, but in the sheer volume of material with which the reader was bombarded, and in the ferocity of the assault on the medieval church that flowed from the printed page.

The dominant theme of Bale's history was the rise and influence of Antichrist within the Roman church. Bale's interests in the application of apocalyptic writings to the history of the church dated from at least the 1530s when he translated Thomas Kirchmeyer's anti-papal drama *Pammachius*, but an additional impetus was provided by his own experiences in exile during the late 1530s and early 1540s. The enterprise culminated in the printing of the first part of Bale's *The Image of Both Churches* in 1541, with the second part following in 1545 and the third in 1547.[26] *The Image of Both Churches* offers a clear demonstration of the extent to which Bale's interpretation of the Christian past was shaped by the prophecies contained in the book of Revelation. History, Bale argued, was the record of the division of mankind into two churches, the true and the false, whose existence could be traced throughout the centuries. Read in the light of Scripture, history provided a record of an ongoing conflict between the true and the false church, and the unfolding of the divine plan for humanity. Historical events were located within the biblical prophecies to provide both a framework for the interpretation of the past and an informed understanding of the significance of events in the present. *The Image of Both Churches* has been described as a 'vigorous and crude typological reading of the scriptural text', but Bale's text was enormously influential in shaping English attitudes to the past and subsequent commentaries on the text of Revelation.[27] The relationship between Scripture and history was reinforced in the first part of *The Image of Both Churches* by the inclusion of detailed marginal notes and documentation that made clear the parallels between the prophetic words of John and the events of the Christian past. The years around the end of the first millennium were cast as a critical period in the history of the church and as an age in which the biblical prophecies of Antichrist appeared to acquire fulfilment in historical events.[28] The notes also identified other texts that Bale had used in the construction of his commentary, and highlighted his indebtedness to a variety of medieval and Reformation writers. Over 100 authors were listed, revealing Bale's particular interest in Joachim's *Expositio in Apocalypsim* and the works of Martin Luther and Francis Lambert.[29]

This basic interpretative framework for the narrative of the medieval past served as the foundation for Bale's other polemical histories in the 1540s. In *Yet a course at the Romyshe Foxe* (1543), Bale dated the release of Satan from bondage to the year 1000, in order to explain and condemn the burgeoning political power of the papacy in the centuries before the Reformation. In turn, this interpretation contributed to the detailed historical narrative of the rise of Antichrist that was advanced in the second part of *The Image of Both Churches*.[30] *The Mystery of Iniquity*, printed in 1545, took as its starting point the assertion that the doctrine and morality of the institutional church had become ever more corrupt throughout its history. The eventual occupation of the throne of St Peter by Antichrist was evidenced by the growing power and pretensions of the papacy in the centuries after 1000. With the history of the church recast as a narrative of the rise of Antichrist, the medieval past became central to the evangelical rejection of traditional religion. The example of the primitive church was valuable, but it was the events of the intervening centuries that provided the bulk of the new historical narrative, as the records and chronicles of the past became a store of evidence and information that could be plundered in the service of polemic and propaganda.

The pattern of history laid down in *The Image of Both Churches* was universally applicable, but Bale retained a particular interest in the history of the English church.[31] His *Actes of the Englysh Votaries*, a vigorous reconstruction of English ecclesiastical history, was published in two parts in 1546 and 1551 and ran to numerous subsequent editions. The principal theme of the work was the exposition of the catastrophic consequences of the imposition of compulsory clerical celibacy upon the clergy of the English church. In many ways, clerical celibacy and morality provided an ideal issue around which Bale could construct the identification of the true church and the false in the English past. A church either permitted clerical marriage or it did not. Clergy were either celibate or they were not, and were either morally pure or they were not. In an interpretation of history that did not allow for shades of grey, clerical celibacy was a near-perfect test of allegiance. As a controversial issue in England in the 1530s and 1540s, the history of clerical celibacy was also a potent weapon in the hands of evangelical writers. Historical evidence that the clergy of the early English church had been married provided proof that it was the medieval church, and not the evangelicals, which was guilty of doctrinal innovation, and gave added support to those English writers who argued that the legalisation of clerical marriage was a necessary part of the restoration of the English church to its apostolic roots.[32]

The history of the imposition of compulsory clerical celibacy allowed Bale to argue that the native British church had enjoyed fidelity to the church of the Apostles prior to the arrival of papal missionaries in the sixth century. The first part of the *Actes of the Englysh Votaries* chronicled the 'rising' of the clergy, the gradual accumulation of ecclesiastical authority over the centuries and the concomitant corruption in the faith of the church. Christianity in England, Bale argued, dated, not from the mission of St Augustine in 597, but from the first century when Joseph of Arimathea had reached the shores, bringing with him a faith that had its origins not in Rome but in Jerusalem. Joseph was a married man and, until the fifth century, Bale claimed, the clergy of the English church had followed his example and taken wives. The early English church was thus the heir to the apostolic tradition and to a faith that had been born 'at ye very spring or first going forth of the Gospel, whan the church was moste perfit and had moste strengthe of the holy ghost'.[33] However, the faith of the early British church had later been undermined, first by the imposition of a diocesan structure, and then by the expansion of the monastic tradition which encouraged a superstitious reliance upon works and especially vows of chastity. It was with the arrival of Augustine and his missionaries in 597 that the purity of the church had first become tarnished. Augustine was 'not of the ordre of Christ as was Peter but of the superstitiouse secte of Benet', Bale protested, and had brought with him a religion that had its roots not in the fertile soil of the Gospel but in the 'duste heape of their monkery'.[34] Candles, vestments, relics and altar cloths were the tools with which Augustine and his monks had constructed a seat for Antichrist in the English church.[35] In deliberately misdating the appointment of Theodore of Tarsus as Archbishop of Canterbury to 666, Bale was able to lend to this narrative an apocalyptic edge of the degeneration of the English church in the aftermath of the Augustinian mission. The arrival of the Roman mission was shown to have ushered in a period of a thousand years in which papal interference in the English church had expanded, while the faith of the church had been corrupted by monasticism, idolatry, the cult of the saints and compulsory clerical celibacy, under the influence of Augustine, Dunstan, Anselm and Thomas Becket.[36] To bolster Bale's interpretation of the ecclesiastical past, medieval hagiography, legends and chronicles were pressed into service as propaganda for the evangelical cause.

Bale was quick to recognise, as Tyndale had been, the polemical capital that was to be gained by using the words of the monastic chronicles to condemn the medieval church. The pages of the *Actes of the Englysh Votaries* made frequent references to the histories of Matthew Paris, John of Salisbury, Roger of Wendover and William of Malmesbury. Although Bale argued that most monastic chronicles had been tainted by the context in which they were produced, some writers, most notably the sixth-century historian Gildas, were reread and reinterpreted as proto-Protestants.[37] But Bale's vigorous condemnation of monastic authors for their uncritical acceptance of the material that they handled was accompanied by a long-standing interest in the English literary and historical tradition. His *Illustrium Maioris Britanniae scriptorum* (1548) presented a chronological listing of English authors, with a summary of the contribution that each had made to English literature and history. The *Illustrium* was greatly augmented and expanded with the publication of the *Scriptorium Illustrium Maioris Brytanniae ... Catalogus* in 1557, in which individual authors were located firmly within Bale's schematic interpretation of history and Scripture. The work was structured to ensure a correspondence between the biographies of individual figures and the prophetic interpretation of history that had been established in the *Image of Both Churches*. Each figure was accorded a role in the historical conflict between the true church and the false. Joseph of Arimathea featured prominently as the missionary who had first brought Christianity to England, Robert Grosseteste appeared as a representative of the true church in a period of error and John Wycliffe emerged as the leading figure in English opposition to the power of the papacy.[38] The *Catalogus* presented the history of the church in England through biographies of those individuals who had shaped and recorded it, and maintained the dominant themes of Bale's historical writings, the rise of Antichrist and the expansion of papal influence in the church.

The iconoclastic attitude with which Bale approached the history of the church was more than matched by his desire to see the records of that history preserved. As Bale's biographer has noted, the theologians and polemical writers of the English Reformation were often antiquaries engaged in the recovery of the medieval past alongside its exploitation as a weapon in controversy.[39] It was the duty of a godly prince, Bale argued, to provide for the completion of the national history project that had been begun by Leland, and to compensate for the loss of the chronicle tradition after the dissolution of the monasteries.[40] Bale had himself amassed a substantial body of materials that related to the history of the church in England and, by the time of his appointment as bishop of Ossory in 1552, his collection amounted to some 350 items.[41] The library was the fruit of Bale's historical and antiquarian endeavours in defence of English religion and culture, and was certainly recognised as a valuable resource for the reconstruction of the medieval national past.[42] However, much of the library had been abandoned when Bale left Ireland and, although Elizabeth I issued a warrant for their return, there is no evidence that Bale was able to recover the lost books.[43] The collection, Bale protested, had fallen into the hands of 'obstinate papists' who continued to conceal the papers in the hope that they would remain out of his reach. The history, and the historical record, of the true church and the false was well worth fighting for.

The historical division between the true church and the false, firmly established in the writings of John Bale, provided the dominant theme for the most substantial treatment of the Christian past produced in Tudor England. John Foxe's *Actes and Monuments*, first printed in English in 1563, exemplifies this 'history-as-propaganda' school of thought.[44] The foundations of the work had been laid in the early 1550s. After the accession of Mary Tudor in 1553, Foxe had sought refuge on the continent and, in 1554, completed a Latin account of the suffering of the heretics and martyrs of the fifteenth and sixteenth centuries. The *Commentarii Rerum in Ecclesia Gestarum*, printed in Strasbourg, was a small octavo volume running to around 200 leaves. Lollard martyrs dominated the narrative, but the volume also included accounts of the life and death of critics of the medieval church in Europe, including Jan Hus and Jerome of Prague. The title page identified the work as the first volume of an intended commentary on the history of the church and an account of the persecutions throughout Europe from the time of Wycliffe to the mid-sixteenth century, but the second volume covering the persecution of the Lutherans was never completed. Between 1553 and 1558, Foxe received a wealth of further information relating to the ongoing persecution in England from evangelicals who had remained at home and from those in exile in Basle, Strasbourg and

Frankfurt. Foxe's work in the city printshops also introduced him to leading evangelical polemicists and historians, including Conrad Gesner and Heinrich Panteleon. The publication of Matthias Flacius' *Catalogus Testium Veritatis* by Oporinus in 1556 provided Foxe with first-hand access to sources and an interpretative scheme for ecclesiastical history that would influence his own work.[45] In 1559 a much expanded history of the martyrs (running to some 750 folio pages) was published in Basle as the *Rerum in Ecclesia Gestarum quae Postremis et Periculosis his Temporibus Evenerunt* (*A Commentary on the Events that have happened in the church in these Latter and Perilous Times*). Again, the title page described the volume as the beginning of a more general history of the great persecutions throughout Europe, the first part of which covered the 'narrative of events in England and Scotland and particularly of the dreadful persecutions under Mary, recent queen'.

The *Commentarii* and the *Rerum* were both dominated by recent events, and it was in the first English edition of his martyrology that Foxe finally fulfilled his intention to produce a more wide-ranging history of the Christian church. Printed in 1563 by John Day, the *Actes and Monuments of these Latter and Perilous Days* included an account of the persecution of the faithful in recent years, but also 'from the year of our Lord 1000 unto the time now present'. The work was vast, running to some 1,500 folio pages, and incorporated extensive accounts of the Marian persecution, a detailed commentary and marginal notes, and woodcuts which depicted the pride of the popes, and, in graphic detail, the suffering of the martyrs. A second edition, printed in 1570, extended to over 2,000 folio pages and presented a detailed narrative of ecclesiastical history that stretched from the age of the Apostles until Foxe's own time. Foxe also took the opportunity to rebut the criticisms that had been levelled against the 1563 edition by Nicholas Harpsfield, whose *Dialogi Sex* (1566) concluded its defence of Catholic theology and practice with a vigorous assault on Foxe's methods and interpretation. Some of the more contentious passages were discreetly removed from the 1570 edition of the *Actes and Monuments*, but others provided the foundation for pugnacious defence of the new Protestant past. A careful examination of history, Foxe claimed, would validate claims that it was the reformed English church, and not the church of Rome, that enjoyed congruity in faith and practice with the primitive church. The preface to the 1570 edition set out a defence of the project and outlined Foxe's purpose. 'For first to see the simple flocke of Christe, especially the vnlearned sort, so miserably abused, and all for ignorance of history,' Foxe told his reader,

> not knowing the course of times, and true descent of the church ... agayne considering the multitude of Chronicles and storywriters ... of whom the most part haue bene either Monkes or clients to the see of Rome, it greued me to behold how partially they handled their stories ... I thought with my selfe nothing more lacking in the Church then a full and a complet history ... faithfully collected out of all our Monasticall writers and written Monumentes.[46]

The title page of the *Actes and Monuments* presented a stark visual representation of the overarching theme of the volume. The title woodcut showed the two churches, the congregation of the faithful and the congregation of Antichrist, in parallel columns on the page. Foxe's narrative placed this conflict between truth and falsehood, faith and persecution, at the centre of a cosmic drama that extended across the whole Christian past. The significance of history to a proper understanding of the present was made clear, with the persecutions of the sixteenth century set firmly within the context of the ongoing battle between Christ and Antichrist, which had followed the loosing of Satan from the pit. The *Actes and Monuments* marked a significant landmark in the development of English historical writing, not least because, as Haller notes, Foxe's narrative incorporated contemporaneous legends concerning the national past into what was a markedly Protestant version of the history of the church and the Reformation.[47] Foxe's narrative used the records of the English past both to remould that past and to construct the present, exploiting familiar myths and legends in order to anchor his history in the popular imagination. The records of the medieval past, for all their monkish fictions, were central to Foxe's reconstruction of that past; alongside his obvious debt to Bale and Flacius, Foxe's vision of church history owed much to the English chronicle tradition.

The narrative of the English ecclesiastical past outlined by Foxe was influenced by the history of the early English church that had been established Bale and Tyndale. Following the interpretative scheme established in Bale's *Actes of the Votaries*, Foxe argued that Christianity had reached Britain prior to the Roman mission sent by Gregory the Great in 597. Foxe provided a list of witnesses to the apostolic faith of the British church, and concluded that it was only with the letter sent from King Lucius to Pope Eleutherius that the first contact had been made between the native church and the church of Rome. Lucius, Foxe argued, had been converted to Christianity prior to his correspondence with the pope, indicating the existence of a Christian tradition and a church in Britain in the second century. John Bale had developed a similar narrative of the early British conversion in his account of the examination and death of Anne Askew.[48] Christianity had been brought to Britain by Joseph of Arimathea, Bale argued, and the letter from Lucius to the pope was simply an attempt to gain advice which might facilitate the dissemination of the faith. There was no sense in which the king had intended to place the native church under the authority of the pope, and the early Christian martyrs in the kingdom had died not for the Roman faith but for the pure faith of Christ.[49] The fact that the king had approached the pope seeking baptism was, for Bale and Foxe, testimony to the antiquity of Christianity in Britain, the pre-Augustinian origins of the national church and the novelty of papal influence over the native religion. In the 1570 edition of the *Actes and Monuments*, Foxe reproduced the letter that was reputed to have been sent by the pope in reply to Lucius, but the legend of the conversion of the second century king was still far from straightforward. The basic narrative had been established by Bede in his *Ecclesiastical History* and popularised in the histories of Geoffrey of Monmouth. However, criticism of

Monmouth's history in the early sixteenth century had combined with evangelical attempts to find evidence of Christianity in Britain prior to the arrival of Augustine to create a legend which was both useful to the evangelical cause and open to a decidedly ambiguous interpretation. The conversion of the king had not been mentioned by Gildas, whose history was the primary source for both Bale and Foxe in their investigation of the roots of the church in England and, even if Lucius had approached the king after his conversion, the precedent provided by an English monarch who had sought spiritual patronage from Rome was less than helpful to defenders of the royal supremacy in the middle decades of the sixteenth century.[50] The development of the Lucius legend by Bale and Foxe highlights the process by which evangelical history writing redefined and reshaped the myths and legends of the English past.

The polemical exploitation of history by Bale and Foxe deserves to be set within the context of Protestant history writing during the Reformation in Europe. The search for records of the medieval past was often a collaborative process, and the resources used by Bale in the construction of his histories were shared and exploited both by Foxe and by the compilers of the so-called *Magdeburg Centuries*, a wide-ranging historical narrative produced in defence of the German Lutheran Reformation.[51] The labours of the Magdeburg Centuriators epitomised the motivation and method that underpinned the Reformation approach to the past. The *Ecclesiastica Historia*, a vast history of the universal church, owed its inspiration to Matthias Flacius Illyricus and a group of Lutheran theologians and polemicists in Magdeburg. The volumes of the *Ecclesiastica Historia* presented a universal history of the church that would stand alongside Matthias Flacius' own catalogue of 'witnesses' to the faith throughout history. This *Catalogus Testium Veritatis*, printed in 1556, had argued vigorously against Catholic claims to continuity with the early church, using the evidence provided by medieval chronicles, ecclesiastical documents and those individuals who had been persecuted by the church. Flacius shared with Bale the principle that history could be interpreted in the light of Scripture and exploited as a store of evidence that could be utilised in polemical debate. The *Catalogus* both used the words and actions of the heroes of the medieval church to attack Catholic doctrine, and anchored the events of biblical prophecy within a historical narrative. The text presented an imposing array of materials, arranged under some 370 headings, which pointed to evidence of shared faith and practice between the primitive church and the Lutheran congregations. In defence of the rejection of Catholic tradition, Flacius cited some 400 'witnesses', including Gregory the Great and Thomas Aquinas, alongside those who had been condemned for heresy by the medieval church, in order to highlight innovation and error in the doctrine and practice of the institutional church.

A similar approach underpinned the work of the Magdeburg Centuriators. In the volumes of the *Ecclesiastica Historia* that were printed between 1560 and 1574, the Christian past was divided into thirteen 'centuries', each containing material that related to areas of controversy between Protestant and Catholic, arranged under sixteen headings. Individual sections addressed key doctrinal issues, including the nature of heresy, the development of rites and ceremonies, and miracles and the supernatural. The determination to demonstrate that the Roman church had been led into error under the influence of the papal Antichrist shaped the selection and presentation of materials, and the appeal to the records of the past was moulded by the virulent anti-papal polemic of the narrative. The materials presented in the *Ecclesiastica Historia*, and their interpretation, exerted a powerful influence over the construction of a Protestant past in Germany and beyond. However, the work remained unfinished. The first thirteen centuries were printed separately in folio volumes, but the final three centuries compiled by Johannes Wigand remained in manuscript form.[52] The thousands of folio pages that found their way into print still presented a coherent body of evidence from which to construct a historical genealogy for the Reformation and challenged Catholic claims to continuity in faith and practice with the church of the Apostles. Its influence on history writing in England should not be underestimated. John Bale described his own *Catalogus* as 'set fourthe by me and Illyricus', and the indebtedness of Foxe to the labours of Bale and the Magdeburg Centuriators is clear.[53]

Matthias Flacius had sought assistance from Bale in the compilation of the *Centuries*, and was clearly well aware of the problems that might be experienced in collecting materials that related to the history of the English church. The fourth volume of the *Ecclesiastica Historia* was dedicated and presented to Elizabeth I, in the hope that the patronage or intervention of the queen might encourage the circulation of crucial manuscript materials and facilitate the recovery of the English past. Flacius certainly received assistance from Matthew Parker, Elizabeth's archbishop of Canterbury, whose own interests in the history of Christianity in England were well known.[54] The creation of a useable English past was as much of a priority for Parker and the Elizabethan church as it had been in the aftermath of the break with Rome. A 'Protestantised antiquity'[55] could provide both a historical justification for the reform of the church and a cogent defence of the particular strain of Protestantism that was embodied in the Elizabethan settlement of religion. Parker's response to Flacius' request for assistance was in sympathy with the archbishop's ongoing acquisition of literature and manuscripts from the English past, and with the compilation and translation of materials relating to the early British church. The dissolution of the monasteries had made available vast reserves of theological and historical sources, but with the opening of the monastic libraries the collections had been dispersed, often without trace. Bale complained that a substantial body of material had been shipped to Flanders in the aftermath of the dissolution, and protested bitterly that the valuable records of the English past had been used for entirely unscholarly purposes by candlemakers and cobblers.[56] Parker was therefore obliged to enlist the support of his colleagues on the episcopal bench, calling upon the bishops to search their cathedral libraries for surviving manuscripts and printed materials that related to the history of the medieval church.

Despite evidence that some individuals were reluctant to deliver their prized possessions to the archbishop, Parker successfully acquired a substantial quantity of material for his collection from a wide variety of sources. His library contained a number of volumes collected from Christ Church and St Augustine's in Canterbury, and from the cathedral libraries in Worcester and Norwich. Bishop Scory provided three volumes from Hereford, John Jewel expressed his regret that the library of Salisbury had yielded little of value, and correspondence with Bishop Davies suggests that the libraries of the Welsh church were also searched.[57] Parker's copy of John of Tynemouth's *Historia Aurea* had been compiled in the scriptorium of St Albans Abbey, and a twelfth-century collection of the *lives* of the saints originated in Dover Priory. A fourteenth-century calendar of the *lives* of the old English saints came from Southwick Priory, and Parker's copy of Bede's *Life of St Cuthbert* was part of the library of Durham Priory.[58] Personal contacts were also important and, despite the loss of the bulk of Bale's library in Ireland, several of the manuscripts in Parker's collection had once passed through Bale's hands. A copy of William of Malmesbury's *Gesta Pontificum* from Norwich may well have reached Parker via Bale, and annotations on first page of the *Chronicon Dictum* of John Brompton suggest that this volume had also been used by Bale. A twelfth-century collection of the *lives* of the saints dating from the late twelfth or early thirteenth century may well be the volume that Bale listed among his own manuscripts as the *Vita Marcialis Apostoli*, and the copy of the chronicle of Thomas Walsingham that Parker used in his edition of Matthew Paris' *Historia Anglorum* contains annotations in Bale's hand.[59]

Parker had sought advice on the recovery of the national past from Bale in July 1560, and Bale's reply included details of manuscripts that he believed would facilitate the archbishop's attempts to demonstrate the independence of the pre-Conquest church in England from the influence of Rome. Arranged under a variety of headings, the list of manuscripts included ecclesiastical histories, biographies of the popes, and details of the works written by and against those heretics who had been condemned by the medieval church.[60] The fruits of Parker's endeavours are visible in the quantity of Saxon texts in his library, which included some 38 manuscripts in Old English. Parker also employed several scholars with interests in Saxon history and philology.[61] Working in the house of William Cecil, William Lambarde produced editions of Bede's *Ecclesiastical History*, sections of the *Anglo Saxon Chronicle*, and collections of Saxon laws and poetry.[62] Laurence Nowell has been credited with the rediscovery of Anglo-Saxon learning and language, and certainly transcribed several important texts that chronicled the history of the pre-Conquest church in England. Nowell was succeeded by Robert Talbot and John Joscelyn, who were responsible for much of the research undertaken by Parker's circle on the history of the Saxon church in the 1560s. Joscelyn had himself attempted to compile a list of potentially useful pre-Conquest books and authors, which included the *lives* of the saints, as well as Eadmer's *Historia Novarum*, used by Parker in his researches into the antiquity of clerical marriage in the English church. These preliminary researches were followed by the creation of a more substantial catalogue, which was informed by the advice on the Saxon past that Parker had received from Bale.[63] Joscelyn also completed transcripts of tracts and treatises by Asser, William Thorne and

Thomas Sprott, and collected manuscripts that related to the history of the Abbey of Abingdon in the pre-Conquest period.[64] To facilitate the printing of materials relating to Parker's historical researches, John Day commissioned the casting of the first Anglo-Saxon font, which was used in his 1566/7 edition of the sermons of Aelfric.[65]

The Anglo-Saxon church was particularly useful to Parker and to other English evangelicals who sought to establish the roots of the reformed church in the early medieval past. The faith and practice of the early British church were presented in opposition to the Catholic piety of the sixteenth century and exploited as evidence that it was the reformed church which was the true heir of primitive Christianity. Parker and his colleagues sought to demonstrate that the Elizabethan religious settlement was in fact the restoration of the early faith of the national church, rescued from centuries of papal oppression and corruption. The library assembled by the archbishop contained several manuscripts of *Saxon Homilies* which provided valuable raw materials for the history and theology of the pre-Augustinian church.[66] The homilies of Aelfric, the tenth-century abbot of Eynsham, were printed in 1566/7 as the *Testimonie of Antiquitie*, in a prime example of Parker's efforts to demonstrate congruity and continuity in the faith and doctrine of the Saxon and Elizabethan churches. Aelfric's homily for Easter Day was particularly useful to Parker, who printed his own copy of the text '*in die Sancta Pasce*' as evidence of English opposition to the Catholic theology of the eucharist. Sections of Parker's copy of Matthew Paris' *Chronica Majora* that covered the pre-Conquest history of England were annotated in order to identify important events, and Parker's distinctive red markings also highlighted passages from Bede's *Historia Saxonice* for further attention.[67] Parker was not the first English writer to prioritise the precedent provided by the early British church. John Bale's *Actes of the Englysh Votaries* had opened with an appeal to Gildas' *De Excidio Britanniae* (c. 540), and Parker also recognised the importance of Gildas as the only surviving source for the period of the Anglo-Saxon conquest of Britain. An edition of Gildas' work was published in 1567, with a preface which extolled the value of the work as a defence of British history from the unwarranted criticisms of foreign Catholic writers.[68]

However, Parker's interests were not limited to the history of the Anglo-Saxon church alone. The library assembled by the archbishop also contained copies of the major English chronicles from the post-Conquest period, including the works of Henry of Huntingdon, William of Malmesbury, Matthew Paris and Florence of Worcester. Several manuscript chronicles were edited and published, including the *Flores Historiarum*, the *Historia Anglorum* and the *Greater Chronicle* of Matthew Paris. Parker and his circle appreciated the value of the records of both the sacred and secular past in the construction of a defence of the Elizabethan church. Key events in the reign of King John were marked with marginal annotations in Parker's copy of Matthew Paris' *Chronica Majora*, and Parker and his secretaries identified crucial passages in the *Gesta Pontificum* of William of Malmesbury. Sections of Book Five of the *Gesta Pontificum*, which covered the history of Aldhelm and Malmesbury Abbey, were heavily annotated, and the marginalia include the caustic comment that the reported vision of a monk of Eynsham was mere fable, '*visio fallax et fabulosa*'.[69] Parker also possessed copies of Ranulph Higden's fourteenth-century *Polichronicon* and John Capgrave's *Chronicle of England to 1417*, and had acquired and annotated a copy of Capgrave's *De Illustribus Henricis* which had already been used by Bale.[70] Parker also made numerous comments and annotations on his copy of the writings of Gerald of Wales, particularly on sections of a dialogue on the history of the church which included references to married priests and clerical concubinage. Gerald's text was clearly of interest to an archbishop for whom clerical marriage was both a personal and a doctrinal issue.[71]

Parker's library contained a variety of books and manuscripts that had belonged to his medieval predecessors in Canterbury, including St Augustine and St Thomas Becket, and his own catalogue of the collection drew attention to those volumes that had come from the libraries of key figures in the English ecclesiastical past. The library also housed copies of the *lives* of the English saints, bishops and archbishops, including Dunstan, Erkenwald, Swithun and Aldhelm.[72] Parker also owned a copy of the *life* of St Guthlac, a twelfth-century *Passio S Aethelberti*, a twelfth-century *life* of St Augustine, Ailred's *Vita S Edwardi* and Eadmer's biography of St Anselm.[73] Such texts appear to have been read in conjunction with other sources, and annotations to the manuscripts provide useful insights into Parker's attempts to compare variant *lives* and histories.[74] Some figures from the past were clearly thought to be worthy of further investigation, and Parker's interest in the *life* of St Dunstan is evident in the annotations made alongside the *life* in a twelfth-century *Vitae Sanctorum*. The title of Obsern's *life* of the saint is provided in Parker's hand, and further annotations are visible in sections of the manuscript that describe key events in the saint's life, particularly the attempts made to impose the discipline of clerical celibacy on the English church. Parker was certainly not afraid to criticise the sources that he used, making a bold note in the margin of the *life*: 'Edmerus corru[]pit hae[] historia[]. Et hic Osbern[] currupte scribitur'.[75] A sixteenth-century transcript of the *life* of St Alban of Mainz was subject to the same critical interpretation and annotation.[76] However, the *lives* of other saints were exploited in the search for proto-Protestants in the national past. Bede's *Life of St Cuthbert* was cited as evidence of the practice of public confession and communion in both kinds in the early British church, and Parker highlighted passages from Archbishop Baldwin's twelfth-century tract on the eucharist as proof that theology of the church had been subject to change.[77] Decades after the suppression of the cult of the saints, the *lives* of the saints that survived in English cathedrals and libraries were to form an essential component of the construction of Parker's history of the national church.

Narratives of the life and works of medieval archbishops of Canterbury were of further value to Parker in his attempts to demonstrate the continuity of the episcopacy throughout English ecclesiastical history. Several manuscripts in Parker's collection were annotated with lists of the names and dates of the archbishops and details of the history of the see of Canterbury. Hand-written additions to sections of the *Anglo-Saxon Chronicle* and Anglo-Saxon laws identified the popes who had sent palls to the medieval archbishops, and a Durham copy of the *life* of St Cuthbert was annotated with a list of the archbishops. The first 21 names were written in the original medieval hand, with further names and numbers being added in a sixteenth-century hand to include Parker as the seventieth archbishop. A further chronology of the English bishops appears to have been checked and corrected by Parker.[78] A similar list of the archbishops of Canterbury appeared in a manuscript containing a *life* of Thomas Becket, in which a Parkerian hand updated the list to include Parker himself. This desire to preserve this appearance of continuity in the succession to Canterbury may well have convinced Parker to adopt a moderate stance in his investigations into the life of one of his more controversial predecessors, Thomas Becket.[79] Parker's collection included copies of letters sent from Becket to Henry II but, while such papers would have provided useful insights into the controversy between the king and the archbishop, there is little evidence of any critical annotations or commentaries from either Parker or his secretaries, beyond faint lines which identify important passages. A number of lines in the *life* of Becket in a fourteenth-century legendary were underlined, but without any hostile comments in the margins.[80] Parker's library also housed a *life* of Becket written in 1497 by Laurence Wade, a monk of Christ Church, Canterbury. The text was hardly helpful to critics of Becket, and opened with a fulsome declaration of the holiness of the cause for which the saint had died:

> O ye virtuous soverayns spiritual and temporal
> And all ye deuoute people both more and lesse
> That thys now shall here hartely I praye yow all
> To support my imperfection of lowly gentylnesse
> For the lyeff here I purpose with your pacience to reherse
> Off seynt Thomas the blessed laureat martir dere
> That dyed for the churchys right onely in Cristys were.[81]

The impact of the early Reformation upon the cult and reputation of Becket is evident in the volume in the sections in which the name of the saint has been deleted from the text, presumably as a result of the Henrician Injunctions of 1538. However, the Parkerian annotations in the margin highlight, not the controversial incidents in the life of Becket but, rather, information that related to the history of the see of Canterbury.[82]

The primary concern of Parker and his circle was the creation of a complete and credible record of the national ecclesiastical past. The archbishop's collection was not simply a labour of preservation but was also a working library. Parker was often an intrusive editor and his heavy annotation of the manuscripts in his possession has attracted criticism.[83] Materials were exchanged between manuscripts and missing sections borrowed from other sources to fill gaps in the narrative. There are copious examples of Parkerian additions and alterations to the manuscript sources that he used. Many changes to the texts were minor: a leaf was added to a fifteenth-century copy of John of Tynemouth's *Historia Aurea*, and missing pages of Matthew Paris' *Chronica Majora* were copied from other extant editions and replaced by

Parker.[84] Volumes were indexed, paginated and provided with a table of contents for future reference.[85] On other occasions, sections from alternative editions and manuscripts were inserted into the original.[86] As May McKisack has noted, Parker and his team did not regard the manuscript text as sacred but, rather, attempted the restoration, both 'physically and conjecturally', of what the author had (or might have) written.[87] Chronicles and manuscripts were read, annotated and plundered for the information that they could provide on controversial issues in the Elizabethan church.

The manuscripts in Parker's collection provided a body of evidence on particular issues that were of vital importance, including the pre-Augustinian origins of the English episcopacy, the vernacular liturgy and scripture of the early church, and the freedom of the English clergy to marry prior to the extension of papal authority over the church. By searching the records of the ecclesiastical past, Parker and his circle sought to identify a precedent for the Elizabethan Reformation, while demonstrating, in common with other evangelical history writers, the degree to which the Roman church had departed from the example of the early followers of Christ. Their labours bore fruit in the printing of the *De Antiquitate* in 1572, which described the faith and practice of the English church prior to the arrival of Augustine in 597 and set out the role that successive archbishops of Canterbury had played in the defence of true doctrine. The volume also celebrated historical writing and scholarship, and emphasised again the value of the rediscovery of ancient texts and the restoration of the national past.[88] There was, Parker believed, a value in collecting histories of the medieval church, and medieval monastic writings, despite the errors that they contained. As Parker explained in the preface to his edition of Thomas Walsingham's chronicle, it was better that the English should have access to their past than that such chronicles be destroyed because they contained errors and superstition.[89] The work of Parker and his circle reflected the crucial developments that had taken place in English Protestant history writing in the middle decades of the sixteenth century, as the medieval past was first rejected, then explored, exploited and employed in the defence of the Reformation.

History was clearly not the preserve of evangelical propagandists alone. The creation of a polemically useful past in the sixteenth century had turned history into a powerful weapon in religious controversy. The importance attached to the possession of the past is evident, not only in the works of Tyndale, Bale, Foxe and the Magdeburg Centuriators, but also in the vigorous response from Catholic controversialists who were determined to reclaim the lessons of ecclesiastical history as their own. Tyndale's attempts to wrest the history of true religion from the history of the institutional church had solicited a strident defence of the faith and practice of the medieval church from Thomas More. Where Tyndale criticised the traditions of the Catholic church and alleged that the church had deviated from the practice of the apostolic church, More argued for the continued presence of the Holy Spirit in the church, evinced in the stability of an unchanging faith in time and space. Tyndale's 'rabble of heretics' stood in stark contrast to the 'common corps of Christendom', whose Catholic faith remained constant across the centuries. The reformers were confused and isolated fanatics, who claimed a precedent for their actions by reference to the history of an invisible church that only its members knew to be real. The location of sixteenth-century evangelicals within a historical congregation of heretics was a vital part of Thomas More's construction of an identity for the institutional church and for its opponents. In this scheme, the unknown church of the heretics was isolated from the historical record and separated from the visible community of the faithful. At the intersection of the absolute authority of the historical and visible church and the imagined authority of the chaotic and demonic other, a clear identity was defined for both.[90] More's arguments have echoes in the criticisms levelled against John Foxe and the *Actes and Monuments* by his Catholic contemporaries, including Nicholas Harpsfield, Thomas Stapleton and Robert Parsons.[91] Harpsfield's *Dialogi Sex* (1566) was a vigorous attempt to answer Foxe on his own ground, by dismantling the ecclesiastical history contained in the *Actes and Monuments* and rebuilding a coherent Catholic narrative of the past that demonstrated both continuity throughout the Middle Ages and congruity with the primitive church. The first book defended the primacy of the pope, the second monasticism, and later sections presented a historical and doctrinal defence of the cult of saints and images. The final dialogue was an assault upon Foxe's history and his construction of Protestant martyrdom. The polemical effectiveness of Harpsfield's work was built upon the mass of information and sources that he rallied in defence of his cause, and upon its clear chronological and thematic structure which repeatedly asserted the legitimacy and longevity of the faith of the Catholic church. By comparison, Harpsfield claimed, the English Protestant church was a flimsy construction, built upon nothing more than the antipathy of its members to the church of Rome. Like More, Harpsfield highlighted evidence of dissension within the ranks of the evangelicals and contrasted the unity of the Catholic church with the disparate and warring factions that made up Foxe's history of the true church in England.[92]

The works of Harpsfield and his contemporaries demonstrate the determination with which Catholic writers in the reign of Elizabeth sought to reclaim the history of the medieval church in England. In 1565, Thomas Stapleton published a translated edition of one of the key texts of the national sacred past, Bede's *Ecclesiastica Historiae Gentis Anglorum*. The commentary on the text also included material from Stapleton's 1565 *Fortresse of the Faith*, which had highlighted the differences between the faith of the Protestant church in England and that of the early British church that it claimed as its ancestor. The true church, Stapleton argued, had been 'planted first among Englishmen' and then reinforced by later papal missionaries. Augustine's mission in 597 had continued the work of the earlier missionaries from Rome, including those who had converted King Lucius, whose example was so central to the narrative of the primitive British church provided by Bale and Foxe.[93] The true faith in England was to be found, not in the history of the martyrs crowned by Foxe, but in the testimony and miracles of the holy men and women of the Catholic church. Bede's narrative of ecclesiastical history not only presented

38

evidence of the worthy witness provided by the faithful in the centuries before Augustine but also identified the church founded by Augustine, and authenticated by miracles, as the heir of this primitive tradition.[94] In order to mount a cogent defence of the antiquity and authenticity of Catholic doctrine against the criticisms of Foxe and other evangelical history writers, Catholic polemicists attempted to wrest the ecclesiastical history of the English people from the pages of Protestant histories. Defenders of the Reformation had destroyed the Catholic past and constructed a new Protestant narrative, which was in turn dismantled by Catholic writers in an attempt to expose once more the original historical foundations of the English church.

Writing in 1581, Robert Parsons protested that his opponents had 'destroied the old memories [and] would now make us new' in their efforts to 'Protestantize' the national past. There was no authority in Scripture or in history for the actions of his Protestant opponents 'but only self will and fansie', Parsons alleged, claiming to have found over 100 errors in just three pages of Foxe's history.[95] The history of religion and politics in England presented in Parsons' works had its roots in the medieval and Tudor chronicles that had been exploited by evangelical history writers. The historical argument in the *Conference About the Next Succession to the Crown of Ingland* (1594) was informed by a close reading of Polydore Vergil, alongside the works of Tudor chroniclers. Other works were more overt in their attempt to construct a history of the medieval church which would expose the errors and falsehoods that had masqueraded as historical fact in the pages of the *Actes and Monumentes*. The *Treatise of the Three Conversions* (1603–4) represented the culmination of Parsons' attempt to demolish the foundations of Protestant history writing that had been laid by Bale and Foxe. Books One and Two used the principles of the evangelical reconstruction of the past as the basis for a new, Catholic narrative of the history of the medieval church. The church established by Augustine in 597, Parsons claimed, was identical in faith and practice to the early church from which the Catholic church in the sixteenth century could chart its descent.[96] The three conversions to which the title referred were the labours of St Peter and Joseph of Arimathea, reinforced by the conversion of King Lucius, and finally brought to fruition in the late sixth century after the arrival of Augustine. It was the Catholic church across the centuries which was the true heir of this Saxon Christianity, founded by the Apostles and established by the papacy. The saints and heroes of this English church had spread this faith across Europe; Christianity in England lay at the heart of the medieval church; and its survival was a visible expression of the unity enjoyed by the true church. The final book was devoted to an investigation of the characteristics of Christian martyrdom, which was intended to discredit the 'martyrs' that had been created in Foxe's *Actes and Monumentes* and break apart the bonds of faith and suffering which had joined the martyrs of the Reformation to those of the primitive church. The Reformation in England was not the restoration of the faith of the early Saxon or British church but, rather, a wilful separation from it, in which the heroes of the medieval church had been displaced by the false saints and pseudo-martyrs created by Protestant history writers.[97] Parsons, Stapleton, Bale and Foxe each sought evidence of the origins of the church in the early British past. The dichotomy between the interpretations of that past that they set forth offers a clear demonstration of the malleability of the historical record in the hands of Reformation controversialists.

Evangelical writing on the ecclesiastical past generated a Catholic response on a grand scale. The publication of the Lutheran *Magdeburg Centuries* was followed by the compilation of the massive *Annales Ecclesiastici* (1588), the fruit of the labours of Caesar Baronius. Structured around the principle of *semper eadem*, 'always the same', the *Annales* were an imposing response to the interpretation of history and dogma that had been advanced by Flacius, Judex and Wigand. The *Annales* had their origins in a series of lectures delivered at weekly conferences in the church of San Girolamo in the 1560s, but the bulk of the work was not completed until the 1580s. Baronius' endeavours coincided with a heightened interest in the history of the church after the Council of Trent and with a growing appreciation of the value of an accurate record of the history of the church, both as a means of validating traditional practices and as a weapon in religious controversy. To this end, Gregory XIII entrusted to Baronius the task of revising the Roman martyrology, in order to accommodate the recent calendar reforms and to present an accurate and verifiable record of the martyrs of the church. The first edition of the martyrology appeared in 1586, but Baronius' work continued and further revisions were printed in 1589. The first volume of the *Annales* appeared in 1588, the same year as the foundation of the Sacred Congregation for Rites and Ceremonies, reflecting the close relationship between the ecclesiastical past and present in the post-Tridentine church. The decades that followed witnessed the emergence of a number of 'Baronio figures', who were inspired to use available manuscript sources to set out and defend the history of their local churches and saints.[98] Baronius' own work was ongoing, with the publication of the second volume of the *Annales* in 1590, five further volumes by 1596 and the final five volumes by 1607. These 12 volumes extended the narrative to the end of the twelfth century. The death of Baronius in 1607 did not bring the project to an end, and continuations were published by scholars within the Oratorian order. By the eighteenth century, full editions of the *Annales* ran to more than 30 volumes, but the text rapidly emerged as a popular work of history, abridged and edited for different audiences and earning for Baronius the title of 'Father of Ecclesiastical History'.

The scale of the response from Baronius was a clear indication of the seriousness with which the Catholic church regarded the threat posed by the evangelical reconstruction of the past. Historical writing in Germany in the middle decades of the sixteenth century had been a crucial factor in the hardening of confessional lines after the Peace of Augsburg, and in England the same period had witnessed the construction of a powerful national and historical identity for the nascent reformed church.[99] The past did much to influence the controversies of the Reformation, but doctrinal debates also did much to shape the appeal to the past.[100] Early sixteenth-century antiquarian interests were largely overtaken by the concerns and controversies of the Reformation, which (sometimes literally) reinvented the Middle Ages and fashioned a useable history from the records and narratives of the medieval church. The interaction of history and Scripture in the search for the roots of English evangelicalism in the national church of the past was most clearly evident in the works of John Bale and John Foxe, but was reflected more widely in polemical defences of the Henrician and Edwardian church. The religious struggles of the sixteenth century were represented as the contemporary enactment of the everlasting conflict between the true church and the false throughout history, and it was in the midst of this conflict that the self-fashioning of the national church occurred. English evangelical identity was shaped against that of an Antichristian enemy, the institutional embodiment of vice and corruption, that was recognisable and identifiable.[101] The reform or the destruction of the false and demonic was predicated upon the ability to discover (or invent) its existence in the past and the present. It was this necessity which energised the application of a genre of polemical writing, based upon polarised opposites, to the history of the church.

This imagery of opposition in history was apparent in the works of the first generation of English evangelical writers. William Tyndale's *Parable of the Wicked Mammon* (1528) was structured around the stark contrast between the true church and the false, the honest and the fraudulent, the simplicity of the word of God and the impenetrability of the doctrines of the medieval church.[102] The history of the two churches had its origins in the conflict between Cain and Abel and encompassed the whole of human history until the last judgement. Membership of the true church or the false was not simply institutional, but was evident in morality, doctrine and action. John Bale's *The Image of Both Churches* identified and exploited the theological and moral opposition between the true church and the false throughout history, while George Joye's *Commentary on Daniel* used the persecution of the faithful in the time of Daniel as the starting point for a narrative of the continued suffering of the true church throughout history. The persecution of English evangelicals in the reign of Mary was a highly visible drama in this ongoing cosmic battle, and this same sense of contemporary events as the latest phase in the historical conflict between truth and falsehood was apparent in the words of some of the martyrs themselves.[103] The members of the congregation of the false church were identifiable by their actions, their morality, their persecution of the faithful and their degeneration into idolatry, which placed them throughout the ages in the historical company of Antichrist.

The attempt to relate history to prophecy was not without precedent. However, the scale of the endeavour in the sixteenth century has encouraged historians to see this period as a critical time in the development of the English understanding of history, prophecy and the biblical Antichrist.[104] The traditional figure of Antichrist in late-medieval religious literature was a composite image of a future figure of evil constructed from indistinct warnings contained in a limited number of biblical texts.[105] In the hands of evangelical writers in the sixteenth century, Antichrist became a permanent spiritual presence within the church. Antichrist was not a

41

figure yet to come, but a force of evil and deception that was already active in the world. The evangelical image of Antichrist is encapsulated in Tyndale's *Parable of the Wicked Mammon.* 'Antichrist is not an outward thing, that is to say a man that should sode[n]ly appear with wonders as our fathers talked of him,' Tyndale claimed, 'no verily, for Antichrist is a spirituall thing. And this is as much to say as agaynst Christ, ye one that preacheth against Christ.'[106] The identification of the actions and influence of this permanent and corrupting presence within the church was accomplished through the application of the scriptural text to the Christian past. History was the arena in which the spiritual actions of Antichrist found visible expression and in which the ongoing conflict between good and evil found an embodiment in recorded events and personalities.

The conflict between true and false religion in the sixteenth century was thus expressed in terms of a vigorous two-church ideology, in which the adherents of truth and error in the present were identified by the application of biblical and historical types from the biblical and Christian past.[107] The visible church had an identifiable history, and the evangelical claim that the true faith resided not in the institutional church but in the invisible congregation necessitated the creation of a plausible past for a church that had no formal record of its existence. The application of biblical prophecy to events in the past and the present lent a legitimacy to this reinterpretation of history. Suffering and persecution at the hands of the false church became the marks of the true congregation, and allowed evangelical writers to invert the traditional Catholic claim that it was visible continuity which secured and substantiated the legitimacy of the church.[108] Protestantism acquired a history as a congregation of the faithful which had resisted the corruptions and persecutions of the Catholic church in centuries past, and acquired an identity in the present as the heirs of the persecuted witnesses to the truth throughout the Middle Ages. Doctrinal continuity among these historical witnesses was more theoretical than tangible, but the 'homogenisation' of medieval heresies condemned by the Catholic church into a body bound together by a shared faith and experience ensured that these groups could provide the Reformation with a past, and one that was rooted in biblical prophecy.[109] The appearance of an English edition of Bernardino Ochino's commentary on the battle between Christ and Antichrist in 1549 reflects the religious and political impulse that underpinned such a reconstruction of the past. The *Tragoedie or Dialoge of the Unjust Usurped Primacie of the Bishop of Rome* not only justified the separation of the English church from Rome but also located the reign of Edward VI within the ongoing conflict between Christ and Antichrist and provided the young king with a pivotal role in the prophetic and historical drama.[110]

The narrative of a medieval past in which the faithful followers of Christ laboured against the growing influence of Antichrist in the church was a crucial component in the construction of religious identities in the sixteenth century and a powerful weapon in polemical debate and controversy. At the most basic level, history writing provided the means by which the ancient practices of the church could be identified and described, and an ancestry found for the Protestant

Reformation. The history of the early church was crucial in this regard as a witness to the practice of the apostolic church and a record of the faith of the first generations of Christians. However, the history of the medieval church was highly significant as the record of conflict between truth and error, orthodoxy and heterodoxy in the centuries before the Reformation. The apostolic church presented a record of the antiquity of Christian practice, but the intervening 1,000 years provided evangelical writers with a pre-history for the Reformation which located their church in a time and space which were broader than the present. Meaning and purpose in the present were to be found in the reinterpretation of the events of the past, a reinterpretation that located contemporary controversies and conflicts within the unfolding pattern of a divinely inspired history. The reformation of the past reached to the heart of the crisis of authority precipitated by the division of Christendom by shattering the link between the visible continuity of the church as an institution and the invisible continuity of the faith of believers. An appeal to Scripture alone might well prove insufficient to inspire faith in a church that had no visible history and might prove to have no future.[111] But history, interpreted in the light of Scripture, provided Protestantism with an existence in the past, a function in the present and a promise of reward in times to come.

The importance of the past lay not only in the fruits of antiquarian endeavour but also in the polemical and interpretative function of history in deciphering the present. History was a kaleidoscope in which both Protestant and Catholic could observe the events of their own time reflected, dissected and rebuilt. The approach to the past was dictated by the priorities of the present, and the changing nature of evangelical history writing in England reflected the changing needs of the nascent English church.[112] The history of the papal Antichrist was popularised by the break with Rome but also served to justify the independence of the English church and provide it with a location within the grand scheme of providential history. English evangelicals, frustrated by what they regarded as the slow pace of reform within the Henrician church, found solace in accounts of the suffering of biblical prophets and true believers throughout history, and saw a justification for their actions in the application of the words of Scripture to the events of the past and the present. Responding to the exigencies of the age, preachers and polemicists drew parallels between the reign and Reformation of the young king Edward VI and the rule of the boy king Josiah, who had destroyed idolatry in his own time and cast down the false altars of the priests.[113] Martyrdom and exile in the reign of Mary inspired a struggle for possession of the precedent of the primitive church, as Catholic writers compared evangelicals to those heretics condemned by the Fathers, while Protestant martyrologists portrayed them as successors to the 'old ancient saints' who had suffered for their faith in the first Christian centuries.[114] Finally, the nature of the Elizabethan church and settlement required a history for the English church that demonstrated the antiquity of the episcopacy yet undermined the legitimacy of Catholic practice.

In the turbulence of Reformation debate, history as a store of moral examples gave way to history as fulfilment of prophecy and history as the building blocks of cultural identity.[115] The attempt to locate contemporary events within the framework of the Christian past, coupled with the polemical reconstruction of that past, yielded results that in turn seemed to justify such an approach to history and controversy. John Dick has noted that Tyndale's *Parable of the Wicked Mammon* 'successfully initiated a mythologizing of current English history that became increasingly a self fulfilling prophecy, providing ideological justification for the widening breach with Rome'.[116] The interdependence of past and present is evident in the construction of a new, evangelical character for the English church. The creation of an ancestry for the reformed church in Christian history, as has been suggested, was made possible only by locating the nascent national church in the same past that it had itself created: 'the Protestant historian produces pasts in which, not surprisingly, he finds himself'.[117] The search for proto-Protestants in the medieval past went some way towards providing evangelicals with an answer to the question of where their church had been before Luther. As a result, the past was rewritten, reconstructed and reformed in order that it might accommodate the demands of doctrinal controversy and polemical debate. But the moulding of medieval history that took place in the middle decades of the sixteenth century also raised more fundamental questions about the nature of the church, the authenticity of its teachings and its location in the past and present conflict between truth and falsehood, Christ and Antichrist. This conflict between past and present, good and evil, presented a potentially devastating challenge to traditional assumptions about the church, the papacy, ecclesiastical authority, and the heroes and wonders of medieval history and hagiography.

3

'LYING HISTORIES FAYNING FALSE MIRACLES'

Monks, miracles and magic in the medieval past

In June 1538, the bishop of Chichester wrote to his commissary describing the conduct of one of his diocesan clergy who, according to the bishop, 'seems to be a very fool'. The bishop's complaints against Cowley focused upon two key issues: first, Cowley had defended from the pulpit the presence of images in churches, and second, he had preached with what might be described as incautious enthusiasm on the miracles of the saints. In particular, Cowley had told his congregation the story of a man who had been miraculously healed by St Martin, but had responded to this act of saintly thaumaturgical generosity by complaining that, now cured, he was expected to work for a living. However, Cowley's comments soon acquired a political dimension when he proceeded to speculate on the possibility of future miracles and predicted that, just as St Martin had cured the man's body of disease, so Henry VIII would remove the disease of the New Testament from the people of England. He had then instructed his parishioners to pray to St Antony for the wellbeing of their cattle, and appeal for the intercession of St Louis on behalf of their horses.[1] The expectation of such miraculous interventions in the world by God and His saints had been a central part of pre-Reformation piety and devotion. Cowley's comments drew upon a long-standing belief in the efficacy of prayer to the saints, but also touched a raw nerve in the controversies of the early Reformation in England. Pilgrimage, relics and miracles had been subjects of heated polemical debate in the preceding decade, and remained a potent weapon in religious controversy. In 1534, Thomas Cranmer had listed miracles, and particularly the ability to 'forge miracles', among contentious topics which were to be avoided by preachers for the space of one year. The popularity of Elizabeth Barton, the Holy Maid of Kent executed in April 1534, reflected the very real threat posed by the political manipulation of miracle and prophecy, and the investigation of the Blood of Hailes and Rood of Boxley in 1538 was indicative of the ongoing determination of the Henrician government to reform attitudes to saints, relics and wonders.[2]

Traditional hagiographical writing had established miracles, both in life and after death, as a clear sign of saintliness. The repeated intrusion of the supernatural into the realm of the material was well documented in the *lives* of the saints, in prophetic discourse and in devotional materials and sermons. A broad range of miracles and cures was attributed to the consecrated host, and such wonders had been used both to inspire devotion to the eucharist and to convince doubters of the validity of Catholic doctrine.[3] The development of the popular pilgrimage shrines of medieval England had been fuelled by the conviction that the relics of the saints both represented and facilitated access to the miraculous. Over 250 miracles were attributed to St Thomas Becket, and the curative powers associated with the primary and secondary relics of the saint had encouraged successive generations of pious and hopeful pilgrims. The same was true of smaller shrines and new pilgrimage sites. Miracles recorded at the Rood of Bromholm included 39 resurrections from the dead, while the miracle collection compiled for the canonisation process of Henry VI detailed numerous incidents of healing and recovery from misfortune.[4] Miracles were treated as evidence of the continued presence of God in His church and divine approbation of its life and doctrines. Their association with saints and pilgrimage, with the identification and promulgation of true doctrine, and as a sign of the true church throughout the centuries, was to ensure that miracles would occupy a central place in the polemic and propaganda of the Reformation.

Writing in 1972, Bernard Vogler commented that the attitude of Protestants to the miraculous was one of 'categorical rejection'.[5] However, more recent research has done much to remind us that the relationship between the Reformation and the supernatural was far more complex than this blunt notion suggests, and that evangelical objections to the saintly miraculous did not carry an implicit rejection of the potentiality of divine intervention in the affairs of the world.[6] Throughout the sixteenth century, evangelical writing on miracles in the past and the present was shaped, not by a simple denial of the possibility that such events took place, but rather by the reinterpretation of the miraculous as fraud, sleight of hand or diabolic manipulation. The miracles of the medieval church were not abandoned, but rather turned into polemical weapons that could be used to condemn Catholicism as a faith which was founded upon deceit, manipulation and credulity. Miracles that had provided the foundation for the cult of the saints were recast as the tools of its destruction. Peter Marshall has argued that the 'false' miracles exposed in the 1530s presented the Henrician regime with a 'valuable hermeneutic prism' through which religious change could be represented as the actions of a godly king lifting the yoke of popery and leading his people from the blindness of superstition.[7] However, the evangelical manipulation of the miraculous was not limited to recent events, but reached back into the history of the church and its saints. The bold assertion that the age of miracles had passed enabled evangelical writers to reject as frauds and diabolic deceptions a multitude of miracles attributed to the saints of the past, and break apart the foundations of the cult of the saints, pilgrimage and sacred thaumaturgy. The exposition of false wonders in the *lives* of the saints and the life of the church lent weight to the argument that the visible and historical church of Rome was the fulfilment of biblical prophecies of the false church, deceived by false preachers and deluded by feigned wonders. Miracles and marvels acquired a historical location, not simply in the narrative chronology of the past, but in the evangelical reading of that narrative as a conflict between truth and falsehood, Christ and Antichrist. The apparent presence of false wonders in the history of the visible church cast doubt upon the veracity of the faith, practice and piety that had been constructed around them, and served to undermine Catholic claims to continuity with the church of the Apostles. As evangelical polemicists turned to the past to interpret the present, the miraculous emerged as a central block in the construction of an identity for the true church and the false throughout Christian history.

Evangelical polemicists argued with vigour that the miracles claimed by the Catholic church identified it as the fulfilment of biblical prophecies of false preachers and feigned wonders. However, the question of whether such wonders were worked by the devil, the saint or the priest was often left open, with the intention that the figures of saint and devil should become blurred in the mind of the reader. Since only the effect of a miracle was visible, the classification of its supernatural source as divine or diabolic was a highly subjective decision, but one that had far-reaching implications. The attack on the cult and shrines of the saints in England in the 1530s acquired a polemical justification through the rhetoric of fraud and diabolic deception. Miracles that had been cited in defence of doctrine were immediately deprived of their function and authority once labelled as false wonders. If it could be demonstrated that the miracles associated with the holy men and women of the past were wonders worked by the devil, then such miracles ceased to substantiate claims that the institutional church and its heroes enjoyed divine approbation. The argument that the age of miracles had passed opened up a broader debate over the interpretation of the past in the light of the prophetic texts of Scripture and the creation of a history for the true church and the false. Evangelical interpretations of the miracles of the saints conferred an eschatological dimension upon the history of the church, but also placed the discussion of the boundary between miracle and magic, saint and sorcerer at the centre of a polemically constructed historical scheme.

The importance of the marvellous and miraculous to debates over the nature of the church was evident in English polemical literature even prior to the break with Rome. Miracles, Thomas More argued, were an essential sign of the true church, and the absence of miracles among the adherents of Luther and Tyndale was sufficient proof that they were not numbered among the true followers of Christ. For More, the defence of the miraculous was part of a broader debate over the continuing revelation of the law of God and the experience of faith outside Scripture. The unwritten word was an important vehicle for the transmission of the faith to the unlearned, More claimed, and, among the unwritten traditions of the church, miracles had been 'specially kept for the profe of ye trouth'.[8] Such signs were not visible in the churches of the heretics, More argued, and Tyndale and his followers remained a disorderly and disunited 'rabble' among whom 'ye light of myracles shall neuer shyne'. Among the 'false sects', More claimed, God had permitted not even the devil to work false wonders. 'As for heretykes which falsly fayne them selfe to be his owne flocke ... ', he claimed that 'these false sectys of them may be dyscernyd & knowen frome hys very true chyrche.[9] Miracles were established as a visible means of delineating the true church and the false across the centuries, in a scheme which enabled More to locate his opponents within a broad chronological narrative of deviance and doctrinal error.

It was therefore vital that evangelical polemicists shatter this link between miracles and doctrinal truth, in order to neutralise the charge that no miracles were to be found outside the Catholic church and to position the reformers as the true heirs to the faith of Scripture and the primitive church. In his *Answer to More*, William Tyndale rejected outright the assumption that miracles were necessary to confirm evangelical preaching. The truth of Scripture, Tyndale claimed, had already been demonstrated by the miracles worked by Christ and the Apostles and, since evangelical doctrine stemmed from Scripture, no further miracles were necessary.[10] In what was to become a commonplace in evangelical writings against the miracles of the medieval saints, Tyndale concluded that the age of true miracles had ceased once 'the scripture was fully received and authentic'.[11] More's assertion that miracles continued to be worked in the Catholic church, Tyndale claimed, suggested that it was in fact the Catholic church which was guilty of innovation in matters of doctrine and which required further miracles to confirm new items of faith.[12] The claim that age of miracles had passed was repeated in evangelical literature throughout the middle decades of the sixteenth century and beyond. Writing in the 1540s, William Turner suggested that divine miracles were evident only where there was 'great cause' for such wonders to be seen, and concluded that he could see no such reason in the sixteenth-century church.[13] In a commentary on the prophecies of Micah, Anthony Gilby argued that there was no need for 'newe prophets' or new prophecies for those who lived in the latter days and needed 'no Miracles, sygnes or tokens'.[14] James Calfhill, responding to John Martiall's *Treatise of the Cross*, set out what had emerged as the standard evangelical viewpoint: 'in the first beginning and gathering of the church many things were necessary which now be needless. Miracles were used then, which outwardly be denied now.' Calfhill likened the church to a newly planted tree which in the first years of life had required the water of miracles but which was now firmly planted and no longer needed such things.[15] Miracles had been necessary for a time but, once that time had passed, such wonders had ceased.

If true miracles had ceased once the faith of Christ had become firmly established, it was suggested, the miracles recorded in the Catholic church were not miracles at all, but rather deceptions, frauds and diabolic wonders. Scripture was far from perspicacious on the subject of the miraculous beyond the era of the apostolic church, but there were ample warnings, both specific and general, of false preachers working wonders that might deceive the faithful. Several evangelical writers exploited the descriptions of false preachers contained in St Paul's second letter to the Thessalonians. Repeating the text of 2 Thess. 2, Tyndale warned his readers that 'Antichrist shall not only come with lying signs and disguised with falsehood, but also with lying miracles and wonders', fuelled by the offerings of the people and intended to 'minister and maintain vice, sin, and all abomination'.[16] William

Turner advised his readers to test recent miracles against the prophecy of Paul, with the promise that 'youre mynde shalbe at rest and certifyed' that such wonders were indeed the works of the devil.[17] John Bale condemned the miracles of the canonised saints as 'strange delusions', and a fulfilment of the prophecy of Paul that God would permit false wonders among the ungodly,[18] and Rudolph Gualther argued that the clergy had promoted false doctrine with 'lyeng wo[n]ders', locating the miracles proclaimed for the saints among the false wonders of Antichrist.[19] Walter Lynne's account of *The beginning and endynge of all popery* opened with a summary of the 'working of Sathan with all lyenge power and signes and wonders', predicted in 2 Thess 2, while the French Protestant divine John Veron detailed the 'lyeng wonders' that marked the fulfilment of Paul's prophecy in the Roman church.[20]

The second Scriptural *locus classicus* in the discussion of false miracles was Matthew 24:24. Tyndale reminded Thomas More that Moses, Christ and the apostles had warned that the latter days would be heralded by the arrival of false preachers, with 'lying miracles'.[21] John Frith identified the operation of Satan in 'lyenge and mervelous signes' that counterfeited the miracles of Christ, and concluded that the false preachers and feigned wonders predicted in Matt 24 were clearly evident in the Catholic church and papacy, and in the 'coniuringes and answeres of sprites by the which it is brought to passe/that the Pope is also made the kinge of them that are dead and raigneth in purgatorye'.[22] The author of the *Confutatio[n] of Vnwritte[n] Verities* warned that Antichrist would come with false prophets who 'shal shewe great miracles/and wonders', and noted that 'Sathan doth chaunge himselfe into an Angell of light/and that their dreames haue deceuyed many me[n]'.[23] John Foxe described in detail a number of the miracles attributed to Thomas Becket, and concluded that such wonders were either false fabrications perpetuated by supporters of the cult, or 'if they were true they were wrought not by God but by a co[n]trary spirit: of who[m] Christ out Lord geueth vs warning in hys Gospell, saying: whose com[m]ing shalbe w^t lyenge signes & wonders to deceaue, if it were possible, the elect: Matt 24'.[24]

Biblical warnings against false prophets working false wonders to delude the faithful added an apocalyptic tone to the evangelical argument that the age of miracles had passed. The claim that the age of miracles had long ceased, combined with the argument that all subsequent recorded wonders were the work of the devil, afforded the opportunity for evangelicals to dismiss the miracles of the saints at one fell swoop, and obviated the need to demonstrate that each and every miracle had its origins in falsehood and deception. However the interpretation of history in the light of biblical prophecy situated the miracles and wonders of the past and present within a chronological framework that lent weight to the claim that Antichrist had become ensconced in the medieval church and papacy. The history of the medieval church, its saints, and their miracles clearly had much to offer evangelical polemicists, and encouraged a polemical engagement with the legends of miracles in the past and present. The influence of Antichrist and satanic illusions provided one explanation for the apparent persistence of the miraculous within the Catholic church, but the argument that 'false' miracles would delude the faithful also left open the possibility of practical manipulation, pious fraud and feigned wonders. There were polemical advantages in making malleable the distinction between Antichristian illusion and human deception, in order to facilitate the representation of Catholicism as a faith grounded on fictions, promoted by forgeries and accepted by a congregation of fools and hypocrites.

The image of the false and feigned miracle was established in the writings of the first generation of English evangelicals. Tyndale alleged that the miracles recorded in the legends of the saints were 'feigned so grossly' that even Thomas More would prefer that they were not celebrated.[25] Such sentiments had an established pedigree in the writings of humanist critics of the excesses of late-medieval religious culture, and the suggestion that some of the miracles attributed to the saints and their relics were of dubious provenance was not unique to Tyndale.[26] However, the vigour with which the pursuit of the false wonder was taken up in the decades that followed provided the trope with a prominent position in discussions of saints, pilgrimage and the miraculous in the sixteenth century. The feigned miracle, manufactured by popes and clergy, became the starting point for a wide-ranging assault upon the traditional rituals and practices of the church. John Bale argued that neither the devil nor his 'unholy vycar in Rome' would be able to supplant the true church with their false miracles, or their 'curssynges and coniurynges, calkynges and coblynges, brawlynges and bablinges, massinges and mutterynges, Images and Idolles, pardons and purgatory, with the deuyl and all of hys other sorceryes, which these graceless papistes co[n]tynually gapeth for yet ones agayne'.[27] The Catholic priesthood, he alleged, were 'dau[n]cing apes, whose natural property is to cou[n]terfaite al thinges that they se done afore them', the successors of the magicians of Pharaoh's Egypt rather than the heirs of the Apostles. The false wonders and feigned holiness of the clergy had placed them in a position of authority over the body and the souls of all men, Bale claimed: 'yea and wyth thy preuye legerdimain, with the iuglinge castes, with the craftes and inchauntments of thy subtyle charmers, were all nacions of the worlde deceyued with lies in hypocrisye, were the great gouernours most miserable blinded and with errours in supersticion the common people seduced'.[28]

The litany of juggling, charming, muttering, conjuring, babbling and counterfeiting with which Bale relentlessly bombarded his reader hammered home the message that the Catholic church was constructed upon invented delusions and not the simple word of God. Other writers were more restrained in their style, but the conclusion was the same. The author of A short treatise of certayne thinges abused in the Popysh Church long used (1548) complained that the faithful had been 'drowned with dreames', led into captivity and deprived of knowledge of the truth. The 'popes church' had presented error as truth and promoted wickedness under cover of hypocrisy and 'great colour of holiness'. Scripture and the word of God had been supplanted by the images and the relics of the saints, and 'feates of legerdemayne, by these iugglers inuented that Gods word shulde not florysshe, the lyght of oure salvation'.[29] George Joye protested that the Catholic church was able to muster in its defence only 'lyes, false miracles, fayned reuelacions', yet still esteemed such 'delusions' above the written word of God.[30] A multitude of false wonders had been worked by the devil and 'fayned and counterfeited of hys lyuelye members / Monkes and Friers with other such hipocrites'. So adept were the priests and monks in fabricating and feigning the holy, Cranmer noted, that Satan had no cause to raise up false oracles and prophets. The devil would be as well to retire gracefully and 'take his ease in his inne', he suggested, 'seeing his subtil servau[n]tes Monkes / Friers / non[n]es / and other pope holye hypocrites/can and do counterfeit such thinges daylye'.[31] The vocabulary of miracle and feigned wonder in evangelical literature drew upon the same lexicon as the official pronouncements of the Henrician and Edwardian regimes on the cult of the saints and images. The Royal Injunctions of September 1538 warned of the dangers of 'feigned' images and relics, Bishop Goodrich ordered the removal of all 'writings and monuments of feigned miracles' from the churches of his diocese in 1541, and the Edwardian Injunctions of 1547 encouraged preachers to warn the faithful of the dangers of reliance upon 'men's fantasies'.[32] A miracle was not a neutral event. Where accepted, it became a powerful sign of the continued presence of God with His church. Where probed by the devout sceptic, it became a vulnerable part of popular devotion, which could be neither wholly rejected nor wholly accepted. Where exposed as clerical fraud at the hands of evangelical polemicists, it became part of an accumulation of evidence of the hypocrisy and deceit that supported the Roman church, its doctrines and its authority.

The image of the feigned miracle and false wonder ran throughout John Bale's narrative of English history in the *Actes of the Englysh Votaries*. Bale proclaimed his intention that his work should enable the reader 'to iudge false miracles that they be no more deuylishly deceyued', and expose 'these holy canonysed deuyls in their own right colours'.[33] The presentation of the legends of the saints and their miracles as works of fiction and deception was informed by the desire to inspire a wider scepticism among the readers, calling into question the veracity of other traditional devotions and inculcating a sense that eyes and ears could be, and had been, deceived by the false miracles of devils masquerading as saints. Bale outlined the miracles associated with the heroes of the English past and used the wonders of these saints to discredit their claims to sanctity and expose the ambition of the Roman clergy. The miracles and prophecies of St Anselm, he argued, were a clear manifestation of the threat posed to political stability and security by the greed and ambition of the priests and monastics. It was claimed of Anslem that he had 'behelde it in a vision at Lyons (they saye) how St Albone, and other Englysh sayntes sent fourth an euyll sprete to slee the seyd kyng Wyelya[m] for oppressynge their abbeyes'. The prophecy of the death of the king was not fulfilled, but this failure of the 'preuy legerdemaynes' of the clergy had not deterred Anselm's supporters, who, Bale claimed, 'feyne in an other fable' that their saint had torn the flesh of Christ from a rood with his teeth in protest against the royal confiscation of the fruits of empty benefices. The miracles attributed to Anselm were presented by Bale as a telling commentary on the relationship between a monastic community and a medieval king who had attempted to appropriate the wealth of the monasteries, a message that would not have been lost on English readers in the 1540s.[34]

The representation of the clerical or monastic community as the perpetrator of fraudulent miracles was a common theme in evangelical polemic. In the *Confutation of Unwritten Verities* it was the friars who were guilty of self-serving attempts to delude the faithful. The author recounted events that surrounded the burial of the wife of the provost of Orleans, who had requested that she be buried without the traditional ceremonies of the church. Fearing that such a precedent might establish a pattern with unfortunate financial consequences for the church, the community of friars had convinced one of their number to hide in the vault of the church and, in a female voice, declare that he was 'the sowle of the Profests wife condemned in hell for contemning of the suffrages of the holy churche', before requesting a second burial in accordance with the traditional rites. The plan failed, and in the narrative presented in the *Confutation,* the angry provost forced the friar to confess. The activities of the friars provided useful evidence of the dangers in relying upon miracles and other 'unwritten verities' in the determination of doctrine.[35] Rudolph Gualther denounced the 'false deceauable varlettes' who feigned miracles, and bemoaned the ease with which the 'ruder sorte of peoples' were deceived at the hands of the 'friers & cloisterers'. Motivated by greed and hunger for power, he claimed, the clergy were wont to claim that the souls of the dead appeared to them, or suggest that they had the ability to summon good and evil spirits. The most common culprits were the Franciscans and Dominicans, who had invented and exploited miracles to serve their own interests. 'How ofte[n] haue the graye friers made lies of their francise?' Gualther demanded, and 'how ofte[n] haue the black friers made lowed lies of ye blessed virgin Mary, of Barbara, Katherine, and of Christ our Lord himselfe?'[36] The reduction of saints and the miraculous to the status of pawns in a long-standing rivalry between two religious orders highlighted both the capacity for clerical manipulation of the lay imagination and the wide scope over which such manipulation might operate.

John Foxe suggested that many of the most well-known miracles recorded in medieval literature and chronicles were either feigned or fiction. The reputation of Archbishop Odo of Canterbury, Foxe claimed, had been damaged rather than promoted by the content of 'our lying histories faining false myracles vp on him'. The miracles associated with the archbishop included the transformation of the eucharistic bread and wine into the visible flesh and blood of Christ, the protection of the cathedral church of Canterbury from inclement weather by the power of prayer alone, and a vision of a sword falling from heaven into the scabbard of King Ethelstan.[37] Such wonders, Foxe suggested, were weak ground upon which to build a claim to sanctity, and provided rather more convincing evidence of the distortion of history by medieval monastic chroniclers. The miracles associated with St Cuthlack, which included imprisoning the devil in a boiling pot and summoning spirits to build houses, were equally dubious in Foxe's eyes. 'Why this Cuthlake shoulde bee sancted for his doings I see no great cause, as neyther do I thinke the fabulous miracles reported of him to be true' Foxe claimed, and he dismissed the wonders linked with the saint as mere monkish inventions.[38] The same was true of the miracles of Bishop Adhelm of Sherborne. Drawing upon the account of the life and works of the bishop provided by William of Malmesbury in the *Gesta Pontificum Anglorum*, Foxe protested that the miracles attributed to Adhelm were 'Monkishe deuises … forged upon their Patrons, to mayntayne the dignity of their houses'. The fictions that lay behind accounts of the miracles of Adhelm were confirmed, Foxe alleged, by the fact that similar miracles were also ascribed to Bishops Adelwold and Swithun at Winchester, where Adhelm had once resided.[39] Foxe's criticisms reached to the heart of the self-perpetuating quality of the *lives* and legends of the saints. It was precisely this re-enactment or repetition of accepted exempla that established the position of an aspiring saint among the community of the holy. The miracles of Adhelm that were recited so dismissively by Foxe, miracles in which infants spoke holy words, material objects changed their shape, mariners were saved from drowning and clothes were hung upon sunbeams, had been the staple of medieval hagiography and an evident sign of holiness. Foxe's rejection of the miracles recorded in Winchester was not merely a rejection of the sanctity of Adhelm, Swithun and Adelwold but a rejection of the commonplaces of traditional writing on the saints and their miracles which had provided the historical foundations of sainthood. Foxe's advice to his readers that the miracles associated with St Swithun would be better 'redde together w^t the Iliades of Homer or tales or Robenhode' had implications that reached far beyond the accounts of the wonders of one ninth-century saint.[40]

It was this possibility that one feigned wonder might be used to justify the demolition of the whole edifice of the miraculous which made the miracles of the saints in the past and present such a powerful weapon in polemical debate. The revelation that one miracle was a fraud provided iconoclasts with a motivation and a defence, and inspired and shaped polemical controversy. Thomas More was well aware of the necessity of dissociating the general miraculous from the particular fraud, and both the *Dialogue Concerning Heresies* and the *Confutation of Tyndale's Answer* reflected a considered calculation of the advantages of conceding that a minority of miracles might be fakes, in order to defend the veracity of the majority. The discussion of the miraculous in the *Dialogue* drew heavily upon More's belief in the existence of a common consensus across time and space that God could and did work miracles. More repeatedly refused to concede that all such wonders were in fact the work of the devil. Tyndale and his followers, he claimed, in their rejection of miracles, stood in stubborn opposition to the traditions of the church and the faith of the Fathers. When pressed by the Messenger on the possibility that the faithful might be unable to discern the difference between true miracle and diabolic fraud, More replied that it would be foolish to ascribe all miracles to the devil, who 'can do nothing but by sufferaunce', unless there were clear and convincing cause 'that can not suffer that worke to be rekened goddes'. Chaos would follow, he protested, if the miraculous were dismissed as an explanation for each and every event that could not be explained by reason and nature, given that reason and nature both demonstrated that miracles could occur.[41]

It was possible, More conceded, that some events which appeared to be miracles might be the work of the devil or human forgery. However, such feigned wonders were still tolerated by God and had a specific purpose. Where evangelical writers saw in one feigned wonder a fault line which stretched across the whole miraculous, More argued that it was more instructive to see the hand of God at work in demonstrating the truth of all other miracles by exposing one as a fraud. False miracles feigned by man and by the devil had been exposed by the saints in the past and the present 'so that always god hath preparyd his trew doctors/to dystroy by playne myracle the false myracles / whereby men were and myght be deceyued'. All miracles had a purpose, whether worked to prove the veracity of others or to demonstrate the miraculous capacities inherent in nature.[42] The Messenger remained doubtful, and presented to More a scenario which was no doubt intended as an allusion to legends of feigned miracles that had become common currency. It would be easy, the Messenger suggested, for

> some preste to brynge up a pylgrymage in his parysshe/may deuyse some false fellow faynyng hymselfe to come seke a saynt in his chyrche/and there sodenly say/yt he hathe gotten his syght. Then shall ye haue the belles rong for a myracle. And the fonde folke of the countrey soone made foles. Than women commyngye thither with their candels. And the person byenge of some lame begger .iii. or .iiii. payres of theyr olde crutches will .xii. pennes spent in men and women of wax/thrust thorowe diuerse placys some with arrowes and some with rusty knyuys/ wyll make his offeryngys for one .vii. yere/worth twyse his tythes'.[43]

More's response was to repeat the argument that, while it was indeed possible that a cult might be created around a fraudulent cure, the very fact that the miracle was exposed as a fraud evinced the veracity of other miracles. Although miracles were exceptional events, there existed a common bond between those miracles 'done by god in olde tyme' and those recorded more recently at places of pilgrimage. Neither miracle nor pilgrimage was a recent invention, and the evidence of the past suggested that miracles had been feigned for many centuries but always exposed by the will of God.[44] True miracles validated one another, while false wonders simply served to confirm the strength of the true.

In support of his argument, More provided the Messenger and the reader with additional examples of miracles that had been revealed as false or feigned. More described what at first appeared to be an example of a common curative miracle at the tomb of one of England's most famous saints. A blind beggar had travelled with his wife to the tomb of St Alban, following a dream in which he had been promised a cure at the tomb of the martyr. The promised cure had not materialised and the blind man had begun to voice doubts that the body of the saint was in the city. However, when the entourage of Humphrey, duke of Gloucester arrived in the town, the beggar proclaimed that his blindness had been cured through the miraculous intercession of the saint. News of the cure spread and 'a myracle was solemply rongen'. The joy of the community was short-lived. The duke exposed the beggar as a fraud after it became clear that he could not only see the colours in the duke's cloak but could also put a name to them.[45] The fact that this one miracle had been exposed as a fraud was for More adequate testimony to the veracity of other miraculous cures that had been widely accepted and proclaimed. However, despite More's confidence that such tales would serve to inspire faith in the existence of true miracles, these same false wonders were to become a staple of evangelical criticisms of the feigned miracles of traditional religion. William Tyndale described the same events at St Albans in the *Practice of Prelates*, and claimed that the wily papists had not stopped at proclaiming a false miracle but had also contrived to bring about the death of the duke, whose capacity to detect such falsehoods posed too great a threat to Catholic piety.[46] An embellished version of the legend was repeated by John Foxe in his accounts of the deeds of the duke of Gloucester, and was provided with a dramatic representation in Shakespeare's *Henry VI*.[47] To More, the fact that one man's false claim to have been cured was exposed as a lie was no reason to doubt the other curative miracles of the saints. However, the conclusions that were drawn from the same incident in evangelical accounts were more hostile, and this more negative interpretation of the events was to become ingrained in the popular imagination.

More's second example of a false miracle that might serve to confirm the truth of others related to events at the priory of Leominster in the reign of Henry VII. The prior had brought a 'strange wenche', Elizabeth, into the church, claiming that she had been sent by God, and had constructed a resting place for her in the rood loft, where she lived without food or drink. Elizabeth was sustained instead by communion bread, which appeared to fly to the loft from the hands of the prior. A local cult developed around the fasting holy maid, until it was revealed that the airborne communion wafers were in fact transported along a specially constructed wire, and that the real source of the maid's food was the prior himself, who spent each night with her in the rood loft. Once removed from the church by the king's mother, Elizabeth had betrayed her true character by demanding food and water, and was subsequently compelled to perform penance for the deception that she had perpetrated. More drew a parallel between the events at Leominster and Daniel's exposition of the false claims that had been made for the idol Baal. 'Bycause no suche faynyd wonders sholde enfame goddys very myracles/hys goodness shortly brought them bothe to knowledge,' More argued, 'so doth his especially cure and prouydence brynge euer shortely suche flashed and faytey to light to theyr shame & confusyon.'[48] The fact that the fraud perpetrated by the prior of Leominster had been exposed was testimony to the potential for divine intervention in the defence of true miracles.

Again, More's confidence in the ability of exposed frauds to animate faith in true miracles seemed to have been misplaced, and the narrative of events at Leominster was repeated in numerous evangelical criticisms of miraculous deceptions. The *Confutatio[n] of Unwritte[n] Verities* included a detailed description of the reputation of the Holy Maid of Leominster, who 'lyued only by Aungels foode … massed into the maids mouth' by the prior. Demands from Lord Abergavenny that the miracle be investigated had led to the discovery of meat bones beneath her bed and fine threads of her hair which led from the rood loft to the altar.[49] The discussion of events at Leominster was accompanied by a list of other such 'holy maids' whose miracles had been revealed as frauds. One young woman had journeyed to St Albans seeking a cure from the saint and bearing a key that she claimed had been given to her by an angel in order to unlock the reliquary. Upon arriving at the shrine, she had prayed openly, pressed the key into the lock, proclaimed herself cured and 'by & by the mo[n]kes would haue had it ro[n]ge for a miracle'. However, some 'wiser men thought it meete to trye the matter better & to examine her further' and imprisoned the maid in a nunnery while they investigated the miracle. The night before the men intended to reveal the cure as a fraud, the maid was apparently 'conueyed awaye' from the scene.

The investigation of the miracles of holy maids continued. The miracles of Anne Wentworth, the 'maid of Ipswich', were argued to be 'proued to be done by necromancy & the deceit of the deuill', while the trances and prophecies of the Holy Maid of Kent were condemned as a 'diuilishe illusion', feigned by Barton and promoted by the clergy.[50] There was a clear polemical purpose behind the selection of holy maids in the *Confutation*. The deception at Leominster provided a useful precedent for the clerical and monastic manipulation of miraculous, and for the leading role of the crown and nobility in the detection and suppression of such cults. The fraud at St Albans presented a further example of monastic credulity and highlighted the ease with which such false wonders might be widely celebrated and 'rung' for miracles. Popular enthusiasm for Anne Wentworth at Ipswich has been described as the 'star cult' of the age, and the last such coalesence of opinion around a female prophet before the controversy surrounding Elizabeth Barton in 1534. The key events were well known: Thomas More detailed the miracles linked with Wentworth and the Ipswich image of the Virgin, and Robert Curzon had provided the king with an account of events.[51] By calling into question the miracles associated with holy maids at St Albans, Leominster and Ipswich, it was possible to represent the Maid of Kent, by far the most politically threatening of the group, as the latest in a long line of women who had been manipulated by clerical patrons and deceived the faithful with feigned miracles. In defending the cause of Elizabeth Barton, her promoters had exploited familiar hagiographical exempla from the lives of holy women and imbued them with a polemical and political purpose. In contrast, the representation of the holy maids in the *Confutation* brought a new interpretative scheme to bear upon traditional images of pious pilgrims and holy women. Medieval hagiography had used the legends of the past to validate claims to sanctity in the present. The reversal of this process, in the use of miracle legends from the English past to discredit the church and its saints in the present, demonstrates the extent to which sainthood and the miraculous remained powerful tools in the hands of evangelical writers.[52]

The discussion of the holy maids and their miracles in the *Confutation of Unwritten Verities* formed part of a wide discussion of the role of miracles in the authentication of doctrine. In response to Catholic claims that the faith of the church had been confirmed and preserved by miracles, it was argued that such miracles were no substitute for Scripture in doctrinal debate. The rejection of the miraculous as either a form or an indication of doctrinal authority was a key part of the evangelical defence of the Reformation from accusations of novelty and innovation, and one which opened up the history and miracles of the medieval church to further scrutiny. The claim that miracles were a necessary part of doctrinal proof and validation had been vigorously articulated by Thomas More in the *Dialogue Concerning Heresy* and the *Confutation of Tyndale's Answer*. Under the heading 'God does not allow the church to err', More argued that the faith of the Fathers, made clear in their writings, was the historical faith of the church. God had accepted the Fathers for saints, '& by myracles openly declared yᵗ theyr fayth & lyuing liked hym'. Scripture described the miracles worked by Christ which served as proof of his preaching, More claimed, and it was incumbent upon Tyndale and his followers to accept as true both these miracles and 'all myracles/those that are tolde and reported as done for the doctours of Crystes chyrche/syth myracles were specially deuysed by god for a knowledge of his trewe messengers/and a profe of theyr message'.[53] This argument for congruity between the miracles of the Apostles and those attributed to the saints of the medieval church was repeated and expanded in the *Confutation*. More argued that God 'hath from the begynnyng ioyned his worde with wonderfull works' and still 'causeth hys chyrche to do myracles styll in euery age, and to be discerned and knowen by the plentuouse workyng of goddys wonders'. It was these same miracles that evinced the Catholic church as the church of God across the centuries, and confirmed 'that the doctrine of the same chyrch is reueled and taught vnto yᵗ by the spyryte of god'.[54] The miracles of Christ were vital in the planting of the faith but, More argued, subsequent miracles were also a visible sign of God's continued presence in the church and the means by which the stony hearts of men were softened and imprinted with the words of the law.[55]

If, as Thomas More claimed, the teachings of the Catholic church had been confirmed by miracles, it was vital that the iconoclasm of the Reformation break apart both the images of the saints and long-standing assumptions about the relationship between sanctity, miracles and doctrine. The re-examination of the *lives* and the miracles of the saints was animated by the desire to bring to light dubious assertions and highlight any inconsistencies or divisions that might undermine their role in the construction and defence of Catholic doctrine. William Tyndale was prepared to uphold the validity of the miracles worked in the name of Christ, which he claimed were intended to move the individual to listen to the word of God and to confirm the truth of the promises contained therein. The 'miracles of antechriste', Tyndale claimed, also inspired faith, but faith in those doctrines which would lead the faithful away from the truth, 'to pull thee from the word of God, and from believing his promises, and to put thy trust in a man or a ceremony, wherein God's word is not'.[56] It was not miracles that provided confirmation of doctrine, but rather the faith revealed in Scripture that confirmed the truth of miracles. The everlasting covenant made in Christ required that the faithful should 'receive no miracles', Tyndale argued, with the result that all miracles that appeared to confirm doctrines contrary to the word of God were in fact 'done of the devil'.[57] Tyndale urged More to reconsider the legitimacy of doctrines and practices that had been 'proved' or promoted by the miracles of the saints, which appeared to defend 'the poverty which ye have feigned' or which encouraged men to pay tithes and offerings. The miracles of the saints were hardly consistent in the doctrines that they were used to support, Tyndale claimed, noting that Thomas Aquinas, 'a saint full of miracles as friars tell', had believed that the Virgin had been born into original sin.[58] There was no proof of doctrine where miracles fermented division and controversy.

Chapter 6 of the *Confutatio[n] of vnwritte[n] verities* was devoted to the argument that 'neyther are miracles abel to proue our fayth'. Just as the magicians of Egypt had worked wonders by 'sorceries' before Pharaoh, so it was argued that it was still possible for men to be deceived into false faith by feigned miracles and delusions. Scripture warned of the dangers posed by prophets and 'dreamers' who worked wonders and encouraged the faithful to 'goe after straunge goddess'. Miracles had never been intended as a proof of doctrine, it was claimed, but false miracles had been used to defend idolatry and false belief where there was no warrant in Scripture. 'They alledge reuelacions of Aungels/of our Ladye and other sainctes/and dead mennes soules appearing to diuers men and wemen,' the *Confutation* claimed, in order to maintain the cult of the saints itself, pilgrimages, relics, the Mass, pardons, purgatory and holy water, and 'tel also of many wonders and straunge miracles to proue their doctrine in all these'. Miracles provided insufficient proof that the 'unwritten verities' of the papists were true doctrine, and it was imperative that any miracles be tested against Scripture if the faithful were to discern the true from the false.[59] The Mass itself was supported only by the 'feigned fables' that the clergy had claimed in defence of error and ignorance.[60] The same themes were explored by other writers. Jean Veron argued that if miracles alone were proof of the validity of the cult of the saints, then 'by the same reason might the Idolatrie of the Gentiles or heathen be vpholden as good'.[61] Rudolph Gualther suggested that miracles and 'devilish wonders' attributed to images were merely a 'craftye conueyaunce' intended to increase the offerings that were made at the shrines and justify the fact that such images were 'set furthe gorgeously with a great light of curses hanged around them'.[62] The author of *A booke called the fal of the Romish Church* argued that the miracles associated with the images of the saints were insufficient proof that there was any warrant for the worship of such images. While they remained within the carver's workshop, images did not work miracles, it was claimed, and 'were neuer holy till these Gentylmen had goten them into their whorysh church'. While the crucifix was worked upon by the goldsmith, it was not worthy of veneration, 'but when these Ipocrytes once finger them, they must be both capped and kneled to, and they themselves wyll goo bellowynge and bleringe after these false Gods'.[63] It was only when images and crucifixes fell into the hands of the clergy that they began to work miracles in defence of Catholic doctrine.

Evangelical polemicists represented false miracles as the invention of the Catholic clergy, feigned and promoted in defence of a variety of false doctrines.

John Bale complained bitterly that the miracles associated with the chastity of the saints detracted from the importance of Christian marriage. The obsession with chastity in the *lives* of the saints, Bale suggested, was reflected in the numerous miracles that were recorded as the saints battled with the temptations of the flesh. Traditional hagiography was replete with examples of occasions on which the devil had apparently appeared in the guise of a woman to tempt the saint, only to be dispelled by holy water, but Bale noted acidly that such miracles did not extend as far as making honest married women of clerical concubines.[64] The biographers of St Oswald recorded several occasions on which the saint had repeatedly plunged himself into cold water to quell the desires of the flesh, but Bale was dismissive of such 'holy actes whereupon the pope hath made y[e] said Oswald a saint'.[65] Capgrave's narrative of the *life* and miracles of St Etheldreda included an account of the sudden death of a married priest who had presumed to touch the relics of the chaste saint, a miracle which Bale suggested had been fabricated by the church in order to promote false chastity over godly marriage. 'For marriage maye touche nothynge that longe to that generacyon,' Bale concluded, 'vnlesse whoryshnesse be good masters vnto it, and came as a mean betwixt both.'[66] Bale's desire to prove that the prohibition of marriage to the clergy was a recent innovation required that the miraculous chastity of the saints be discredited and their wonders shown to be frauds perpetrated to defend the indefensible. In the eyes of Bale, compulsory clerical celibacy was the invention of Antichrist, instituted by his monastic servants and supported by false wonders. After reciting a litany of feigned miracles associated with clerical celibacy, and the apparently miraculous means by which the saints had defended themselves against temptation, Bale concluded sardonically that 'colde water was of great vertu in thys age byleke'.[67]

Bale condemned monastic vows of chastity as 'apte instrumentes to work many myracles by, in the vprearynge & further mayntenau[n]ce of that myghty monarchy of Antichriste'.[68] Not even the magicians of Pharaoh or the 'soothsayers of Egypte', he alleged, had used such devious means to delude and persuade the people. Throughout the *Actes of the Englysh Votaries*, Bale repeatedly blurred this distinction between miracle and magic, and represented the miracles of the saints as magical acts, worked to uphold the dominion of Antichrist in the institutional church. St Augustine and his companions, he claimed, arrived in England well armed with 'Aristotles artillery, as wyth logyck, Philosophy and other crafty sciences'. Sebba, king of the East Saxons, was 'so by wytched of the bishop of Londo[n] and his calking collygenes' that he became a monk and left his wife and property to the church. St Oswald, in Bale's narrative, 'had stodied necromancy at Floryake' and become 'so wel armed with deceytes as euer were Pharaoes sorcerers'. Following the account provided by William of Malmesbury, Bale described the deeds of Palumbanus, a priest of Rome as 'a great Necromanser and a myghty worker of knaueries spiritual', who had 'wrought innumerable sorceryes & legerdemaynes of lecherie for y[e] holy chast prelates there'.[69] Elmer, a monk of Malmesbury, was similarly suspect in Bale's eyes, being 'so wel seane in Necromancy that he coulde with wynges flye abroade and work many wonders'.[70] Saints emerged from the pages of Bale's history as sorcerers, monks as magicians, and miracles as false wonders feigned by the clergy to defend the doctrines of Antichrist. Miracles were not proof of true doctrine but, rather, evidence of the degree to which the faith and practice of the church had become corrupted by false preaching and magical manipulation. However, the process by which the English past was reclaimed and reworked in evangelical polemic was to be dominated by images of saintly sorcerers and the same false miracles that Bale had denounced as mere 'tayles'.[71]

The evangelical contention that miracles recorded after the apostolic era were the work of the devil was buttressed by references to saints, monks and popes who could be shown to be magicians and conjurors, manipulating the magical to give a show of the miraculous and deluding the faithful with false wonders. St Dunstan, Archbishop Odo of Canterbury, St Augustine, Elmer the flying monk of Malmesbury and – by the time John Napier compiled his list – some 21 medieval popes were represented in evangelical history writing as necromancers, their miracles cast as magic and fraud.[72] For evangelical writers, the presence of clerical conjurors and monkish sorcerers in the Catholic church was testimony to the fulfilment of biblical prophecies of Antichrist in Christian history, and the identi-fication of diabolic wonders in the *lives* of the saints was a critical part of this interpretation of the past. The identification of ecclesiastical magic across the spread of Christian history was central to the shaping of a past for the nascent reformed churches, but writers such as Bale also made a concerted attempt to demonstrate the simple absurdity of traditional wonders, in order to call into question the doctrines and practices that they supported. By undermining the foundations of individual miracles, it was possible to cast doubt upon the validity of all miracles; with key bricks removed, the edifice would crumble. The mockery of medieval miracles not only discredited the individuals responsible but also broke a link in the hagiographical chain that linked the heroes of the past with the Apostles and with the church of the present.

However, it was not only the miracles of the saints that were subjected to re-interpretation and re-evaluation in evangelical polemic, and the assault on the miraculous was to reach into the heart of Catholic piety and doctrine. The Mass lay at the centre of pre-Reformation religion, and the moment of the elevation of the consecrated elements lay at the heart of popular devotion. Over time, the elevation had come to be identified as the moment of the miraculous transforma-tion of the substance of the bread and wine into the body and blood of Christ, and had thus acquired a devotional, pastoral and propagandistic purpose.[73] It was at the moment of the elevation that the laity encountered the sacred, and the importance of the act was marked in the liturgy by the ringing of the sacring bell and the lighting of torches. Representations of the Mass in devotional art and literature were dominated by the image of the elevation and further reinforced the centrality and significance of the event in popular devotion.[74] The ceremonial elevation, and the meanings that were attributed to it, encouraged the belief that presence and participation in the ritual moment enjoyed a sacramental status and efficacy. Limited lay access to the consecrated species helped to focus popular devotion upon this 'sacramental viewing', which was itself believed to carry spiritual and practical benefits. The importance of witnessing the elevation was emphasised in sermons and devotional and pastoral literature, including Mirc's *Festial* and John Lydgate's *Merita Missa*.[75] Participation in the ritual was the physical embodiment of the shared belief that bound together the community of the faithful, a belief that was reinforced by the institution of the feast of Corpus Christi in 1264, the commemoration of which located the theology of the church within the civic life of the community.[76]

The doctrine of transubstantiation required a willing acceptance of a miraculous transformation which was both unseen and unfelt, and it was at this intersection of the visible and invisible, clerical and divine power, that the pressure of its critics was felt most strongly. This same difference between the seen and the unseen had provided the inspiration for much of the traditional devotional literature on the Mass, intended to inculcate faith and to dispel critics. Miracles associated with the consecrated host were collected and circulated in Gregory the Great's *Dialogues* and Bede's *Ecclesiastical History*, and more widely disseminated in sermons which extolled the manifold merits of the Mass. Miri Rubin has counted 46 miracle collections associated with the Mass that were produced in the three centuries before the Reformation, including the Dominican *Alphabetum Narrationem* which alone detailed more than 800 miracles.[77] Manuscript editions of the *Legends of the Holy Rood* circulated widely between the eleventh and fifteenth centuries, and John Mirc's *Festial* included accounts of various miracles that were intended to inculcate orthodox piety and convince critics. Many of the miracle stories associated with the host were clearly intended to persuade doubters and critics of the veracity of Catholic teaching on the sacrament. *Gregory's Chronicle* recorded an edifying tale of misconduct and repentance in order to reinforce beliefs in the miraculous powers of the host. In 1467, a London locksmith who had conspired with thieves to remove pixes from churches discovered to his horror that he was no longer able to see the host at Mass. After visiting several churches, the locksmith was driven to confess his crime and his sight was restored.[78] In the more common form of the eucharistic miracle narrative, the bread and wine were either visibly transformed into flesh and blood at the moment of consecration, or the infant Christ was seen to appear upon the altar. The most famous such encounter was the sixth-century Mass of St Gregory, which was widely represented in devotional art on the eve of the Reformation.[79] Robert Mannynge's *Handlyng Synne* described in detail the appearance before three monks of Christ in the form of a child, his blood running into the chalice, and the image of the bleeding host was also a common trope in polemic directed against heretics and Jews.[80] The physical appearance of flesh and blood on the altar was by its nature a rare and miraculous event, but by their repetition in *legenda* and sermons, such miracles became engrained in the popular imagination and acted as a useful reminder of the reality and veracity of Catholic teaching.

The same visible eucharistic miracle, which had been exploited by the church to

Plate 1 The Mass of St Gregory, Stoke Charity parish church, Hampshire

convince its opponents, emerged as the focal point for criticisms of the Mass in English evangelical polemic. The rhetoric of novelty, fraud and feigned miracle that had been directed against the cult of the saints was also turned against the central rite and sacrament of the church and used to justify the rejection of traditional teaching on the theology of the eucharist. Opposition to the Mass was evident in the writings of English evangelicals in the 1520s, including William Tyndale's *Answer to More*, and in scurrilous attacks on the clergy and the sacrament such as the *Burial of the Mass*. In 1536, the Lower House of Convocation complained that the 'sacrament of the altar is not to be esteemed', and a steady trickle of anti-Mass sentiment could be heard throughout the 1530s.[81] However, the application of vocabulary from the Henrician propaganda against false shrines and feigned relics to the theology of transubstantiation continued to be dangerous, especially in the aftermath of the Act of Six Articles of 1539 and its prohibition of further speculation on the subject of the Mass. It was with the accession of Edward VI in 1547 that anti-Mass polemic found its voice. Within days of the death of Henry VIII, there were reports in London of open preaching against the Mass, and debate over the sacrament was not silenced by the Act Against Revilers of the Sacrament passed by Edward's first parliament. Opposition to the Mass provided the dominant theme in the literature of 1548 and 1549, as anti-Mass tracts flooded from the presses; in 1548 alone, 31 separate treatises were published, and numerous satirical broadsides posted on the doors of churches.[82] Popular liter- ture encompassed a wide range of criticisms of the Mass, including the sacrificial focus of Catholic theology, private Masses, the deception of the laity by conjuring priests and defamatory attacks on clerical morality.[83] Transubstantiation, the moment of elevation and the miracles attributed to the Mass were recast as evidence of false religion and the illusory and delusory nature of Catholic theology and its conjuring clergy.

The personification of the Mass as the debased character of 'Mistress Missa', and the judgement of the Mass by a comparison with the chaste maid 'Lord's Supper', was a common polemical image. In William Turner's *A newe dialogue wherein is conteyned the examinations of the Messe and of that kind of priesthode*, Mistress Missa admitted that she was the 'popes daughter' who had driven the Lord's Supper from the churches, and bemoaned the fact that there were now so many who despised her. In the ensuing dialogue, the character Fremouth demanded that the Mass be put on trial for heresy and blasphemy. Justice warned that Fremouth's views were in violation of the Six Articles, only to be corrected by the character Knowledge, who reminded the audience that persecution under the Act had ended and that the new king intended to purge the church of enormities and abuses. Encouraged by the promise of the reform of false religion under Edward VI, the trial proceeded. Witnesses alleged that Mistress Missa was guilty of promoting idolatry by encouraging the worship of a god that had been created from bread and wine, despite the knowledge that 'bread and wyne are not god, wither is ye offering vp of breade and wyne any ordinaunce of God'.[84] Throughout the trial, the character Porphyrius urged caution and warned that, if the Mass were to be abolished, all other ceremonies and rituals of the church would follow, given that the 'multitude' continued to hold the Mass in such credit.[85] Such fears were in fact the very foundation of evangelical writing against the Mass. In anti-Mass polemic, it was the Mass which supported the powers and pretensions of the clergy, required that the faithful accept invisible miracles as items of faith, and encouraged the proliferation of rites and ceremonies in church and community. The Mass lay at the centre of the life of the church, and it was only by removing this keystone of traditional theology and practice that false religion would be destroyed.

Miracles recorded in medieval *legenda* and hagiography had detailed the fate of those who had ritually defiled the consecrated host, and it was therefore vital that evangelical writers rupture this association between Mass and miracle. In response to this imperative, anti-Mass tracts portrayed the Mass as a cult of bread and wine, presented for worship on the altar by false priests, who mumbled Latin words of consecration to conjure feigned miracles in order to delude the faithful. The allegation that the clergy had conspired to deceive the faithful was a staple of the Edwardian anti-Mass tracts. Jean Veron denounced the theology of transubstantiation as idolatry and superstition, and alleged that the faithful had been deceived by the clergy into believing that it was true doctrine.[86] In *A Declaration of the Masse*, Marcourt complained that the Mass had 'seduced and begyled' the world 'under shadow and colour of holynesse', a feigned miracle that fulfilled the prophecy of false preachers in Matthew 24. The theology of the Mass was the 'doctrine of deuyls', he argued, 'procedinge of vanite and of dreames', which deluded the faithful into believing that the body of Christ in heaven could be present in the bread and wine on the altar.[87] Thomas Cranmer portrayed the Catholic clergy as charlatans, peddling religion for lucre and deceiving the world with their 'merchandise of glistering glasses and counterfeit dredges'.[88] Randall Hurlestone complained that the priests had long deceived their flock, 'beatinge into their heades a sorte of beggarly ceremonies fetched out of the bottome of hell' and enforcing with persecution doctrines for which there was no scriptural warrant.[89] The figure of Mistress Missa admitted that, while her clergy claimed to be able to bring Christ from heaven in order to free men from Hell, 'truly neyther I nor my daughters, haue anysuch poure to fetch any soule from hell. Yea I feare me rather lest we haue sent thousands thyther.' Her father the pope, she conceded, had created her merely to advance the power of the bishops and clergy, bring wealth into the church and bolster the reputation of the 'Ihon lacklatyne' priests, who could find no other gainful occupation.[90]

The representation of the Catholic clergy as false preachers and deceivers was a central part of the condemnation of traditional religion as a false theology, supported by feigned miracles. The transformation of the bread and wine into the body and blood of Christ, it was argued, was the most common manifestation of the feigned wonders of the devil.[91] If the clergy were guilty of manipulating and deceiving the faithful, it was with the miracle of the Mass that their delusions were most often accomplished. In a series of tracts directed against the Mass, Luke Shepherd argued that the even the Mass priests were unable to provide a cogent defence of the doctrine that they preached against the reasoned objections of their flock. The traditional theology of the Mass had emphasised the disparity between the visible accident and invisible substance, but it was this very contrast which was to form the basis of evangelical criticisms. In the dialogue between *John Bon and Mast Person*, the naïve questioning of John Bon bewildered the ignorant priest. John Bon had raised a number of practical objections to the doctrine of transubstantiation, suggesting that the consecrated host was too small to contain the body of Christ, and that the species still tasted and looked like bread and wine even after the consecration. In response, the priest had no answer except to fall back upon the argument that John Bon was a heretic who should reform his ways.[92] Shepherd's *Cauteles preseruatory* mocked the priest who claimed to be able make God in the Mass but could not prevent that same God from becoming stale and mouldy, and parodied the rituals used in the church to preserve the host.[93]

Similar arguments were repeated in Shepherd's *A Pore Helpe*, in which the narrator suggested that the invisibility of the body of Christ in the elements was ample proof that Christ was not physically present. The consumption of the consecrated host by animals or its destruction by fire, it was argued, was sufficient evidence that the substance of the bread remained after the consecration.

> And some there be that saye
> That Christ could not all daye
> Be kept within a boxe
> Nor yet set in the stockes
> Nor hidden lyke a fox
> Nor presoner vnder lockes
> Nor clothes with powdred armyne
> Nor bredyth stynkyng vermyne
> Nor dwelleth in a howse
> Nor eatyn of a mouse
> Not rotten is nor rusty
> Nor moth eaten or musty … [94]

Accounts of the apparent corruption of the host by nature, or its ingestion by animals and insects, provided a stark contrast to traditional legends which detailed the miraculous survival of the consecrated elements.[95] Anti-Mass tracts repeatedly presented the belief that Christ was bodily present in the host as counter-intuitive, given the obvious visible corruption of the bread even after its consecration. Robert Crowley argued that the very corruptibility of the consecrated elements was proof that the eucharistic bread remained bread, and demanded that his opponent explain why 'the bodie of Christe doe suffer these thinges eatinge of the mouse, burneinge and corruptinge'. If no bread remained after the consecration, Crowley asked, what substance filled the belly of the mouse, burned in the flames or became putrid with mould?[96] Thomas Cranmer dismissed Stephen Gardiner's 'ungodly feigned doctrine' of transubstantiation, arguing that the validity of the miracle was called into question by the experience of the eyes, which saw bread and wine, and of the tongue, which tasted stale bread and sour wine. Gardiner, he alleged, had turned to miracles as a defence where all other arguments had proved untenable, but the only true miracles reported of the Mass were 'when the form of wine turns into vinegar, and when the bread mouldeth, or a man doth vomit it, or the mouse eateth it, or the fire burneth it, or worms breed in it'.[97]

The rejection of the veracity of Catholic doctrine by English evangelicals raised the same questions of the 'miracle' of the Mass that had been asked of the wonders of the saints. The words of consecration uttered by the priest were represented either as an act of ecclesiastical magic and diabolic manipulation, or as a deliberate fraud intended to defend the indefensible argument that man could make God. The allegation that Catholic priests feigned the miracle of the Mass in order to claim for themselves the ability to create their Creator lent further weight to the portrayal of Catholic theology as false and delusory. References to priests as 'godmakers' permeated evangelical polemic against the Mass.[98] Thomas Cranmer argued that the theology of the Mass contradicted the word of God and the laws of nature in its assumption that it was possible for the priest to make both God and man on the altar.[99] Luke Shepherd brought his inimitable poetic style to bear on the same issue:

> As verely as bread is made of the maker
> So verely by gods worde we consecrate our maker
> As verely as gods worde did tourne Moses rod
> So verely gods worde consecrate the body of god.[100]

The same argument was explored at length in the treatise *Here begynneth a booke called the fal of the Romish Church,* which contrasted the faith and practice of the Catholic church with that of the Apostles. The Roman clergy, it was claimed, revealed themselves as 'Antichristes' in their claim to make God in the Mass and repeat daily the creation of the God who had created them. It was impossible to create the divine: God the Father was Creator, not created, Christ the Son was begotten, not created, and the Holy Spirit proceeded from Father and Son. If the priest could make God, it was argued, it followed that the pot would be able to make the potter, yet the clergy, 'coninge artificers', although 'they can nother make beaste not foules, yet will they make the maker of all these thinges'.[101] By claiming the power to make God, the Catholic clergy had betrayed the weak foundations of the theology of the Mass, and had been driven to work feigned wonders in support of false doctrine.

The favoured example of the forged eucharistic miracle among evangelical writers in the 1540s was that of the Surrey priest, Nicholas Germes. Determined to demonstrate to his congregation the veracity and reality of the teaching of the pre-Reformation church on the theology of the eucharist, Germes, in John Bale's account of the incident a 'popysh priest', pricked his fingers with a pin at the moment of the consecration to give the illusion of Christ's blood on the altar.[102]

The visible eucharistic miracle had been a common feature of late-medieval devotional literature, but in the context of the Henrician Reformation of the 1530s and 1540s the exposition of a false miracle of this kind had an even stronger polemical purpose and effect. Conservative clergy such as Germes might well have viewed such wonders as a powerful tool of propaganda and persuasion; certainly in the standard medieval exempla, the miracles surrounding the host had often involved a sceptic or critic. However, the fact that such legends of eucharistic wonders had a powerful and popular resonance in late-medieval devotion ensured that a miraculous fraud which deluded and deceived the faithful, such as that perpetrated by Germes, could be an equally potent weapon in the hands of evangelical propagandists such as Bale. The continued capacity of the miracle of the Mass to act both as an inspiration to faith and as a focus for critics was reflected in the list of false and feigned wonders described in the *Confutation of Unwritten Verities*. A description of Germes' false miracle was followed by an account of the efforts of an Edwardian priest to feign a similar miracle, and of the actions of a Marian preacher, who had attempted to demonstrate the veracity of Catholic teaching by feeding a consecrated host to a horse which piously refused to consume the body of Christ.[103]

Examples such as that provided by Germes supplied evangelical writers with evidence of clerical frauds in the present, but Bale and others also turned to examples from the past in order to provide such feigned wonders with an ancestry in the history of the false church. Familiar miracles recounted in medieval sermons and miracle collections took on a different form when viewed through the prism provided by evangelical writings on the Mass. Mirc's *Festial* had described a miracle attributed to Archbishop Odo of Canterbury, in which the doubting clergy were convinced of the real presence of Christ in the consecrated elements when blood was seen to run over the fingers of the archbishop and into the chalice.[104] The veracity of the miracle was called into question by Bale and Foxe, who interpreted the event as evidence of devious practice on the part of the archbishop and his supporters. In Bale's account, a number of clergy had argued against Odo's monks that the bread and wine were simply figures of Christ's body and blood. Close to losing the argument, the monastic party had resorted to magical manipulation to secure victory in the debate. When scriptural support for their belief was found wanting, Bale claimed, the monks 'were driuen to false miracles or playne experymentes of sorcerye. For Odo, by a cast of legerdemayne, shewed vnto the people a broken host bledynge.'[105] In Bale's hands, the miracle was not a didactic tool to convince the hesitant secular clergy but useful evidence of a persistent division of opinion over the eucharist in the medieval church and a clear indication of the possibilities for fraud and the deception of the faithful at the heart of traditional devotion.

Accounts of attempts to feign the eucharistic miracle added weight to the evangelical argument that the doctrines that lay at the centre of the debate were fundamentally false. The suggestion that the flesh and blood of Christ were made present only by the sleight of hand of the priest was accompanied by the representation of the priest as a conjuror, using magic rather than miracle to effect the transformation. The vernacular ballad, *The Ymage of Ypocresye* (1533), had denounced the 'Lernynge invocations', 'crafty in-cantacyons' and 'inchauntment' by which the Catholic clergy 'gett thyr avauncement', and this image of priest as conjuror featured repeatedly in the evangelical polemic of the 1540s.[106] Thomas Crowley likened the ritual gestures of the priest at Mass to the movements of a magician, 'full of turnes & halfe turnes, beckeinges and duckeinges, crosseynges, tosseynges and tumblings' and contrasted the elaborate liturgy Mass with the simple celebration of the Lord's Supper. At the Last Supper, Crowley complained, Christ had taken bread, broken and distributed it, but the priests 'take bread & blowe vpo[n] it breathinge out certaine wordes in the maner of enchau[n]ters & sorcerers, to turne the substaunce therof'.[107] John Bale condemned the prayers of the Mass as 'legerdemaynes' and 'Dreamynges', and suggested that the clergy were 'very connynge worke menne' in their claims to be able to transform bread and wine into the body of Christ by 'sorcery'.[108]

The Edwardian image of the priest who practised magic was not simply invented for popular consumption, but reflected a growing interest in the boundaries between miracle and magic, religion and the illicit supernatural. The autobiography of Edward Underhill described his meeting with one 'Alene', portrayed in the text as a prophet and soothsayer. Allen had cast the nativity of Edward VI, and had predicted the death of the king with such confidence that that 'his conselars the papists bruted it all over', forcing Edward VI to travel through the city of London in order to dispel the rumour. Underhill claimed that he had preserved a paper that he had found in Allen's possession, which included what appeared to be evidence of clerical dabbling in magic.[109] One William Wycherley admitted that he had conjured at Yarmouth with a sword and a ring, and that his priest companion had fled before the spirit that he summoned had appeared.[110] Robert Brian, a priest and former hermit, was alleged to have 'conjureth with a syue and a pair of sheeres invocating Saint Paule and Saint Peter. And he also useth the psalter and the key with a psalme.'[111] Such reports of priests who engaged in dubious practices lent a degree of authenticity to evangelical allegations that the clergy were guilty of deluding and deceiving the faithful by magical manipulation, and perhaps helped to set the sweeping claims of the polemicists within the microcosm of local and individual experience. Keith Thomas has drawn attention to the 'magical' beliefs that, mingled with official sacramental teaching, created the illusion that the medieval church acted as a repository of supernatural power. Of all the sacraments of the church, he suggests, it was the Mass which was most closely associated with magic, an association for which he held the institutional church at least partly responsible.[112] Popular attitudes to the Mass credited the recitation of the eucharistic liturgy with the mechanical efficacy of prayers and incantations, and the miracle of the Mass in particular acquired a magical interpretation. The central role of the priest, and the *sotto voce* recitation of the Latin words of consecration, encouraged this use of vocabulary from the realm of popular magic to describe the sacrament and to identify the celebrant as a conjuror.

The condemnation of priests as magicians was accompanied by a criticism of the miraculous properties that were attributed to the consecrated host. Again, the miracles cited and parodied in evangelical literature had their origins in well-known examples of wonders associated with the eucharist. Such miracles were widely recorded in medieval sermon collections, including Caesarius of Heisterbach's *Diagolus Miraculorum* (1223), and in the *Golden Legend*, which inspired the repetition of these familiar *topoi* across Europe, coloured and contextualised by local concerns.[113] At the popular level, the miraculous powers of the consecrated host were called upon in the context of the judicial ordeal and for medicinal and prophylactic purposes, in practices which were often tolerated, if not approved, by churchmen.[114] Luke Shepherd presented a graphic list of the wonders linked to the consecrated host:

> Some say she is a leache
> To make whole scabes and bleache
> Some say she is good for byles
> And some for humbles heles
> And good for kowe or Oxe
> That chafid be wyth yockes
> And good for hens and cockes
> To keep them from the fox
> … they say she bringeth rayne
> She seaceth thonder lowed
> And scattered euery cloude
> They say the plage and pestile[n]ce
> The papist messe expelleth he[n]ce.[115]

William Turner presented and condemned a similar catalogue of miracles linked with the Mass, including the ability to deliver souls from purgatory, rescue the souls of the damned from hell and 'to make faire wether and rayne to heale sycke horses, mesaled swine and the French poxe to bring souls to rest that are in torment and payne, to deliuer soules out of hell'.[116] The repetition of long lists of familiar miracles served to highlight the expansive claims that had been made for the consecrated host, while simultaneously devaluing each miracle by trivialising its effect. In the eyes of evangelical polemicists, this material use of sacred objects was symptomatic of a more general predisposition within Catholicism towards the magical manipulation of the world by words and rituals, and served to justify the root-and-branch reform of the sacramental system. The mundane and the material, in the form of mouldy bread, were exploited in evangelical polemic to expose doctrinal errors in the theology of the Mass, which in turn revealed Catholicism as a religion upheld by the magic and manipulation of the clergy, peddling false sacraments and feigned wonders.

Recalling the account of the *life* of Bishop Adelmus offered by William of Malmesbury, John Foxe concluded that William had been over-credulous in his acceptance of 'monkish devices' as miracles, but celebrated the fact that, despite the efforts of the wily William to delude his readers by the 'dexteritie of his stile', 'father experience hath taught the worlde now adaies more wisdom', the wisdom not to put faith in such delusions.[117] Evangelical writing on the miraculous was constructed, not only upon the outright rejection of the miracles of the saints and the church, but by the reinterpretation and re-evaluation of these miracles, and their exploitation in the service of nascent reformed church. James Calfhill described how 'these wicked spirits do lurk in Shrines, in Roods, in Crosses, in Images: and first of all pervert the Priests, which are easiest to be caught with bait of a little gain. Then work they miracles.'[118] The work of the devil was intimately entwined with the deeds and artefacts of the saints, and his agents were identifiable in the history and hagiography of the church. The condemnation of medieval miracles, and the repetition of accusations of magic and necromancy in the church, were part of the search for a Protestant historical identity in the events and personalities of the past. In the construction of a historical legitimacy for the English church in the 1530s, the miracles of the saints ceased to be the guarantor of true doctrine, and individuals, like the vicar of Ticehurst who revered the saints and celebrated their miracles, were criticised and condemned. Miracles merged with magic, the *lives* of the saints with superstition, in a rhetoric of reformation that used the vocabulary of fraud and deception as a shorthand for traditional religion. Such rhetoric justified an assault on the central constructs of Catholicism in the present and the past. The identification of the false miracle enabled evangelical writers to highlight what they most despised in Catholicism, and to emphasise the stark contrast between the true church and the false throughout history. The language of miracle and marvel was not abandoned but, rather, manipulated and exploited, with the result that the water of miracles that had sustained the primitive church became a wide ocean that separated the reformed churched from the church of Rome. Despite the Reformation appeal to the authority of Scripture and the church of the Apostles, evangelical writers were quick to recognise the importance of reclaiming the Middle Ages from the pages of 'lying histories fayning false miracles'.[119]

4

'ENTIQUE GARGLES OF YDOLATRY'

Saints, images and hagiography in Reformation polemic

Thanne longen folk to goon on pilgrimages,
And palmeres for to seken straunge strondes,
To ferne halwes, kowthe in sondry londes.
　　　　Geoffrey Chaucer, *The Canterbury Tales*, Prologue

The *lives*, legends and images of the saints were among the most popular and prominent features of pre-Reformation Catholicism. The cults of local saints and the commemoration of their lives embodied the communal identity of their participants, and provided a link with generations past, and protection in the present and future.[1] On the eve of the Reformation, Europe was 'drenched in saints', a cultural saturation that acquired visual expression in the dedication of churches and in the images that were erected in churches and chapels.[2] Representations of the saints in churches frequently outnumbered representations of the divine. By 1530, the images of the saints in the parish church of Ashburton in Devon included the Virgin Mary, Andrew, John, Christopher, Thomas Becket, Erasmus, George, Roche, Nectan of Hartland and King Henry VI.[3] The feasts of the saints punctuated the liturgical year and the ritual calendar; indeed the number of such festivals more than exceeded the number of days in the year. By the late fifteenth century, there were more than 50 days designated as *festa ferianda*, on which the saints were commemorated and all but the most vital work was prohibited.[4] Saints were not remote figures, models of holiness and piety that could be approached only in imitation but, rather, friends to the individual and community, and guardians whose protection was available to those who honoured them. The personalities of the saints became familiar through the repetition and recitation of their deeds and miracles in sermons and in print. The Sarum Rite, reinforced by primers and popular hagiographical literature, repeatedly reminded the faithful of the intercessory powers of saints, while vernacular accounts of pilgrimages undertaken in England and abroad fuelled further devotion to the saints and their relics.[5]

The devotional map of England on the eve of the Reformation suggests that, while the geography of the holy might have shifted in the preceding centuries, the saints continued to exert a powerful influence over the church and its people. Revenue at the shrine of St Hugh in Lincoln had peaked in 1364, but the decline in the value of offerings was far from terminal, and the income in each of the first two decades of the sixteenth century exceeded that of the 1490s.[6] Several other English cults declined in the fourteenth century, but the saints as a whole still enjoyed a prominent presence in the church. Oblations at the shrines of St Thomas Cantilupe, St Etheldreda and St Cuthbert had dwindled long before the storm clouds of Reformation had gathered, their places taken by a new generation of saints, cults and pilgrimage destinations.[7] Just as the early medieval cult of martyrs had given way to the veneration of saintly confessors, so this process of change in images of sainthood was to continue, as the saints revered in the late-medieval English church came to include a number whose cults had their origins in the thirteenth century and beyond. The cult of Thomas Becket at Canterbury had attracted vast numbers of pilgrims in the twelfth and thirteenth centuries, but by the fourteenth century the revenue raised at the shrine had begun to decline from its peak in the 1220s. By 1535, the annual offerings totalled £36, a mere shadow of an income of more than £1,000 in 1220. In the twelfth century alone, some 700 miracles were attributed to the archbishop, yet in 1445 the Canterbury monks saw fit to make a public announcement after just one miracle was recorded. The last cure attributed to the saint before the Reformation came in 1474.[8] However, this apparent collapse in the popularity of England's most famous medieval martyr in the century before the Reformation should not be seen as an indication that the cult of the saints had lost its hold over the imagination of the faithful. Miracles were not the only function of the saint and, even after the number of pilgrims to the shrine dwindled, the name of Becket continued to live on through the commemoration of his feast in devotional art and literature and in the dramatic re-enactment of his death.[9] Even after a century of declining revenue, the cult of Becket had received a boost in the late fourteenth century as pilgrims preoccupied by a fear of the Black Death sought his protection and intercession.

The waxing and waning reputations of individual saints was a process in which history, politics and even fashion played a part. Eamon Duffy has noted the growing importance on the eve of the Reformation of saint cults that had their origins in the political conflicts of the fifteenth century. 'Martyrs' were created by Angevins and Plantagenets from those who had fallen victim to civil war, and the cult of Henry VI was more than once appropriated to political ends, first in anti-Yorkist propaganda, and later by Henry Tudor. The fifteenth century had also witnessed a rise in the popularity of the virginal saints Katherine and Margaret, and a variety of 'cloned and identical' saints whose legends were popularised in Osbern Bokenham's *Legendys of Hooly Wummen*.[10] The 1516 printed edition of John Capgrave's *Nova Legenda Anglie* incorporated 13 saints whose *lives* had not appeared in the earlier manuscript editions, including two saints canonised in the fifteenth century. Other cults were growing in popularity on the eve of the Reformation. The cult of St George, established in 1415, had a national appeal throughout the fifteenth century, while other more localised cults continued to attract a steady stream of pilgrims.[11] The cult of Our Lady of Woolpit fuelled requests for pilgrimages in wills from the late fifteenth and early sixteenth centuries, and St Sidwell and St Michael remained popular figures of devotion in the West Country.[12] In 1536, Dr John London reported to Thomas Cromwell that the Marian cult at Caversham remained the object of 'great pilgremage', and the image of the Virgin at Cardigan still attracted pilgrims as late as 1538.[13]

Expenditure on the upkeep of the shrines and statues of the saints fluctuated as new saints were introduced into the local community and the national calendar, but images continued to be cast, clothed and cultivated in the early decades of the sixteenth century. Pressure from 'above' to participate in the veneration of the saints, Duffy notes, was more than matched by lay enthusiasm, and the cult of the saints had an appeal that reached across social and cultural boundaries, with shrines devoted to national heroes, regional figures and individual saints who offered protection for specific trades or cures for specific maladies.[14] Many cults and shrines withstood the test of time, but even where the phenomenon of popular pilgrimage was short-lived, faith in the spiritual significance of an individual, relics or place could endure well beyond the point at which the last pilgrim visited or the last miracle was recorded. It was for this reason that the assault on saints, their cults and their legends emerged as a priority for the proponents of English Protestantism and the Henrician Reformation. The destruction of the images and the shrines of the saints in the 1530s removed these representations of traditional piety from the physical landscape, but this work of official iconoclasm was accompanied by a vigorous polemical campaign to subvert the foundations of the mental image of sanctity that had been constructed over the centuries. At the heart of the evangelical campaign against the cult of the saints lay the determination to expose the powerful as powerless, the miraculous as magical, and holy legends as lies. The centrality of the cult of the saints to traditional piety ensured a prominent role for the heroes of the past in the construction of an identity for the national church in the present.

The cult of the saints on the eve of the Reformation was not without its critics. A small but vocal chorus of voices hostile to the veneration of the saints, images and pilgrimage can be heard in the writings of the Lollards, in the examinations of those accused of heterodoxy, and in the humanist critique of popular religious practice.[15] In 1531, Grace Palmer of St Osyth's in Essex was reported to have refused to contribute towards the cost of lights set before images, and condemned pilgrimage as a wasted journey 'to a piece of timber painted'.[16] In the mid-sixteenth century, John Foxe's *Actes and Monuments* did much to establish the rejection of the saints and the destruction of images as the identifying mark of late-medieval proto-Protestants, and celebrated a number of pre-Reformation assaults on roods, images and cults, including the wonder-working rood at Dovercourt.[17] The physical assaults of Foxe's iconoclasts were matched by the verbal critique of the cult of the saints by humanist writers. German scholars of the late fifteenth century had unravelled the *lives* of the saints in an attempt to purge the written record of its more fanciful accretions, while Desiderius Erasmus' edition of the *Life of St Jerome* included a vigorous denunciation of the historical inaccuracies contained in medieval hagiography.[18] In the *Pilgrimage for Religions Sake*, written in 1526, Erasmus attempted to steer a course between the moderate critics of the cult of the saints and those who had engaged in acts of iconoclastic destruction.[19] The three characters in the dialogue personified different shades of opinion on the cult of saints and relics. Menedemus placed his trust in the teachings of Scripture and wholeheartedly rejected the intercession of the saints. Pullus, perhaps modelled on Erasmus' own pilgrimage companion John Colet, continued to visit the shrines of the saints but baulked at the veneration of blooded bones and secondary relics of dubious provenance. The defence of pilgrimage and relics fell to Ogygius, whose respect for the views of his colleagues was tempered by the belief that the veneration of the saints still contributed to the defence of communal values. Even 'this piece of shoe', he suggested, supported a house of poor men.[20] However Erasmus was especially critical of those who 'rely on certain magic signs and prayers thought up by some pious imposter for his own amusement or for gain'. Among these 'pious imposters' were those who promoted the cult of individual patron saints or invented relics that were presented for popular veneration. The consequence of this misdirected devotion was a 'sea of superstition' whose floodgates had been opened by the young, the old, the women and the 'simpletons' who took the greatest delight in the worship of holy objects.[21]

This disdain for the veneration of material sacred objects had echoes in the writings of English evangelicals in their assault on the cult of the saints in the 1530s and 1540s. In the years after the break with Rome, English writing on the cult of the saints struck at the heart of beliefs in the intercession of the saints, their miracles and their role as spiritual patrons. The denunciation of the shrines and the relics of the saints as the physical embodiment of false doctrine was accompanied by the destruction of the images of the saints that had been erected in the hearts of men, leading them into idolatry and false religion. Robert Barnes argued that the cult of images was a violation of the first commandment, invented by the clergy, the 'new godmakers', to encourage the faithful to place their trust in 'feyned and invented mediators'.[22] The Catholic response, that the reverence offered to the saints was of a different order from that due to God, was rejected by Barnes, who argued that the very fact that the people 'ranne from place to place to seke the[m]' demonstrated that it was the physical image rather than the memory of the saints which was the subject of popular devotion.[23] William Tyndale used the example of Elisha to condemn the veneration of the bones of the holy dead. The miracle by which Elisha's bones had restored a dead man to life was 'not done that men should pray to him … ', Tyndale wrote, 'neither to put their trust in his bones. For God, to avoid all such idolatry, had polluted all dead bones.'[24] William Turner's translation of Rhegius' *A co[m]parison betwene the olde learnynge [and] the newe* used the veneration of the saints as an example of the contrast between true faith, which worshipped Christ as the sole mediator between man and God, and false religion, which held that 'the sayntes worke miracles. For how many being syck wt diuerse sicknesses haue be[n] holpen at ye monume[n]tes & to[m]bes of the saintes.'[25]

George Joye complained that the people were all too willing to forsake the worship of God and 'runne after straunge goddess, into hylles, wodes and solitary places, where to worshype stokes and stones', refusing to honour God in their home but travelling on pilgrimages to worship objects manufactured by men.[26]

The saints were not without their supporters. In response to evangelical criticisms, Thomas More had defended both the general cult of the saints and images, and the specific role of individual saints as protectors and patrons. Human reason, he argued, could not penetrate the divine mind, neither understand 'why God dothe in some place myracles/and in some place none/yet is it no doubte but he dothe'.[27] God worked miracles at His pleasure at specific times and in specific places, More argued, not to honour the place, but to honour the saint and encourage faith.[28] In response to the criticisms of the Messenger that ridiculous petitions were made to individual saints who were believed to have the ability to cure certain diseases, More defended the position of the patron saint. Conceding that there were some instances in which petitions to the saints were either ill-informed or of dubious merit, More argued that there was still good reason to associate saints with specific problems. The intercession of St Appollonia, for example, was sought for the alleviation of toothache, on the basis that the saint's teeth had been pulled as a test of her faith. While devotion could be excessive or ill-conceived, this was not in itself a justification for the rejection of the principle and custom.[29] However, More's Messenger was not alone in his ambivalent attitude to the cult of patron saints, and the debate in the *Dialogue* no doubt had at least some basis in the reality of controversy over saints and sainthood in the 1520s and 1530s.

Despite More's efforts, the role of specific saints as patrons and protectors was repeatedly condemned by evangelical writers. Both Tyndale and Barnes confidently rejected the notion that one place could be thought to be more holy than another, or that prayer would be more efficacious if offered at the shrines of the saints. Barnes suggested that such beliefs were superstition, invented by the devil to delude the people.[30] Tyndale, in his controversy with Thomas More, likened the obsession with proximity to relics and sacred objects to magic, alleging that such 'imagination bindeth a man to the place with a false faith as necromancers trust in their circles'.[31] In *The Image of Both Churches*, John Bale identified the proliferation of superstition with the cult of saints and their miracles, and more specifically the cult of patron saints with particular functions:

> Sayncte Job for the poxe, Saynt Roke for the pestilence, Sayncte Germyne for the ague, Saynct Appolyne for the ake, Saynct Graciane for thrift losynge, and Saynt Barbara for gone shote. That ladye in that place and that ladye in that. This rode here and that rode there. And he that dyd myracles here coulde do nothynge there. Thus was all changed into deuylishnesse.[32]

The example of St George was exploited by George Joye in a humorous satire on the problems that might be created by the appeal to patron saints. The invocation of individual saints in specific circumstances was unscriptural, Joye claimed, and made false gods of the saints. In the case of St George, whose assistance was called upon by armies in battle, Joye pondered which side the saint would fight on if both the English and the French summoned his help in the field. Taken to its logical conclusion, Joye argued, traditional faith in the intercession of the saints would compel St George to wage war with himself if both sides were to claim him as their holy patron. But in reality, he concluded, the cult of the patron saint was a mere delusion that deceived the faithful into calling upon St George 'and suche lyke saintes dead which nether heare ne knowe us'.[33]

The contention that the saints were beyond the reach of human influence, and deaf to the prayers addressed to them, was argued to be apparent in the seeming inability of the saints and their relics to defend themselves in times of trial. The 'testing' of the miraculous powers of the saints and their relics, whether by neglect or by physical harm, had ample precedent in the ritual humiliation of relics, most common during the eleventh and twelfth centuries. Patrick Geary has identified the miraculous protection afforded by the patron saint of a monastic community as a vital part of its defence from its enemies. The alienation of the 'honores' of a monastery, by occupation or confiscation, was tantamount to the alienation of the 'honores' of the patron saint, who was then expected to work miracles of vengeance in defence of the community. If the saint failed to act, the community was permitted to engage in a liturgical act of humiliation, removing the images or relics of the saints from their usual position and laying them on the ground before the altar in an attempt to force the saint to fulfil his duty to protect the community.[34] The expectation was that the physical humiliation of the remains of the saint would prompt a dramatic miracle, forcing those who threatened the community to retreat and reaffirming the position of the saint in heaven. Such punitive miracles were a staple of medieval sermons and art; a series of paintings in Eton College portrayed the death of a man who had attempted to damage an image of the Virgin.[35] However, the inverse was also true: a continued failure to act could irreparably damage the reputation of the holy dead. Evangelical polemic against the cult of the saints and propagandists for the Henrician government therefore capitalised upon the apparent inability of the saints to defend themselves from attack in the 1530s and 1540s. Randall Hurleston exploited an example of such saintly inactivity in Gottinga, where thieves had entered the chapel of St Nicholas and removed a quantity of gold and silver. On hearing that the thieves had escaped, a local cobbler demanded an explanation: 'why shulde I seke for helpe of this saincte?'. St Nicholas, he recalled, had been hailed as the liberator of prisoners, yet 'how chaunceth it that he whiche hathe delyuered many out of stynkyng prisons and from punyshmentes that they shulde haue suffred could not loke to hym selfe?'. One bystander made the sarcastic suggestion that perhaps the saint had simply been persuaded to relinquish his wealth in order to follow Christ. The apparent inability of St Nicholas to act in defence of his own church, Hurlestone concluded, suggested that the faithful had simply been deluded by 'satans subtiltie' into believing the miracles attributed to the saint.[36]

The unresponsiveness of saints and images in the face of attack was a common feature of evangelical polemic in England in the middle decades of the sixteenth century, and a prominent part of the official Henrician and Edwardian campaign against the objects of cults. In 1536, the Londoner William Collins appeared before the Common Council, accused as a 'common brawler' after railing against the sacrament of the altar and 'shooting despitefully at the picture of Christ at St Margaret Pattens', challenging the rood to prove its worth by defending itself.[37] Others pricked the images of the saints removed from London churches, claiming that their failure to bleed exposed them as mere 'stocks and stones'.[38] William Gray's *The Fantassie of Idolatrie*, a celebration of the destruction of the shrines of the saints, derided images that had fallen prey to iconoclasts:

> For when they bored holes
> In the roodes back of poles,
> Which, as some men saye, dyd speake,
> Then lay he still as a stocke,
> Receyved there many a knocke,
> And did not ones crie 'creake.[39]

'Throw them down thrice,' Gray demanded, 'they cannot rise, not once to help themselves.' John Foxe noted that the iconoclasts responsible for the removal of the rood at Dovercourt in 1532 were blessed with 'a sondrous goodly night, both hard frost and fair moonshine', a sure sign that their actions were favoured by God. The vandalism was accomplished 'without any resistance of the said idol' and the task made all the easier by the fact that among the miraculous powers associated with the rood was its ability to prevent the closure of the church door.[40] Hugh Latimer carried the figure of St Rumwold to the doorway of St Paul's, shattering the popular legend that the image was impossible to move.[41] By contrast, events surrounding the removal of the rood and images in St Paul's Cathedral were seized upon by conservative clergy as evidence that the destruction of the images of the saints would not go unavenged. Workmen charged with the removal of the images entered the church under cover of darkness in order to avoid public opposition, but the destruction was carried out with such haste that two men were killed by falling masonry and several others were injured.[42] For some observers, events in the church were testimony to the vengeful power of the saint and a warning of the dangers inherent in even officially sanctioned iconoclasm.

The Reformation attack on the images of the saints was not only a work of vandalism but also an inversion of the traditional act of ritual humiliation, intended, not to spur the saint into action, but to disprove the very idea that the material might be used to manipulate the holy. The breaking or burning of images and roods was a powerful piece of propaganda, in which objects that had been publicly venerated were publicly destroyed.[43] Images, like relics, were believed to have the ability to choose and protect their location, with the result that the simple removal of the image was often enough to cast doubt upon the miraculous powers of the saint.[44] In June 1538, the statues of the Virgin from Ipswich and Walsingham were cast into a bonfire in Chelsea, along with a number of other images, as a potent demonstration of the inability of images to work miracles in their own defence.[45] The ease with which the statues were removed and destroyed provided a public exhibition of the emptiness of images and served to undermine traditional assumptions and beliefs around the power of the saints. It is not surprising then that the vigorous campaign against saints and images in the 1530s also sought to capitalise on the identification of fraudulent claims surrounding the ability of saints and images to work miracles, and expose any fiction in the legends that surrounded them. This concern to locate and expose incidents of deception, Peter Marshall has argued, was a 'thread which can be found running through the course of the Reformation in Henry VIII's reign' and one which was clearly evident in the campaign against saints and miracles that began in 1534.[46] In June 1534, preachers were instructed to avoid contentious subjects including purgatory, the veneration of the saints, clerical marriage, pilgrimage and *forged miracle*, on the basis that sermons on such topics would merely engender 'talk and rumour'.[47]

The same concern over the saints, relics and miracles is evident in the Injunctions issued for the royal visitation of the smaller monasteries in July 1535, which ordered that religious houses 'shall not shewe no relyques or fayned myracles for the encrease of lucre but that they exhort pylgrymes and strayngers to geue that to the poore that they thought to offere to ther images or reliquies'.[48] Reports returned to Cromwell by the commissioners suggested that the monasteries were in possession of a significant number of relics, many of which were not only retained because of their historical reputation but continued to be venerated and used by those seeking to tap into the thaumaturgical generosity of the saints.[49] Richard Layton promised Cromwell that he would send from Maiden Bradley 'a bage of reliquis, wherein ye shal see straingeis thynges', including 'Godes cote, Our lades smoke, Parte of Godes supper in cena domini … belyke ther is in Bethelem plenty of stones and sum quarrie, and makith ther maingiernes off stone'. He also promised to provide Cromwell with 'oure lades gyrdell of Bruton, rede silke, wiche is a solemne reliquie sent to women travelyng wiche shall not miscarie in partu'. Layton also made reference to 'Mare magalens girdell and that is wrappyde and coveride with white, sent also with gret reverence to women travelling, wiche girdell Matilda thempresse fownder of Ferley gave unto them as saith the holy father of Ferley', suggesting that the relic enjoyed a well-developed historical pedigree and was still used by women in labour.[50]

The debate over saints and images continued. Hugh Latimer's Convocation sermon delivered in June 1536 was a call for further action against the deceit and 'juggling' that supported the cult of the saints, accompanied by a vigorous denunciation of images and pilgrimages, particularly the 'preferring of picture to picture, image to image' and the veneration of 'pigs bones' as relics.[51] The response in Convocation was mixed, and the doctrinal formulary that resulted, the Ten Articles, was rather less aggressive in its tone in discussing cult objects. Images were permitted as 'kindlers and firers of men's minds', although preachers were still encouraged to warn against the perils of idolatry. Prayer to the saints was permitted, but the expectation that one saint might be more merciful than another, or act as a specific patron, was condemned.[52] Although the Ten Articles upheld the keeping of holy days 'unto God in memory', the Act for the Abrogation of Certain Holy Days, issued one week later, reached into the heart of traditional devotional observances by abolishing all feast days that fell within the harvest season and the Westminster law terms, preserving only those associated with the Apostles, the Virgin and St George, alongside the Ascension, the nativity of John the Baptist, All Saints Day and Candlemas.[53] The legislation of June 1536 was reinforced by Cromwell via the Injunctions issued later in the year, which ordered that the clergy should not 'set forth or extol any images, relics, or miracles for any superstitious lucre, nor allure the people by any enticements to the pilgrimage of any saint, otherwise than is permitted in the Articles lately put forth'.[54] The Injunctions, and the abrogation of holy days, had a substantial impact on the parish calendar, and concern that the legislation of 1535–6 amounted to an attempt to remove the saints from the religious landscape was evident in the complaints made by rebels in the Pilgrimage of Grace. The *Bishops Book* of 1537 was vigorous in its condemnation of images, and the dismantling of the shrines of saints and their cults continued throughout 1537 and 1538. John Hussee noted in March 1538 that 'pilgrimage saints go down apace', and this public destruction of images provided evangelicals with further polemical ammunition in their denunciation of false relics.

John Hilsey's denunciation of the rood of Boxley and the Blood of Hailes in a sermon at Paul's Cross in February 1538 is perhaps the most famous example of the transformation of objects of traditional devotion into a piece of evangelical propaganda. Hilsey claimed to have heard from the mistress of the abbot of Hailes that the relic of the True Blood was in fact nothing more sacred than blood taken from a duck. Tradition held that the Blood had been purchased in 1267 by Edmund, earl of Cornwall, and brought to Hailes.[55] A new apse and five chapels were added to the abbey after the arrival of the precious relic, and pilgrim traffic was encouraged by a Papal Indulgence. The relic was clearly popular on the eve of the Reformation, despite the common belief held that the Blood was only visible to those who were of a suitably pious aspect.[56] But the Blood also had its critics, and some of the punitive miracles that were publicised in the early sixteenth century were perhaps part of a more general campaign to silence detractors. The Blood of Hailes certainly provided the Henrician regime with the ideal tool with which to start chipping away at the cult of relics. The official denunciation of the Blood as a fake not only drew upon a long-standing debate over its authenticity but also exploited the popularity of the relic as a springboard for a more general investigation of cultic objects. Likewise, the dismantling of the famous rood of Boxley offered Hilsey the opportunity to turn an object of popular devotion into an object of popular ridicule. Hilsey described how the movement reported in the rood was made possible by a mechanism of strings and joints, and invited his audience to demonstrate with their own hands the powerlessness of the rood by participating in its destruction.[57] The mechanism behind the Boxley rood was presented before Henry VIII who, it was claimed, did not know 'whether to rejoice at the exposure or to grieve at the long deception'.[58] It scarcely mattered; evidence that the Catholic clergy had been engaged in the perpetration of fraudulent miracles with the intention of deceiving the faithful could be readily turned to justify a more widespread investigation of the claims made for images and shrines.[59] A king who grieved that his people had been deceived, and who exposed feigned miracles and idolatry, was a king who exercised his supremacy over the church not as a schismatic but as a defender of true religion.

The same process is evident in William Barlow's account of the destruction of a 'false' relic in Cardigan in March 1538. Barlow promised to send Cromwell a selection of relics from his cathedral, including 'two rotten skulles stuffed wyth putrified clowtes', two arm bones, a 'worme eaten boke' and 'our ladyes taper of Cardigan', which he viewed as evidence of the 'develish delusyon' perpetrated upon the faithful by the clergy. Barlow's letter to Cromwell also detailed his examination of Thomas Hore, the prior of Cardigan, on the subject of the miraculous taper, which had reportedly been discovered burning in the hand of an image of the Virgin floating on the river. Hore testified that the taper had burned continuously for nine years after its discovery and had been revered as a valuable relic upon which men swore oaths. However, the previous prior had placed additional wood in the taper to prolong its life after fragments had been removed by pilgrims. Barlow demanded that the cathedral clergy preach before the people and denounce 'the abhominable idolatrie and disceetfull jugglinge of their predicessours there in worshippinge and causing to be worshipped a pece of old rotten tymber'. The clergy were also enjoined to remove anything from the church that might lead the people to idolatry and to make an inventory of the offerings left at the shrine and convert it into a money payment to the poor.[60] Barlow's message was all the more significant because the taper was not only revered by pilgrims to the cathedral but was also respected by the wider community who, as Hore observed, had used the taper as the basis for legal transactions.

The search for false relics continued. In June 1538, Hugh Latimer celebrated the burning of the image of the Virgin of Worcester, 'our great Sybill', suggesting that a 'jolly muster at Smithfield' might be made of this statue and her 'sisters' of Walsingham, Doncaster and Penrice.[61] Richard Pollard informed Cromwell of the preservation of 'roten bones that be called reliques' at Winchester and Hyde and, in September 1538, John London wrote to Cromwell with a description of the relics at Nutley abbey, where one canon 'wasse acostomyd to shew many pretty relykes among the wiche wer (as he made report) the holy dager that kylled kinge Henry and the holy knife that kylled seynt Edwarde'. In December, London was in Oxford, from where he wrote to Cromwell describing the 'two heddes of seynt Ursula, wich bycause ther is no manner of syluer abowt them, I reserve tyll I have another hedd of hers, wich I shall fynd in my waye within these xiiii dayes as I am creadably informyd'.[62] The sheer quantity of relics preserved in monastic communities, and especially those of dubious provenance, was presented as evidence that the religious had long exploited the credulity of the people for profit and led the faithful into idolatry. The Royal Injunctions of September 1538 provided a justification for what had been a long summer of iconoclasm, and demanded the removal of all 'feigned images' and 'feigned relics' that were visited by pilgrims.[63] The tenor of the Injunctions was echoed and reinforced in vernacular pamphlet literature, most notably Nicholas Wyse's *Consolacyon for Chrysten People*, and the publication of the first English translation of Heinrich Bullinger's commentary on Antichrist.[64] In less than a decade, the English church and government had moved from the condemnation of image-breakers and the persecution of iconoclasts to a campaign of destruction that was accompanied by the public humiliation of false relics. Such destruction was unprecedented, and therefore highly shocking and highly visible.[65] The ritual disproof of images and relics both reflected and enacted a brutal rupture between the present and the past, true religion and false.

The 1547 Royal Injunctions, issued in the first months of the reign of Edward VI, reinforced many of the official pronouncements on images and idolatry made in the 1530s,

> to the intent that all superstition and hypocrisy, crept into divers men's hearts, may vanish away, they shall not set forth nor extol any images, relics, or miracles for superstition or lucre, nor allure the people by any enticement to the pilgrimage of any saint … .

At his coronation, the young king was reminded of his duty to uphold true religion, as 'God's vice-gerent and Christ's vicar within your own dominions, and to see, with your predecessor Josiah, God truly worshipped, and idolatry destroyed, the tyranny of the bishop of Rome banished from your subjects and images removed'.[66] Throughout Lent of 1547, Edward's court preachers hammered home the message of reform.[67] In autumn, the Council instructed London authorities to direct the aldermen to visit each church in the city in order to determine which images remained as objects of veneration and ascertain the fate of those that had already been removed. Surviving images were to be removed under cover of darkness.[68] The erosion of the liturgical position of the saints that had begun in 1536 was continued in the calendar that accompanied the 1549 Book of Common Prayer, which removed the feasts of all non-scriptural saints. The feasts of the saints were pared down to include only the feasts of the Evangelists, John the Baptist, the Apostles, Mary Magdalen and the Virgin, alongside the commemoration of Christmas, Easter and Whitsun.[69] Court preachers in Lent of 1550 continued to preach on the need for reform and repentance, casting Edward VI in the role of a second Josiah and constructing a model of kingship based upon the precedent provided by the godly rulers of the Old Testament.[70] The 1552 Parliament accepted a longer list of holy days as authorised by the king and not ordained by the timeless will of God, on which harvest labourers and others were permitted to work if necessary. Knights of the Garter were permitted to celebrate the feast of St

George, but this was certainly not a general rehabilitation of the national saints of the past, and no mention was made of figures such as Hugh of Lincoln and Swithun.[71] The 'Homily Against the Peril of Idolatry' condemned as 'madness' the actions of those men who were prepared to squander their wealth on pilgrimage to Rome, Jerusalem and Santiago 'to visit dumb and dead stocks and stones', throwing their families into poverty as a result.[72] In the eyes of Edwardian evangelicals, the power of the pope and his clergy had been built upon an enduring delusion in which dead images were manipulated to give the illusion of life. However, this was a delusion that could be readily exposed by stripping away the layers that protected the saints and their cults, and exposing their 'dumb stones' to the light of the Gospel.

There was a plentiful supply of relics that could be tested by the words of the Gospel. The cartulary of Christ Church contained a list of some 400 relics garnered from a multitude of saints, and the descriptions provided by the monastic Visitors of the 1530s detailed the numerous relics that were in the possession of the religious houses.[73] The reputation of the relics of a saint had its roots in the collective memory, reinforced by the existence of written documents that testified to the authenticity of the relic and identified it with a specific saint.[74] It was therefore vital that the assault on the physical remains of the saints in the 1530s should be accompanied by an assault on the written and oral tradition that perpetuated their cults. The interruption of this tradition of belief broke the crucial link which bound the relic to the saint and the saint to the community. Although the social and legal functions of relics had diminished in the centuries before the Reformation, the continued existence of a multitude of undocumented relics provided Henrician propagandists with a vast and valuable range of polemical material.[75] Feigned and dubious relics had long been a cause for concern, and the potential for even innocent error was exacerbated by the vibrant medieval trade in the fragmented bodies of the saints.[76] Erasmus' satirical account of pilgrimage to Walsingham and Canterbury was reprinted as propaganda for the Henrician Reformation, and his criticism of the relics with which he was presented had resonances in both the 'pigges bones' of Chaucer's Pardoner and the 'old rotten bones' criticised by Thomas More's Messenger.[77] The theme was taken up and expanded in the service of the Reformation. In 1535, Richard Layton alleged that the monks of Bath were in possession of a collection of relics 'haveyng therof no writyng' nor any oral record of their provenance.[78] John Calvin's 1543 *Advertissement tres-utile du grand proffit qui reviendroit à la Chrestienté, s'il faisoit inventoire de tous les corps sainctz, et reliques* ... , translated into English in 1561, complained that every church contained 'a heap of bones and other small rubbish', and suggested that all relics should be collected together in order to demonstrate the scale of the deception. So keen were the faithful to find relics, Calvin claimed, that they accepted without question those items that were presented to them, although 'even a child could see how the devil had been mocking the world' with unverifiable and fraudulent objects.[79] Divorced from their historical and geographical context, the relics of the saints became objects of ridicule and justified their own destruction.

Commenting on medieval *furta sacra* (thefts of relics), Patrick Geary has argued that the very act of removal broke the cultural context which had provided the relic with meaning, a meaning that would then be reinvented and restored by its new community.[80] The saints continued to 'live among their people' in their relics, with the result that the historical record of the possession of a relic was evidence of the continued life of the saint in the community.[81] The removal of the relics and images of the saints from English churches in the 1530s, like traditional *furta sacra*, shattered the cultural context of the sacred object. However, when these sacred objects were then imbued with a new meaning, it was as evidence of Catholic deception, idolatry and superstition. The immediate effectiveness of the destruction of images and relics was constrained by the fact that the scope of such activity extended only as far as that which was breakable and combustible. In going further, and breaking apart and reconstructing the cultural and historical meaning of the sacred objects, English evangelicals not only celebrated material iconoclasm but also sought to purge idols from the hearts and minds of the faithful. The destruction of the images and relics of the saints was accompanied by the reconstruction of the legends and histories that had encouraged and authenticated their cults. In a campaign of iconoclasm that reached beyond the physical remains and representations of the saints into the very nature of sainthood itself, evangelical polemicists took apart the edifice of traditional hagiography and reassembled its component parts to present a new image of medieval sanctity. Saints traded places with sinners and the heroes of the past emerged as villains in the present. Traditional attributes of sanctity such as miracles, chastity and the defence of the liberties of the church were recast as the fruit of doctrinal error, clerical greed and magical manipulation.

The legends of the saints reflected an ongoing battle of acceptance and displacement, in which individual saints' *lives* were remodelled to established patterns of sanctity, and images of sanctity reconstructed in the light of the *lives* of individual saints. Hagiography was strongly self-referential and, within the rich tapestry of medieval hagiography, common threads run through the *lives* of the individual saints. The existing corpus of the *lives* of saints provided a reference point for future writers, and a collection of *topoi* and exempla from which new saints could be constructed. Hagiographers had at their disposal a 'veritable thesaurus' of examples of holy life and action that could be employed to cast their subject in the historical mould of sanctity. Bede's *Life of St Cuthbert* was replete with parallels between the life of his subject and those of figures whose place within the Christian pantheon was well established, including recognised saints and biblical figures.[82] Miracles and manifestations of the sacred in the *lives* of the saints defined and confirmed a pattern of holy life, in which the birth of the saint was either anticipated by wonders (Cyrus, Hild, Edward the Confessor), or marked by miracles and radiance (Patrick, Gerald, Dominic). The miracles of the saints echoed those with an already-established scriptural or historical precedent, such as extinguishing or raising fire, resisting temptation or foretelling death. The writing of legends of the saints thus not only reinforced the past record of human holiness but also helped to shape that record by becoming part of the tradition of sanctity that it recorded.[83]

Peter Burke has demonstrated that the sacred was often contagious, with individuals canonised if they conformed to the pattern established by another canonised saint, or had been associated with a canonised saint.[84] The perception of holiness acted as a mirror for the social and religious values of the community, with the result that hagiographical literature reflected not so much the society that produced the saint but the culture that produced the written record of the *life* of the saint.[85] Individual saints served as a witness to the age in which they lived, but their *lives* witnessed to the age in which they were composed, and their canonisations reflected the concerns of the age in which their cult gained official sanction.[86] Saints and sainthood are continually constructed and reconstructed in the communal and historical perception, and images of sanctity acquire a fullness of meaning within the context of the culture that produced them. However, despite the frequent repetition of common exempla, there was still scope for substantial divergence in the attributes of sanctity across space and time, highlighting the role of the concerns of the present in shaping the construction of holiness in the past. In a study of the cult of Hemma of Gurk, Edmund Kern has charted such a changing relationship between the 'historical' Hemma of the eleventh century and her life as represented in the *vitae* produced in the centuries that followed. The hagiographic Hemma was represented variously as a model of female piety and a miracle-worker, and her cult and legend were exploited and twisted by the town of Gurk in its relations with the archbishop of Salzburg.[87]

Late-medieval hagiography came to be dominated by the written and printed *life*, in a process that culminated in the humanist and Bollandist catalogues of the *lives* of the saints and the rising status of hagiology over traditional *vitae*.[88] This trend was reflected most obviously in the popularity of the *Golden Legend*, first compiled in the late thirteenth century by Jacobus de Voraigne, archbishop of Genoa. Voraigne gathered together a collection of *lives* that exemplified the piety and virtue of sanctity, and attempted to steer a path between the multiple variations, expansions and compressions in the *lives* of the most popular saints. The text circulated widely in French monastic communities, and a full French edition was printed early in the fourteenth century. The first printed English edition was compiled and edited by William Caxton in 1483. Caxton removed four chapters from the 182 in Voraigne's text, but added ten new entries on the feasts and *lives* of recently canonised saints, and an entirely new section on the *lives* of the biblical saints. Two editions of the *Golden Legend* appeared in Caxton's lifetime, and a third edition was printed by Wynkyn de Worde.[89] The popularity of the *Legenda Aurea* is reflected in the vigorous assault on its contents by humanist and Protestant writers, who complained that it obscured rather than illuminated Christian history. Jan Luis Vives condemned the collection as '*ferrei oris, plumbei cordis*', and repeated efforts were made by Bonino Mombritius, Jacques Lefevre d'Etaples and Caesare Baronius to reground the *lives* of the saints in historical accuracy, in a labour that eventually bore fruit in the work of the Bollandists.[90]

Although evangelical writers were quick to condemn medieval hagiography, evangelical engagement with the legends of the saints was not confined to a simple rejection of their content. The fluctuating reputations of individual saints and their cults had reflected the development of different models of holiness and ongoing changes in medieval religious culture. The era of the Reformation was no exception. The denunciation of medieval hagiography as fraud and fiction was accompanied by a polemical rereading and rewriting of the *lives* of the saints. Virtues were redefined as vices and miracles dismissed as magic. The corpus of medieval writing on the saints was used to construct an image of the past in which the *lives* of the saints emerged as evidence of doctrinal error, moral corruption and political treason in the church of Rome. With the destruction of the physical cult of the saints in the 1530s came an attack on the traditional structures of sanctity, one which appropriated the history of the church and its holy men and women in the service of the Reformation. In his *Actes of the English Votaries*, John Bale complained that 'the spirituall sodomites in the legends of their sanctyfyed sorcerers diffamed the Englysh posterite with tayles', but it was these same 'tayles' that were so vital to Bale and others in the formation of a Protestant narrative of English 'posterite'.[91] Medieval hagiographical writing has much to offer the historian of the religious culture of the age, and the destruction and reconstruction of the same texts in the era of the Reformation sheds light upon the nature and priorities of religious change.

Evangelical polemicists made much of the intersection of fact and fiction in the *lives* of the saints. William Turner's translation of Rhegius' *A Comparison between the Learnynge and the Newe* (1537) complained that the defenders of the new faith 'bring forth old wyues fables for sounde and true thynges', and John Bale alleged that the only support for the cult of the saints was to be found in 'manyfest lyes and knaueries'.[92] Reginald Scot protested that his Catholic opponents persisted in presenting a version of the past 'so grosse and palpable that I might be thought as wise in going about to confute them as to answer the stories of Frier Rush, Adam Bell, or the Golden Legend'. Raphael Holinshed recorded the miracles that were attributed to St Germane but alleged that they were mere fables, an illustration of

> what stuffe our old historiographers haue farced up their huge volumes not so much regarding the credit of an historie, as satisfieng the vanitie of their owne fond fantasies, studieng with a pretended skilfulnesse to cast glorious colours upon lies.[93]

John Bale suggested that the saints of the Catholic church were no more than idols created to fill the vacuum left by the rejected pagan gods. Jupiter, Saturn, Mercury, Mars and Diana, he claimed, had been replaced in the medieval church by 'Wenefryde, Cuthbert, Dunstane, Oswalde, Anselme, Becket, Brigyde, Audreye, Modwen, Edith, Osith and Ethelberge'.[94] Inconsistencies within the legends and canonisation processes were exploited to suggest that faith in the role of saints as heavenly intercessors was misplaced. 'The pope canonizeth and uncanonizeth,' de Valera claimed, pointing to the example of Boniface VIII who had canonised St Louis, but 'uncanoniseth Herman of Ferrara, commaunded him to be vntombed, and after he had been buryed thirtie yeares, to be burned'. When the clergy appealed to the saints in the canon of the Mass, he suggested, they were all too often seeking the intercession of those 'whose souls were burning in Hell'.[95]

Traditional marks of holiness were strongly criticised by evangelical writers. Robert Barnes complained that the medieval church had made saints of those who had resisted the will of the monarch and rebelled against princes in defence of spiritual liberty, yet had refused to honour those who obeyed the temporal powers and defended the word of God. Neither a tradition of veneration, nor the wealth and popularity of a shrine, could prove a saint to be a member of the church of Christ, Barnes argued. 'S Thomas of Canterburys holy showe,' he claimed, 'wyth alle the holy botys of holy martyrs & all these to gether can not make one crumme of holynes in you/nor helpe you one prycke forward/that you may be wyth in this churche.'[96] John Bale protested that saints had been canonised for their defence of the authority of the traditions of men over that of the Gospel, and mocked the legends of the saints that celebrated miracles worked 'in contempt of their christe[n] gouernours'.[97] Reginald Scot made light of the miracles associated with individuals whose saintly reputation was built upon their chastity. A marginal note, 'Saincts as holie and chaste as horses & mares', appeared beside Scot's account of the *life* of St Christine, who had offered to sleep in the bed on a maid who was troubled by an incubus in the night. Scot promised to enlighten his reader with further tales of 'divers saints and holie persons which were exceedinge bawdie and lecherous and by certeine miraculous meanes became chaste', including St Syren, Helias and the abbot Equicius, all of whom had been apparently been castrated by angels after praying for the gift of chastity.[98]

Among the characteristics of sanctity that had been prized by medieval hagiographers, it was chastity that was most vigorously denounced by evangelical writers. The polemical defence of clerical marriage was accompanied by a sustained assault upon the morality of the celibate clergy and the chastity of the medieval saints. Bale complained that the Popes had

commaunded unto us whoremongers, bawds, bribers, Idolaters, hypocrites, trayters and most filthy Gomoreanes, as Godlye men and women, but also haue they canonysed the[m] for most holye sayntes, set them vp gylt Images in their temples, commaunded their vigils to be fasted, appointed them holy dayes and the peoples to do them honoure with euensonges, howres, processio[n]s, lights, masses, ryngynges, syngynges, sensynges and the deuylls and al such hethenyshe waies.[99]

The *lives* of the saints, he argued, were hardly a ringing endorsement of either Christian marriage or the chastity of the regular and secular clergy. The legend of St Patrick, for example, described him as the son of a priest. Bale also directed his readers to the *lives* of St Dubrice, later archbishop of Careligion, and St Kentigern, whose mothers both refused to confirm the name of the father of their saintly sons, and St David, whose birth, predicted by angels 30 years previously, still took place out of wedlock.[100] 'Neuer were the sonnes of Abraham, Isaac and Jacob, of Moyses, Eleezar and Phinees, so paynted out with miracles and wonders nor yet so pranked up with tabernacles and lightes, sensinges and massinges, as these whores birdes,' Bale protested, 'thus iudge they whoredome holiness and wholesome marriage sinne.' Further examples followed. St Iltute was esteemed as a saint, despite the fact that he had sent his wife away and put out her eyes when she returned to him, St Drithelm had abandoned his wife and children to enter the monastery of Melrose, and St Cuthbert was reputedly 'so cruel ... vnto women' that none were permitted to enter the sanctuary of his church after his death.[101]

The exaltation of celibacy over marriage by the medieval church, Bale claimed, had distorted the image of true sainthood and filled the *lives* of the saints with stories of temptation by women. All too often, saints were either unmarried or had relinquished their wives in the pursuit of holiness.[102] Bale's rendering of the traditional legends was largely accurate, and readers were frequently referred to John Capgrave's *Nova Legenda Anglie* as the original source for examples of false miracles that were associated with the feigned chastity of the saints. Bale cited the legends of Milburga, Mildred and Etheldreda who, he claimed, had laboured to dissuade men from marriage. Details were repeated from Capgrave's *life* of Etheldreda, which described how the saint had married one Tonbert, and 'when she came into the chaumber she committed her virgynyte to our Lorde', with the result that her husband feared to touch her.[103] Milburga's legend described her entry into monastic life and her flight from the son of a king who was determined to marry her.[104] Capgrave's *life* of Mildred recorded her suffering at the hands of her abbess who had attempted to force her to marry, and the saint's determined rejection of her many suitors.[105] Bale's handling of the legends of these female models of chaste sanctity is instructive. His exploitation of one of the most popular collections of medieval saints' *lives* in the condemnation of holy chastity exemplifies the close engagement of evangelical writers with the legends of the saints that they sought to reject. Bale's work demonstrated the polemical capital to be gained in using the Catholic records of the past to condemn the version of the past that they had been composed to commemorate. Evangelical polemicists used the medieval *lives* of the saints to mock and deride those same saints, engaging in a process of desanctification that had as its primary weapon the popular hagiographic record.

This process can be observed in the reconstruction of the *lives* of other English saints in evangelical history writing. John Bale narrated the legend of St Wulstan of Bawburgh, a lay aristocrat who had relinquished his inheritance to pursue a life of chastity and poverty. The legend of Wulstan does not feature in any surviving calendars and liturgical texts, and the cult was initially confined to the area around his burial place at Bawburgh. Until the late fifteenth century, Wulstan's name was not included in standard collections of English *Vitae*, but by 1516 the saint and his cult had become important enough that a detailed account of his *life* appeared in Capgrave's *Nova Legenda Anglie*.[106] Bale's account of the miracles and reputation of Wulstan drew heavily upon the account in Capgrave's collection, reflecting his indebtedness to the *Nova Legenda Anglie* for the histories and biographies of the saints. Eamon Duffy has highlighted the extent of clerical management behind the cult of Wulstan, in order that the saint might be represented as a layman who led a godly and pious life as a son of the church.[107] This reputation as a chaste and obedient miracle-worker was unlikely to endear Wulstan to evangelical writers, but Bale's attention may also have been attracted by the apparent popularity of the cult on the eve of the Reformation. The cult had helped to finance the rebuilding of the church in the 1470s and had inspired the foundation of a guild of St Wulstan in the late fifteenth century. Offerings left at the shrine, and will preambles, continued to name Wulstan as a patron in the early sixteenth century.[108] Wulstan was revered as a protector of the farmers of Norfolk, a reputation that was reflected in Bale's blunt condemnation of the saint as 'the god of their feldes'. The bucolic miracles associated with Wulstan were ridiculed by Bale, in an attempt both to devalue the legend of the saint and to encourage a more sceptical attitude to the miraculous among his readers. Capgrave's legend claimed that 'both man and beastes which had lost their preuy partes had newe members agayne restored to them' by the saint, prompting Bale to recommend that his reader 'marke thys kynde of myracles for your learnynge'.[109]

Other *lives* received similar treatment. The legend of St Ursula and the 11,000 Virgins had enjoyed great popularity in the later Middle Ages. However, the combination of this popularity and the apparently dubious foundations of the cult provided Bale with invaluable polemical material in his denunciation of the legends of the saints and the cult of virginity in the medieval church. According to legend, Ursula and her 11,000 companions had set sail from Britain and visited Cologne and Basle, before journeying on land to Rome. Upon their return to Cologne, they had suffered martyrdom for their faith and chastity. Later versions of the legend claimed that they had been killed by the Huns, who had then fled, terrified by the miraculous powers of the martyrs. They were enshrined as patrons and protectors of the city of Cologne, and the relics of Ursula and the virgins attracted pilgrims and their cult flourished. However, the legend that supported the cult was not recorded until well after the events that it purported to describe. It was only in the ninth century that the passion of Ursula was commemorated in the liturgy and her name and those of her companions entered into the canon of German martyrology.[110] The new cult of the 11,000 was well provided with relics, especially after the discovery of a necropolis under the convent of St Ursula in Cologne in 1106.

The written legend circulated widely, and the journey and death of Ursula and her companions was recorded by English chronicle writers, including Gildas, Fabian, Polydore Vergil and Geoffrey of Monmouth. A full account of Ursula and the 11,000 was reproduced in the *Golden Legend*, which detailed several miracles attributed to the women.[111] Thomas Hardyng's *Chronicle* summarised the legend, describing the martyrdom of the virgins in Cologne at the hands of the Germans, who

> slue them al through cruelte and hate
> Which now be sayntes & merters euery chone

88

In nonnes munster, conserued in Coleyn
That nombred bene, both wyth frend and foone
XI.M. Virgins of Great Britayn.[112]

Jesuit interest in the cult and the shrine encouraged the wider dissemination of the
legend and relics of Ursula and her companions in the second half of the sixteenth
century, and the traditional tale of their chastity and martyrdom was repeated in
Hermann Crombach's *Ursula Vindicata* in 1647. However, the basis of the legend
was far from secure, and contradictions in the various medieval texts were seized
upon by evangelical writers. John Bale challenged both the historicity of the tale
and the assumptions about sanctity which it helped to propagate. 'Of Ursula and
her xi thousand compansions haue the spirituall hypocrites by helpe of their
spiyrituall father the deuyll practised innumerable lyes by them,' Bale alleged, 'to
make their newly sought out virginitie to apere sunwhat gloriouse to the worldly
dodypolles that neuer wyll be wise.'[113] The cult was part of a wider cult of chastity
that Bale was determined to dispel, and unpicking the foundations of the legend of
Ursula and her companions was a useful part of the process. Bale summarised the
basic core of the legend, but argued that the cult had its origins only in the fables
of monastic chroniclers, and in their 'co[n]ueyau[n]ce … in playstering vp their
unsauoury sorceries'. There was no proof, he alleged, that the women had ever
reached Rome. Instead, the women had set sail in order that they might be 'honest
wives' to the British troops in France, but had instead become 'byshoppes
bonilasses or prestes playeferes'. The bones of Ursula and her companions were
buried, not in Cologne, but at the bottom of the sea, Bale argued, making the cult
of their relics 'a uery straunge procuringe of sayntes'. Despite factual inconsistencies in the legend and the lack of verifiable relics, Bale protested, the feast of Ursula
and the 11,000 'is yet no small matter in their Idolatrouse churche'. In Bale's eyes,
the legend provided no justification for the veneration of a multitude of saints, and
offered no support for the exaltation of virginity over marriage in the church.[114]

The cults of several English saints were similarly subject to Bale's scrutiny. The
life of King Edward, Bale alleged, was a 'legende of lyes', but one which was nonetheless 'solemnly to be redde' in English churches.[115] The biographers of St Anselm
had feigned numerous fables, Bale protested, and constructed 'legendes of
abhomynable lyes' around him.[116] The legend and cult of St William of York was a
'very straunge thynge' in Bale's eyes, not least because William had died a martyr
but was venerated as a confessor in the liturgy. Drawing upon Roger Hoveden's
chronicle, Bale claimed that William's 'martyrdom' had occurred at the hands of
one of his own chaplains who had poisoned the saint's chalice, with the result that
William's name could not be officially numbered among the martyrs of the church.
The enthusiastic promotion of the cult, Bale alleged, reflected, not the honourable
death of the saint, but the fact that York lacked a recognised 'shryned patron'
whose cult could be promoted for financial gain.[117] Bale dismissed as 'knavery upon
knavery' the legend of St Drithelm who, after his miraculous restoration to life, had
recounted a vision of the afterlife that encouraged the faithful to view him as a

prophet. Drithelm, Bale claimed, had simply 'feyned himself on a tyme to be dead' and had then exploited his new-found fame in order to deceive the king and encourage practices such as fasting, confession, Masses and the endowment of monasteries that were profoundly antithetical to the religious climate of Edwardian England. Drithelm and his abbot Cuthbert had deluded the 'foles of thys worlde' with 'lyes and illusions', but both had been exalted as saints and commemorated on solemn feast days.[118] Bale's account and condemnation were repeated by John Foxe in the *Actes and Monuments*. 'Lying myracles', Foxe claimed, punctuated the *life* of Drithelm, in the account of his death, resurrection, and particularly in the 'wonders of straunge thinges' that he described to his audience.[119] The legend of Drithelm upheld doctrines and practices that could not be accommodated within Bale's and Foxe's understanding of true religion; Drithelm's miraculous vision confirmed the truth of Catholic teaching on purgatory, and his advice to pilgrims that they should endow monasteries sat uncomfortably alongside the dissolution of the English religious houses in the 1530s.

In his account of the Kentish church, William Lambarde recounted the legend of St William of Rochester, and concluded that his cult had been cultivated by monks for the sole purpose of enriching their coffers. Lambarde directed his readers to the narrative of the *life* of William in the *Nova Legenda Anglie*. William, a Scottish baker, had been robbed by his servant in Rochester while undertaking a pilgrimage to the Holy Land. His body was carried to St Andrews by monks, who declared him a saint and proclaimed miracles worked by his relics. The monkish propaganda had the desired effect, and generous offerings were left at the shrine of the saint 'euen until these latter tymes'. In Lambarde's eyes, the promotion of the cult revealed the ease with which the faithful could be deluded, but also confirmed 'to what hard shift of Saints these good fathers were then driven'.[120] Lambarde's account of the genesis of the cult and legend suggested that sainthood was all too readily bestowed in the service of monastic greed, and that the foundations of a popular cult could easily be established by fiction and fraud. The medieval *lives* of the saints provided Bale, Foce and Lambarde with a readily accessible store of familiar legends which could be transformed into vehicles for the dissemination of the Reformation. The collective construction of medieval hagiography, in which the events and miracles in the *life* of one saint echoed established exempla and shaped future trends, was exploited by evangelical writers in their commentaries on medieval sanctity. By disparaging the *life* and miracles of one saint, it was possible to cast doubt upon the whole structure of sanctity and expose the *lives* and actions of the saints as scant ground for centuries of veneration and supplication. The familiarity of the hagiographical legends upon which they drew enabled evangelical polemicists to utilise a widely understood lexicon of words and images in order to inspire and enact the suppression of the cult of the saints.

In April 1538, William Barlow, Henrician bishop of St Davids, protested to Thomas Cromwell that the patron saint of his diocese was a papal invention. Barlow requested that the seat of the bishop be moved from St Davids with its remote and 'desolate angle', which attracted as its main visitors only crowds of 'vacabounde pilgremes' to the shrine of the saint. St David, he alleged, was an unworthy patron of Wales, a saint 'whose legende ys so uncerten of trueth and certently full of lyes that not only his sayntly holynesse ys to be suspected but rather to be dowted whether any soch person was ever bishop there'. Barlow's investigations of the cults of other Welsh saints reinforced his views of St David: 'semblable case latly tried owte by Dervelgaren, Conoch, and such other Welsch Godes' had revealed these saints and images to be 'entique gargles of ydolatry'. The reform of the Welsh church, he argued, necessitated the complete severance of its link with the papal saint David.[121] Barlow's plea that his cathedral be relocated to more amenable surroundings fell on deaf ears. However, his observation that the purification of the Welsh church would be possible only after the destruction of both the 'entique gargles of ydolatry' and the historical myths and legends that linked it to Rome highlighted a central issue in the relationship between the Reformation and the cult of the saints. The destruction of the images and relics of the saints removed their physical presence from churches. If the iconoclasm of the Reformation was to reach into the minds of the faithful, however, it would be necessary to demonstrate that 'sayntly holynesse' was a deception, and that the histories and hagiographies of the medieval church were legends and lies.

5

'LYING HISTORIES FAYNING FALSE MIRACLES'

Reformation *lives* of St Thomas Becket and St Dunstan

The rejection of medieval chronicles and hagiography as 'lying histories fayning false miracles' did not exclude the saints and their *lives* from the controversies of the Reformation. The process by which the heroes of the national past were recast as traitors, deceivers and conjurors both inspired and reflected the changes that had taken place in attitudes to sanctity, the supernatural and the sacred past. As true and false doctrine clashed in evangelical interpretations of the history of the church, so the defining characteristics of sainthood, including miracles, chastity and the defence of the church were subject to the same iconoclastic impulse that saw images of the saints removed from the churches. The reinterpretation and reconstruction of the *lives* of the saints in Reformation polemic is highly revealing of the changing priorities of evangelical writers and the national church. A detailed study of the Reformation reputation of two English saints exposes several common themes in evangelical writing on medieval saints and their miracles. The representation of St Thomas Becket and St Dunstan in the works of English evangelicals reveals the central role that was played by figures from the ecclesiastical past in the creation of a religious, political and historical identity for the English church in the sixteenth century.

'Savagery also upon the dead': the cult of Thomas Becket in Tudor England

Late in 1538, Pope Paul III pronounced a sentence of excommunication upon the king of England. A bull had been prepared, although not promulgated, three years earlier, but the actions which Henry VIII had taken against the Catholic church in England were now laid before the faithful and condemned. In the years prior to the papal pronouncement, the monasteries had been plundered, the Ten Articles had promulgated heretical doctrine, and the *Bishops Book* had set out the new faith of the national church. The pope condemned what he referred to as the 'cruel slaughter of living priests and prelates', presumably a reference to the execution of John Fisher and the assault on the London Carthusians. But Henry's authority as

Supreme Head of the church was not limited to the church of the present. Paul III complained that Henry had 'not been afraid to exert his savagery also upon the dead, even upon saints whom the universal church has revered for many centuries'.[1] Henry's crime, perhaps even his greatest crime, was his assault upon one of the heroes of the English church and western Christendom, an archbishop whose cult had turned his cathedral at Canterbury into one of the greatest pilgrimage centres of the medieval church.

The pope outlined his case against Henry VIII. The king had summoned St Thomas Becket to trial, he had declared the saint to be a traitor and he had ordered that the bones of Becket be exhumed and burned, and his ashes scattered to the wind. Unfavourable comparisons were drawn between the actions of Henry VIII and those of the unnamed heathen, who had at least shown a modicum of respect for the bodies of the dead. Apart from the wilful disregard that the king had shown for the bones of Becket, the pope also complained that Henry had appropriated the treasures of the shrine at Canterbury, many of which had been bequeathed by his predecessors on the English throne, and had turned the cloisters of the monastery of St Augustine into a deer park.[2] Paul III was not alone in his recognition of the importance of Becket to the debates of the Reformation. Becket may well have been the favourite English son of the medieval popes, but from the earliest days of the Reformation, English evangelicals had been quick to question his sanctity and challenge his reputation. A crescendo of criticism of Becket's *life* and cult echoed in the words of writers from Tyndale to Foxe and beyond, and the eradication of the sight and memory of Becket was a preoccupation of the Henrician church. The smashing of stained glass, the breaking of statues and the blacking out of Becket's name in the service books are familiar features of the Reformation of the 1530s, and the merciless uprooting and destruction of the cult was visible not only to the pope but also to pilgrims and in the parishes.

Becket's reputation as a saint had followed rapidly on the murder of the archbishop in his own cathedral, and miracles were quickly reported in Canterbury and beyond. As early as 1171, the monks of Canterbury had started to record the wonders associated with their saint. Indeed the first reported miracle occurred on the very night of Becket's death, with further cures proclaimed in Gloucestershire and Sussex by the following January, and repeated by the monks as testimony to the holiness and sanctity of their hero.[3] The murder of the archbishop had awoken the attention of Christendom, and from its earliest manifestations the cult of Becket was the cult of a martyr. On 12 March 1173, a papal bull promulgated by Alexander III announced to the church the canonisation of 'that saintly and reverend man, Thomas your archbishop'. Alexander listed his reasons for counting Becket among the legions of the martyrs, including 'the glorious merits by which his life was so highly distinguished [and] the public fame of his miracles', and proclaimed that he should be 'numbered in the roll of saintly martyrs'. The bones of Becket were translated to a position in proximity to the altar in his cathedral, and the faithful were encouraged 'by devout supplication' to obtain the intercession of Becket for the 'salvation of the faithful and the peace of the universal church'.[4] Within half a century

Plate 2 St Thomas Becket, 13th-century wall painting, south side, Hauxton parish church, Cambridgeshire

of Becket's death, over 20 biographies of the archbishop had been written, and the events in the cathedral had become embedded in its fabric and liturgy.[5] The *vitae*, including those written by men close to Becket, made little attempt to present evidence of sanctity in his early life, and only William fitzStephen attempted to furnish a detailed narrative of Becket's youth.[6] The reputation of Becket was constructed around the circumstances of his death, and the cult of the martyr owed more to the models provided by the heroes of the early church than to the example of the 'confessor' saints of the later Middle Ages. The cult of Thomas Becket depended upon the manner of his death, and his status as martyr rested upon the claim that the cause for which he had laid down his life was the cause of God.[7]

However, the cult of Becket was controversial even before his reputation began to trouble to defenders of the Henrician Royal Supremacy in the 1530s. Within 50 years of his death, there was already evidence of some disquiet about Becket's status as a saint. In a debate with Peter the Cantor in 1220, Roger the Norman criticised the assumption that Becket had died a holy death for the church, and proposed instead that he deserved to be damned for his traitorous behaviour towards the divinely appointed king, Henry II. Other thirteenth-century accounts were equally ambivalent, reflecting a violent difference of opinion between those who 'said he was a lost soul as a betrayer of his country, [and] others that he was a martyr as a defender of the church'.[8] The cult of Becket loomed large in Lollard opposition to the cult of the saints in the fourteenth and fifteenth centuries, and those who were summoned before the ecclesiastical courts charged with heresy were frequently critical of Becket and his status as a hero of the church. Lollards denounced the prodigious wealth of the churches that housed the shrines of the great pilgrimage saints, and claimed that Becket had died in defence of ecclesiastical avarice.[9] In 1429, William Emayn of Bristol alleged that Thomas Becket was no more of a saint than William Wycliffe, while one Margery Backster denounced Becket as a liar and a coward whose miracles and prophecies were heresies.[10] As J.F. Davis has shown, such views persisted into the sixteenth century and were to inform the criticisms of the cult that were voiced in the 1530s.[11] In 1531, the bishop of London acted to condemn a book that had impugned the character of Becket, and two years later William Barlow confessed that he was the author of a polemical dialogue against the saint.[12]

However, the reconstruction of the national past during the Henrician Reformation ensured that the cult and reputation of Becket would be reshaped by royal concerns and preoccupations. If the wealth of the shrine was not enough to attract the attention of Henry VIII, the legend of Becket and the basis of his status as a martyr ensured that his position as national saint and hero was unlikely to survive the assertion of the royal supremacy over the church. His death, and therefore his cult, was a clear assertion of the powers of popes and prelates to resist princes, and a declaration that a death in the name of resistance to the king was the death of a martyr. The cult of Becket was a 'cult of the oldest and most traditional kind', informed by a hagiographical and popular tradition that encouraged the veneration of the martyr on the spot hallowed by his death.[13] The definition of sainthood which emerged from the cult of Thomas Becket inspired the assumption that defiance of the will of the king was an ingredient of sanctity, and that defiance to the point of death constituted martyrdom for the sake of the church. The vigorous assertion of the historical rights of the kings of England in relation to the church in the 1530s sat uneasily alongside the presence of a national saint whose reputation was built around his resistance to the will of the crown. As Diarmaid MacCulloch has argued, from the moment that Henry VIII discovered that he was the head of the English church, he detested Becket.[14] Almost everything about the cult and its hero was repugnant to the Reformation of the 1530s: a bishop who disobeyed his king, pilgrims seeking forgiveness at the shrines of the saints, the accumulation of monastic wealth through the promotion of the cult, the veneration of relics of dubious provenance but with a history of miracles of healing and punishment. The suppression of the cult of Becket and the destruction of his shrine in 1538 was therefore a multifaceted piece of iconoclastic propaganda which spoke volumes for the theological direction of the English church. The assault on Becket's reputation said much about the mind of the king, the nature of religious change and the value of 'savagery upon the dead' as a means persuading the living.

Contained within the printed Letters and Papers of Henry VIII is a document dated 24 April 1538, charging Thomas Becket with contumacy, treason and rebellion.[15] According to the text, Becket had been summoned to appear in person before Henry VIII to justify his actions, with the promise that he would be provided with a legal representative at the expense of the crown. Thirty days elapsed, during which time the dead archbishop maintained his silence. According to the written account, the case was heard in the absence of the accused, and the attorney general secured a decision in favour of Henry II. Sentence was pronounced: the offerings that had been made at the shrine of Becket were to be forfeited to the crown, the bones of the saints were to be exhumed and his remains burned, to 'admonish the living of their duty by the punishment of the dead'. One extant document does set out the case against Becket in some detail, with reference to the controversial Constitutions of Clarendon of 1164,[16] but there has long been doubt over the validity of the story of Becket's posthumous trial. The most obvious problem is that of chronology. In the most glaring inaccuracy, the document refers to Henry VIII as king of Ireland, making it impossible that the account was written as early as 1538. The relics, according to the document, were burned in August 1538, but on 1 September, the head of Becket was offered for veneration to Madame de Montreuil, suggesting that the date, if not the fact of their destruction, was untrue.[17] Yet even if the text was an elaborate fake, it told a story which was to spread around Europe like wildfire. By October 1538, news had reached England that the pope had denounced the actions of the king in despoiling the shrine of Becket and scattering his ashes to the wind.[18] The reform of the church in England, it seemed, had become synonymous with the burning of the bones of saints.[19] Early in 1539, Wyatt wrote to Cromwell from Toledo, complaining that the news of Henry's actions against anabaptism was drowned out by the news of the 'burning of the bishop's bones'.[20] Reginald Pole complained to Emperor Charles V of the outrage committed against Becket's tomb, and described his horror that Henry 'should pluck from it the bones of a man who had died so many centuries before him, should cast them into the fire, and when they were reduced to ashes should then scatter them in despite to the wind'.[21] The claim that the bones had been 'scattered to the wind' was to surface again in Catholic commentaries on the actions of Henry VIII from Pole to Stapleton, although for later writers the main source of information on the fate of Becket was probably the papal bull outlining the charges against Henry VIII, rather than first-hand experience.[22]

It was evident from the response to the events of autumn 1538 that there would be a world of difference between the destruction of the remains of Becket and the obliteration of his cult. Becket's fame and reputation were such that, regardless of whether the bones of the bishop were burned or simply removed, the king of England would have to justify his decision to unseat the popular hero of the English church. The legend of Becket was well grounded in the popular imagination, in the commemorations of the church and in secular celebration. As Becket's biographer suggests, 'Chaucer's Canterbury Tales kept the saint's memory green' after the Reformation, and the drama of his death has repeatedly attracted the attention of authors and playwrights. The saint's legend, of course, changed with the times, and each age interpreted the events in accordance with its own preoccupations.[23] However, recasting the reputation of Becket in Reformation England marked a sudden rupture with the tradition of the past. After his protestations against the acts of sacrilege committed by the king, Reginald Pole demanded, '[W]hat then will this godly king say, this avenger of the wrongs of his ancestor? Will he rewrite history?'[24] Pole was right: this was exactly what Henry did. Becket's *life* was rewritten, the events of the twelfth century were re-examined and the dangers that Becket and his memory posed to the security of church and state in the 1530s laid bare.

In the autumn of 1538, Thomas Cranmer invited Cromwell to investigate the claim that the phials of Becket's Canterbury water did not contain the blood of the martyr but, rather, nothing more miraculous than red ochre.[25] The investigation was accompanied by a vigorous assault on the cult and, on 16 November, a proclamation was issued outlining the new interpretation and assessment of the *life* and character of Thomas Becket.[26] The archbishop, it was claimed, had determined 'stubbornly to withstand the wholesome laws established against the enormities of the clergy by the king's highness' most noble progenitor, king Henry II'. The proclamation noted that the death of Becket was 'untruly called martyrdom': untruly because it was clear that Becket had antagonised the knights who had approached him and had used violence against them, and also because 'his canonization was made only by the bishop of Rome, because he had been a champion to sustain his usurped authority'. The cause, not the penalty, made the martyr. Becket's name was to be deleted from the service books, his images were to be removed from churches, and his feast day was to be abrogated 'to the intent that his grace's loving subjects shall no longer be blindly led and abused to commit idolatry'. The proclamation was part of a sustained propaganda campaign against Becket and his memory in late 1538 and early 1539. A comparison between the draft of the

Cromwellian Injunctions of 1538[27] and the version which was promulgated[28] indicates that the Becket question had become increasingly important: the main alterations and additions relate not only to the destruction of the cult of Becket but also to the re-evaluation of his reputation. However, statute and proclamation were not the only weapon in the king's armoury. At the time that the shrine itself was removed, John Bale and his players were in Canterbury performing a drama entitled 'On the Treasons of Becket', while the campaign against Becket was gathering force in London, with the removal of his likeness from churches.[29] If the assault on the shrine was to do any more than scratch the surface of the cult, it would need to be backed up by a polemical reconstruction of the past that would vilify the saint and unravel the threads of his reputation in the popular imagination.

The campaign against Becket in the autumn of 1538 was unique. Other saints had been mocked and derided in print, and the relics of other heroes of medieval English Catholicism, from Richard in Chichester and Swithun in Winchester to Cuthbert in Durham, had been subjected to scrutiny. But the memory of Becket was more powerful and more potent, and thus the effort to shatter his image – in plaster and in memory – was all the more intense. Aside from the general assault on the abuses that were associated with the veneration of the saints, there were other reasons why Becket should be singled out. In general terms, the actions of Becket and the nature of his quarrel with his king were unlikely to endear him to the new Supreme Head of the Church in England. The emphasis on Becket's disloyalty to the crown, and allegations that he died a traitor and not a saint, made up the bulk of the Henrician representations of his life. However, the cult and legend of Becket also threatened to land some better-directed blows against the new national English church and its Supreme Head. The demands of Henry II to which Becket had objected were far too close for comfort to the official pronouncements of the English Reformation in the 1530s. Becket had argued that church lands which were in the possession of the laity should be restored to the church, a recommendation which was unlikely to meet with the approval of a king who had just dispossessed the monasteries. Becket had also opposed key articles in the 1164 Constitutions of Clarendon, articles which had a clear resonance in the England of the 1530s. The Constitutions had allowed recourse from the courts of archbishops to the king alone, effectively denying the right of appeal to the pope. Becket's opposition to this principle was unlikely to endear him to a king whose parliament had, in March 1533, passed the Act in Restraint of Appeals to Rome. As an archbishop who had struggled to uphold independent ecclesiastical jurisdiction, Becket's actions provided an equally unwelcome contrast with the tone of the Submission of the Clergy that had been extracted from Convocation in May 1532.

In the draft of a speech prepared for parliament early in 1532, Archbishop Warham had presented an outline of the liberties of the English church and painted a bleak picture of the decay in religion that would ensue if these privileges were ever undermined. The speech contained references, not only to recent events, but also to the events of the past, and particularly to the *life* and death of Thomas Becket. Warham believed that the powers over the church that had been claimed by Henry II were the same as those for which Henry VIII now laboured, and he reminded Henry of the fate of other English rulers who had sought to appropriate the authority of the church to the crown. The articles contained in the Constitutions of Clarendon had led, not only to Becket's death, Warham warned, but also to the humiliation of the king, who had been compelled to withdraw his demands and perform penance at Becket's tomb.[30] The model of a powerful Henry II, a monarch who had condemned as a traitor any individual who brought papal interdicts into the realm, and a king who had siphoned Peters Pence into royal coffers, would certainly be attractive to Henry VIII. However, it was an image and a precedent which for centuries had been tarnished by the accusation that Henry had been party to the murder of his sainted archbishop of Canterbury. In legend, Becket had played David to Henry's Goliath,[31] and if a Tudor monarch was now to identify himself with the biblical king David, then history would have to be rewritten and another role found for the archbishop.

The evangelical assault on the reputation of Becket had in fact preceded the dismantling of the cult by royal decree. William Tyndale's *Practice of Prelates* used Becket's early military career to condemn the rise of the saint 'from bloodshedding to a bishoprick', and drew parallels between the secular service offered by Becket and that of Tyndale's contemporary, Thomas Wolsey.[32] Much was made of the worldy preoccupations of both men; Tyndale noted that there were more profitable comparisons to be made between the *life* of Becket and Wolsey than between either churchman and Christ. On his appointment as chancellor, Tyndale suggested, Becket had managed to surpass the 'pomp and pride of Thomas cardinal as far as the one's shrine passeth the other's tomb in glory and riches'.[33] Under the heading 'the freshe and lusty beginninges of Thomas Becket', Bale's biography of the saint in the *Actes of the English Votaries* claimed that Becket had committed robbery, rape and theft while serving the army at Toulouse.[34] Bale presented a detailed account of events in the 1160s, engaged with the legal disputes over the status of criminous clerks and contrasted the characters of the sober Henry II and Becket, who was 'more like a mad Bedlem than a sober preacher'.[35] Becket fitted neatly into Bale's schematic history of the church, which marked the gradual rise of Roman power and pretensions in the period after the end of the first millennium. Bale was to identify this as the date at which Antichrist was loosed on earth, and claimed that Becket was intent 'by all trayterouse meanes to brynge the kinge under and to exalte the tyrannouse kyngedome of Antichrist to the very heauens'.[36] Bale cast further doubt upon the legitimacy of Becket's status by suggesting that the archbishop had plotted his own end and deliberately sought the crown of the martyr.[37] He bemoaned the sheer volume of ink that had been spilt in lauding the saint in the multiple *lives* written over the centuries. The promotion of the miracles at Canterbury, and the repetition of the legend of the saint, he claimed, were for one purpose: 'to blemish the king and to depresse ye high power both in him and in all his successors kinges after him'.[38]

The claim that Becket had coveted the title of martyr, and that the cause for which he had died was unworthy of sainthood, was developed at length in Bale's *A*

Brefe Chronycle concerninge the Examynacyon and death of the blessed martyr of Christ syr Johan Oldcastell, printed in 1544. After an examination of the character and suffering of Oldcastle, Bale concluded the tract with a direct comparison between Oldcastle and Thomas Becket, and encouraged his reader to 'conferre the causes of this godlye man[n]ys death with the poyntes that Thomas Becket died for an other Popishe martyrs besides'.[39] Oldcastle had died, he claimed, imprisoned in chains in London at the order of the bishop, while Becket had died in the apparel of a bishop 'by his owne sekynge'. Oldcastle had been persecuted and condemned by the clergy for his demands that there be a Christian reformation of the church, in contrast to Becket the martyr who had sought his own death for the sake of the 'wanton lybertees and superfluouse possessions of the Romyshe church'. At the moment of death, Oldcastle had bequeathed his soul to God in the manner of David, Christ and Stephen before him, whereas Becket had commended his soul to the patrons of his church in Canterbury. Although the Roman church had canonised Becket as a saint, Oldcastle had been canonised by the Gospel.[40] Bale demanded of his reader 'which of these two semeth rather to be the martyr of Christ/and which the Popes martyr?'[41] Like the Old Testament destroyer of idolatry Josiah, Henry VIII had 'perceyued the synnefull shrine of Becket to be unto his people a most pernycyouse euyll/and therefore in the worde of lorde he destroyed it'.

The new version of the English past was not universally accepted, either in England or abroad. If Becket emerged from official histories as a villain of the Catholic past, he remained a hero in the present for those who opposed the Reformation of the 1530s, including one unnamed individual who had sworn in the name of Becket and denounced the activities of the vicegerent.[42] It was clear that the cult of Becket still maintained a hold on the popular imagination. Information reached Cromwell that the 'pardon of St Thomas' continued to be preached, and that it was still believed that Becket had died for his resistance to the will of the king.[43] Thomas Tyrell, parson of Gislingham, was reportedly celebrating the service of Thomas Becket in January 1539, despite the issuing of royal injunctions condemning the saint, and later that year Coverdale informed Cromwell that the image of Becket still remained on view in the parish church in Henley. Reluctant to destroy a statue of the saint, one church had simply attempted to disguise Becket by replacing his episcopal cross with a woolcomb.[44] The official assault on the cult was slow to overcome the authority of ecclesiastical tradition. One Canterbury friar argued that, even if Becket were a devil in hell, he was still a canonised saint of the church and therefore deserved the veneration of the faithful.[45]

A recognition of the relevance of twelfth-century disputes to events in England in the 1530s and beyond was not confined to the official pronouncements of the Reformation. The example of Becket's *life* ensured that his ghost would haunt the dealings between Henry VIII and those who opposed the Reformation that he enacted. The damage done by Becket's prolonged exile in France and his repeated appeals to Rome would be all too fresh in the mind of those who heard Reginald Pole's denunciation of events in England from the relative safety of the continent. A troublesome critic at home was an irritant, but the last years of Becket's *life* set an uncomfortable precedent for a life of exile, political scheming and eventual martyrdom. The fact that Becket had pursued a successful career in the service of the crown might also have given Henry VIII cause for further discomfort. Becket owed his early advancement to the patronage and favour of Henry II; it was Henry who had secured his appointment, first as chancellor and then as archbishop of Canterbury in 1161. The king, it appeared, had initially viewed Becket as a supporter of strong monarchical government until Becket gave a clear indication of his own understanding of the relationship between church and state. Upon appointment as archbishop, Becket resigned from the office of chancellor, a gesture which might have been seen as an indication of his commitment to religious principles, but which was understood, not least by the king, as a hostile declaration of intent. When Thomas More resigned from the Lord Chancellorship in May 1532, and was executed three years later for opposing the claims of the king to supremacy over the church, the parallels would have been all too visible. It should come as no surprise that Thomas More entered the works of Catholic polemicists in the same breath as Thomas Becket.[46] The message would certainly not have been lost on the king. The execution of John Fisher was similarly fraught with historical meaning, and the death of a bishop in defence of his church invited just the kind of comparisons with the events of the twelfth century that the Henrician settlement could have done without.[47] Friar Forest's declaration under examination that 'St Thomas of Canterbury suffered for the rights of the church as many holy fathers have suffered now of late as that holy father the bishop of Rochester' was an audible warning of the power that the past still wielded in the present.[48] Forest was not alone in applying the precedent of Becket and his conflict with Henry II to the events of the 1530s. Henry Totehill was foolhardy enough to claim in 1539 that 'it were pity and naughtily done to put down the pope and St Thomas for the pope was a good man and St Thomas saved many such as this deponent from hanging'.[49] Richard Panemore, cautioned for criticising the sermons of the reformist bishop Latimer, replied that he would be prepared to die for his beliefs, 'and if I did I shall die as St Thomas of Canterbury did, in a rightful quarrel'.[50] Even the persuasive power of drama was limited: Thomas Cranmer took action against a member of the audience who spoke in Becket's favour during the performance of an anti-papal play at Ford.[51]

The controversy over the reputation of Becket continued beyond the destruction of his shrine. In William Thomas' *Il Peregrino Inglese* of 1552, the pilgrim attempted to respond to critics of Henry VIII's treatment of Becket and his relics by arguing that the shrine had been a drain on royal finances, with seldom a king of England crowned without making some donation to the saint. Parallels were drawn between the godly ambitions of Henry II and Henry VIII to reform the English church. Henry II had begun 'by good occasion to perceive the errours of this malignaunt church', he claimed, 'and lyke a good Christian Prince, wold gladly have reformed it first with the correction of the ministers abhominable lyfe, and after with due consequent remedies'.[52] However, the refusal of Becket to compromise over the legal status of the clergy had provoked Henry II to further action, and Becket's apparent criticism of his king had resulted in his death. Thomas was in no doubt that it was the exploitation of the circumstances of Becket's death by his monastic supporters, and not the character of the dead archbishop, that had led to his canonisation.[53] The cult of Becket, he claimed, was founded upon false claims of martyrdom and feigned miracles that had been recorded by the monks to proclaim the sanctity of a dead traitor. Such was the scale of the deception that not only were the 'ignoraunt multitude' convinced by the false wonders but the king himself had been persuaded to perform penance at Becket's tomb. By contrast, Henry VIII had recognised the flaws and fictions in the legend of Becket and the accounts of his miracles. Thomas described how the king, finding 'the maner of this saintes lyfe to agree evil with the proportion of a very sainte' and marvelling at the number of miracles attributed to the healing water and blood, had determined that the lack of any substantial proof of Becket's sainthood showed the miracles to be false.[54]

The legend of Becket continued to be contested in the decades that followed the break with Rome. John Foxe, following Bale, ruthlessly exploited accounts of Becket's quarrel with the king, and medieval criticisms of the saint. Foxe positioned his account of the *life* and legend of Becket in the 1570 edition of the *Actes and Monuments* close to an illustration of Pope Alexander treading upon the head of Emperor Frederick. This theme of antagonism between popes and princes, spiritual and temporal authority, dominated Foxe's treatment of the relationship between king and archbishop in the reign of Henry II. Becket, he claimed, deserved the title of martyr 'no more than any other whom the princes sword doth here temporally punish for their te[m]poral desertes'. To die for the faith would indeed be a glorious death, but the martyrdom of Becket had been a death for 'possessions, liberties, exemptio[n]s, priuileges, dignities, patrimonies & superiorities' and not a death in defence of true faith and doctrine. Becket was 'a new saint made of an old rebel', a traitor canonised for his false miracles, and the centre of a lucrative cult constructed as a 'light sport so impudently to deceaue the simple soules of Christes church with trifling lyes and dreaming fables'.[55] Caesarius' *Dialogues* was cited as evidence that the sanctity of Becket had been called into question as early as the thirteenth century.[56] Of the 270 miracles that were credited to Becket, Foxe concluded that several were manifestly ridiculous, others monstrous, more blasphemous, and some so shameful that the honest writer should not describe them. The healing waters of Canterbury were claimed to cure almost every disease, he protested, enriching the wealth of the monastery but, by dint of their sheer quantity alone, Becket's miracles called their own truth into doubt. The legends of miracles were but 'triflyng lyes' and weak ground on which to build the shrine and reputation of a saint.

Writing in the reign of Elizabeth, a quarter of a century after the destruction of Becket's shrine, Matthew Parker avoided such overt criticism of the saint. In his *De Antiquitate Britannicae Ecclesiae*, Parker endorsed the suppression of the shrine and the cult in the 1530s, but the primary purpose of his work was to establish a historical continuity among the occupants of the see of Canterbury, Becket included, and the tenor of his history of Becket was therefore less stridently polemical than that provided by Foxe. The narrative of the *life* and death of Becket in the

De Antiquitate drew heavily upon the medieval chronicles in its description of the controversy over the treatment of criminous clerks, the intervention of the papacy and the flight of Becket into France. The murder of Becket in his cathedral was passed over briefly, and there was certainly nothing hagiographic in Parker's tone. The volume of pilgrim traffic to the shrine and the numerous miracles attributed to Becket were noted, and Parker praised the liturgy that had been composed by Aquinas in honour of the saint. However, the references to the canonisation of Becket and the historical foundations of the cult were far from positive. Becket, Parker claimed, had been 'canonised by the papal clergy for his famous death for the privileges of his church in Canterbury'. His status had altered dramatically in the reign of Henry VIII, however, when enquiries had been made into the legend, and further details discovered, of the 'troubles and miseries' that Becket had fomented for his king. Becket's fame, Parker claimed, derived from the 'intolerable arrogance' with which he had exalted himself and promoted the authority of the church over that of the king and the common law. Parker took comfort from the fact that the passage of time had brought the truth to light, exposing the fraudulent errors embodied in the cult and leading to the destruction of the shrine.[57]

Other Elizabethan writers were more damning in their judgement, rehearsing the themes that had dominated the construction of Becket's *life* in the 1530s and 1540s. Raphael Holinshed celebrated the obliteration of the shrine, devoting space in his *Chronicles* to the collapse of the cult and the destruction of the bones of the saint. 'What remembrance is there now of Thomas Becket,' he demanded of his readers, 'where be the shrines that were erected in this church and that chappell for perpetuities of his name and fame? Are they not all defaced? Are they not all ruinated? Are they not all conuerted to powder and dust?' The pope might have deemed Becket to be a saint, Holinshed claimed, but English chronicles proved him to be a 'Romish rakehel' with an 'ambitious and traitorous heart'.[58] Among the Elizabethan writers, it was the antiquarian and divine Francis Godwin who provided one of the most detailed accounts of the *life* and fate of Becket. In the *Catalogue of the Bishops of England*, Godwin described Becket's rise to royal favour and his appointment as chancellor. When elevated to the archbishopric, he claimed, Becket 'altered the whole course of his life; became so graue, so austere, and so deuout in all outward shewe', declaring his determination to uphold and defend the rights of the church.[59] The spark to the powder keg had come with the dispute over the legal position of criminal clerks, and Godwin provided his reader with a summary of the king's Constitutions, which he claimed were grounded in historical precedent and informed by the immediate need to restrain clerical misconduct, given the outrages committed daily by churchmen. Becket's attempted reconciliation with Henry II floundered as the archbishop abused his authority to excommunicate, turning on those English bishops who had opposed him. In turn, Henry II had expressed regret that he had appointed Becket to Canterbury, and sought the means with which to make the archbishop an example to all others who might be tempted to disturb the peace of the realm.[60] The primary focus of Godwin's account was the treasonable and unreasonable conduct of the king's servant. Although Godwin outlined the circumstances of the death of Becket, he refrained from comment on the question of martyrdom and paid no attention to the development of the cult and the proliferation of miracles.

The *life* of Becket featured prominently in the polemical controversy between Francis Hastings and Robert Parsons in the 1590s.[61] Echoing the words of Foxe, Hastings argued that Becket was no more than 'a newe saint made of an olde Rebell'. The assumption that a death in defence of the liberties of the church was the death of a martyr was erroneous, Hastings claimed, not least because the liberties for which Becket had died were not spiritual, but 'of Antichristes devising'. The canonisation of a traitorous bishop was, for Hastings, confirmation that 'many are worshipped for saints in heauen, whose soules are burning in Hell'.[62] The miracles associated with Becket, he claimed, were the 'shameless inuentions of the Munkes idle braines', and so numerous that it must be clear to the observer that they were false.[63] Parsons countered by criticising the inaccuracies in Hastings' representation of the *life* of Becket. The accusations of treason against the saint, he claimed, were 'manifest slaunder': Becket was no traitor, and his resistance to the secular magistrate had ample precedent in the *lives* of John the Baptist and St Ambrose. A multitude of miracles witnessed to the sanctity of Becket, and the continued veneration of the saint and pilgrimage to the shrine over the centuries confirmed his status as a 'glorious martir'.[64] Parsons turned to the medieval chronicles to add weight to his arguments, citing Matthew Paris, John of Salisbury and Peter of Blois in defence of Becket's reputation as saint and martyr.[65] Becket's fame also ensured him a prominent place in the defence of medieval Catholic heroes and sainthood outside England. The continental Catholic history writer Caesare Baronius was sufficiently moved by evangelical revisions to the historical reputation of Becket that he produced his own '*life*' of the saint, translated into English in 1639. Becket was worthy of veneration, he claimed, by virtue of his holy life and his willingness to lay down his life for his flock in a time of trial.[66] Condemned as a traitor by the knights, Becket was, Baronius claimed, a 'confessor of Christ now instantly to be crowned with Martyrdome' who had died for the defence of justice and the liberties of the church.[67] The shock of the archbishop's murder had reverberated around Europe, and news of the suppression of the cult and the accompanying efforts to rewrite national history were to find an audience almost as wide. Becket's popularity endured among English recusants in the reign of Elizabeth and beyond, and the determination of Harpsfield, Stapleton, Parsons and Baronius to keep his memory alive ensured that his act of defiance against his monarch remained current among Catholic opponents of the Elizabethan church and settlement. The shrines of other saints could be destroyed as monuments to superstition, but the broken tomb of Becket still stood as a shrine to political activities and historical events which were more dangerous still.

The destruction of the shrine of Becket was in itself a monument to the priorities and pitfalls of the English Reformation. The events of 1538 are a clear demonstration of the Henrician concern to drive out abuses, expose false relics and lead the faithful away from the temptations of superstition. However, while the assault on the cults of other saints was a simple assertion of the right of the monarch to expunge idols from his church, the campaign against Becket suggested rather more. The rewriting of Becket's *life*, not just in popular polemic but in the official documentation of the Reformation, implied that the king could 'unsaint' the saints, reverse the judgements of the popes, and reach back into the past and examine the consciences of its heroes. Reginald Pole had doubted whether the king would find new evidence with which to discredit Becket by searching the intervening 300 years, and predicted that Henry's solution would simply be 'to tell the story otherwise than history has recorded it'.[68] The propaganda of the early English Reformation may well have sought precedents in the events of the past, but the construction of a new history and a new past was rather more important. At the end of the sixteenth century, Robert Parsons defended the cult of Becket by arguing that 'all the Christian world for these foure hundred yeares have holden him for a glorious martir'.[69] However, for evangelical writers, ecclesiastical history was not a unified or continuous whole: the past might provide a precedent but it did not have to be prescriptive. Pilgrims had travelled to Canterbury for centuries, but Becket and his cult were still an affront to the supreme headship, one of the few unchanging features of the English Reformation of the 1530s and 1540s. To defend this supremacy, and to impress its reality upon his people, to admonish the living by the example of the dead, Henry VIII was prepared to do what the pope complained that he had done – to 'exert his savagery also upon the dead, even upon the saints whom the universal church has revered for many centuries'.

Fact and 'abhominable fiction' in Reformation *lives* of St Dunstan

In the fourth chapter of *A Child's History of England*, Charles Dickens takes his reader back to the tenth century, to the reign of King Edgar, the growth of monasticism and the reform of the church. The ambitions of the higher clergy dominated royal policy and for seven years the archbishop of Canterbury had refused to crown the king. Married priests had been expelled from the cathedral churches and their protests quashed by the archbishop of Canterbury, after what appeared to be divine intervention on the side of the St Dunstan and the monastics. For this and other actions, Dickens contended, 'when he died, the monks settled that he was a saint, and called him Saint Dunstan ever afterwards. They might just as well have settled that he was a coach horse, and could just have easily have called him one'.[70]

Dickens was not the first writer to question Dunstan's legend. Saints, after all, were human beings, and their reputation for sanctity depended upon the actions and beliefs of other mortals. As these beliefs changed, so the reputation of the individual saint waxed and waned as the saint as martyr gave way to the saint as monk and the image of the saint as powerful statesman gave way to the image of the saint as obedient subject. Reformation debates over miracle and magic had narrowed the accepted wonder-working capacity of the saint and, as the case of Thomas Becket demonstrated, obedience to Rome had become a vice rather than a virtue. The transformation of Dunstan's fortunes in the sixteenth century reflected changes in models of sanctity, in the role and nature of miracles and in the perception of the correct relationship between church and state. The events of the tenth century had done much to change the shape of the church in England, and were also to feature prominently in the histories of the church which were written during the Reformation. Dunstan's involvement in political affairs had a powerful resonance in the sixteenth century, and his role in the prohibition of clerical marriage was to place him at the heart of the violent Reformation debate on this issue. Models of sanctity formulated in previous centuries had created saints whose actions and beliefs were profoundly antithetical to the expectations of the reformed church. The *life* of a medieval bishop was not necessarily a prototype for godliness in the sixteenth century and, in the case of St Dunstan, the very actions which had made him a tenth-century saint were to identify him in the sixteenth century as the agent of Antichrist. The detail with which Reformation writers recorded Dunstan's actions offers valuable insights into their concerns and objectives.

St Dunstan was born in 909, at Baltonsborough near Glastonbury, into a noble family of royal descent. His birth and learning brought him close to King Athelstan, but the jealousy of his enemies resulted in his expulsion from court in 935. Dunstan took monastic vows and led the life of a hermit in Glastonbury, until King Edmund, attributing to Dunstan his miraculous escape from a hunting accident, appointed him abbot. Again, Dunstan rose to a position of prominence at court, and the death of Edmund left him virtually in control of the kingdom. However, his fortunes changed dramatically with the accession of Edwy in 955, and Dunstan fled the country after quarrelling with the king at his coronation feast. He remained abroad until King Edgar invited him to return to court and appointed him bishop, first of Worcester and then London and, in 960, archbishop of Canterbury. Dunstan and his associates, Aethelwold and Oswald, were the driving force behind the English church reforms of the tenth century, the promotion of monasticism and the subsequent expulsion of married clerks from the cathedrals. In the later years of his life, Dunstan's involvement in politics and government declined, but he continued to play an important role in the affairs of the church until his death on Ascension Day, 988. He was almost immediately recognised as a saint.[71] Six medieval *lives* of Dunstan survive, spanning the centuries from his death to the fifteenth century.[72] The modern editor of the *lives* identifies Dunstan as the 'favourite saint' of the English church for a century and a half, before his fame was eclipsed by that of Thomas Becket.[73] However, little effort was made to promote the cult of Dunstan; the relics of the saint were not accommodated in an imposing shrine and there is nothing to suggest that any attempt was made to record or publicise the miracles which were reported at the tomb.[74] His cult did not extend much beyond Canterbury and the cathedral and monastic churches with which he had links in his lifetime. Political and religious turmoil in the aftermath of the Norman Conquest threatened to undermine the foundations of Dunstan's reputation: the Norman Archbishop Lanfranc questioned the factual foundation of the cults of several Anglo-Saxon saints, and his scepticism was to lead to the removal of Dunstan's name from the Kalendar.[75]

After fading from view in the centuries after his death, the memory of Dunstan was revived in the fifteenth century. As a loyal adviser to successive monarchs, he was held in esteem by Henry VI, and Henry VII was sufficiently interested in Dunstan to erect a statue of the saint in Westminster Abbey, which depicted the famous miracle in which he had held the devil captive in a pair of tongs.[76] This revival of interest in Dunstan may have contributed to the renewal of the rivalry between Glastonbury and Canterbury, with both communities claiming possession of the relics of the saint in the early sixteenth century.[77] Glastonbury legend described the arrival of the relics at the abbey after the bones had apparently been removed from Canterbury for safe keeping under the threat of Danish invasion. William of Malmesbury, albeit under the aegis of the Glastonbury community, provided an account of this translation of the relics and their eventual burial in a secret location in the church at Glastonbury.[78] When the Canterbury coffin was opened in 1508, however, it was found to contain the relics of Dunstan, marked by an identifying plaque. Archbishop Warham called upon the abbot of Glastonbury to appear before him with evidence in support of the abbey's claim, but the abbot, claiming to be too ill to travel, replied that, while it was possible that there were relics at Canterbury, Glastonbury still held the greater part, and protested that, in any case, he could do nothing to prevent their veneration. Warham was unimpressed by such cavillation and demanded that the abbot indicate on whose authority the relics had been removed from Canterbury, warning that the lapse of time alone did not lessen the offence.[79] The final chapter of the saga, if it was ever written, is lost, but the controversy is certainly testimony to growing interest in the saint and his relics on the eve of the Reformation in England.

Dunstan's reputation was to undergo a rapid and dramatic transformation at the hands of English evangelicals. The example of Dunstan certainly had much to offer Reformation controversialists who sought to defend theological and ecclesiological developments in the sixteenth-century English church. The relationship between Dunstan and successive monarchs was to prove pertinent in debates over the balance of power between church and state in the early decades of the century. The role of the saint in the suppression of clerical marriage in the tenth century was to imbue his words and actions with a powerful resonance in the sixteenth century, when the compulsory celibacy of the clergy came under fire from evangelical polemicists. The miracles associated with Dunstan, and particularly those miracles which appeared to validate the imposition of clerical celibacy, were germane in the context of debates over providence, witchcraft and the nature of the supernatural throughout the era of the Reformation. Dunstan's *life* and cult attracted the attention of writers in England and on the continent, and their interpretation of the *life* of this tenth-century saint offers further evidence of the international nature of Protestant history-writing in the sixteenth century. In the early years of the Reformation, references to the saint were highly favourable: Dunstan's defence of the liberties of the English church from the predations of Rome won him a favourable mention in the divorce tracts of Henry VIII. However, after these promising beginnings, Dunstan was to fall foul of the priorities of the later

Reformation in England and was instead portrayed as a magician, the agent of Antichrist and the persecutor of married priests. The rewriting of Dunstan's *life* during the Reformation gives a clear indication of ongoing changes in perceptions of sanctity, attitudes to saints and their miracles and, in more general terms, to the history of church and the polemical value of the past.

The printed edition of the *Censurae Academiarum*, the conclusions of the universities on the validity of the first marriage of Henry VIII, included in its seventh chapter a critique of the role of the bishop in the English church, both in enforcing the laws of marriage and in determining the nature of relations between the church in England and the papacy. It has been argued that this section reflected the central preoccupations of the king in the final months of 1530 and the early months of 1531, and particularly the authority of the bishops to pronounce upon the validity of the Aragonese marriage.[80] In the search for a model to support such claims, the authors of the tract turned to the history of the English church and to the deeds of a tenth-century archbishop. St Dunstan, as his biographers recorded, had excommunicated an earl who had refused to repudiate his wife, despite the fact that that the marriage was within the prohibited degrees of consanguinity. In the text of the *Censurae,* it was noted that Dunstan,

> after that he had excommunicat and cursed the erle Edwyne, bicause he had maried his brothers wyfe, coulde not be moued by no meanes to obei the pope, that desired him charged and commande hym most sharply and streitely to assoyle the sayde Edwyn: vntyl he hadde forsaken his vnlefull wyfe. And more ouer it is written that he was euen wont to haue this saieng on his mouth: God forbid that I shulde, for any mortall man, not regarde the law of my God.[81]

In general terms, Dunstan's refusal to conform to the demands of the pope presented those who promoted the cause of the king against Rome in 1531 with an interesting precedent, but the fact that the case apparently revolved around the validity of the marriage of a man to the wife of his brother made the incident more valuable still. In a matter in which parallels with the crisis of 1530 were unmistakeable, an English saint and bishop had stood in direct and obstinate opposition to the papacy. To hammer the point home, the text of the *Censurae* continued:

> truely if the pope do suffre bi his auctorite and power incest marriages to be made or wyll not breake them, when they be made, which (as Gregory saith) be abhominable to God & to all good men, it shall be the dutie of a louing and a deuout bisshop not only to withstande the pope openly to his face, as Paule dyd resist Peter, bicause the pope verili is to be reprehended & rebuked; but also with all faire meanes & gentylnesse, and lernynge, in tyme and out of tyme, oucht to crye upon hym, to rebuke, reproue, besche, exhorte hym that the persons so couples to gether maye forsake suche maryages.[82]

The same story of Dunstan's dealings with Edwyn was repeated by Edward Foxe. The papacy, he argued, had 'vexed & perturbed this realme of England', but Archbishop Laurence, Bishop Grosseteste and Dunstan 'kepe & defended there own Iurisdiccion & authorite and excluded all such fore[n] power'.[83] The example of Dunstan served to validate the claim that the question of Henry VIII's marriage could be settled in England by English bishops in defiance of the will of the pope; indeed the incident could also suggest that this solution was not only possible but was also incumbent upon any godly bishop. Dunstan's place as defender of English jurisdictional independence from Rome appeared secure, his reputation in the emerging national church averred.

Within two decades, however, the 'Protestant myth of St Dunstan' had been born.[84] The loyal defender of the English church had become the archetypal proud prelate of evangelical polemic, the promoter of idolatry, worker of false miracles and usurper of temporal authority. The example of Dunstan might have been useful in the rejection of the papal power of dispensation, but in defining the relative authority of church and state, still more in marking the boundary of the true church and the false, Dunstan was a highly controversial figure and one whose reputation was to suffer at the hands of evangelical history writers in the middle decades of the sixteenth century. Dunstan had not merely acted against the marriage of Count Edwyn, but had interfered in the personal affairs of two kings and had even refused to crown King Edgar until he had fulfilled the terms of the penance which Dunstan had imposed. Dunstan had come to dominate the king and court, and the extent of his influence attracted the hostile attention of sixteenth-century commentators who were quick to suggest exactly how this position of pre-eminence had been gained.

The seeds of scepticism had already been sown by Polydore Vergil in his account of the *life* of the saint in the *History of England*. Dunstan had played an important role in the tenth-century reform of the church in England, encouraging the promotion of celibate monastics at the expense of the married secular clergy who had been expelled from their cathedrals. At the Council of Winchester held in 975, the married secular clerks complained against the treatment which they had received at the hands of the monastic reformers, Dunstan included, and appealed for restitution to their churches. An argument ensued, but it became apparent that the issue would not be resolved by discussion alone. Dunstan then suggested that those present should pray before a crucifix and entrust the resolution of the issue to divine will. In his *life* of the saint, Osbern described the events which followed. Those present followed the instructions of Dunstan, and were terrified and astonished to hear a voice emanating from the image which instructed them to leave the matter as it stood and reject the complaints of the married clerks.[85] The miracle of the speaking crucifix became part of the traditional legend of the saint and was repeated without question in the sixteenth century by the Catholic historian Nicholas Harpsfield in the *Historia Anglicana Ecclesiastica*.[86] The miracle had appeared to provide a divine mandate for the expulsion of married clerks from English cathedrals, and confirmed that the will of Dunstan was at one with the will of the deity. Not all writers were as willing to accept the miracle as fact, however, and just as the story of the miraculous voice had become commonplace in accounts of the *life* and miracles of St Dunstan, so the issues which it raised were to dominate the analysis of his *life* in the sixteenth century and beyond.

Polydore Vergil was certainly willing to entertain the possibility that miracles and prognostications could be genuine, but his attitude to the miraculous Winchester rood was far less accommodating. After describing the expulsion of the married clerks from Winchester and Worcester, he outlined the events at the council called in 975 'for the reformacion of relligion'. When the judges appeared to be on the verge of resolving the issue in favour of the married clerks, he wrote, a voice was heard to emanate from the crucifix, declaring that 'they are not well in their wittes that beare so muche with priestes'. At this point the course of the narrative departs from the traditional medieval legends. Polydore continued:

> neverthelesse, forasmuche as an ymage of Christe standing before them seemed to haue spoken these woordes; the poore prelates loste their sewte, and all the broyle was appeased. Thus the monckes bie divine helpe, or rather human subtiltie, withheld still thease gotten gooddes, for eeven at those dayes there weare diverse who rather surmised it to bee the oracle of Phebus then Godd, that is to say, rather craftelie cowntrefayted bie men then uttered of the Lorde.[87]

The judgement in favour of the monastics was the altogether predictable result of human forgery and not an example of the involvement of an angered deity in the affairs of the world against the married priests who presumed to serve Him. The miracles of the saints were not to be accepted without further investigation, especially where they appeared to serve the needs of one party or the interests of an individual, whatever their reputation for sanctity.

The account of the 'miracle' at Winchester provided in the *History of England* raised doubts over the miracles and motives of Dunstan, but the story was to receive an added twist at the hands of later writers. The invocation of the divine will to justify the enforcement of celibacy upon the clergy was unlikely to go unchallenged by a generation of evangelical polemicists seeking to prove the validity and antiquity of clerical marriage in the English church.[88] Despite the initial promise of reform after the break with Rome, aspects of English religious life continued to trouble personalities such as William Turner and John Bale, who had hoped for vigorous action to remove Catholic influences from the national church, not only in word but also in deed. The continued prohibition of marriage to the clergy suggested that the English church was as yet unreformed, while the practice of true religion remained obscured by the remnants of the Catholic past. As English evangelicals sought evidence to support their interpretation of history as a narrative of the rise of Antichrist in the church, the prohibition of marriage to the clergy emerged as compelling evidence of the increasing influence of Rome over the national church. The enforcement of compulsory clerical celibacy provided a chronological framework against which to measure the decline of the church into false doctrine and superstition. The history of the church was testimony to a gradual falling away of faith and the assertion of the primacy of the laws of the God over the laws of man. The church had been rent by schism, new doctrines had been formulated and a myriad of ceremonies introduced. Chief among these 'unwritten verities' was the prohibition of marriage to the clergy. In evangelical polemic, both Scripture and the councils of the early church had spoken with one voice on the subject, in a unanimity of belief which was only to be shattered by subsequent innovations. The debate over clerical marriage had become a central theme of Catholic and Protestant polemic in England and on the continent by the middle decades of the sixteenth century, and the decision of a church to allow its clergy to marry was a highly visible sign of its doctrinal allegiances.

Such was the importance of the issue to John Bale that he devoted virtually an entire work, *The Actes of the Englysh Votaries*, to the history of clerical celibacy and the apparent moral consequences of the prohibition of marriage to the clergy. Bale's works, and particularly the *Votaries*, made clerical celibacy and morality a dominant theme in the history of the church, and his interpretation of the ecclesiastical past was to exert a powerful influence over other evangelical history writers, most notably John Foxe. The expulsion of married clerks from the cathedrals was, in Bale's view, 'the very doctrine of deuyls', inspired by Antichrist and motivated by greed and ambition.[89] Dunstan's role in the introduction of clerical celibacy in England was itself enough to tarnish his reputation in the sixteenth century, but the exact circumstances surrounding the decision did still further damage. Ironically it was these same events and miracles that had contributed much to his reputation for sanctity in his lifetime which were reduced to the status of diabolic magic in the hands of the evangelical history writers. With the objective of preventing the triumph of the pro-marriage party, Bale claimed, Dunstan had 'sought out a practyse of the old Idolatrous prestes, which were wont to make their Idolles to speake, by the art of Necromancy, wherein the monkes were in those dayes expert'. At the instigation of Dunstan, those present knelt down before the crucifix. 'In the myddes of their prayer,' Bale wrote,

> the roode spake these wordes, or els a knaue monk behynde hym in a truncke through the wall, as Boniface did after for the papacy of Celestyne. God forbyd (sayth he) ye shuld change this ordre taken. Ye shuld no do wele now to alter it. Take Dunstanes wayes unto ye, for they are the best. At thys worke of the deuill at al they were astoyned, that knewe not therof the crafty conueyance. If this were not cleane legerdemayne tell me.[90]

The fabrications of Dunstan had then been widely accepted as a miracle which confirmed divine approbation for the expulsion of the married priests, leading Bale to lament that, 'if there had bene but one Thomas Cromwell, they had not so clerely escaped with that knauery'. Instead, Bale complained, 'in remembraunce of this knauery (myracle they say) were afterward written upon the wall undre that roodes fete these verses following: Humano more, crux presens edidit ore, Coelitus affata, que perspicis hic subarata, Absit ut hoc fiat & cetera tunc memorata'.[91] In a reversal of the traditional claim of the Catholic church that its teachings were validated by miracles, the prohibition of clerical marriage on the basis of a false miracle and a speaking idol confirmed, rather, that the celibate priesthood was a symptom of the perversion of true religion by the medieval church. The association of clerical celibacy with idolatry and false religion allowed Bale to present the legalisation of clerical marriage as a necessary part of the reform of religion by Edward VI, promoted as the new Josiah, who had reformed the church in his day.[92]

Dunstan's involvement in the case of Edwyn's marriage had contributed to his reputation as the defender of the liberties of the English church and to the favourable representation of his actions in the *Censurae*. However, in other respects, Dunstan's *life* was far from being the ideal mirror for the relationship between spiritual and secular powers in the sixteenth century. The exaltation of the power of the state over that of the church, the authority of the king over the clergy and the vindication of the traditional imperial rights of the English monarch presented an interpretation of the rightful place of the clergy which was far removed from the position which Dunstan had occupied at the court of his king. In defences of the royal supremacy over the church, the example of a bishop who interfered in the personal and political affairs of the monarch served as a warning to those who might doubt the dangers of an over-mighty church. Under the heading 'that Idoll is crowned king of England', Bale described how King Cnut, out of respect for the miraculous power of the rood, had travelled to Winchester and placed his crown at its feet. Such acts of abasement, he protested, made monarchs 'verye Idolles & no kinges'.[93] There could be no clearer manifestation of the subjugation of the king to the church than the surrender of the symbol of his regnal authority to this feigned symbol of the supernatural power of that church.

Relations between Dunstan and the Anglo-Saxon royal house did not always run smooth. Indeed Dunstan had been expelled from court by King Edmund, but was reputedly recalled after the king was persuaded that the intercession of Dunstan had preserved him from near-certain death after a hunting accident.[94] The 'miraculous' preservation of the king, and the equally sudden rehabilitation of Dunstan, smacked to Bale of superstition and witchcraft, and implied a weakness on the part of the monarch which the power-hungry monk had exploited. Bale made his point bluntly:

> by hys sorcery, he [Dunstan] alwayes made the kynges fytt for his ghostly purpose … specyally by kynge Edmonde … whom by his necromancye he broughte to the poynt inuysyblye to haue bene torne in peces.[95]

The near-death of the king, Bale suggested, was the work of Dunstan, and his survival was far from miraculous, despite the fact the 'the Pope's armye … allowe this still for a miracle'.[96] In Bale's history, the boundaries of the miraculous had been redrawn and, from the perspective of the 1550s, no longer encompassed supernatural acts which promoted the authority of the priest over that of the prince.

Dunstan's relations with Edmund's heirs were no less fraught. On the death of Edmund, the throne had passed to his son Edwin, a minor, under the protectorship of his uncle Edred. In the early days of the reign, however, Dunstan had clashed with Edwin, after claiming the right to intervene in the personal affairs of the king. At the feast to celebrate his coronation, the young king had retreated to his chambers, along with Elfgifu, his future wife, and her mother Aethelgifu. Shocked by Edwin's behaviour, Dunstan followed him into the room, forcibly removed him from the company of the women and brought him before Archbishop Odo. John Bale, vigilant as ever for signs of impropriety, seized on this event, noting of Dunstan that 'he vexeth king Edwine, retayning his concubine'.[97] This was hardly the conduct of a saint, but neither was it a model for the authority of bishops under the Henrician royal supremacy. Bale concluded that he could find no precedent for such action, since 'neuer were the co[n]cubines of Dauid & Solomon thus ordered of Samuel and Achimelech, Abiathar & Sadoch, the byshop of yt age'.[98] It was not the place of the bishop to seek to dictate morality to the king, a salutary warning to any of Bale's contemporaries who might have hoped to trouble the conscience of Henry VIII.

If Dunstan's relations with Edmund and Edwin made his position as a model English bishop uncomfortable, from the perspective of Reformation polemicists his activities in the reign of King Edgar were to make it untenable. The coronation of the new king was delayed by Dunstan after Edgar admitted that he had defiled Wilfrith, a nun from the convent of Wilton. Bale noted that Dunstan had refused to take the hand of the king as a protest against his sin and had ordered that Edgar should not wear the crown for seven years. Edgar's admission of guilt presented Dunstan with the opportunity that he had been seeking to promote the monastic life in England, to the detriment of the married cathedral clergy. Under the influence of Dunstan, Bale claimed, Edgar was not be crowned until 'he had fully graunted to the vtter condempnacion of priestes maryage through out al hys realme, and fyrmelye promysed to put the monkes in their rowmes in the great cathedrall churches, wrytyng to the pope for the same'.[99] The authority of the king had been usurped by the bishop, Bale alleged, as Dunstan 'fashyoneth the kynge to his purpose' and 'so mocked hys kynge to make of hym a very dysarde fole'.[100] Dunstan as advocate of independence from Rome appeared now as Dunstan the presumptuous prelate, who had subjected the authority of the king to the laws of the church and exploited his influence over the king to impose his will on both church and kingdom. Given the fate of that other defender of the liberties of the church, Thomas Becket, at the hands of the king and reformist propagandists in the late 1530s, it is hardly surprising that the actions of Dunstan were treated with such asperity in subsequent decades. His harsh reaction to the incestuous marriage of a knight had served the purposes of royal propagandists in the period between 1529 and 1531, but his interference in the marital affairs of princes and in the government of the realm as harder to accommodate within the notion of the royal supremacy over church and state.

In the works of evangelical polemicists, the legend of Dunstan had been reconstructed, and the history of the tenth-century church rewritten, to facilitate the construction of a evangelical narrative of the past in the middle decades of the sixteenth century. A bishop whose fame owed much to the fact that he had prepared the ground for the imposition of clerical celibacy in the English church and made images speak was the antithesis of the ideals of the Edwardian church. The new evangelical image of Dunstan, rebuilt from the fragments of his shattered reputation for sanctity, was to exert a powerful influence over later interpretations of his life and miracles. In particular, Bale's account of Dunstan's *life* was to provide the basis for John Foxe's interpretation of the tenth-century reform movement and his vilification of its heroes. With the accession of Mary, married priests had been expelled from their benefices and the polemical debate had been renewed, securing a prominent place in Foxe's history for the issue of clerical marriage. Foxe shared Bale's assessment of the significance of the tenth century in the chronology of the degeneration of the English church, and was not only highly critical of the church reforms attributed to Dunstan but also highly suspicious of the miracles which had accompanied them. Foxe suggested that the voice heard speaking from the crucifix might well have been that of 'some blynde monke behynde him in a trunke', and, like Bale, lamented that there had been no Thomas Cromwell present at the council to test the veracity of the tale.[101] The absence of any reports of the miracle in several chronicles, Foxe argued, cast further doubt upon the veracity of the tale. In fact, the miracle was recorded in the *Polychronicon* and Foxe was clearly aware of this, having drawn attention to the reporting of the incident in the margin of his own copy. The marginal note, the only one of its kind in Foxe's hand in the manuscript, paraphrases Higden's text and reads simply: '*ymago crucifixi locuta est de pariete*'.[102] Foxe's suspicions had clearly been aroused and he was adamant that the 'speaking' crucifix should not be regarded as a manifestation of the divine will. If it proved anything at all, the voice emanating from the crucifix 'proueth in thys matter nothing els but Dunstane to be a sorcerer'.[103]

It was not only English history writers who were interested in the reconstruction of the *life* of an English bishop. The accounts of events provided by Bale, and later repeated by Foxe, have clear parallels in the works of the German Lutheran Magdeburg Centuriators. The Centuriators appeared no more predisposed than their English counterparts to accept the miracle at Winchester as the work of God or to regard it as a divine sanction for the expulsion of the married canons. The married priests had presented a case against Dunstan which was based upon the word of God in Scripture and the example of the primitive church, but Dunstan had remained unrepentant. The miracle that followed, it was argued, was not therefore an act of God but, rather, accomplished by the agency and particular powers of Dunstan. After outlining the protests against the treatment of the married priests, the Centuriators attributed the 'miracle' to Dunstan's skill in the art of magic and contrasted the purity of the primitive church with the influence of the devil in the decrees of the council. The account in the *Ecclesiastica Historia* made use of the medieval *lives* of Dunstan, the Polychronicon and the work of Polydore Vergil. The Centuriators were to give greater credence than Foxe to the antiquity of the story, but still shared the view of Bale and Foxe that the voice, if it was not that of another monk, was generated by diabolic magic.[104] Despite minor differences of interpretation, both English and continental history writers recognised the polemical capital which Dunstan's *life* afforded. Bale, Foxe and the Magdeburg Centuriators not only shared the same fascination for the history of the medieval church but also shared the resources from which this history could be constructed, lending an international character to Protestant history-writing in the sixteenth century.

The rejection of the miraculous powers of the medieval saints was certainly not a complete denial of the influence of the supernatural in the material world. What mattered was the source of that power, and in this respect the miracles of St Dunstan provide a useful illustration of the willingness of English evangelicals to manipulate the medieval past in order to meet the polemical requirements of the present. The miracles of Dunstan were recast as diabolic wonders, worked in support of false doctrine and commemorated and celebrated by the congregation of Antichrist. The pronouncement of the miraculous rood at the Council of Winchester, whether the voice of God or of a false monk, had not been regarded as the last word on the subject of clerical marriage. The issue was raised again, and hotly debated, at the Council of Calne. Alferus of Mercia, seeking to promote the cause of the married clergy, had sent to Scotland for assistance from a learned bishop who had argued the case of the deprived canons before the council. On this occasion, Dunstan, confined to a stretcher by poor health, grew impatient with the debate and referred the issue to divine judgement. Once again, God was on the side of the monastics: as Dunstan spoke, the joints beneath the floor in the council chamber collapsed, leaving Dunstan still supported, but killing or injuring those who had attempted to defend the married priests. The miracle at Calne was no more acceptable to evangelical writers than the miracle at Winchester. Bale made his opinion clear from the outset, describing the incident under the heading 'Dunstane disputeth with sorcerye and murther'. The saint, he claimed, 'in a great fury' had made the pretence of committing the cause to God, but had instead 'sett the Deuill by his necromancy to worke', causing the floor to collapse.[105] The Magdeburg Centuriators, following Bale, were equally willing to see the devil at work in the miracle. John Foxe presented a variety of explanations for the miracle, suggesting that it might have been either a portent of the ruin of the realm or a fabrication on the part of 'monkish writers', but left the reader to make the ultimate decision as to 'whether it was so wrought by Dunstanes sorcerye (as was not unpossible)'.[106] Bale, Foxe and the Centuriators were all prepared to accept that the events described in the chronicles were real and that they could be ascribed to more than simply human agency. The Roman church and its agents were not impotent; supernatural forces could be summoned and channelled to the service of the church and its saints, and the miracles at Calne and Winchester were prime examples of this

Plate 3 Archbishop Dunstan, Corpus Christi College, Cambridge, MS 161 fol. 1r

potential. The accusations that were levelled against Dunstan in Protestant histories even had some support in the views of his contemporaries. Dunstan had been expelled from the court of Athelstan following accusations that he was guilty of sorcery, and such accusations were grist to the mill of Reformation propaganda. Bale claimed that Dunstan was 'founde very connynge in wanton Musyck, in sorcery and in Image making', and viewed the miracle in which Dunstan's harp played without being touched as evidence that the saint was 'geuen to yll science and wroughte many thynges by the deuyl'.[107] Foxe was more sceptical and suggested that the legend of the miraculous harp had been cast 'out of the same mint' as that from which Dunstan's biographers had forged tales of angelic voices and visions. The miracles that had been cited as proof of the sanctity of Dunstan were, Foxe claimed, 'prodigious fantasies', fabrications and forgeries that had been invented or exaggerated by the chroniclers.[108] However, it was on the veracity of such 'fantasies' that the reputation of an individual would stand or fall. Bale made the same point explicitly towards the end of his account of the *life* of Dunstan: 'if those their sorcerers be sayntes as they say they are', Bale argued, 'then may the Deuyls of hell be sayntes also. Let Dunstanes deuyll stande than checkmate with Dunstane hys master, and be a popish saynt as he is.'[109]

The fluctuating reputation of Dunstan in the sixteenth century reflected the determination of evangelical writers to locate the conflict between miracle and magic, Christ and Antichrist, in Christian history. Evidence of disunity, innovation and sorcery in the history of the medieval church and its saints had been a crucial part of attempts to endow the nascent national church with an historical identity after the break with Rome. However, the study and reinterpretation of the past continued to play an important role in the debates of the sixteenth century, not only in defining the identity of the reformed churches in relation to the church of Rome but also in defending the established English church from the assaults of radical Presbyterianism. It was for this purpose that Matthew Parker as archbishop of Canterbury sought to compile a history of the English church which would offer a historical validation for the Elizabethan settlement and present a cogent defence of the English episcopacy and of the primacy of the see of Canterbury.[110] Parker's history was not without its contradictions. While it was clearly important to uphold the history and the pre-Augustinian origins of the English episcopacy, it was equally vital to distance the national English church from the contaminations of Roman doctrine and practice and to ensure that the spread of Christianity in England was not associated too closely with prelates who, in Protestant myth at least, were the agents of Antichrist. The case of Dunstan would clearly be problematic. Dunstan the necromancer and usurper of temporal authority was certainly not the ideal weapon against Presbyterian critics, but it would hardly serve Parker's purpose to start expunging weak links from his historical chain. Parker thus chose to tread the middle course. He noted that Dunstan had been forced to flee after antagonising King Edwin, and drew attention to the promotion of monasticism in England by Dunstan, Oswald and Aethelwold. Dunstan, he wrote, '*ad Iohannem Papam pro pallio profectus, petiit authoritate papali eiiciendi e coenobiis coniugatos clericos Monachos inducendi sibi concedi potestatem*', a summary which perhaps reflected Parker's personal interest in the question of clerical marriage in the English church. The biography of Dunstan was distinctly less fulsome in praise of its subject than other *lives* in the volume, but more moderate in its approach than the interpretations advanced by Bale and Foxe.[111]

Dunstan's actions in defence of the jurisdiction of the English church and her bishops in the tenth century had brought him to the attention of those who sought the answer to Henry VIII's 'Great Matter' in the precedents provided by English history. By the second half of the sixteenth century, Dunstan had fallen foul of that same preoccupation with the past. The direction of the history of Christianity in England to the service of the nascent national church operated with different criteria and objectives to the defence of the right of the king to settle his marital problems within his realm. Evangelical writers became increasingly preoccupied with the desire to trace the roots of their church to the primitive church of the Apostles and its pre-Augustinian roots in England, and new issues – clerical marriage, idolatry and image-worship, miracle and magic – came to dominate debate. In the process of constructing a new history of the English church, victors traded places with the vanquished, and centuries-old heroes became the villains of the present. Images of saints were destroyed as idols, and images of sanctity were smashed and reassembled to represent the beliefs and practices of subsequent generations. Medieval beliefs in the efficacy of the magic of the church and the miracles of its holy men against the powers of the devil were shattered as the devil was seen to be active in both the church of Rome and its saints, and divinely inspired miracles became false wonders of Antichrist. The implications of such shifts in perception have visible expression in the construction of the 'Protestant myth' of St Dunstan in the sixteenth century. Dunstan had been declared a saint by his followers, but images of sanctity were subject to the pressures of time and circumstance. For many in the sixteenth century, and indeed beyond, the decision of the church to declare a man a saint was not in itself incontrovertible proof of his sanctity; as Dickens had claimed, the monks 'might just as well have settled that he was a coach horse and could just have easily have called him one'.[112] The rewriting of the *lives* of the saints in the sixteenth century is testimony to the extent of the influence of human perception in assessing the character of the individual. The medieval *lives* of Dunstan and Becket were replete with incidents and exempla which reflected contemporary idea of saintliness; the sixteenth-century *lives* of these saints indicates the paradigmatic shift which had occurred in the perception of holiness, not only between the tenth century and the sixteenth, but also between the beginning of the sixteenth century and the end. John Foxe was to cite the miracles attributed to Dunstan by medieval hagiographers as examples of 'the impude[n]t and abominable fictions of this romishe generation'. The creation of a new legend for Dunstan and for Becket in the sixteenth century, however, suggests that the boundary between fact and 'abominable fiction' was not always simple to define.

6

'ANTICHRIST, & NOT THE TRUE SUCCESSOUR OF PETER'

Popes, miracles and necromancy in Reformation polemic

In 1518, John Stilman was condemned by the bishop of London as a relapsed heretic after his repeated denial of the Real Presence of Christ in the eucharist, and criticism of pilgrimage and the veneration of images. In particular, it was alleged, Stilman had

> spoken against our holy father the Pope and his authoritie, damnablie saying that he is Antichrist, & not the true successour of Peter, or Christes vicare in earth: and that his pardones and indulgences whiche he graunteth in the Sacrament of penaunce, are naught, and that you will none of the[m]: And likewise that the colledge of Cardinals bee lymmes of the said Antichrist: and that all other inferiour Prelates and Priestes are the Sinagoge of Sathan.[1]

Within two decades, the authority of the pope in England had been overturned, the name of the pope had been expunged from the service books of the English church and the image of the papal Antichrist had become a staple of evangelical propaganda against the Catholic church and its adherents in England. The official pronouncements and propaganda of the Henrician church in the 1530s were profoundly anti-papal in tone. The Act of Appeals (1533) proclaimed the historical independence of the English church and nation from 'foreign princes and potentates', and the Act Against Papal Authority (1536) ordained that it was no longer heresy to speak against the 'pretended power' of the bishop of Rome. The *Institution of A Christian Man* (1537) undermined papal claims to primacy and asserted that the authority of the bishop of Rome was an invention of man, contrary to the word of Christ and in violation of the decrees of the councils of the primitive church. Claims that the Henrician regime had rejected, not the true church, but an institution whose claim to authority rested upon fictions and fraud were reinforced by the publication of William Marshall's edition of Lorenzo Valla's exposition of the Donation of Constantine (1534), and a translation of Marsiglio of Padua's *Defensor Pacis* (1535). Polemical tracts such as Thomas Swinnerton's *Little*

Treatise Against the Muttering of Some Papists in Corners, and the Treatise vvherin Christe and his techynges, are compared with the pope and his doings, both printed by the king's printer Thomas Berthelet in 1534, spelt out in popular vernacular tones the flawed foundations of papal primacy and the dangers that were posed by allegiance to Rome. A comparison between the teachings of Christ and the actions of the popes in the past offered a historical justification for the actions of the king and parliament in the present.

The formal abrogation of papal authority in England, the persecution of those individuals who remained loyal to Rome and the obliteration of the name of the pope from service books are suggestive of a vigorous effort on the part of the Henrician regime to destroy the political, physical and spiritual presence of the pope in the English church. Yet the figure of the pope was to remain an essential component in the construction of the nascent national church. Conflict between king and pope dominated royal iconography in the reign of Henry VIII and his son Edward VI, and the image of the clash between crown and tiara was instrumental in the definition of new English polity. Traditional Catholic imagery was exploited and inverted in the service of royal propaganda through the manipulation of visual images that were well established in the popular mind.[2] The appeal of the Lutheran *Passionale Christi und Antichristi* or Walter Lynne's *The Begynning and end of all popery* (1548) relied upon the familiarity of the images of the papacy that they presented to the reader, and the effectiveness of anti-papal propaganda lay in the fact that its visual and verbal vocabulary was widely understood.[3] The polemical defence of the English church in the 1530s and 1540s accorded the papacy a prime position in the history of the church and in the determination of truth and falsehood. Evangelical writers described an expansion of theological error throughout the history of the church and attributed this corruption of doctrine by innovation and idolatry to a succession of medieval popes. Justification for the rejection of Catholic doctrine came via the construction of a history of error and innovation in which the medieval papacy was ridiculed and rejected. The invention of a plausible identity for the Henrician church in the past and the present ensured that the name of the pope would have a prominent position in the polemical literature, histories and commentaries of the Reformation. It should not be surprising then that the break with Rome coincided with, and indeed helped to spawn, a renewal of interest in the history of the papacy, the deeds of the popes and the character of the successors of St Peter in the past and the present.

Histories and biographies of the medieval popes featured prominently in the literature of the early Reformation. The reconstruction of the history of the medieval church in the middle decades of the sixteenth century included a radical re-evaluation of the origins and development of papal primacy, in which the popes were recast as the agents of Satan rather than as the vicars of Christ. Antichrist, as exposed by English evangelical writers, was not a single, future figure of evil, but a permanent and spiritual presence in the world, one whose actions could be witnessed in the present and identified in the events of the past. Interpreted in the light of Scripture, ecclesiastical history became a record of the conflict between the true followers of Christ and the historical Antichrist, a spiritual presence identifiable by the application of scriptural texts to the events and personalities of the past. Evangelical histories of the medieval church and papacy located the deeds of the bishops of Rome within the framework provided by biblical prophecies of Antichrist. The identification of the papacy as the seat of Antichrist enabled evangelical polemicists to explain the apparent degeneration of the institutional church from its apostolic origins, and provided the spiritual Antichrist with a physical and tangible location in the persons of those who claimed to act as the successors of St Peter.[4] The polemical justification for the abrogation of papal authority in England was built around the identification and exposition of the threat that the medieval papacy had posed to the integrity and purity of the national church. A narrative of national resistance to the growing influence of Rome provided the English church with a genealogy for the royal supremacy, which could then be exploited to defend doctrinal reform set forth in the name of the king. The papacy emerged from such literature as a potent rival to the temporal power of the English monarchy, responsible for the fall of the Roman Empire, the expansion of Islam and the rebellion of the people against their legitimate ruler.[5] English monarchs, most notably Henry II and John, who had resisted the authority of the church and upheld the rights of the crown, became the heroes of the English past and provided prototypes for the formal declaration of royal supremacy over the church in the 1530s.[6]

However, the actions of Henry and John were not merely a precedent for the Henrician supremacy. In their resistance to the expansion of papal power in the centuries before the Reformation, English kings were argued to have played a crucial role in the ongoing conflict between Christ and Antichrist, and the defence of the true church from the predations of the false. The identification of members of the true church by their participation in disputes of the past had as its necessary concomitant the exposition of the false church and its adherents in this same past. The suffering of Henry II and John at the hands of the church were small episodes in a broader ecclesiastical history that charted the expansion of papal power and pretensions, and identified within that expansion the presence and influence of Antichrist in the church of Rome. This representation of the papacy as the seat of Antichrist emerged as a commonplace in the polemical works of early English evangelicals. In the writings of William Tyndale, the papal Antichrist was a composite image, constructed from evidence that successive popes had promoted falsehood as truth. Such deceptions were evident in the erroneous interpretation of Scripture and in the legitimacy that popes had bestowed upon fraudulent documents, most notably the Donation of Constantine, which had been used to justify the enforcement of papal domination over secular princes. In his *Answer to More*, under the heading 'a sure token the that Pope is Antichrist', Tyndale identified the popes as the false preachers of 2 Thess. 2, and the workers of feigned miracles described in Matthew 24. Where 'M.More feleth that ye Pope is holy church,' Tyndale concluded, 'I feele that he is Antichrist.' It was simply the expansion of the false spiritual and temporal authority of the church that had required that the primacy of the pope be established in law, Tyndale claimed, for 'when the kingdome of Antichrist was so enlarged that it must haue an head they set vp our holy father of Rome'.[7] The exposition of ecclesiastical history presented in Tyndale's *Parable of the Wicked Mammon*, and more rigorously in *The Practice of Prelates*, was rooted in his conviction that the conflict between the medieval church and the empire revealed the extent to which the papacy was responsible for the promotion of treachery and immorality. His characterisation of history as the battleground of truth and falsehood did much to establish the polemical possibilities inherent in the identification of heroes and villains in the events of past and present. History acted as a repository of moral examples which could be tied to the biblical text to offer compelling evidence that the medieval papacy had become the dominion of Antichrist.

Other writers were more direct in their application of biblical prophecies to the history of the medieval papacy. The term 'Antichrist' appears on only two occasions in the Bible, in 1 John 2:22 and in 2 John 7. The most fruitful texts for evangelical writers were therefore those which contained more general references to false preachers, alongside the Old Testament prophecies of Daniel and the Revelation of St John. John Frith's *The Revelation of Antichrist* (1529) exploited the prophecies of Daniel as a tool for the interpretation of the universal past. Essentially a commentary on the eighth chapter of the book of Daniel, the *Revelation of Antichrist* explored the expansion of error and corruption across the centuries from the ancient empire to the eventual embodiment of Antichrist in the Roman papacy. Antichrist was identified as a false prophet who persecuted the faithful and withheld the truth of the Gospel, planting illusions in the consciences of men that drew them away from true religion. The popes, cardinals and bishops, Frith argued, by virtue of their actions, revealed themselves to be 'reprobate/and Antichristes'.[8] The Catholic church was characterised as the fulfilment of biblical warnings against false preachers, who would invent their own doctrines and counterfeit the Gospel in order to lead the faithful into error.[9] The veneration of relics, promoted by popes and clergy through the centuries, provided concrete evidence that the spiritual worship of Christ had been supplanted by the physical worship of Antichrist.[10] Early evidence of the infiltration of the see of Rome by Antichrist had come with papal claims to primacy over the Greek church. However, as Antichrist became more powerful, the popes had begun to intervene more forcefully in temporal affairs, Frith claimed, to the point where they claimed dominion over the empire.[11] False doctrine condemned in scriptural prophecies had eventually prevailed in the kingdom of the papacy, where wealth was prized over poverty, fables were preferred to gospel truth and the proud tiara replaced the humble crown of thorns.[12] George Joye's *The Exposicio[n] of Daniell the Prophete* (1544) echoed Frith's interpretation of the prophecy as a reference to the growing power of the papacy after the collapse of the Roman Empire. The little horn described in Daniel 7, Joye claimed, had its historical embodiment in the bishops of Rome, whose rise to dominance and eventual primacy in the medieval church marked the fulfilment of Daniel's prophecy. Claiming power over princes and empires, the popes had deceived and bewitched the temporal powers, convincing them to unleash persecution upon the faithful members of Christ's church.[13]

English evangelical writers such as Frith and Joye were able to draw upon an image of Antichrist that was already familiar in medieval tracts and sermons. However, as Richard Bauckham has demonstrated, the Antichrist legend had already become a complex motif by the early sixteenth century.[14] The prophecy of Antichrist had continued to have a popular appeal throughout the Middle Ages, and Adso's tenth-century *Life of Antichrist*, which had done much to establish the image of the Antichrist as a single, future figure of evil, was among the works printed by Wynkyn de Worde in the 1520s.[15] English evangelical interpretations of scriptural prophecy and history also had much in common with the native Wycliffite tradition of anti-papalism, in their representation of the miracle of the Mass as the abomination foretold in Daniel and in the use of Revelation in the identification of the Roman Antichrist.[16] The articles laid against heretics arrested in the Lincoln diocese in the 1520s suggest that Lollard interpretations of Revelation still enjoyed common currency among critics of the church on the eve of the Reformation. The evangelical image of Antichrist as a spiritual opposition to Christ throughout the ages of history, informed by the literal interpretation of history as the fulfilment of prophecy, also had a precedent in the late twelfth-century writings of Joachim of Fiore. Joachim's *Expositio in Apocalypsim* was widely read in the sixteenth century, and its influence is evident in the writings of Sebastien Meyer, Martin Luther, Francis Lambert and, in England, John Bale. However, as Bauckham has noted, this medieval heritage was to be 'Protestantised' by Reformation commentators, whose application of the prophetic texts to the English and universal past required a radical renegotiation in the understanding of the nature and presence of Antichrist in the church.[17]

Evangelical writers presented a historical narrative in which the gradual extension of the influence of Antichrist in the papacy was reflected in the degeneration of the church from its apostolic purity and in the expansion of the political and material interests of the popes. The repeated identification of the pope and the Roman clergy as the congregation of Satan helped to build the association between Catholicism and false religion in the popular imagination, and the description of the Catholic church as the 'synagogue of Satan' or the spouse of the devil was rapidly established in the vocabulary of evangelical polemic.[18] English writing on Antichrist was influenced not only by native traditions, but also by continental, particularly Swiss, commentaries on biblical prophecy. Heinrich Bullinger's exposition of 2 Thess. was translated into English in 1538, and his 1554 sermons on the Apocalypse were popular among English evangelicals in exile in the reign of Mary.[19] The Latin text of the sermons was printed at Basle in 1557 and the first English translation appeared in 1561 as *A Hundred Sermons vpo[n] the Apocalips of Iesu Christi*, with a second edition in 1573.[20] Rudolph Gualther's sermons on Antichrist were translated by John Old and printed in English in 1556 as *Antichrist. That is to saye a true reporte that Antichriste is come*. The first homily, a commentary on Matthew 24, identified the 'teachers of popery' as the false prophets and miracle-workers condemned in the Gospel. The second homily charted the rise of Antichrist in the medieval papacy and listed those popes in whose pontificate the church had fallen prey to the influence of Satan, most notably Gregory the Great, Boniface III and Benedict II. The third homily set out the marks of Antichrist which were evident in the *lives* of the popes, and the fourth defined the works and weapons of Antichrist, including false wonders, feigned holiness and hypocrisy, and a faith that was founded upon human tradition. Drawing upon the description of the adversary in 2 Thess. 2, Gualther argued that by their living and doctrine 'it shall also manifestly appear that the B. of Rome is necessarily that very right and great Antichrist'.[21] Gualther's fifth sermon held out the promise of the eventual destruction of the papal Antichrist, in fulfilment of the promises contained in Scripture. The sermons clearly exerted a powerful influence over Old's own commentary on Antichrist, addressed to the nobility of England in the reign of Mary.[22] The publication of English and continental commentaries on Antichrist in the middle decades of the sixteenth century did much to establish the image of the papacy as the tool of Satan and provide the spiritual Antichrist of evangelical literature with a historical location and reality.

The application of imagery from biblical prophecies to the events of the past enabled evangelical writers to locate the growth of moral corruption and doctrinal error in the institutional church at precise moments in Christian history. The image of the Roman Antichrist as the fulfilment of biblical prophecy encouraged a greater interest in the medieval narratives of papal history. As a result, the *lives* of the popes were re-examined and reinterpreted in the search for identifiable marks of Antichrist that would lend support to the claim that the medieval church had become the synagogue of Satan. Evidence of innovation in matters of doctrine and practice provided a framework for the analysis of the gradual corruption of the church by error and falsehood. The anonymous author of the *Sum of the Actes and decrees made by dyuers Byshopes of Rome* (1539) complained that the popes had invented for themselves new laws which would defend and advance their usurped authority, and had enacted decrees that marked them out as 'mysty aungelles of Satan' who had constructed their power upon the ordinances of man rather than God. The liturgy of the Mass was represented as an accumulation of inventions and innovations over several centuries, to which each pope had made his own contribution.[23] On a larger scale, Robert Barnes' *Vitae Romanorum Pontificum* (1535) listed the innovations that could be ascribed to individual popes, in order to undermine Catholic claims to antiquity and authenticity in doctrine and expose what Barnes viewed as the human foundations of the primacy of Rome. Examples in the text were layered one upon another and accompanied by polemical annotations in the margins which hammered home the message that successive popes had deviated from the truth of Scripture and from the practices of the primitive church. The chronological arrangement of the material allowed Barnes to argue for the expanding and cumulative influence of Antichrist in the church, reflected in the affinity between the deeds of the popes and the biblical warnings of false prophets and preachers. Barnes' identification of the papal Antichrist was not accomplished by the application of specific prophetic texts to the history of the church but by a methodical and detailed examination of the *lives* of the individual popes which made up the composite image of the corrupted papacy.

Among the evangelical writers of the middle decades of the sixteenth century, it was John Bale who made the most wide-ranging efforts to locate individual popes and key events within the historical framework provided by biblical prophecies. The identification of the papal Antichrist was a common theme in most of Bale's works but dominated the narrative of the *Actes of the Englysh Votaries* and *The Image of Both Churches*. Like Tyndale, Bale saw the widening jurisdiction claimed by the medieval papacy as a reflection of growing corruption within the church and symptomatic of the gradual occupation of the papacy by the agents of Antichrist. Bale's *Opening and Disclosing of the Manne of Sinne* (1543) had vigorously denounced the accumulation of temporal power and false doctrine in the Catholic church, and alleged that the growth of theological and moral corruption could be identified as early as the seventh century.[24] The *Mystery of Iniquity* (1545) presented a history of the rise of Antichrist within the institutional church, and alleged that it was the popes who had been responsible for the release of Satan after 1,000 years of captivity. The wealth of the popes and their thirst for spiritual and temporal power, Bale argued, had culminated in the eventual occupation of the papal throne by Antichrist and his agents.[25] Since the Ascension, the church had been subject to the working of this 'mystery of inquity' but it was in the most recent 500 years that the power of Antichrist had come to fulfilment. Bale offered a 'genealogy' of false religion, tracing the descent of the Catholic clergy from Cain, through the priests of Baal and Bell and the New Testament figures of Judas and Simon Magus, to the 'false/filthy/fleshlye … and abhominable generacion' of the present.[26] The power of the popes and the clergy, Bale argued, had been constructed upon the false foundations of superstition, 'blessynges/bones/belles/candelstyckes/cuppes/curettes/oyle/waxe/light/ashes/palmes/and holyewater', with the result that the Catholic church had become the 'synagogue of Sathan' and the 'spowse of the deuyll'.[27] Chief among the agents of Antichrist within the church were the popes themselves, more particularly in the aftermath of the confirmation of Roman supremacy by the emperor Phocas, after which date, Bale claimed, the popes, clergy and 'hypocrytyshe monkes' had worked false miracles to expand the influence of the clergy.[28]

The key part played by the popes in the expansion of the influence of Antichrist in the church was laid bare in Bale's *Acta Romanorum Pontificum* (1558). In his history of the occupants of the throne of St Peter, Bale established the loosing of Satan after 1,000 years of captivity as a significant date in the history of the church, and emphasised the key role played by the popes in permitting the rise of Antichrist in the church after this date. Papal history in the *Acta Romanorum Pontificum* was divided into three sections. The first ran from the time of the Apostles to the pontificate of Silvester I (324) and was accepted as a period in which the doctrine of the church had remained pure. The second period ran from the pontificate of

Silvester to Boniface III (606), by which point the temporal ambitions of the popes had been revealed and the purity of the church tarnished by popes who 'made a plaine way to Antichriste'.[29] The final period ran from Boniface III to the pontificate of Julius II and encompassed the *lives* of those popes who were 'Antichristes not departinge from the steps of their fathers in all kinde of pryde, tyrannye, lying and filthines'.[30] The history of the papacy in this final period was divided into four sections, each of which corresponded to one part of the prophecies of Revelation. The first, the kingdom of the Beast, covered the history of the papacy between Boniface III and John VIII. The second, the rule of the Harlot, extended until the pontificate of Silvester II and the loosing of Satan from the pit. The third, the age of Dragon, ended with the pontificate of Innocent IV, and the final age, the age of the Locusts, brought the history and commentary into the sixteenth century. The biographies of the popes drew heavily upon medieval commentaries, most obviously Platina's *Vitae Pontificum*, but Bale was prepared to reject those sources which could not be accommodated in his interpretation of the past or which seemingly confirmed the antiquity of doctrines that Bale regarded as papal innovations.[31] The *Acta Romanorum Pontificum*, while sharing some common ground with Robert Barnes' *Vitae Pontificum*, went much further in its attempt to isolate individual popes whose pontificates marked a crucial era in the history of the church, and in its application of biblical prophecy to the events of the past. The underlying principle of Bale's work, that Scripture provided the key to the interpretation of the chronicles, encouraged and facilitated the identification of the spiritual and universal Antichrist in specific historical events and personalities.

Yet a course at the Romyshe Foxe (1543) had provided a general exposition of the rise of Antichrist in the historical church, in which Bale located the binding of Satan at the time of Christ and provided the loosing of Satan with a historical location at the end of the first Christian millennium. The significance of this date in Bale's mind influenced his interpretation of the history of the English church and the narrative of the ecclesiastical past that was presented in the *Romyshe Foxe* and in the *Actes of the Englysh Votaries*. However, it was Bale's *The Image of Both Churches* that was to offer the clearest demonstration of the polemical value that could be gained from the use of biblical prophecy as a means of identifying the specific agents of Antichrist within a general papal history. In Bale's commentary on the book of Revelation, the prophetic text was applied to the full span of Christian history. The first part of *The Image* established a sevenfold division of the past, constructed around the opening of the seven seals described in the book of Revelation. The opening of the third seal was accompanied by the first stirrings of false doctrine and corruption in the church in the seventh century, which had witnessed the expansion of papal power, the rise of Islam and the growth of the Islamic Empire. The fourth seal had ushered in an age of hypocrisy during which the doctrine of the church had deviated from Scripture, in the enforcement of compulsory clerical celibacy, the articulation of the doctrine of transubstantiation and the expansion of the temporal power of the popes, who trampled under foot the authority of princes and persecuted the faithful. The opening of the sixth seal had seen this papal power challenged, in the first instance by Jan Hus and John Wycliffe and later by Bale's evangelical contemporaries, prior to the expected overthrow of Babylon and the binding of Satan at the dawn of the seventh age.

The re-evaluation of the relationship between history and the Scripture encouraged the identification of the influence of Antichrist, not only in the history of the papacy in general, but also in the actions of specific popes whose pontificates acted as beacons in the understanding and rewriting of the ecclesiastical past. This image of the papal Antichrist was constructed by the application of the characteristics of Antichrist set out in biblical prophecies to the history of the church and the papacy. It was these marks, including temporal power, false preaching, feigned wonders and idolatry, which were to become central to the identification of successive bishops of Rome as the agents of the spiritual Antichrist. Evangelical commentaries on Antichrist wove these common threads into their representations of the medieval papacy. Antichrist, Tyndale claimed, would feign holiness in order to deceive the people.[32] Heinrich Bullinger exploited Gregory the Great's declaration, 'I affirm boldly that whosoever he be that calleth himself the universal priest is a forerunner of the Anti-christ', to condemn papal pretensions to supreme spiritual and temporal power as an indication of the presence of Antichrist in Rome.[33] Anthony Gilby argued that doctrinal innovation and the perversion of Scripture were characteristics of the false congregation that marked out the Catholic church as the church of Antichrist.[34] John Ponet, at the close of a discussion of the issue of clerical celibacy, used the same issue of innovation in doctrine and practice to distinguish the false church from the true: 'the Apostles taught one thyng: the byshop of Rome brought in another. Nowe iudge you whether it is beste for vs which professe Christ to follow the Apostles of Christ, or the Romish Antichrist.'[35]

John Foxe's description of the papal Antichrist exploited the work of his contemporaries, Bale and Flacius, alongside a selection of earlier chronicles and treatises that were interpreted to provide evidence of the usurpation of temporal power and corruption of doctrine by the medieval papacy.[36] The representations of the medieval papacy in the dramatic comedy *Christus Triumphans*, and more particularly in the tract *Ad Inclytos ac Proponentes Angliae Proceres Supplicatio*, were to provide the foundation for Foxe's history of the popes in the *Rerum in Ecclesia Gestarum* (1559).[37] His *Solemne Contestation of Divers Popes*, published in 1560, described the historical expansion of papal power and claims to authority over princes, the power to determine rightful rulers, the capacity to determine doctrine, the imposition of interdicts and the prohibition of marriage to the clergy.[38] The text of the *Solemne Contestation* was reprinted in the 1570 edition of the *Actes and Monumentes* as a postscript to Foxe's description of the 'Proud Primacie of the Popes'. Among the 'Romish counterfeyt trash' that marked out the papal church as the false church, John Foxe included 'Masses, Sacrifices, … monkish vowes, Purgatory, merites etc. … '.[39] The enforcement of compulsory clerical celibacy was repeatedly cited by evangelical polemicists as a mark of the presence of Antichrist in the Catholic church. Marriage, it was argued, had been praised in Scripture, and the prohibition of marriage to the clergy was evidence that the Catholic church had departed from the truth of the Gospel. The conduct of the clergy who failed to keep to their promises of celibacy revealed the Antichristian origins of the papal decrees that prohibited marriage. Indeed the *lives* of the popes suggested that the obligation to celibacy and chastity was not observed even by the bishops of the church and lent further weight to the comparison between the counterfeit chastity of the clergy and the hypocrisy and deceitfulness associated with Antichrist in Scripture.[40] The papal Antichrist, he claimed, 'to colour his crafty iugling ... annexed to the premises a sweete and amiable countenance of hypocritical holinesse, a counterfeit sinceritie of unspotted life, yea outward resemblance of true religion, thereby to dazel more easily the eyes and heartes of the unlettered'.[41]

Foxe was not the only evangelical writer to make reference to the 'crafty iugling' of the popes. William Tyndale complained that numerous popes had offered dispensations and licences to the clergy to 'vse Nichromancy, to hold whores, to diuorce themselues, to break the fayth'.[42] In the second part of *The Image of Both Churches*, John Bale had characterised both Mohammed and the papacy as 'false Christs' who 'both have wrought suche wonders and such signes in superstition, as myght deduce into errour (yf God were not mercifull) the very elect persons'.[13] The locusts of Rev. 9 were identified as the Roman clergy, the 'coniurers of Egypt', whose 'supersticyons and sorceryes' would eventually be overturned by the preaching of the Gospel.[44] In fulfilment of the prophecy of Rev. 13, Bale argued, the 'monstrouse kyngdome of antychriste' had become established in the papacy where 'vayneglorie and couetousenesse, sorcerye, supersticion and unfaythfulnesse' reigned unchallenged.[45] However, amid the general accusations that the popes had laboured to deceive the faithful, it is possible to identify a number of more specific and focused allegations that individual popes had engaged, not just in deception, but in diabolic conjuring to advance their position and increase the power of the church. A narrative of papal necromancy emerged in evangelical polemic in the middle decades of the sixteenth century, grounded upon the re-reading of medieval chronicles and papal histories, and their re-interpretation in the light of Scripture and the requirements of evangelical history writing. The canon of papal necromancers that had become established by the end of the sixteenth century took shape in the writings of John Bale but was expanded and augmented by later writers, whose works lent an air of historical legitimacy to the interpretations advanced by their predecessors. Two medieval popes dominate in the evangelical histories of papal magic and necromancy, and the reconstruction of their pontificates in the literature of the Reformation is a prime example of the utilisation and exploitation of the records of the medieval past by evangelical writers in the sixteenth century. Both were controversial figures in their own time, popes whose activities left their mark upon the medieval church and who had done much to advance the prestige of the papacy. Both were well respected by many of their contemporaries but criticised and condemned by others for their character and their conduct. The significance of these two individuals in the history of the papacy was established well before the attack on their reputation in the sixteenth century, and their pontificates were sufficiently well documented that evangelical polemicists were able to amass a substantial quantity of information in the reconstruction of their *lives*.

The short pontificate of Gerbert, Pope Silvester II, spanned the years between 999 and 1003, but these four years were to provide a common thread in sixteenth-century evangelical narratives of papal history. Silvester had been a proponent of ecclesiastical reform, a distinguished scholar and an accomplished technician, credited with the creation of the pendulum clock, the steam-powered organ and a complex globe which depicted the celestial and terrestrial spheres.[46] However, this image of the dynamic, educated and reforming pope is in stark contrast to the representation of the *life* of Silvester in the literature of the Reformation. At the hands of evangelical history writers, Silvester became the first of a generation of papal necromancers, a wily manipulator who betrayed his patrons and protectors, an ambitious bishop who made a pact with the devil in order to gain promotion to the papacy, and a pope whose death and burial provided striking testimony to his evil life. The radical recasting of the *life* of Silvester in evangelical histories was facilitated by three factors that conspired against the reputation of the pope. The first, and most obvious, is the date of his pontificate. The interpretation of the ecclesiastical past through the lenses of biblical prophecies emphasised the significance of events around the end of the first millennium to the history of the church. In part this was a self-fulfilling prophecy: closer inspection of events around the year 1000 revealed a convenient coalescence of date and event which exposed to evangelical writers a series of papally led reforms which ran contrary to the priorities of the reformed church. The second factor behind Silvester's negative reputation in the sixteenth century was the reforms that he proposed and implemented, most notably in the expansion of the political influence of the papacy and the promotion of clerical celibacy in the attempt to improve the moral standards of the clergy. The third factor underpinning the Reformation recasting of the reputation of Silvester was the fact that the image of the demon-pope did not have to be invented but could be built upon a tradition which had its roots in the medieval chronicles.[47] Bale and others were quick to realise the polemical value of Catholic histories that seemed to suggest that a tenth-century pope had made a pact with the devil, histories that lent weight to the historical identification of Silvester as the papal Antichrist in Reformation polemic.

The reputation of Silvester II as a magician and a necromancer was established in the early evangelical literature of the English Reformation. The author of the *Mustre of Scismatyke Bishops of Rome* claimed that, after 1,000 years of bondage, the devil had been loosed from the pit 'by the suffraunce of God'. Silvester, it was alleged, had then entered into a pact with the devil, but the pope was ultimately 'disceyued by ye same answere of dyuels wherewith he disceyued many other by the great iustyce of God'. Swinnerton recorded the promise made by the devil that Silvester would not die unless he visited Jerusalem. However, the pope had then made a fatal error in celebrating the Mass in the Temple of Jerusalem in Rome, before realising his folly and repenting of his sins. Swinnerton described a dramatic

scene in the church in which Silvester had instructed those around him to ampu-
tate his hands and remove his tongue from his head, 'wherwith he dyd sacrifice to
ye devil & dishonoured God omnipotent'.[48] The basic narrative in the *Mustre of
Scismatyke Bishops* was repeated in more detail by Robert Barnes in his history of the
deeds of the popes. Silvester, Barnes claimed, had been rescued by Satan from his
enemies in Spain, who had carried him across the sea and secured his appointment
as archbishop of Ravenna. The pope had long been recognised for his learning in
the magical arts and, Barnes suggested, had reputedly dedicated his soul to Satan to
secure his appointment to Rome. Once safely ensconced in Rome, Barnes alleged,
Silvester had secured from the devil the promise that he would not die until he had
visited Jerusalem, a promise that ultimately led to his downfall.[49]

John Bale's account of Silvester went further, alleging that it was none other
than Pope Silvester who had loosed the devil from the pit after the 1,000 years of
bondage indicated in the Revelation.[50] The period of the binding of Satan had
lasted from the Ascension until the pontificate of Silvester, who 'ded fatche the
deuyll from hell by his nicromancy', an art that Bale claimed that he had learned 'of
a saracene' during his sojourn in Spain.[51] Silvester's motivation was a simple lust for
power and a desire to become 'not only Christes vicar in earthe but also to be equall
with him in mayeste and poure'.[52] After releasing the devil from the pit, Bale
alleged, the pope had promoted 'olde wyues fables' above the word of God in Scripture, deluding and deceiving the faithful and facilitating the proliferation of ecclesiastical laws and superstition and the expansion of papal power. The necromancy
of Silvester, Bale claimed, had placed the power of the two swords in the hands
of the devil and enabled him to 'worke in the worlde all myschefe'.[53] Silvester's
reward for his help in providing the devil with power over the church was the
promise that he would continue as pope until he said the Mass in Jerusalem. But
the pope's interpretation of the promise was rather more literal than the devil's,
and Bale repeated the legend of the death of Silvester after he had celebrated the
Mass in the Temple of Jerusalem in Rome. In Bale's account, Silvester repented of
his sins and, in a variation on the narrative in the *Mustre of the Scismatic Bishops of
Rome*, ordered that his remains be divided and scattered around the city by horses.
In a final twist to the tale, the horses remained where they stood and the body of
the pope was buried in the Lateran where, according to Barnes and Bale, the bones
were said to rattle in anticipation of the death of subsequent popes.[54]

The repetition of the Silvester legend in polemical writings throughout the
1540s and 1550s helped to establish the image of the papal necromancer in Reformation histories of the papacy. Rudolph Gualther named Silvester among the
bishops of Rome who had become the servants of Satan, and alleged that the pope
was 'a practicer of naughtie artes'. Silvester, he claimed, was guilty of the very crime
of simony that he attempted to prosecute among the clergy, having purchased his
appointment as archbishop of Ravenna. Describing the death of the pope in the
Jerusalem chapel, Gualther commented that even 'the masse could not defe[n]de
the pope him selfe from the Deuil'. The activities of Silvester were sufficiently well
known, Gualther believed, that 'the com[m]on people doo knowe evidently that

the most conyngest doctours and maistres of magical artes and other sciences forbidden by Goddes lawes were always either sacrificeing priestes or elles monkishe or frierishe cloisterours marked with the beastes marke'.[55] The account of Silvester's pontificate in the Lutheran *Magdeburg Centuries* echoed the legend of Pope Silvester that had been outlined by Swinnerton and Bale, and included the allegation that Silvester had obtained a promise from the devil that he would survive as pope until he said the Mass in Jerusalem. The Centuriators also printed the story of the portentous rattling of the pope's bones, although this did not appear in Matthias Flacius' own *Catalogus Testium Veritatis*.[56] John Foxe also identified Silvester II as a sorcerer who had kept familiars and made a pact with the devil to obtain and retain the papacy. Silvester, he claimed, had been elevated to the papacy 'through wicked and unlawful means' and 'gaue himselfe wholly to the devil' in order to fulfil his ambitions'.[57] The legend was also repeated by John Napier in his commentary on the Revelation and at the start of the seventeenth century in Cipriano de Valera's treatise on the *lives* of the popes.[58]

The similarity between the various Reformation accounts of the pontificate of Silvester II reflects both the sharing of material and manuscripts among evangelical history writers and the degree to which a consistent legend of the demon-pope Silvester had already been established in medieval chronicles and commentaries. In their biographies of Silvester II, Bale, Gualther and Foxe all cited Bartolomeo Platina's account of his pontificate in the *Lives of the Popes*. Platina described how Silvester had 'got the popedom (as they say) by ill arts', a turn of phrase which served to support evangelical claims that Gerbert's elevation to the papacy could be ascribed to his skill in necromancy. Platina had outlined Gerbert's education in Fleury and his subsequent journey to Spain to study human sciences and, it was alleged, to follow the devil. Gerbert had secured his appointment to the archbishopric of Rheims through simony before his promotion to Ravenna, after which 'at last the devil helping him with an extraordinary lift he got the popedom, upon this condition that after his death he should be wholly the devil's'. The devil assured Silvester that he would survive as long as he did not visit Jerusalem, and Platina recorded the unfortunate events that followed Silvester's celebration of the Mass in the Temple of the Holy Cross of Jerusalem. Fearing death, the pope had repented, called upon those gathered around him to resist the temptations of the devil and ordered that his body be placed in a cart and carried by horses to its final resting place. 'By divine will and providence,' Platina claimed, the horses remained still, and the body of the pope was buried in the Lateran. Platina then repeated the legend that the bones of the pope would rattle in their tomb to foretell the death of other popes, and observed that from such events 'people are wont to gather presages'.[59] The congruence in Platina's account of Silvester and those of Bale, Foxe and others suggest that Platina provided his evangelical successors with an ideal vantage point for their interpretations of papal history.

However, it is clear that Platina was not the inventor of the legend of Silvester; indeed his scepticism over the rattling bones suggests that he was repeating a myth that was already well established. Much of the material contained in the *Lives of the Popes* had already been presented in William of Malmesbury's *Gesta Regum Anglorum*, a source which John Bale had certainly used in his *Actes of the English Votaries* and which provided a readily accessible store of information on the church in England and abroad. William presented a brief narrative of the *life* and career of Silvester, around which he inserted a mass of information about the inventions, discoveries and scientific learning of the pope. Gerbert, he suggested, had learned 'astrology and other sciences of that description from the Saracens' and was educated in astronomy, music, mathematics and, significantly for future biographers, 'the art of calling up spirits from hell'.[60] In return for safe transport from his hostile hosts, Gerbert placed himself under the dominion of the devil, William claimed, in an account of the *life* of the pope that provided much of the staple of evangelical narratives of his life. The narrative made no direct comment upon the means by which Gerbert secured elevation to the papacy, but did record that, after his arrival in Rome, Silvester had discovered 'by the art of necromancy' certain treasures that had been buried by previous inhabitants of the ancient city. William alleged that the pope had used 'his accustomed arts' in order to gain entry to an underground chamber, but then reminded the reader that even Solomon, favoured by God, had knowledge of the occult and compared Gerbert's discoveries with similar stories of underground caverns that had been opened by men.[61]

William also provided substantial detail surrounding the prophecy that Silvester would survive as pope unless he visited Jerusalem. Silvester, he claimed, owned a statue in the form of a head to which he reportedly addressed questions. The statue responded only with affirmative or negative answers, and it was Silvester who first posed the question of whether he would die before he said the Mass in Jerusalem. Assured by a simple negative that he was safe in Rome, Silvester did not anticipate that death would strike as he prepared to say the Mass in the Jerusalem Temple. In the account presented in the *Gesta Regum Anglorum*, the pope repented as he realised his mistake and ordered that his body be torn apart and scattered around the city by horses. It was this last wish which persuaded William that Silvester had indeed been guilty of some devilish crime, and which led Protestant writers some 400 years later to assume that the pope had indeed been outwitted by the devil. Yet even the narrative of the death of the pope is shrouded by confusion, exacerbated by the fact that William had erroneously identified Silvester with Pope John XVI, the anti-pope to the imperially sanctioned Gregory V.[62] The brief description that William provided of the mutilation of Silvester's body at the pope's request certainly has a more solid grounding in accounts of the humiliation inflicted upon the corpse of Gregory V. If this was indeed William's error, it was one which Bale and others were more than content to reproduce in their condemnation of the demon-pope. Whatever William's own views, the inclusion of accusations of necromancy in his account of the *life* of Silvester made him an invaluable source for those seeking evidence with which to blacken the reputation of the pope.[63]

William of Malmesbury's account of the *life* of Gerbert was not the only source for the accusations that were levelled against the pope. Evangelical polemicists found additional support for the claim that Silvester was indeed guilty of necromancy in other monastic chronicles, most particularly in the writings of another favoured source for evangelical history writers, Benno of Osnabruck.[64] Benno had supported the imperial anti-pope Clement III and had made a concerted attempt to blacken the reputation of his rival Gregory VII with allegations, published *circa* 1080, that the pope had practised magic and necromancy.[65] The similar accusation that Silvester had entered into a pact with the devil served Benno well in his attempt to claim that the papacy had become corrupted by diabolic magic by the end of the eleventh century. As part of his denunciation of the contemporary papacy, Benno described Silvester's concourse with the devil which had culminated in the release of Satan from the pit after 1,000 years of captivity and Silvester's accession to the papal throne.[66] The devil had promised Silvester that he would remain as pope until he said the Mass in Jerusalem, and Benno recorded the subsequent death of the pope in Rome after his failure to appreciate the true nature of the promise. In Benno's narrative, Silvester ordered that his body be dismembered and that his hands and tongue, with which had had dishonoured God, be removed.[67] Benno's account of Silvester does not seem to have been used by William of Malmesbury[68] but it was certainly widely used by evangelical writers in their recasting of Silvester as the pope who loosed the devil from the pit, and it emerged as the prime source for evangelical polemicists in their condemnation of Gregory VII.

The legend of Silvester was sufficiently well known that Catholic historians in the sixteenth century clearly recognised the need to defend the reputation of the pope. Whatever the circumstances that surrounded Gerbert's appointment to Rheims and to the papacy, it was essential that the legitimacy of his pontificate should not be called into doubt if the unbroken chain of apostolic succession were to be defended. The account of Silvester that appeared in Baronius' *Annales Ecclesiastici* was far from a ringing endorsement of his life, but Baronius argued that the myths surrounding the pope were simply the result of hostile rumours that had circulated after his sudden and apparently unwarranted promotion to the papacy by Emperor Otto III. Baronius was well aware that Benno and others had believed the pope to be guilty of magic and necromancy but suggested that the distinction between science and magic was sufficiently blurred in the tenth century that Silvester's interests might well have been entirely innocent.[69] However, the medieval legend, reinforced and repeated by evangelical polemicists may well have attracted enough credence to warrant the opening of the tomb of Silvester II in 1648. Canon Caesar Raspo confirmed that the body of the pope was found to be complete and dressed in full pontificals, thus disproving claims that the corpse had been dismembered, although once the tomb was open the bones were reported to have fallen to dust and filled the air with sweet perfume.[70]

Whatever its origins, the legend of the Silvester and his pact with the devil had an enduring appeal. Key events in the *life* of Gerbert, and the learning that was traditionally associated with the pope, could be readily interpreted to provide evidence of forbidden knowledge and demonic activity. For Benno, the identification of Silvester as the antichristian predecessor of Gregory VII provided a useful avenue from which to attack Hildebrand and his reforms and mount a defence of the imperial anti-pope. For William of Malmesbury, the legend offered an opportunity to debate the boundaries between learned science and demonic magic and to explore some of the more dramatic myths and legends associated with the pope. As a pope responsible for the promotion of clerical celibacy, Silvester's apparent pact with the devil encouraged Bale to identify the prohibition of clerical marriage as a mark of the false church that had its origins in the activity of Antichrist in the church of Rome. The existence of a long-standing chronicle tradition in which the image of the papal necromancer was already established facilitated the characterisation of Silvester as the pope who loosed Antichrist from captivity and enabled Bale and Foxe to cite Catholic historians and chroniclers in their attacks on the historical papacy. For evangelical polemicists and history writers, Silvester was important as the pope whose pontificate spanned the crucial year of 1000, after which the influence of Antichrist came to be felt in the church. In Reformation histories of the papacy, Silvester became not only the pope who loosed the devil from the pit, unleashing the rule of Antichrist, but also the pope whose reputation helped to ground evangelical apocalyptic in a firm historical narrative.

Alongside Silvester II, a second eleventh-century pope stands out in evangelical writing on the medieval church and papacy. The pontificate of Hildebrand, Pope Gregory VII, spanned the years between 1073 and 1085 and was marked by the robust implementation of the moral reform of the clergy and the determined defence of the rights and authority of the papacy. These years were dominated by Gregory's prolonged quarrel with Emperor Henry IV over the question of lay investiture, a conflict that was only briefly brought to an end when Henry was absolved by Gregory VII, standing barefoot outside the papal residence at Canossa in 1077. Gregory was to die in exile, still protesting against the actions of the emperor.[71] Like Silvester, Gregory VII was to emerge as an archetypal villain of Protestant history-writing. His pontificate had witnessed the vigorous articulation of papal claims to authority over temporal powers, and his treatment of Emperor Henry IV at Canossa became the *locus classicus* for evangelical writers seeking evidence of the subjugation of kings and princes to the pretensions of the popes. The 1563 edition of Foxe's *Actes and Monuments* included a striking visual representation of the humiliation of the emperor before the pope.[72] Gregory's determination to impose celibacy upon the clergy also marked him firmly in evangelical polemic as an enemy of true religion and as the pope who had forbidden Christian marriage to the priesthood. Robert Barnes identified Gregory as 'Satanae organu[m]', on the basis of the reforms implemented in his pontificate, particularly the prohibition of clerical marriage. In his description of the enforcement of clerical celibacy in the pontificate of Gregory VII, Philip Melanchthon vigorously condemned the 'deuillish decrees' that had forbidden marriage to the clergy.[73] John Bale held Gregory responsible for the immoral conduct of the priesthood which he claimed had followed the prohibition of clerical marriage, and denounced the pope as 'a superstytyouse monke, a nycromanser,

Plate 4 Gregory VII and the Emperor Henry IV, John Foxe, *Actes and Monuments*, 1596/7

a murtherer … '.[74] The 'Hellysh Hildebrande', Bale claimed, had passed a 'most deuylysh decre' that deprived the married priests of their benefices, although Bale noted sardonically that the legislation merely prohibited clerical marriage and did nothing to prevent priests from fathering illegitimate children. Compulsory celibacy ensured that the clergy were 'iudged terrestryall aungelles of the folyshe worlde', Bale complained, when the Catholic priesthood was in reality 'the very drose of the deuyll and poyson of all Christyanyte'.[75]

The enforcement of the prohibition of clerical marriage was rapidly established in evangelical polemic as a clear sign of the corruption of the faith and practice of the church, and Bale's *Mystery of Iniquity* (1545) provided Gregory with a key role in this process. The imposition of clerical celibacy was a prime example of the influence of Antichrist, Bale claimed, informing his reader that it was 'holy pope Hyldebra[n]de which was a Necromanser [who] made this constitution'.[76] The condemnation of Gregory VII as the embodiment of Antichrist in the church was justified, he declared, by the close correlation between the pope's actions and the warnings contained within the seventh Psalm, 'hee altered the lawes of God, for where the Scripture lice[n]ceth al estates to marrye, he barred ye clergy therof, forcing the[m] to vow single life aboue their abilitye'.[77] John Foxe's account of the Gregorian reforms and the imposition of compulsory clerical celibacy followed that provided by Bale, and by Matthias Flacius in the *Catalogus Testium Veritatis*. Until the late eleventh century, Foxe argued, priests 'had wyues opnelye and lawfullye', but Gregory VII had declared clerical marriage to be heresy and instructed the faithful to withhold tithes from married priests. The Gregorian decree, he claimed, ran contrary to Scripture, the practices of the early church and the laws of nature in demanding that priests live like angels. Foxe referred the reader to the protests that had been made by the clergy of the French church and reproduced from the *Catalogus Testium Veritatis* a copy of the pope's letter to the bishop of Constance, in which he denounced the married clergy. Foxe described the opposition to clerical marriage that had been voiced by the imperial clergy at the Council of Erfurt, and used the narrative provided in the chronicle literature as evidence that Gregory's decrees marked a departure from the traditional faith of the church.[78]

The association of the Gregorian reforms with the expansion of the influence of Antichrist in the church was not limited to the role played by the pope in the imposition of compulsory clerical celibacy. Accusations that Gregory had engaged in more specific diabolic practices also featured heavily in evangelical literature in the 1520s, and these allegations were repeated and expanded upon in the middle decades of the sixteenth century. The translator of the *Mustre of the Scismatyke Bishops of Rome* claimed that the pontificate of Gregory VII provided ample evidence that the pope could err in matters of doctrine and noted that Hildebrand's sympathy for the Arian heresy had been widely recognised.[79] Criticism of Gregory's doctrine was accompanied by a description of his apparent involvement in conjuring and necromancy which, it was alleged, had been exposed by a trusted servant who had opened a bound volume which belonged to the pope, only to be confronted by a 'multytude of dyuelles' ready to do their master's bidding.[80] The pope's skills in diabolic magic provided the basis for the miracles that were attributed to Gregory. Among these 'monstrouse wytchcraftes' worked by his demons was the apparent ability to 'shake a payre of manacles of his arms (were they neuer so fast) and leape and spring in the lykenesse of sparkes of fyre'.[81] The account of Gregory's pontificate presented in Barnes *Vitae Romanorum Pontificum* detailed the role of the pope in the prohibition of clerical marriage and repeated the accusations that Gregory had developed interests and abilities in magic. Gregory was not alone: Barnes suggested that the pope had been inspired by the same interests in the magical that had animated the careers of Silvester, Laurence and Benedict IX.[82] It was Gregory's capacity to delude the faithful with false miracles and magic which informed the Swiss preacher Rudolph Gualther's condemnation of Hildebrand among the popes who had been willing to 'bynde them selues holly to be the seruantes of Sathan'.[83] Gregory VII was the 'hellhound hildebrande, called Gregorie the .7. the varlet of all wickednesse and mischief'.[84]

Hildebrand's name followed that of Silvester II in John Bale's list of papal and clerical necromancers in the *Apology agaynst a rank papist*, and Bale's condemnation of the necromancy of Pope Silvester had echoes in his treatment of the pontificate of Gregory VII. The magical practices of the popes far exceeded those of the 'soothsayers of Egypte or Pharaoes calcers', Bale claimed, in the 'incantacio[n]s and necromancies' upon which their power rested.[85] It was in the *Actes of the Englysh Votaries* that Bale's analysis of the role of Hildebrand in the establishment of the rule of Antichrist was first developed to its full potential. Bale posited a link between the loosing of the devil from the pit by Silvester II in 1000 and the necromancy of subsequent popes, including Hildebrand. The influence of Antichrist in the papacy after the death of Silvester had been assured, he claimed, by Silvester's disciples, including Theophylact and Laurentius.[86] Under the tutelage of Silvester and his successors, Gregory had acquired the ability to manipulate the supernatural and had been observed shaking his 'sleues or mittaynes, to delude the eyes of the simple, many tymes he sent out sparkes of fyre, whyche was iudged a wonderfull myracle and a signe of holynesse in hym'.[87] The devil, Bale claimed, was not able to persecute the faithful at will, but the 'false monk' Hildebrand provided an ideal agent.[88] Bale's depiction of Hildebrand did much to shape later evangelical biographies of the pope. John Foxe identified Gregory as a sorcerer whose activites were the 'first and principall cause of all this perturbation that is now and hath bene since his tyme in the church'.[89] It was Gregory VII, Foxe alleged, who had introduced into the papacy the pride and thirst for power that had led to the suppression of princes and aroused antagonism between bishops and emperors 'under the prete[n]ce of chastitie'. The account was far from original, and Foxe's narrative drew heavily upon the history of the pontificate of Gregory that had appeared in Bale's *Catalogus* and in Flacius' *Catalogus Testium Veritatis*. Indeed Tom Freeman has demonstrated the extent to which the Hildebrand that emerged from the pages of the *Actes and Monuments* was very much the creation of Bale, not least in those sections where Foxe repeated Bale's own errors and deliberate omissions.[90] Foxe emphasised the association between Hildebrand and his predecessor Silvester and repeated the tale of the demons that had appeared from the library of Gregory as evidence of the satanic underpinnings of his pontificate.

By the late sixteenth century, the image of Gregory VII as magician and necromancer had become well established in evangelical histories of the papacy. The Huntingdon preacher Thomas Beard denounced one of Gregory's miracles in which he had cast the consecrated communion bread into the fire, 'that hee might have thereby some diuine answer or signe against the Emperor Henry IV'.[91] Other miracles commonly associated with the pope were repeated, including the legend that Gregory was able to send sparks of flame from the sleeves of his cloak. Such wonders, Beard claimed, had deceived the faithful people to the point where they had come to regard Gregory as a saint, enabling the devil to continue in the perversion of true religion through his agent, the 'false monk'.[92] Richard Sheldon, in his *Survey of the miracles of the church of Rome*, alleged that the ability to bring fire from heaven was a sure mark of Antichrist and one that was visible not only in 'Antichrist himself but his ministers', including Gregory

VII in his dispute with Emperor Henry IV.[93] In the recasting of the history of the papacy that took place at the hands of evangelical propagandists, the pontificate of Gregory VII had come to provide a vital marker in the rise of Antichrist within the Catholic church. Gregory was one of the more imposing and prominent figures on the landscape of the medieval church and his reputation was well worth fighting for. His pontificate marked a crucial period in the history of the church and had also witnessed the expansion of papal power and the codification of doctrines and disciplines that were unacceptable within the reformed church of the sixteenth century. In evangelical polemic, Gregory became a false monk, a proud bishop who dabbled with demons to secure his position by feigned wonders, in an attempt to tarnish his character and justify the rejection of the reforms implemented in his name. The value of the reputation of Hildebrand to evangelical history writers is perhaps indicated by Catholic attempts to repossess his reputation and influence, which culminated in the beatification of Gregory in 1584 by Gregory XIII, in order that his pontificate might be reclaimed and exploited as a model for the post-Tridentine papacy. The English Catholic writer Robert Parsons certainly attempted to salvage something of Hildebrand's reputation in the *Treatise of the Three Conversions*, defending the actions of the pope with reference to more favourable medieval chronicles.[94]

Part of the appeal of Gregory VII to evangelical polemicists lay in the fact that his life and his actions were well documented by medieval writers. Not all contemporary commentaries on his pontificate were entirely positive, and evangelical writers were able to exploit earlier criticisms and condemnations of Hildebrand to great effect. The similarity between various accounts of Gregory's *life* and pontificate suggests that there were sources common to many of his critics in the sixteenth century, the most obvious being the biographical letters of Benno, first exploited by Thomas Swinnerton and later by Bale, Flacius, Foxe and Beard. As a supporter of the imperial cause against Gregory VII, Benno's writings were overtly hostile to the pope in their vigorous defence of Henry IV and in their representation of Hildebrand as a magician who had learned his art from Silvester II. It was Benno's account which provided Bale and Flacius with material that related to Hildebrand's tempestuous relations with the emperor and with the allegations that the pope was guilty of heresy and sacrilege.[95] Benno had identified Gregory as the fulfilment of the prophecy of false preachers by Paul in 2 Timothy, and denounced the decrees and reforms of the pope as contrary to Scripture and the Christian faith.[96] The miracles of Gregory VII that were derided by evangelical writers in the sixteenth century had also featured in Benno's account, suggesting that it was this text which provided the foundation for the accusations of magic and necromancy that were levelled against the pope in the era of the Reformation. The legend that a host of demons inhabited Gregory's library, repeated by Barnes, Bale, Foxe and Flacius, also had its origins in Benno's denunciation of the pope. Benno had identified the role of Theophilact and Laurence in educating Hildebrand in the magical arts, and the phrasing of his descriptions of the miracles and illusions worked by Gregory was identical to that of Swinnerton, Bale and Foxe.[97] The text of Benno's biography of Gregory was printed in English in Swinnerton's account of the deeds of the 'schismatic' popes and became a staple of evangelical writing on the Gregorian reform movement.

The ongoing conflict between Gregory VII and Emperor Henry IV also provided evangelical history writers with polemically useful material in the form of the allegations that were levelled against Gregory by the Imperial party. At the Council of Worms in 1076, the bishops and abbots of the empire pronounced a sentence of deposition upon the pope. A variety of charges were levelled against him, many of which were later repeated in sixteenth-century evangelical polemic. Hugh Blancus, a deposed cardinal with more to gain from allegiance to emperor than pope, accused Gregory of treason and witchcraft, and claimed that the pope had entered into a covenant with the devil. Henry IV claimed power by 'God's holy ordinance' over the 'false monk' Hildebrand, and alleged that Gregory had obtained the papacy by unjust means, 'craft, bribery, and force'.[98] At the Imperial Synod of Brixen in 1080, Henry IV again sat in judgement over the pope. Complainants alleged that Hildebrand was a false monk who 'strove to procure position for himself over men through vain glory, without the support of any merits, to set dreams and divinations, his own and those of others, ahead of divine dispensation'. The council convicted Gregory of the murder of four previous popes, an accusation that was to be repeated by Bale in his denunciation of Gregory, and later by Flacius and Foxe.[99] The pope, it was claimed, had thrown the empire into turmoil by his actions, which were themselves ample testimony that he had not been elected in accordance with the divine will. Echoing the denunciation of Gregory at Mainz, the bishops ordered his canonical deposition and alleged that he was an 'open devotee of divinations and dreams, and a necromancer working with an oracular spirit' who defended perjurers and murderers, and sympathised with the heretical theology of Berengar on the eucharist.[100] The list of signatories was headed by another opponent of the Gregorian papacy, Hugh Candidus, which gives some indication of the origin of the accusations that were levelled against the pope. Candidus' allegations against Gregory provided ammunition for the condemnation of the pope in Barnes' *Vitae Romanorum Pontificum*.[101] The condemnations of Gregory issued at Mainz and Brixen were key declarations in the imperial propaganda campaign against the pope and reflected the sheer force that lay behind the ongoing conflict between church and empire. However, in the hands of evangelical polemicists, such declarations became valuable evidence in the condemnation of the medieval papacy as the seat of Antichrist in the world.

In evangelical histories of the medieval papacy, it was Silvester II and Gregory VII who were most often singled out for particular attention. Their pontificates spanned a crucial period in the history of the church, and their activities and reforms touched upon some of the most contested issues in the debates of the Reformation. However, the polemical capital that was to be gained in the identification of magicians and necromancers among the medieval occupants of the throne of St Peter also encouraged evangelical writers to point more generally to other examples of popes whose conduct might be called into suspicion. Although the majority of the text of the *Mustre of Scismatike Popes* was devoted to Benno's account of Gregory VII, Thomas Swinnerton also included Benedict IX among a long list of papal necromancers, alleging that he was 'gyuen holly to the sacrifice of dyuels in woodes and mountaynes by his wytch craftes and nycromancy' which caused 'sely women' to seek him out.[102] In a catalogue of magician popes, John Bale included not only Silvester II and Gregory VII but also Anastasius II, Boniface VIII, John XIII, Paul III and Benedict IX, repeating the claim that the last had used magical powers to conjure devils and draw women to him.[103] John XII, pope between 955 and 964, was labelled as 'the holye vycar of Sathan and successour of Symon Magus'.[104] Once again, Bale was able to draw upon records of a dispute between empire and papacy to colour his account of the pontificate of John XII, whose deeds had been described and condemned by the imperial historian Liutprand in his history of the reign of Emperor Otto.[105] Rudolph Gualther claimed that Boniface VIII had obtained the papacy 'through naughtie sciences', and Thomas Beard added Gregory VI to the list of papal magicians following Platina's condemnation of the pope, echoing Benno's suggestion that Rome had become a school of demonic practice in the eleventh century.[106] William Perkins highlighted the pontificates of Silvester II and Gregory VII and added several other popes to his list of necromancers and 'sundrie malcontented priests of Rome [who] aspire unto the chaire of the supermacie by Diabolicall assistance'.[107]

In the late sixteenth century, John Napier claimed that he had identified some 22 popes who were recognised necromancers, and protested that they had managed to deceive the faithful with 'fained fables and alleged miracles'.[108] Napier's chronology for the application of the prophecies of Revelation to the Christian past differed from that of Bale and the mid-century writers in its emphasis upon the year 1300 as the crucial date at which Satan was loosed in the church. This date coincided with the pontificate of Boniface VIII, whose character loomed large among the popes that Napier believed had conspired with Satan to obtain power on the earth. Evangelical opposition to Boniface VIII was constructed upon the same argument over the relationship between church and state which had fuelled the condemnation of Gregory VII in his treatment of Henry IV. The papal bulls *Clericos Laicos* (1296) and *Unam Sanctam* (1302) presented an unambiguous view of the place of the secular powers in relation to the church, one which had no place in the literature of the Reformation. In his conflict with Philip of France, Boniface had set out a vigorous defence of the rights of the church in the bulls *Salvator Mundi* and *Ausculta Fili,* which withdrew the king's rights to revenues from the French church and established the authority of the vicar of Christ above that of kings and kingdoms. Such pronouncements were unlikely to find favour among the defenders of the English Reformation. After the death of Boniface VIII, Philip of France had alleged that the pope was guilty of heresy and compelled the weaker Celestine V to open a formal process against Boniface, demanding that his bones be disinterred and his ashes scattered to the wind.[109] Again, the reputation of individual popes among their contemporaries was to provide powerful ammunition for evangelical polemicists in their condemnation of the papacy. Reginald Scot reminded his readers of the 'popish visions and conjurations' that had been invented by the clergy and the bishops, and drew attention to the actions of Boniface VIII who, Scot alleged, had feigned an apparition in order to prompt the resignation of his predecessor.[110] The example of Boniface VIII, like that of Silvester and Gregory VII, was especially valuable to evangelical writers in their attempts to discredit a colossus of the medieval papacy by placing a particular inter-pretation upon contemporary, if highly subjective, records of controversies and events.

The identification and condemnation of popes who were alleged to have engaged in magical and demonic practices were central parts of evangelical attempts to root the prophecies of Scripture in the events of the past and construct an identity for the two churches of the false and the godly throughout Christian history. At one level, necromancy was simply another charge to bring against the much reviled figure of the pope, and one more means by which to justify the rejection of papal authority in the sixteenth century.[111] John Bale denounced 'the deuyls unholy vycar at Rome wyth all hys curssyinges & coniurynges, calkynges and coblynges, brawlynges and babblings, massinges and mutteringes, Images and Idolles, pardons and purgatory, either the deuyl and all hys other sorceryes which these graceless papists co[n]tynually gapeth for yet ones agayne', a list of grievances which was polemically effective primarily because it was seemingly all-encompassing.[112] Yet there was something more significant and more damaging in specific accusations of sorcery and necromancy. Witchcraft and holiness represented two poles in the geography of the supernat-ural, yet they existed in a complex network of theological and historical intercon-nections. The demonic and the saintly were the mirror image of each other, the unholy was the perversion of the holy and witchcraft the inversion of true reli-gion.[113] However, the identification of the demonic was accomplished within the framework provided by the vocabulary of true religion and the wonders of the saints were repeatedly defined in opposition to pagan and demonic magic. Richard Kieckhefer has identified a medieval clerical underworld of magic and demonic practice where Latin liturgy came into contact with learned magic, a world in which necromancy seemed to lie at the intersection of the two extremes of true and false religion.[114] The survival of a medieval friar's manuscript which explains 'how to see ye spirites of ye aier', or 'constrayne any sp[i]rit to answer you and fulfil your entente', might well suggest that the late-medieval supernatural was not neatly divided between the ecclesiastical and the magical.[115]

In the identification of the true church and the false in the past and the present, some questions proved invaluable to the Reformation controversialists because they were issues over which there could be no shades of grey: a priest was either married or he was not, the liturgy was either in the vernacular or it was not, an individual either upheld the supremacy of the pope or he did not. In the words of Bale, there could be no compromise between the true church and the false, 'since eyther we are citize[n]s in the new Hierusale[m] wyth Jesus Christ, or els in the old supersticious Babylon with antichrist the vicar of

Sathan'.[116] But in the separation of miracle from magic, science from necromancy, it was the very difficulty of making such a distinction that made the issue so polemically powerful. Where the boundaries between saint and sinner, cleric and conjuror were malleable, it was possible to adopt a polemical approach and adapt, twist or exploit the evidence to a highly persuasive end. John Bale clearly recognised this potential and encouraged the reader to see magic, necromancy and demonic influences at almost every turn. In his description of the appointment of Theodore of Tarsus as archbishop of Canterbury in 668, Bale was not prepared to let the blunt facts stand in the way of a convincing analogy. The arrival of Theodore, he suggested, was portentous, especially once the date of the archbishop's consecration was surreptitiously altered to 666, which had a more obvious significance in Christian history. Bale's account of Theodore's foundation of a school at Canterbury followed that which was contained in John Capgrave's *Nova Legenda Angliae* in almost every respect. Both Capgrave and Bale noted that Theodore had intended that the school advance the learning of logic, rhetoric and philosophy. However, Bale added to this list the disciplines of 'magyck, sortilege, phisnomy, palmistry, Alcumy, Necromancy, Chyromancy, Geomancy & witchery'.[117] In Bale's history, the boundary between religion and magic in the English church had become blurred as early as the seventh century.

The identification of magicians and necromancers in Rome was a prominent part of the evangelical assault on the papacy in the middle decades of the sixteenth century. By drawing upon elements of ambiguity and subjectivity in the chronicles, evangelical history writers elided the distinction between religion and magic in the past, and then established miracles and false wonders as the means by which to distinguish the true church from the false in the present. Medieval narratives and propaganda which hinted that individual popes had interests in magic or science were exploited as evidence that papacy had become the seat of Antichrist, given power over the church by a generation of popes who had practised necromancy and entered into pacts with devil to secure their own position. The evangelical image of Antichrist as a permanent spiritual presence raised the possibility that the signs of this presence in the church might be identified in the past, as well as in the present and future. An ecclesiastical history which took the form of a narrative of the slow corruption of the doctrine and practice of the church under the influence of this spiritual Antichrist was enhanced by the possibility that this spiritual force for evil might be given a physical and chronological location. By attributing a key role in the loosing and empowerment of Satan to the popes, individually or collectively, evangelical writers were able to argue the precise point at which the institutional church had become the false congregation, and justify the abrogation of papal authority and the rejection of Catholic doctrine. The history of the papal Antichrist was therefore a vital part of the construction of an identity for an English church independent of Roman jurisdiction. Justification for the break with Rome came via the uncovering of the true nature of the papacy as the historical seat of Antichrist and the representation of the popes as politically ambitious tyrants and magicians. The construction of a past and present for the national

English church was facilitated by the existence of its papal antithesis in that same past and present, with the result that the abrogation of papal authority in England could not displace the popes from the foreground of polemical debate. The Act of Supremacy established the position of the king as the head of the church in England, but propaganda and polemic in defence of that position drew heavily upon a traditional lexicon of words and images in which the authority of the pope was unchallenged.

CONCLUSION

In 1577, William Harrison described the 'ancient and present estate of the church of England' and summarised the transformations that had taken place in its shape and faith as a result of the religious changes of the sixteenth century. His *Description of England* paints a picture of a church calendar which had been purged of the majority of its festivals, and a map of a liturgical year which was devoid of many of the landmarks and signposts which had guided the faithful on their annual pilgrimage.[1] Shrines, images and reliquaries that had provided tangible testimony to the continued presence of the saints of the past in the church of the present had been destroyed and the legends of the lives and actions of the heroes of the medieval church expunged from the record. Decades of religious change threatened to create a vacuum in the immediate moment by depriving the people of England of the rituals and objects that linked them to their past.[2] Communal liturgical participation in the commemoration of a local or national saint had forged a link between the past and the present, and the repetition or recreation of the *life* of the saint provided both the saint, and those who sought his intercession, with a shared historical context. The loss of ritual, which had included the celebration of the *lives* of the saints, the commemoration of their miracles and the re-enactment of community traditions, was closely allied to a loss of historical memory. As Ronald Hutton's account of the *Rise and Fall of Merry England* has demonstrated, ritual, tradition and history were never immutable, but the iconoclastic approach to the past in Reformation England brought with it a new understanding of the present.[3] Reformation attitudes to the records of the medieval church highlight the complexity of the relationship between the past and the present in the religious turmoil of sixteenth-century England.

The destruction of the cult of the saints, the dissolution of the monasteries and official iconoclasm in the reigns of Henry VIII and Edward VI changed both the physical appearance of the English church and the nature of its relationship with the past. David Cressy has argued that a 'calendrical consciousness' permeated people's lives, and the transformation of this calendar – the period between 1530 and 1570 – was therefore a highly visible and potentially powerful manifestation of doctrinal change.[4] The abrogation of the festivals of the saints in the calendar was accompanied by the visible dismantling of the cult of the saints at a local level, as lights were no longer burned before images, relics and shrines were suppressed and the images of the saints were removed from churches and destroyed. Among the great pilgrimage centres of medieval England, it was only the shrine of Edward the Confessor which survived the predations of Henry VIII and Edward VI, and was repaired and restored in the reign of Mary. The resurrection of the saints was short-lived. Public bonfires fuelled by the images that had been erected under Mary were held in London in 1559 and the Elizabethan *Book of Homilies* preached of the dangers of idolatry, while successive visitations enquired into the presence of images and roods in local churches.[5] David Sacks notes that the celebration of the feasts of St Katherine and St Clement, which had played such a prominent role in the life of the city of Bristol, had all but ended in the 1540s, with little attempt made at revival after the accession of Mary. Such community celebrations had served a specific purpose but attracted little interest once any plausible context was pulled from beneath them.[6]

The liturgical calendar both shaped, and was shaped by, the interchange between the past and the present; the abrogation of the feasts and festivals of the saints not only impacted upon the life of the mid-century church but also articulated a shifting relationship between the national church and medieval Catholicism. The festivals of the liturgical year had provided a vehicle for the communication of the theology and faith of the medieval church. The celebrations of the Christmas and Easter season impressed upon the popular imagination the key events in the life of Christ, while communal participation in Corpus Christi processions both reinforced the doctrine of transubstantiation and cemented the relationship between church and community. The commemoration of the saints served not only as a reminder of the life of the individual saint but also as a spur to faith in the intercessory prayers of the saints, and as an illustration of their place in the community of the living and within the wider *communio sanctorum*.[7] The revisions made to the calendar exemplified and exploited the pedagogic functions of festival. Gaps in the calendar, days left empty by the abrogation of feast days, were a stark and visible reminder of religious change, while new festivals, which marked the accession day of Elizabeth I or the failure of the Gunpowder Plot, helped to establish a new series of important dates and events in the life of the Protestant nation. Likewise, the *lives* of the saints and narratives of their miracles, which had reinforced faith in the divine supernatural, saintly thaumaturgy and the holiness of the church, became the vehicle by which such faith was overturned. The familiarity of the liturgical calendar made it an ideal format for the dissemination of a new version of the past, and the popularity of the *lives* and legends of the saints ensured that traditional hagiography would enjoy a prominent position in the propaganda of the English Reformation. The utilisation of words and images from the past in the justification of change in the present is indicative of a flexible process of reformation, in which the traditions of the past were permitted to survive, or even appropriated, by the proponents of reform. Meanings invested in religious symbols were malleable, and the capacity to reinvent traditions and images was a crucial component in the creation of a post-Reformation culture in the English church.[8] The representation of the *lives* of the saints, the history of the papacy and the theology of the Mass in evangelical polemic in the middle decades of the sixteenth century helped to paint a new image of the Catholic church upon the familiar landscape provided by medieval chronicles, histories and hagiography.

However, the reformed calendar also reflected the fundamental challenge that the Reformation posed to the sacramental system of the pre-Reformation church and, in particular, to the belief that there could be holiness in specific objects, dates and places. In severing the link between the natural and the supernatural, evangelicals acquired a further motivation and mechanism for their vigorous assault upon the cult of the saints, images and miracles. If miracles were no longer miracles, a new explanation was needed in which the wonders of the saints were recast as magical and diabolic illusions. If the theology of the Mass was false, the prayers of the priest became manipulative deceptions. The result was that, by the end of the century, the term 'conjuror' had become synonymous with the recusant priest, with complaints made against a 'nest of conjuring mass-mongers' and clergy who mingled 'mass-matters' with 'magic and conjuration'.[9] In Reginald Scot's *The Discouerie of Witchcraft*, Catholicism and magic were represented in overlapping layers, in which the caricature of mass-monger and witch merged to provide evidence of the 'peevish trumperie' of medieval magic and religion.[10] King James VI's *Daemonology* (1597) exploited the polemical potential of the rhetoric of magic as a weapon against fundamental aspects of Catholic piety and devotion, drawing upon a long-standing tradition in evangelical writing which represented Catholicism as a religion that was derived from witchcraft.[11] Stuart Clark has argued that witchcraft was both an important issue in the works of Protestant reformers and an integral part of the culture of those who were to be 'reformed'.[12] The same was abundantly true for the saints and their miracles, which continued to feature prominently in the rhetoric of the Reformation. Pre-Reformation saints emerged in evangelical polemic as a mouthpiece for the Reformation and as a justification for the construction of a new ecclesiastical history. Traditional assumptions that the Reformation brought about the 'desacralisation' of European culture have been effectively debunked in recent years, as the boundaries between sacred and material, religion and superstition have been shown to be permeable.[13] This permeability, evinced in the difficulties in separating miracle from magic, history from hagiography, saint from sinner, suggests that the spiritual oppositions between truth and falsehood established in polemical debate neither reflected nor resulted in divisions that were as tangible in reality.

In a court sermon delivered before Edward VI, Hugh Latimer described his arrival at a church to preach, only to discover that the church was locked and the congregation absent. Upon enquiring of a passer-by, Latimer was informed that 'this is Robin Hood's Day. The parish are gone abroad to gather for Robin Hood: I pray you let them not.'[14] The tales of Robin Hood acted as a convenient shorthand for fable and legend by the mid-sixteenth century: Latimer's concern that his intended audience was more interested in the myth of an outlaw than the word of God has parallels in John Foxe's equation of the *lives* of the saints with the 'tales of Roben hode', and indeed in the confession of the drunken chaplain in William Langland's *The Vision of Piers Plowman*, that he could recite the rhymes of Robin Hood more readily than he could remember his *Pater Noster*. Edward Dering condemned the *lives* of the saints and the legend of Robin Hood in the same breath as tales that 'hell had printed'.[15] The proclivity of the faithful to recall and cherish the legends of the past rather than the pedagogy and preaching of the present was not only a problem for Latimer. Evangelical polemicists were engaged in a delicate balancing act, deriding popular myths and histories and superstition, while using the same images as the means of communicating the message of the Reformation. The creation of a Protestant past might enable English reformers to lay claim to the history of the church, but it also perpetuated the legends that they sought to condemn. In some areas, traditional practices and memories of long-standing customs were certainly slow to die out. At Sherwell and Pilton in Devon, there were reports in 1586 that people still 'travelled as they did when they were on pilgrimage'. Statues of the saints had been preserved into the 1560s in the Lincolnshire parishes of Thurlby and Bassingham, and investigations in the diocese of York unearthed images in churches and private dwellings.[16] Keith Thomas observed that while the practice of visiting holy wells in the hope of better health was an acceptable post-Reformation activity, the cures recorded at the waters bore the hallmarks of medieval miracle collections, while the popularity of the wells kept alive the names and the memory of the saints after which they were named.[17]

Other practices and beliefs were memorialised in oral tradition and in the 'pleasant histories' contained in popular pamphlets, which reproduced narratives and myths from the past and repeated legends of the saints, chivalrous knights, and monks and friars. The lecherous friar satirised by pre-Reformation critics of the church survived in popular literature a century after the dissolution, while priests continued to celebrate the Mass in the world of the seventeenth-century chapbook.[18] Local memories were often well rooted. The royal Visitors at Ripon in 1568 demanded the closure of St Winifred's Needle, a narrow passage in the parish church which was still commonly believed to be so narrow that only Christ could pass through.[19] The holy thorn of Glastonbury that was reputed to have grown from the staff of St Joseph of Arimathea was still widely recognised when it was destroyed by an outraged Puritan in 1653.[20] Miracles continued to be recorded at the shrine of Thomas Becket four decades after its destruction by Henry VIII, and John Stow was able to present a detailed and vivid description of the missing shrine in 1592.[21] In 1564, the villagers of Seaton were reported to have gathered to celebrate the vigil of the feast of the translation of the relics of Becket, nearly 30 years after those same relics were alleged to have been scattered to the wind. The legend of St Dunstan, comprehensively rewritten in the mid-sixteenth century at the hands of Bale and Foxe, was still common currency at the turn of the seventeenth century, perhaps as a result of the very same process of reinvention. Thomas Fuller presented an account of the conflicting opinions of Dunstan's miracles, and especially the incident at Calne, in which the floor of a building had collapsed leaving only Dunstan standing. Fuller claimed that, while some blamed the devil for the accident, others believed that the events had been orchestrated by Dunstan himself, while others still denied the veracity of the whole legend. But the miracle was to acquire an added twist in Fuller's account. The collapsing floor of the council chamber provided an ideal backdrop for a discussion of events at Blackfriars in London in 1623. On this occasion, a large crowd had gathered in a garret adjoining the residence of the French ambassador, in order to hear a sermon by the Jesuit preacher Robert Drury. In the middle of the sermon, the floor of the building collapsed, killing 90 spectators and injuring others. Alexandra Walsham has discussed the incident in the context of anti-Catholicism and providentialism in seventeenth-century England, but Fuller's use of the miracle at Calne to provide a parallel example also highlights the extent to which the legends of the medieval saints provided a useful mirror for the interpretation of the present.[22]

Reginald Scot despaired at some of the miracles and legends that were attributed to the medieval saints. Readers of the *Discovery of Witchcraft* were urged to reject the 'old wiues fables' and 'lieng vanities' which Scot claimed were to be found in abundance in the *Golden Legend* and in the writings of Bodin. The *life* and miracles of St Margaret were 'incredible, foolish, impious and blasphemous', and there was little to choose, Scot alleged, between the miracles of St Loy and the prophecy of 'Mother Bungie'.[23] Such legends were not merely the stuff of ages past, however, but '*are* of more credit with many bewitched people than the true miracles of Christ'.[24] For Scot, the miracles of the saints were not neglected relics of past superstition but were still retold and even afforded credence in his own day. Many of the histories of saints and miracles that the jurist and antiquary William Lambarde reproduced in the *Perambulation of Kent* were the fruit of his own investigations of the records of the past, but he was also able to narrate numerous traditional local legends and myths that were still current among the inhabitants of Kent in the 1570s. His account of the miracles of St Mildred of Thanet was based upon the narrative of her *life* in the *Nova Legenda Anglie*, although Lambarde attributed the popularity of her cult to the local clergy of the church of St Gregory and St Augustine, who 'bothe made marchandize of her miracles'.[25] Lambarde was similarly sceptical of the miracles that were linked with St Augustine, which he claimed had been invented by the local monastery in order to divert pilgrim traffic from the more famous cult of Thomas Becket.[26]

Even where the process of iconoclastic destruction had been highly visible, the memory of the relics and shrines, and their destruction, often persisted. In his description of Boxley, Lambarde suggested that events surrounding the removal of the famous rood in 1538 were still 'fresh in mynde to bothe sides', Catholic and evangelical. Lambarde expressed his hope that the image of the destruction of the rood might be imprinted upon the popular memory 'to all posteritie', as a reminder of the 'impostures, fraud, juggling and Legierdemain' with which the Roman clergy had deceived the faithful. He provided a basic narrative of the history of the rood, and the exploitation of its moving parts by generations of 'craftie' monks to delude pilgrims who visited the abbey. Lambarde rejoiced in the removal of the rood at the instigation of Cranmer and Cromwell, and the destruction of the 'wooden God' at

Paul's Cross. However, the simple removal of the object, even when reinforced by a public demonstration of the mechanism with which it had been operated, had not been enough to undermine its position in popular memory. The immediate physical act of iconoclasm had not been accompanied by the destruction of the popular mental image of the rood or the memory of the miracles associated with it. Lambarde protested that the events at Boxley 'yet remayneth deepely imprinted in the myndes and memories of many a liue, to their euerlasting reproche, shame and confusion'.[27] The removal of the rood had been imprinted upon the popular imagination, but had yet to conceal the footprints left by pilgrims and the traditional cult.

Other accounts of the miracles and legends of the saints had become embedded in the oral traditions of Lambarde's Kent. In Chetham, Lambarde heard reports of a 'popish Illusion', which he repeated for the benefit of his readers in the hope that it would serve the 'keeping vnder of fained and superstitious religio[n]'. The corpse of a dead man, Lambarde claimed, had been washed up in the parish and had been buried in the local churchyard. However, the actions of the community had apparently caused offence to 'our lady of Chetham', who had appeared to the parish clerk in the night and threatened to withdraw her miracles from the church unless the body was removed. The parish was proud of its miracle-working cult and the Virgin's threat was sufficient for the clerk to order that the body be exhumed and returned to the river. However, in an added twist to the tale, the same corpse was later washed up at Gillingham, where it was reburied in the churchyard. Again, the sins of the unknown victim posed a threat to the local cult: the site of the burial sank beneath the level of the surrounding ground and no further miracles were recorded for the famous rood of Gillingham. This legend had been 'receaued by tradition from the Elders', Lambarde claimed, but was still spoken and 'faithfully credited of the vulgar sorte … and many of the aged remember it well'.[28] As far as Lambarde was concerned, such tales were evidence of the mingling of fact and fiction in the works of 'clerkly talewriters and fableforgers' and merely reflected the ongoing rivalry between the two pilgrimage sites. However, the role of the 'elders' and 'aged' in the perpetuation of myths was recognised by other writers. In the late seventeenth century, John Aubrey listened as the 'old men of Malmesbury' retold the *life* and miracles of St Adhelm, while a few decades later, Daniel Defoe heard the legend of St Chad repeated in Alcester and tales of King Arthur retold in Tintagel.[29] Indeed the bell of St Adhelm continued to be rung in Malmesbury in the seventeenth century to ward off lightning.[30] The survival of such legend in local tradition offers some indication of the problems faced by English evangelicals and reformers in purging the past of its legends of saints and miracles, while the memory of those saints and miracles remained very much alive in the popular traditions of the present.[31]

Discussion of the *lives* and the miracles of the saints and heroes of the medieval past did not come to an end with the suppression of the major national and regional cults by Henry VIII and Edward VI. Indeed the legacy of some of the most contested saints from the medieval past continued to be debated and disputed in the second half of the sixteenth century and beyond. Official and popular invective against the cult of St Thomas Becket in the 1530s had culminated in the destruction of the shrine of Becket at Canterbury and the obliteration of verbal and visual images of the saint from the English church and liturgy. However, Becket's reputation continued to be hotly contested, and the *life* and miracles of the archbishop were twisted to a variety of ends by writers on both sides of the confessional divide in the reign of Elizabeth.[32] The figure of the pope loomed large in evangelical polemic several decades after the break with Rome. Thomas Beard, in his description of the influence of Antichrist in the Roman church, drew upon examples which had been a staple of evangelical writings against the papacy in the 1530s and 1540s. Beard described several wonders associated with Silvester II, including the rattling of his bones in his tomb to foretell the death of the pope, and repeated the legend of the pact made between Silvester and the devil that had resulted in his promotion 'to the popedom by diabolical arts'. In his account of the pontificate of Gregory VII, Beard listed the miracles that had been commonly claimed for the pope, including his ability to send sparks of fire from his fingers.[33] The history of the pontificates of Silvester and Gregory presented in Beard's *Antichrist* detailed the same events and miracles that had dominated the history of their pontificates in medieval chronicles and in the works of Bale and Foxe.[34] The construction of a new ecclesiastical history in the middle decades of the sixteenth century exerted a powerful influence over later writing on the medieval popes, and the continued exploitation of images from the ecclesiastical past almost a century after the break with Rome suggests that the evangelical construct of the papal magician had become firmly rooted in the national memory. Indeed the timing of the publication of Barnaby Googe's *The popish kingdome or reign of Antichrist* (1570), a translation of Thomas Kirchmeyer's earlier work, suggests that the new Protestant mythology of the papacy had come to be recognised as a powerful polemical weapon in times of heated conflict between England and Rome. The repeated presentation of a narrative of papal magic and necromancy need not be seen as evidence of failure on the part of English evangelicals to expunge the name of the pope from the face of the national church, but rather as an indication of the extent to which new Protestant myths could be successfully constructed upon the foundations laid in medieval chronicles and hagiography.

The reputation of the holy men and women of the past could both help and hinder the progress of religious change. Where the history of the cult of the saints, or the memory of their miracles, remained ingrained in the local or national imagination, they appeared as a visible expression of a process of religious change that was as yet incomplete. Yet these same memories and legends could also become a powerful and persuasive tool in the construction of new religious identities and histories. Even where continuity appeared to be the abiding principle in religious practice, the messages inherent in apparently traditional images were often more complex than a basic survival of long-standing beliefs. The seven 'champions' of Christendom commemorated in a seventeenth-century ballad, 'Saint George for England, Saint Denis for France, Saint Patricke for Ireland … Saint Anthonie for Italie, Saint Iames … Saint Andrew for Scotland and Saint David for Wales', were not invoked as saintly protectors, but recast as classical heroes more appropriate to a culture purged of holy intercessors.[35] As Muriel McClendon has demonstrated, the traditional cult of a national saint might well survive in the reformed English church, but imbued with new and more appropriate meanings. The cult of St George, which had been a prominent feature of the celebrations of the pre-Reformation church in Norwich, underwent a process of transformation and reinvention at the hands of reformers and magistrates after its official suppression by Edward VI. Despite the reappearance of the feast of St George in the Elizabethan calendar, McClendon notes, the traditional pre-Reformation celebrations were not revived in the city. Instead, the commemoration of the saint was incorporated into a broader programme of civic events as part of a new city calendar in which local political landmarks dominated the ritual year. The fact that the original legend of St George had its origins in an invented fictional context facilitated this process of reconstruction in the aftermath of the Reformation. With a limited grounding in historical events, the cult of St George could be readily appropriated to changing political and religious circumstances.[36]

Likewise St Peter, whose cult had been criticised as part of the polemical assault upon the papal supremacy in the early years of the English Reformation, enjoyed something of a revival in the last decades of the sixteenth century. However, the reformed St Peter was not intended to serve as a defence for the primacy of Rome but rather as a model for reformed piety, a familiar figure whose reputation both created a sense of continuity with the past and acted as a conduit for the transmission of evangelical ideology.[37] The fluctuating fortunes of the cult and reputation of St Dunstan in Reformation England, as champion of the independence of the crown from the interference of Rome and as a prime example of the presence of magic and superstition in the *lives* and miracles of the saints, offer a clear demonstration of the multiple meanings that could be ascribed to individual figures in the history of the church in an age of religious turmoil.[38] Bridget Heal's study of Marian devotion in Protestant Nuremberg provides an indication of the potential for the transformation of superstition and idolatry into 'legitimate' devotion, once traditional images were reinterpreted to accommodate the doctrinal and social concerns of the reformers.[39] Even pilgrimage, that archetypal expression of devotion to the saints, survived the Reformation, albeit as a metaphor for the journey of the individual through life.[40] The continued presence of saints from the past in the life of the post-Reformation community could therefore reflect both the survival of symbols of traditional religion and the successful exploitation of those symbols in the service of religious reform. The traditional cult of the miracle-working saint appeared to have withered by the mid-sixteenth century, but the commemoration of the saint was to become an important part of the reformed civic calendar.

The assertion that the age of miracles had passed emerged was a commonplace in evangelical writing and preaching on the saints, but the continued discussion of the intrusion of the supernatural into the realm of the material represented more than just the survival of long-standing belief in the continuation of miracles in the post-apostolic church. Beliefs in portents, prodigies and providences were less the remnants of popular superstition than they were a central part of a reformed understanding of the relationship between the natural and the supernatural.[41] As Alexandra Walsham has suggested, providentialism was one area in which the Reformation did not simply eradicate elements of traditional religion but, rather, infused such beliefs with a greater intensity and exploited them in the service of confessional conflict.[42] Tensions between Catholic miracle and Protestant providence were softened in the construction of a reformed moralised universe in which the supernatural remained a potent and significant force. Where the understanding of the distinction between miracle and providence was uncertain, there was ample scope for the manipulation of traditional images of the miraculous as a vehicle for the dissemination of reformed theology. John Foxe vigorously defended the miracles of vengeance and judgement that had been visited upon those who had persecuted the true church, but would have been well aware that such miracles were a common *topos* in medieval hagiography. The familiarity of the image of the miraculous punishment of the wrongdoer enabled Foxe to shift the ground of truth and falsehood in the representation of what appeared to be the judgement of the Catholic persecutor at the hand of God. For Foxe, such wonders were testimony to the providential protection of the Protestant martyrs but, as Tom Freeman has argued, they also acted as an inspiration to the faithful to believe that there was a fairness and even-handedness in divine justice. In later editions of the *Actes and Monuments*, such providences served as a supernatural form of pastoral guidance, as punitive wonders were visited upon not only the persecutors but also the drunkards and adulterers.[43] The representation of medieval Catholicism as a religion of clerical conjurors and magic-working saints had been informed by the assertion that the age of true miracles had passed, but the traditional assumption that moral causes might have material effects was to remain a powerful pedagogic and persuasive tool.

The deployment of providential tales in the dissemination of religious change and moral reform had clear advantages for English evangelicals, but the repeated assertion that the age of miracles had passed was not merely a springboard for the discussion of divine intervention in defence of the Reformation. The traditional miracle, adjusted to accommodate the concerns and priorities of the reformed English church, enabled evangelical writers to clothe familiar images in new garb, but the argument for the cessation of miracles was part of a more general response to repeated Catholic accusations that the absence of miracles and wonders marked out the reformed church as the false church. Debate over the nature of the miraculous, and the identification of true and false miracles, was reinvigorated in the final decade of the sixteenth century by the publication of two accounts of the miracles that had been reported at the shrine of the Virgin in Halle and Montaigu in the Low Countries.[44] The author of the tracts, Justus Lispius, was a respected humanist scholar, and his description of the miracles worked by the Virgin in defence of Dutch Catholicism was an unwelcome addition to Reformation representations of the miraculous. Lipsius was occasionally critical of the miracles that had been claimed by visitors to the shrines, but his work, like that of the medieval hagiographers, was intended to inspire faith as much as record the historical event and therefore included the full panoply of wonders. Miracles of vengeance visited upon those who reviled or defaced the images of the Virgin provided precisely the kind of evidence of saintly intervention in defence of their cults that had been lacking in England in the 1530s, and the legends were hotly contested. The account of the miracles at Montaigu was translated for an English audience and dedicated to the king by Robert Chambers in 1606. In the same year, George Thomas produced a refutation of Lipsius' work, and three years later Robert Tynley issued a reply to Chambers in *Two Learned Sermons*. The miracles recorded by Lipsius and Chambers soon found their way into other controversial works and featured prominently in the debate between John Floyd and Richard Sheldon.[45]

Robert Chambers' account of the miracles at Montaigu opened with a bitter complaint that Scripture had been deliberately misinterpreted by Protestant heretics who had undermined the reputation of the saints and martyrs and cast aspersions upon the faith of the Fathers of the church. Miracles, he argued, had been a mark of the true church since the age of the Apostles and had continued to provide a sign of God's presence among the faithful. Medieval chroniclers had detailed the abundant miracles of the saints, miracles which had been essential to the propagation of the faith across Europe. In contrast, he alleged, the congregations of the heretics could present no evidence of true miracles in their church, but instead forged tales of 'diuers miracles' worked by their martyrs. At Halle and at Montaigu, however, God had 'powred down from heauen whole showres and streames of heavenly miracles' that provided ample testimony to the true faith of the Catholic church. An image of the Virgin had been seen to bleed copiously after a blow from a Calvinist sword, and those who had mocked the pilgrims to the shrine had themselves fallen lame. The miracles recorded at the shrine were a potent rejoinder to Protestant critics of the cult of the saints. Indeed Chambers suggested that the site had been chosen by God precisely because the miracles and pilgrims would be in full view of the Dutch heretics and might serve as the instrument of their reconversion to the Catholic faith.[46] Chambers' analysis had echoes in the views expressed by John Floyd in his debate with Edward Hoby. The miracles recorded at Halle were, he claimed, ample evidence of the truth of Catholic doctrine and wonders which might serve to 'dissolue the smoky mysts' raised by critics of the church. To divert attention from the lack of miracles worked among the heretics, he claimed, Hoby had attempted to disparage the miracles recorded at Halle and had repeated the 'toyes and trifles' claimed for English Protestant martyrs by Foxe and others.[47] The age of miracles might have passed, but miracles were to remain a source of conflict between Catholic and reformed, and provide valuable ammunition in polemical debate.

For evangelical writers, the miracles at Montaigu and Halle were simply the most recent evidence of the promotion of false wonders and false doctrine by the church of Rome. Robert Tynley's *Sermons* opened with a warning to the faithful to beware of false prophets, and the miracles recorded at Halle featured prominently in his denunciation of the feigned wonders of the false church. Where Chambers had pointed to evidence of the continued presence of miracles in the Catholic church in centuries past, Tynley argued that 'all such histories are fictions' and protested that his opponents had 'stuffed the historie of their saints' with implausible accounts of false miracles. Edward Hoby's *Curry-combe* denounced the 'forged and feigned fopperies' that had been described at Halle, and used this condemnation as an excuse to rehearse some of the miracles of the saints that had been condemned in evangelical histories in the 1540s and 1550s.[48] Richard Sheldon's *Survey of the Miracles of the Church of Rome* also took a broad chronological sweep and included, not only a response to the miracles claimed by Floyd for the shrine at Halle, but also a more general history of the wonders attributed to the saints of the medieval church.[49] Sheldon repeated some of the more popular miracles from the *Golden Legend*, and dismissed as mere fictions the multitude of miracles that had been claimed for the saints. The *Golden Legend* itself, he suggested, was collection of 'copper fables', 'fond lyes and imaginations', which had been feigned by the clergy for material gain.[50] Many of the miracles of the saints condemned by Sheldon were familiar; he repeated, for example, the claim that Gregory VII was able to throw sparks of fire, as part of a comparison between the wonders of the saints and the miracles described in biblical prophecies of Antichrist. Other miracles, he claimed, were so humorous as to betray their false origins. Claims that St Hyacinth had raised a calf to life, that St Dominic had convinced a devil to hold a candle for so long that his fingers were singed or that St Anthony had once preached to an audience of devout fish, Sheldon suggested, were a ridiculous proof of doctrine.[51] While the publication of work of Lipsius and Chambers might well have been responsible for igniting a new interest in the miracles of the saints, the repetition of miracles from the *lives* of the medieval saints in evangelical polemic at the turn of the seventeenth century suggests that images from the past still had a powerful resonance in the present. The *Golden Legend*, which provided much of the material for Sheldon's history of the Catholic miraculous, did not enjoy an extensive publishing history in Reformation England, but the *lives* of the saints that it contained were clearly not so far removed from popular consciousness as to be meaningless referents in polemical debate.

The vigour with which the debate over miracles was conducted in the decades after the Reformation reflected not only the importance attached to the false wonders of saints in evangelical histories of the medieval church but also the determination with which the Catholic church and its propagandists defended the *lives*, legends and miracles of the saints. Humanist and evangelical criticisms of the cult of the saints had placed the issue in the foreground of doctrinal controversy, and the role of the saints and their miracles in the life of the church was debated at the Council of Trent. A *Decree on the invocation, veneration, and relics of saints, and on sacred images* was issued in the 25th session of the Council (1563). The decree was a broad and forceful defence of traditional Catholic practice. The council confirmed that the cult of the saints sat 'agreeably to the useage of the Catholic and Apostolic church received from the primitive times of the Christian religion', and instructed the faithful

> diligently concerning the intercession and invocation of saints; the honour (paid) to relics; and the legitimate use of images: teaching them, that the saints, who reign together with Christ, offer up their own prayers to God for men; that it is good and useful suppliantly to invoke them, and to have recourse to their prayers, aid, (and) help for obtaining benefits from God, through His Son, Jesus Christ our Lord, who is our alone Redeemer and Saviour.

The bodies and relics of the martyrs were to be venerated by the faithful, and the council condemned those who opposed the practice of pilgrimage. Images of the saints were to be retained in churches as an inspiration to faithful imitation, as a means by which the mind might be turned to the contemplation of higher things and as a commemoration of the wonders and miracles that God had worked through His saints. In a passage that attempted to ensure that the cult of the saints would no longer be open to abuse, the council demanded that

> every superstition shall be removed, all filthy lucre be abolished; finally, all lasciviousness be avoided; in such wise that figures shall not be painted or adorned with a beauty exciting to lust; nor the celebration of the saints, and the visitation of relics be by any perverted into revellings and drunkenness; as if festivals are celebrated to the honour of the saints by luxury and wantonness.

No new images were to be introduced into local churches without official consent, and no new miracles were to be acknowledged, or new relics recognised, without the approval of the local bishop.[52] The Council of Trent conceded no theological ground to the evangelicals on the question of the intercession and miracles of the saints, but the decree issues in 1563 perhaps reflected a growing awareness of the need to bring the popular devotions associated with the saints under the control of the church, while defending the cult of saints and relics from accusations of superstition and idolatry.

The 1563 decree was accompanied by a more general reform of the cult of the saints, in which the influence of the institutional church was brought to bear upon local cults and traditions. In the decades after Trent, the process of canonisation was tightened, a new breviary, missal and martyrology were issued, the liturgical calendar was vigorously pruned and a Congregation for Sacred Rites and Ceremonies established. By the end of the fifteenth century, the sheer quantity of feast days celebrated in the church had come to dominate the liturgical year. The institution of some 200 new feasts in the period between 1100 and 1558 had required that several days be set aside for the commemoration of multiple feasts, but the reform of the breviary left over 150 days clear of festivals. The new calendar was dominated by the feasts of the uncontested martyrs of the early church, with a preponderance of saints from the city of Rome itself.[53] Efforts were also made to control the circulation of the relics of the saints. However, amid the turmoil of religious division, relics were vigorously promoted as evidence of continuity between the past and the present, and the opening of the catacombs had certainly created a plentiful supply of new relics for the missionary church. Attempts were made to ensure that all relics sent out from Rome were provided with a notice of their authenticity but, as Trevor Johnson has noted, the veneration of the relics of St Anonymous might suggest that the process was not altogether foolproof.[54]

Evangelical pressure upon the theology and practice that underpinned the veneration of the saints has been seen as the root cause of a 'crisis of canonisation' in the middle decades of the sixteenth century; the last papal canonisation before Trent took place in 1523, and no further saints were created until 1588. The canonisation of St Didacus in 1588 hardly opened the floodgates and, when compared to the new cults of the high Middle Ages, the numbers of saints recognised by the universal church remained low throughout the early modern period, with six canonisations in the sixteenth century, 24 in the seventeenth and 29 in the eighteenth.[55] The canonisation process was placed under stringent scrutiny. Pope Sixtus V's foundation of the Sacred Congregation of Rites created a central body responsible for the promotion of universal uniformity in the externals of worship and with control over the processes of beatification and canonisation. The articulation of papal demands for greater control over the creation of saints culminated in the decrees of Urban VIII, issued in 1625 and 1634. Urban ordained that no religious *cultus* should be paid to any person recently deceased, however great their virtue and numerous their miracles, and prohibited the honouring of any person as a saint without the consent of the pope. The decree of 1634 also forbade both the publication of literature describing the miracles and visions of the aspiring saint without papal or episcopal approval, and the representation of any individual with the nimbus of sanctity, other than the beatified or canonised.

The expansion of papal authority over the creation of new saints was accompanied by a developing interest in the histories and *lives* of the saints of the past. As the process by which saints were recognised came to be dictated by the presentation of valid evidence that testified to the holiness, orthodoxy and miracles of the individual, so the post-Tridentine authors of hagiographical texts demanded that the *life* of a saint be subjected to a similar process of investigation and verification. Such efforts were to bear fruit in the writings of the Bollandists and in the emergence of a more critical, even scientific genre of saintly biography.[56] The *lives* of the saints were still intended to inspire devotion and imitation but were to be provided where possible with a more solid grounding in history and reality. The divergence between saint and legend which had been ruthlessly exploited by evangelical opponents of the cult of the saints was also recognised by those who sought to reform from within the popular legends of the medieval saints. A formal report addressed to Pius V warned that the *lives* of the saints included much that was apocryphal, even evidently untrue, and in 1592 Cardinal Bellarmine concluded that the established corpus of hagiography perpetuated long-standing errors that had been uncorrected for centuries.[57] Despite his misgivings about the content of the *lives* of the saints, however, Bellarmine was one of the most determined defenders of the importance of relics and miracles in the life of the church and in the battle to regain ground that had been lost to the Reformation. The importance of the cult of the saints to the theology and piety of the church, and the key role that might be played in the promotion of Catholicism by the saints, their relics and their miracles, was not lost upon the Tridentine church. Concerns that the miracles of the saints that were recorded and celebrated in their legends and cults should be verifiable certainly did not result in a diminution of enthusiasm for the miraculous on the part of either hagiographers or missionaries.[58] Jesuit Mariology was rather more subdued than late-medieval homiletic on the life of the Virgin, but the value of the example of Mary in the inculcation of a popular piety based upon obedience, humility and inward experience was widely exploited.[59] The printed accounts of the miracles at Montaigu and Halle that circulated in England were but one visible manifestation of attempts to regain the saints, their images and their miracles for the Catholic church.

The religious turmoil of the sixteenth century had not only thrust the cult of the saints into the spotlight of religious debate but had also animated the already bitter controversy over sanctity, history and the miraculous by creating a new generation of martyrs. After several centuries in which the figure of the confessor-saint had dominated perceptions of holiness, the sixteenth century saw the revival of the cult of the martyr and the reinvigoration of debates over the nature of martyrdom and suffering for the faith. Where Catholic writers attempted to denigrate Protestant theologies and martyrs by drawing parallels between the views of the reformers and the beliefs of condemned heretics, Reformation polemicists turned medieval opponents of the church into proto-Protestants and downplayed any internal inconsistencies in this new historical scheme.[60] The composition of reformed martyrologies by Bale and Foxe in England, Jean Crespin in France, and Adriaan van Haemstede in the Low Countries emphasised the continuity between the early Christian martyrs, those persecuted by the medieval church and those who died in defence of the Reformation.[61] Perhaps the most obvious example of the representation of the evangelical martyr as the heir to the apostolic tradition is to be seen in John Bale's account of the examination and death of Anne Askew, late in the reign of Henry VIII. Bale located Askew within a broad narrative of ecclesiastical history and associated her suffering with the death of the martyrs of the early church, particularly the second-century martyr Blandina, who had died after a steadfast defence of her faith. Set against the backdrop of the persecution of the early church, the *life* and death of Anne Askew not only acquired a historical perspective but also provided a link in Bale's chain of witnesses to the true faith in the past and present.[62] The narrative of the death of Anne Askew, and the suffering of the Marian martyrs in Foxe's *Actes and Monuments*, reflected this same concern to position the martyrs of the Reformation within the broader context of Christian martyrdom. Foxe's description of the deaths of Ridley and Latimer resonated with images culled from the accounts of the suffering of the early Christian martyrs, while his narrative of Cranmer's martyrdom concluded with the assertion that the archbishop was more worthy to 'bee numbred amongst *CHRISTES* Martyrs' than St Thomas Becket.[63] The iconoclastic attitude of evangelical writers towards the saints of the medieval church was accompanied by a vigorous attempt to reclaim early models of sanctity as the foundations for a new ecclesiastical history.

The representation of the Askew, Cranmer and other Reformation martyrs as the imitators and successors of the martyrs of the early church allowed Bale and Foxe to graft the reputation of those who had died in defence of the Reformation onto a widely recognised model of heroic conduct with a long-established pedigree. The dignity of the Protestant martyr was articulated both in their actions and in the degree to which these actions conformed to the patterns of sanctity and martyrdom that had been established in the first Christian centuries. In the same way that medieval hagiographers had used the *lives* of earlier saints to validate the life and miracles of their subject, so Reformation martyrology used the *lives* of the early martyrs as a precedent for the suffering of the 'true church' in the present. Comparisons between the martyrs of the primitive church and those of more recent times served to anchor the events of the Reformation more firmly within the evangelical narrative of the ecclesiastical past, and mediated their message through familiar forms and structures of writing. As Damian Nussbaum has demonstrated, the Kalendar of martyrs printed in the *Actes and Monuments* provided the ideal means with which to ridicule and reject the popish saints of the past while at the same time exploiting the traditional format of the calendar to define and promote the character of the reformed English church. The Kalendar was both a commentary upon the ecclesiastical past and a pattern and inspiration for the future.[64] Its basic format was comfortably familiar, and the Kalendar included the festivals that were sanctioned in the Prayer Book calendar. However, the empty dates were filled with the names of Protestant martyrs, ranging in the 1583 edition from the famous (Wycliffe and Bucer) to the obscure ('an old man of Buckinghamshire'). The Kalendar effectively 'unsainted' the heroes of the medieval church and, by replacing them with the martyrs of the Reformation, laid bare the shape of the new evangelical history of the church. The appropriation for the Reformation of texts and images that were associated with the Catholic cult of the saints was a powerful weapon of persuasion, which at the same instance revealed the depth of the fracture between the past and the present and served to bridge that gap by linking evangelicalism with the faith and practice of the primitive church.

Neither Foxe's kalendar nor the image of martyrdom represented in evangelical histories of the Reformation went unchallenged. Writing in the reign of Mary Tudor, Miles Huggarde complained that his evangelical opponents had elevated their heroes to the status of martyr and had attached legends and miracles to the narratives of their death in order to promote them as saints. Evangelical criticisms of the relics of the saints, he suggested, were more than matched by the enthusiasm of those who gathered the remains of the martyrs from the ashes. Huggarde mocked those who had derided the miracles recorded in the *lives* of the saints and yet were all too willing to see the miraculous in the death of English martyrs. Claims that the Holy Spirit had appeared in the form of a dove at the death of Rogers were mere fancy, he suggested, and volunteered that the incident might be better explained as the flight of pigeons driven from their nests by the smoke.[65] Nicholas Harpsfield was strident in his criticisms of the Kalendar in the *Actes and Monuments*, and complained bitterly that Foxe had usurped for himself the authority of the pope to create saints in his deliberate parody of the red and black lettering of the traditional calendar.[66] Both Robert Parsons and Thomas Stapleton echoed Huggarde's complaint in their accusations that evangelical writers had claimed for their false martyrs the same miracles that they had refused to accept in the *lives* of the saints.[67] Parsons protested that Foxe had made 'diuers wicked blasphemous and distracted men to be of his martyrs and patro[n]s in heauen', and endeavoured to break apart the links that bound together the martyrs of the Reformation martyrs by highlighting differences in opinion in crucial matters of doctrine. Barnes, Garrett and Jerome, Parsons suggested, were unlikely to find themselves welcome bedfellows, given their varying views on the theology of the eucharist.[68] Foxe's Kalendar was reprinted in the *Treatise of the Three Conversions*, as Parsons set the saints and histories of the two churches side by side as a stark demonstration of the chasm that existed between truth and falsehood. Where the saints of the Catholic church were monks, priests, doctors and virgins, the saints of the Protestant calendar, he claimed, were mere artisans, heretics and incontinent priests.[69] The controversy unleashed by the form and content of the Kalendar in the *Actes and Monuments* suggests that sanctity, albeit shorn of its miraculous and intercessory powers, still exerted a powerful influence over hearts and minds, not least in the creation and perpetuation of religious division.

The exploitation of such traditional images in the service of the Reformation was testimony to the continued influence of the past in the invention of an identity and culture for the post-Reformation church. However, if the construction of reformed calendars and martyrologies upon the foundations of traditional Catholic texts was a potent polemic weapon, so too was the vacuum created by the abrogation of the feasts of the saints, the suppression of cults and pilgrimages and the possibility that new myths might be created from old legends. Participation in the destruction of images and shrines inculcated in individuals a sense that they had been involved in the work of the Reformation; as Margaret Aston has noted, the practice of laying altar stones as paving slabs in churches provided a visible reminder of the break with the past and broadened participation in the destruction of the old religion through the simple act of walking upon the sacred objects of the past.[70] Whether they were making a virtue out of a necessity, or deliberately engaging in acts of iconoclastic destruction, those who removed fixtures, fittings and fabric from the monasteries in the late 1530s had become involved in the process by which the face of the English church was transformed.[71] The 'bare ruin'd choirs' of English monasticism not only stood as a memorial to the cloistered life but also as a visible reminder of the speed and effectiveness with which the monasteries had been suppressed. The empty and broken tombs of the saints were a reminder of the passing of the heroes and legends of the past and of the shattering of myths and superstitions by the iconoclasm of the Reformation. When John Lyly described the arrival of two pilgrims in Canterbury, the shrine of Becket had long since been removed, but the void left by the disappearance of visible monuments to the past remained imposing nonetheless.[72] The English landscape, both architectural and topographical, not only bore the marks of cultural change but also imprinted these changes upon the collective memory.

The passage of the year continued to be punctuated by the names and feasts of the saints in the decades after the break with Rome. Legal terms still operated on the timetable laid down by the festivals of the pre-Reformation church and the sessions of ecclesiastical courts followed in the footprints of the saints and feasts of the old church. Printed almanacs continued to use the feast days of the saints as familiar markers in the passage of time throughout the sixteenth century.[73] The willingness of their readers to rely upon landmarks provided by the old church while participating in the devotions of the new is suggestive of a syncretic religious culture in which apparently competing world views were able to overlap and intersect despite their inherent contradiction. Just as the survival of sections of monastic buildings cannot be seen as evidence of the survival of that same eremitic impulse that had inspired successive generations of monks, so the enduring presence of the saints in word and image cannot always provide testimony to an enduring belief in the intercession and miracles of the holy men and women of the past. The polemical writings of English evangelicals had established in print an image of a true church and a false, a spiritual division between truth and error that had its physical embodiment in doctrinal conflict, religious persecution and the construction and defence of competing orthodoxies. It is clear that the desacralisation of Catholic space and time did not immediately create a reformed religious culture, but neither did the continued exploitation of the images and legends of saints and popes reflect the simple survival of traditional beliefs surrounding saints, miracles, images and relics in the reformed English church.

The verbal and visual images of saints, popes and miracles were not expunged from the religious lexicon but, were rather, appropriated, reformed and deployed in the service of the English Reformation. Throughout the history of the church, the *lives* and legends of the saints had not only acted as cultural indicators, reflecting the priorities of the society that had produced them, but had also served as the means by which new models of holiness and piety had been planted in Christian society. Traditional, familiar images had been repeatedly exploited as a means of promulgating and legitimating the new, and the era of the Reformation was to be no different. The rejection of the traditions of the past was accompanied by the creation of a new history and, in the process of constructing a new narrative of the past, familiar emblems and images were once more pressed into service, reinvented or reformed. Religious divisions acted as a spur to historical research and writing in the sixteenth century, but the past that was exposed in the works of evangelical history writers was one which was both fashioned and formative. Saints traded places with sinners, heroes with villains, in the creation of a plausible and persuasive past for the English church. The miracles that dominated the pages of medieval hagiography were dismissed as magic in the pages of evangelical polemic, but the assertion that the age of miracles had passed did not preclude the discussion and repetition of saintly wonders and divine providences in defence of a national church that proclaimed itself devoid of such wonders. The vigorous rejection of the universal authority of the bishop of Rome was accompanied by the detailed investigation of the history of the medieval papacy and the construction of a narrative of the ecclesiastical past which ensured a prominent position for the popes in the history of the national church. If it was in the person of the saint that the many worlds of medieval religion coalesced, it was also in the person of the saint that Reformation debates over history, miracle and magic coincided. In a turn of phrase that encapsulated the crux of the debate over history and sanctity, Robert Bellarmine concluded that the authority of the pope to judge a heretic derived from his authority to judge a saint. The distinction between sanctity and heresy lay in the eye of the beholder and, for Bellarmine, ultimate authority rested with the pope. For evangelical writers, however, the distinction between sanctity and heresy, true and false religion in the present required a re-examination of the underlying assumptions that had shaped history and hagiography in centuries past. The iconoclasm of the English Reformation, it has been suggested, made forgetfulness the 'central sacrament' of doctrinal change.[74] Edwardian Injunctions issued in 1547 demanded the removal of 'all shrines … pictures, painting and all other monuments of feigned miracles, pilgrimage, idolatry and superstition; *so that there remain no memory of the same* in walls, glass-windows, or elsewhere within their church or houses'. In the determination to ensure that 'no memory of the same' remained, a new narrative of the sacred past was constructed, a narrative in which shrines, images and feigned miracles played a prominent part. If the memory of popes, saints and miracles survived, it was a memory which was coloured and imbued with a radically different interpretation by the generation of evangelical polemicists who had constructed a new history for the national church in England.

NOTES

1 INTRODUCTION

1 For an introduction to the cult of the saints in medieval religion see Brown 1981; Abou-el-Haj 1994; Wilson 1993; Weinstein and Bell 1982; Finucane 1995; Vauchez 1997; Heffernan 1988; Scribner 1987, Chapter 1; Duffy 1992, Chapter 5.

2 See for example the presentation of the offerings left at shrines as an indication of the continued vitality of the cult of the saints (Bernard 1998; Watts 1998; Whiting 1989). For an analysis of the changing levels of offerings made at shrines and images see Duffy 1992; Duffy 2002; Finucane 1995; Sargent 1986.

3 Wycliffe 1922; Jones 1973; Phillips 1973; McHardy 1972; Tanner 1977; Hudson 1978; Swinburn 1917; Aston 1984, 1988, 1993b.

4 Muller 1933.

5 Huizinga 1954: 177.

6 For example Dickens 1989.

7 Duffy 1992; Duffy 2002; Haigh 1993; Scarisbrick 1984; Kumin 1986; Brown 1995; Litzenberger 1997.

8 Hutton 1990; Whiting 1989; Whiting 1982; Walsham 1993: 17. Shagan 2003: 25 argues, for example, that 'the English Reformation was not done to the people, it was done with the people'; Duffy 1992; Haigh 1993; Scarisbrick 1984.

9 See especially Bernard 1998.

10 Bernard 1998; Marshall 2003; Heming 2003.

11 See especially Heming 2003; Marshall 1995, 2003; Scully 2002; Parish 2001.

12 On the representation of Henry VIII as David see Rex 1993; on Edward as Josiah see King 1982, 1989; Bradshaw 1996; Aston 1993a; White 1963.

13 For a useful discussion of the relationship between word and image in the English Reformation see Cummings 2002.

14 Betteridge 1997, 1999; Bynum 1978; Cameron 1993; Davies 1987; Freeman 1997, 2000; Freeman and Wall 2001; Knott 1993.

15 Fairfield 1971.

16 Levy 1967; McKisack 1971.

17 Bouwsma 1990; Cressy 1989; Gordon 1996; Greenblatt 1980; Gregory 1998; Hadfield 1994; Helgerson 1992; Kelley and Sachs 1997; Mason 1997; Pocock 1985; Williams 1970.

18 Anderson 1984; Koebner 1953; Levin 1980, 1988; Lock 1996.

19 Alford 2002; see also Davies 2002; Bradshaw 1999.

20 See for example Jones 1981; and particularly Pineas 1962a, b, 1964, 1968, 1972, 1975b, 1980.

21 Leland 1549, 1964; Flower 1935; McCusker 1936; Robinson 1998; Wright 1951; see

Chapter 2 below.
22 Woolf 2003; see also Woolf 2000.
23 Fox 2000; see also Fox 1996; Thomas 1984; Harris 1995.
24 Fox 2000; Chapter 4 highlights, for example, the legends which grew up around wells, trees and prominent geological landmarks.
25 See, for example Parish and Naphy 2003.
26 Bruhn 2002; Sacks 1986; McClendon 1999.
27 Nussbaum 1998.
28 Walsham 1999: 231–2; see also Buell 1950; Kay 1999; Walker 1988.
29 See Chapter 2 below.
30 Thomas 1991: 45–57.
31 See for example Clark 1993, 1997; Daston 1999; Eamon 1983, 1994; Sluhovsky 1995; Vogler 1972; Webster 1995.
32 See Chapter 2 below.
33 See Chapter 3 below.
34 For a discussion of Reformation attitudes to Becket and Dunstan, see Chapter 5 below; Parish 2001.
35 See Chapter 6 below.
36 See for example Weinstein and Bell 1982: 239–4; Finucane 1995.
37 Olsen 1980: 407; Wilson 1983: 1; Gibbon 1952: I.467, Colgrave 1958: 42; Power 1914; Graus 1965.
38 Heffernan 1988: 20, 116–7.
39 Heffernan 1988: 7; see also Walter Daniel's *life* of Ailred of Rievaulx, Olsen 1980: 410.
40 Heffernan 1988: 22–34; Stancliffe 1990; Delehaye 1962.
41 Heffernan 1988: 3–4.
42 Olsen 1980: 410; Heffernan 1988: 14; Weinstein and Bell 1982.
43 Delehaye 1962; Farrar 1973: 84; Heffernan 1988: 5–6. As an example of the incorporation of alien materials into the *life* of the saint, Delehaye, highlighted SS Barlaam and Joasaph, whose legends were effectively a Christianised version of the life of Buddha. Delehaye 1962: 51.
44 Kern 1994: 412–6; Delooz 1983: 194–9; Burke 1984: 45.
45 Brown 1981; Sox 1985: 9; Sumption 1975: 22; on early medieval pilgrimage see Webb 2002; Sumption 1975.
46 J.M. McCulloh 1975; Sumption 1975: 23; Webb 2002; Finucane 1995: 18–20; Brown 1977: 3–4; Wilson 1983.
47 *Acta Sanctorum* 1643–1867: May.
48 Finucane 1995: 27–33; Sumption 1975: 27–31; Sox 1985: 15–16, 56.
49 There is an extensive and informative body of literature on the medieval cult of the saints. See for example Weinstein and Bell 1982; Vauchez 1997; Delooz 1969; Sorokin 1950; Blumenfeld-Kosinksi and Szell 1991; Heffernan 1988: 41, 152ff; Mecklin 1941; Finucane 1995; Hertling 1933; Goodich 1982; Walker Bynum 1987; Cazelles 1991; Horstman 1901; Bokenham 1938; Golden Legend 1527. On the development of the official canonisation process, see Woodward 1996; Burke 1984; Blaher 1949.
50 Heffernan 1988: 253 suggests that virginity eventually came to eclipse martyrdom as the most worthy form of 'imitatio Christi'.
51 For a further discussion see Geary 1978: 5–7.
52 Brown 1977: 14; see also Geary 1978: 5–7.
53 Geary 1983.
54 Finucane 1995; Ward 1987; Murray 1992; Frazer 1993; Thorndike 1923–58; Flint 1991; Malowinski 1948; Kieckhefer 1994b; Jolly *et al.* 2002.
55 Hilton 1516: 4.

56 Mirk 1905.

57 On the importance of miracle to the canonisation process, see Cheney and Semple 1953: 27–8.

58 Several saints, for example, engaged in miraculous duels with their opponents, including Augustine of Canterbury and St Berach: Bede 1907: I.25. Other saints performed miracles that had scriptural precedent. Morse 1975: 77, for example, describes Erkenwald parting the waters of the Thames. For helpful discussion of medieval ecclesiastical attitudes to the miraculous see Ward 1987; Heffernan 1988: Chapter 3; Brown 1967: 413–8; Daston 1999; Clark 1997. Key contributions are to be found in Augustine of Hippo 1990; *De Civitate Dei* 22:8; Aquinas 1928: c.II, III.ii.65ff; 1947: I.520; Forester 1863; Caesarius 1851; John of Salisbury 1909.

59 Augustine of Hippo 1990; *De Civitate Dei* 10:9; Clark 1997: 167; Herzog 1931; Kieckhefer 1994, 2000, 35ff; Murray 1992; Jolly, Raudvere and Peters 2002.

60 Aaron transformed his rod into a serpent before the Pharaoh, and Pharaoh's magicians did the same, only to see their rods consumed by Aaron's serpent. A similar clash between prophet and magician is recorded in I Kings 18.

61 Acts 8:9–24.

62 Kieckhefer 1994a; Herzog 1931: 140 argues, for example, that 'magic is always other people's faith'; Remus 1983.

63 Among the most useful surveys of Christian attitudes to magic are Jolly *et al.* 2002; Kieckhefer 1994a; Murray 1997; MacNeill and Gamer 1990; Gurevich 1988. Biblical prohibitions of magic are numerous: Leviticus 20:6, 27; Deuteronomy 13; 1 Sam 15:23; 1 Cor 10:20; 2 Thess 2; 1 Tim 4:1. See also Augustine of Hippo 1990; *City of God*: 9; Origen 1953: II.51; Bede 1907: I.25; and the condemnation of magic and clerical magic at the synods of Elvira (309), Carthage (398) and Orleans (511).

64 Talbot 1954; Bede 1940: 184.

65 For the role played by miracles in attracting converts to Christianity see MacMullen 1983; Rydberg 1879: Chapter 2; Colgrave 1935. Augustine claimed to have been impressed by the miracles that were worked at the shrines of Protasius and Gervasius in Milan, prior to his own conversion, and quickly perceived the value of the relics of the saints and their miracles in the propagation of the faith in North Africa. See Finucane 1995: 18–20. Augustine produced an account of the miracles worked by the relics of St Stephen after their translation: Thomas 1991: 25–6.

66 Kieckhefer 2000: 35; see for example the story of Ananias and Sapphira in Acts 5; Brown 1970: 28; Finucane 1995: 17; Frazer 1993: 460.

67 Murray 1992: 192; Flint 1991: 359–64; Wilson 2000: xxviii; Frazer 1993: 460ff.

68 Jolly *et al.* 2002; Clark 1997: 552; see also Brown 1970; Kee 1983.

69 Bartlett 1986; Franz 1909: II, 364ff.

70 Thomas 1991: Chapter 2. See also the discussion between Thomas and Geertz over the nature of religion and magic: Thomas 1975; Geertz 1975; Gentilcore 1992, 1998; Cameron 1998: 165; Jolly et al. 2002: 2; Flint 1991; Klaniczay 1990; Hill and Swan 1998; Dinzelbacher 1990.

71 Klaniczay 1990, 1997: 241–2; Kieckhefer 1994a; Kleinberg 1989.

72 Kieckhefer 1994a: 356–8. The dispute over the sanctity and historical reputation of Joan of Arc provides another example: Jones 1980.

73 Klaniczay 1997: 49–65.

74 See Chapters 3, 4 and 5 below for a full discussion of these themes.

75 Brown 1977: 2.

76 See Chapter 6 below.

77 See Chapter 5 below.

78 For a complete discussion of the uncomfortable relationship between historians and hagiography see pp. 17–20 below. On the controversy between Tyndale and More see

for example Daniell 1994: 250–280; Butterworth and Chester 1962; Fox 1993; Harris 1940.

79 King 1982; King 1966–7; Duffy 1992: 459–60; Davies 1987; Greenblatt 1980.

80 Rex 1989; Baskerville 1979; Clebsch 1980: 25ff; Gillett 1932; Loach 1975; Loades 1964.

81 See for example Watt 1991; Spufford 1981; Myers and Harris 1990; Cressy 1997; Barry 1995; Walsham 1999, Chapter 1.

2 'BROUGHTE OWTE OF DEADLY DARKENES TO LYVELY LIGHTE'

1 For further discussion of the construction of Protestant history and identity see Gordon 1996; Bouwsma 1990; Fussner 1962; Hadfield 1994; Helgerson 1992; Levine 1987a; Woolf 2000, 2003.

2 Hobsbawm and Ranger 1992: 4–5.

3 Hobsbawm and Ranger 1992: 1–2. This same interest in the reinvention of the past in periods of upheaval can be identified at the turn of the first millennium: 'when traditional relationships between past and present break down, those most affected by this rupture respond by reshaping an understanding of that which unites past and present in terms of some new continuity in order to defend themselves from the effects of this rupture': Geary 1994· 8

4 Southern 1962: 50; Ridyard 1987, 1988.

5 For the enduring influence of, for example, the miracles associated with William of Malmesbury in the seventeenth century see Fox 2000: 232.

6 Rhegius 1537: C6r; Bacon 1892: III.288. Juan Luis Vives, in *De Causis Corruptarum Artium*, Antwerp, 1531, Chapter 2, claimed that medieval hagiography was more subjective than truthful.

7 Owst 1965: 115.

8 Delehaye 1962: 53–60; Heffernan 1988: 13–20. The store of exempla exploited by medieval hagiographers included christianised biographies of holy figures from other traditions. The desire to ground the cult of the saints on more reliable foundations was the primary motivation behind the work of the Bollandists (Delehaye 1922).

9 Collinson 1997: 37.

10 Congar 1966: 86–9; on the idea of 'sacred text' outside Scripture see Ditchfield 1995.

11 Williams 1970: 8.

12 Bale 1550b: I.A4v.

13 Letters and Papers VI 1077, VII 776, IX 846, X 365; Levin 1988: 70; Jaech 1985: 296; Lock 1996.

14 Hay 1952: 111–2, 153. Levy 1967: 56–61. Polydore's *De Inventoribus Rerum* (1499) had also charted the history of profane and Christian customs, some of which (for example images, relics and clerical celibacy) were to feature heavily in the debates of the Reformation.

15 25 Henry VIII, cap. 19.

16 Flower 1932: 47.

17 Leland 1549: A2r–6r. For a further discussion of these themes see Alford 2002: 5ff.

18 Bacon 1927: 2.

19 For a discussion of Tyndale's approach to history and its influence on later writers see Pineas 1962a, b, c.

20 Williams 1970: 23.

21 Levin 1988: 75; Pineas 1968: 120ff; Levin 1988: 83.

22 See Chapter 6 below.

23 Fairfield 1976: 58.

24 Fairfield 1976: 8, 50–58. Bale's sympathy with the evangelical cause would seem to

date from the early 1530s. In 1531 he was alleged to have denied the real presence of Christ in the eucharist, and in 1534 was examined by Archbishop Lee under suspicion that he held unorthodox attitudes to the lives of the saints. There are few sympathetic biographies of Bale, although a number of attempts have been made to chart his career and interpret his dramatic and prose writings. See for example Fairfield 1976; McCusker 1942; Harris 1940; Pineas 1962d; Bauckham 1978.

25 Hadfield 1994: 51; Harris 1940: 13. King 1982: 61 notes that Bale was little read by the end of the sixteenth century.

26 *Pammachius* was performed at Christ's College, Cambridge, in Lent 1545, and the anti-papal satire was sufficiently blatant to encourage Gardiner to approach the vice chancellor to demand an investigation of the circumstances which surrounded the performance.

27 Hadfield 1994: 55. An abbreviated version of Bale's commentary on Revelation appeared in the English Bibles printed by John Day in the reign of Edward VI, the Matthew Bible of 1551 and the marginal notes to Revelation in the Geneva Bible of 1560. The *Image* was reprinted four times in the reigns of Edward VI and Elizabeth, and cited by John Foxe, Thomas Cranmer and John Hooper (see Bauckham 1978: 22; Davis 1940).

28 For further detail on Silvester II and Bale's depiction of his role in the loosing of Satan see Chapter 6 below. Bale was not the first writer to emphasise the significance of the millennium in this way. The Lollard *Fasciculi Zizaniorum* claimed that the church had been in error since the end of the first millennium, and John Wycliffe also identified this as a crucial period in the history of the church. Bauckham 1978: 28; Fairfield 1976: 70.

29 Bauckham 1978: 23. Joachim's work may well have been available to Bale via Sebastian Meyer's commentary on the Apocalypse.

30 Firth 1979: 52.

31 Bale 1543, 1544; Fairfield 1976: 88.

32 For a more detailed discussion of the debates over clerical marriage during the Reformation in England see Parish 2000a; Carlson 1994.

33 Bale 1551: I.A5v-6r; 1553: B4v; Pineas 1962a, b, 1972, 1980.

34 Bale 1551: I.C7v.

35 Bale 1546: A6v-7r.

36 Bale 1551: I.D6v. There are clear echoes of Tyndale in Bale's analysis of the English past, and particularly in the assertion that the English clergy had fomented rebellion against the legitimate authority of the king (Tyndale 1573: 181, 364, 374ff; Pineas 1962a).

37 Bale 1557: 19.

38 Bale 1548c: 13v (Joseph), 106 (Grosseteste), 154 (Wycliffe).

39 McCusker 1942: xi.

40 Leland 1549: E1v-2, F3.

41 McCusker 1942: 32–47; Bale 1553.

42 The contents of Bale's library have been listed by McCusker 1936, 1942, and include many of the sources used by Bale in the *Votaries*, and indeed by his contemporaries, including Matthew Parker. See 65–76 below.

43 *Calendar of State Papers Relating to Ireland 1509–1573*: I.158.

44 Levin 1988: 114. For further information on Foxe and the history of the *Actes and Monuments* see Mozley 1940; Haller 1963; Loades 1997; Freeman 2004, 2004a; Collinson 2004.

45 Freeman 2004 provides the best recent overview.

46 Foxe 1570: I.2v. Two further editions followed in Foxe's lifetime (1576, 1583). For the publishing history of the *Actes and Monuments* see Haller 1963; Freeman 2004.

47 Haller 1963: 141.

48 Bale 1546, 1547; Haverfield 1896.

49 Bale cited the example of Alban, Julius and Emerita in his list of 'true' martyrs: Bale 1547: 3r-v.

50 Bede 1907, Chapter 4. A fuller discussion of the Lucius legend and its place in the controversies of the Reformation may be found in Felicity Heal's forthcoming article in *English Historical Review*.

51 The *Magdeburg Centuriators* were not the first to attempt to construct a history that met the demands of confessional polemic. Others worthy of note include Johannes Sleidan's *Commentaries* (1555) which located German history against an international backdrop, Heinrich Bullinger's history of the Swiss Confederation to 1519 and history of the Reformation in Switzerland 1519–32, Melanchthon's biographies of Luther (1546) and Bugenhagen (1558) and Theodore Beza's Life of Calvin: Dickens and Tonkin 1985: Introduction.

52 Volumes I–III were printed in 1559; IV in 1560; V and VI in 1562; VII and VIII in 1564; IX in 1566; X and XI in 1567; XII in 1569; and XIII in 1574.

53 Jones 1981; Freeman 2004a.

54 Jones 1981: 35; PRO SP70/26 fol. 92; Luard 1879: 173; Graham and Watson 1998.

55 Robinson 1988: 1061.

56 See Bale's preface to Leland's *Laboryouse Journey* (Bale 1549); Luard 1879; Graham and Watson 1998.

57 Robinson 1988: 1067–8.

58 CCCC MSS 5, 42, 145, 183.

59 CCCC MSS 43, 96, 161, 195; James 1912; Bale 1557: 85, 161; Thomas Walsingham 1866–9: I.lxvi.

60 Graham and Watson 1998: 2–4.

61 The most recent surveys of Parker's work on the history of the Saxon church are Robinson 1988 and Graham and Watson 1998. James' catalogue of the Corpus Christi library remains an indispensable tool.

62 Flower 1935: 52. Parker had acquired manuscripts that included sections of the *Anglo Saxon Chronicle* and legal codes, including CCCC MS 173.

63 BL Cotton MS Nero C iii 208r, 208v–12r; Graham and Watson 1998: 5–8.

64 Robinson 1988: 1073.

65 Aelfric 1566; Robinson 1988: 1601; Bromwich 1962.

66 CCCC MSS 302, 303, 419, 420, 421.

67 CCCC MS 26, fol 37ff; the homily may be found in the Worcester collection of Saxon Homilies, CCCC MS 198, James 1912; CCCC MS 41, fol. 11, 25, 393. Parker's annotations on Bede's history of the Saxon church highlighted particular passages that described the historical succession of the archbishops of Canterbury: see for example Book 5, Chapter 8 (the death of Theodore).

68 Robinson 1988: 1065–7; Giles 1848.

69 CCCC MS 16, fol. 21ff, 43 fol. 107r; William of Malmesbury 2002.

70 CCCC MSS 164, 167, 408. Bale and Parker's annotations can be seen on a flyleaf list of contents. Higden's *Chronicle* was a familiar text, and had been printed by Caxton in 1482, and by Wynkyn de Worde in 1495.

71 CCCC MS 400. See especially part II, *Dialogues Giraldi Cambrensis de Ecclesia Meneue[n]si*, fol. 16v–17r. Parker was the author of a defence of clerical marriage in 1567 (*A Defence of Priestes Mariages against T. Martin*); Parish 2000a; Carlson 1994.

72 For a further discussion of the library and its origins, see de Hamel 2000.

73 CCCC MSS 307, 308, 312, 318, 389.

74 See for example the flyleaf to the *lives* of St Katherine and S. Aelphege, CCCC MS 375, and Parker's comparisons between the narrative of the English history in MS 174 and MS 182.

75 CCCC MS 42, especially fols 62v, 76r, 76v and 77r; see also the *life* of Dunstan in

CCCC MS 338 and in Matthew Paris' *Chronica Majora* MS 26, fol. 75–6. For a more detailed discussion of sixteenth century representations of St Dunstan, and his role in the introduction of compulsory clerical celibacy, see Chapter 5 below.

76 CCCC MS 100, fol. 365: 'fabulosa haec historia in quinque paginis enarrat vitam nescio cujus Albano qui ex incesto thalamo procreatus et in Hungarium deportatus ibique expositus regi defertur et ab eadem in filium adoptatus'.

77 CCCC MS 183, fol. 16r, 21v; 200.

78 CCC MS 173, fol. 54ff; 183, fol. 61, 62. See also a Parkerian list of the succession of the bishops in Gerald of Wales's history, CCCC MS 400, fol. 2.

79 For a further discussion of the treatment of Thomas Becket at the hands of English evangelical writers, including Parker, see Chapter 5 below.

80 CCCC MSS 45, 111 no.142, 295.

81 CCCC MS 298, fol. 1.

82 CCCC MS 298, fol. 6r, 7r, 7v.

83 May McKisack 1971: 40 notes that Parker was not skilled as an editor, but deserved credit for the efforts that he made in recording the past *Tudor History*. Galbraith 1937 is more negative, accusing Parker and his circle of vandalising the chronicles with their annotations and references.

84 CCCC MSS 5, fol. 293; 16 after fol. 3; 103, and 232.

85 CCCC MS 9, flyleaf, 408, 419, 421.

86 CCCC MS 162, a collection of Anglo Saxon Homilies includes material from MS 178.

87 McKisack 1971: 34–5.

88 Pearce 1925; Greg 1935; Wright 1951; Flower 1935.

89 Robinson 1988: 1067.

90 More 1973: 248, 480–1, 660, 679, 942; 1981, 434; Martin 1554: A2v–3v; Gogan 1982: 96–100; Greenblatt 1980. John Headley has commented upon the similarity between More's trust in the unity of the common corps of Christendom and the German polemicist Thomas Murner's use of the notion of *gemeine Christenheit* against Luther. Headley 1967: 80–90.

91 Harpsfield 1573; Stapleton 1565b; Parsons 1603; Sanders 1585; Hamilton 2002; Parry 1997.

92 Harpsfield 1566, especially Dialogue 6, Chapters 14–15.

93 Stapleton 1565b: 3v–4v.

94 Stapleton 1565b, dedication, 2v–3v.

95 Collinson 1997: 48; Parsons 1599: 6; 1581: 4–5; 1603: III.412–451, headed: 'a note of more than a 120 lyes uttered by John Foxe in lesse than three leaves of his Acts and Monuments'.

96 Parsons 1603: I.3.

97 Parsons 1603: I.230–4; II.43–48.

98 Ditchfield 1993: 283–7 gives an excellent introduction to this topic, and a detailed examination of Catholic history writing in Italy in the early modern period. See also Ditchfield 1995; Soergel 1993; Kamen 1993.

99 Polman 1932: 213–34; Cochrane 1981: 445–78.

100 Fueter 1968: 246.

101 King 1989: 153; Greenblatt 1980.

102 This theme can also be identified in earlier Christian literature composed during periods of turmoil and persecution (Dick 1991: 72; Cohn 1993a).

103 Bauckham 1978: 54.

104 Firth 1979: 1–6. Dawson 1994: 75 argues that 'apocalyptic ideas lay at the very heart of British thought throughout the early modern period'.

105 1 John 2:22; 2 John 7; Matt.24:24; 1 Tim.4; 2 Tim.3; 2 Pet.2.

106 Tyndale 1573: 60.

107 Bradshaw 1999; Parish 2000a, Chapter 5; Bauckham 1978; Firth 1979.

108 The image of the false church as the persecuting church was evident in Lollard writings, and in the works of early English evangelicals. The *Lanterne of Lyght* (1530) made reference to the 'synagoge of Satan', and the traditional belief that Antichrist would persecute the faithful was reflected in John Frith's *A Pistle to the Christen Reader* (1529). For further discussion of the apocalyptic content of English Reformation literature, see Bauckham 1978; Betteridge 1999: 13ff; Firth 1979; Dawson 1994.

109 Cameron 1993: 198–207 emphasises the repeated representation and misrepresentation of the beliefs of Lollards, Waldes and Hussites by sixteenth-century Protestant martyrologists and historians.

110 Ochino 1549; Alford 2002: 101–2; MacCulloch 1999: 52–3.

111 Mason 1997: 56.

112 Lock 1996: 153; Parish 2001.

113 King 1989; Aston 1993a: 1–96.

114 Coverdale 1564: A2v; Brooks 1553.

115 Pocock 1985: 155–6.

116 Dick 1991: 79.

117 Betteridge 1999: 27–8.

3 'LYING HISTORIES FAYNING FALSE MIRACLES'

1 LP XIII.i.1199 (17 June 1538).

2 Shagan 2001, 2003: 64; Rex 1991; Neame 1971; Marshall 1995, 2003; MacCulloch 1986: 143. On the importance of the miraculous to an understanding of early modern religious culture, see Marshall 2003; Clark 1997; Walsham 1999; Walker 1988.

3 See for example Rubin 1991: 108–47; Duffy 1992, especially 101–8. For further discussion of the Mass see 124–42 below.

4 On Bromholm see Thomas 1991: 27. On Henry VI see Knox and Leslie 1923; for Becket see Finucane 1995, Chapter 7.

5 Vogler 1972: 145; Walsham 1999; Buell 1950.

6 Clark 1997; Marshall 2003; Parish and Naphy 2003; Walker 1988; Walsham 1999; Parish 2001, 2002.

7 Marshall 2003: 61.

8 More 1973: 270, 275, 479, 690–1, 735, 739.

9 More 1981: 242, 432; 1973: 246, 251–3, 274, 608, 611, 792.

10 Tyndale 1850: 129.

11 Tyndale 1850: 130.

12 Tyndale 1850: 129–30.

13 Turner 1555: A8r–v.

14 Gilby 1551: A2r; Calfhill 1846: 332–3; Cooper 1617: 298; Walker 1988.

15 Calfhill 1846: 333; cf. Perkins 1608: 10.

16 Tyndale 1848: 286, 289; cf. Tyndale 1850: 129.

17 Rhegius 1537: C7v.

18 Bale 1551: A5r.

19 Gualther 1556: U3v: 'for sometyme they feynes that soules appeare & made mone vnto them, sometyme they declare miracles wrought by ymages, sometyme they preache of wonders, wrought by the bread God of the aultare & infinit suche other trickes they ymagine dayly, wherby theymay the more easily cheoppe men downe into the kyngedome of darkenesse'.

20 Lynne 1548: B1r; Veron 1562: B7v–8v. See also Jewel 1845–50: II.894; Daneau 1589, Chapter 36; Napier 1594: D6v.

21 Tyndale 1850: 89–90, 128.

22 Frith 1529: 45v–48v, 82v–84r.
23 E.P. 1556: I3r–7v, I4r–v.
24 Foxe 1570; see also Hastings 1600: I.2r.
25 Tyndale 1850: 129.
26 Marshall 2003: 46–50; Erasmus 1965: 288–310.
27 Bale 1552: B5r; cf. 1545: B5v; 1548: I.Q1r–v alleged that the Roman church had bolstered power by the invention of 'all kyndes of supersticions in blessynges/bones/belles/candelstyckes/cuppes/curettes/oyle/waxe/lught/ashes/palmes/and holyewater/with soche other lyke. They dedicated stonewalles/they cristened belles/they consecreated vestime[n]tes they anoi[n]ted chalyces/they hallowed aultares/they tabernacled Images/they shrines dead mennes bones/they coniured/crossed/senses/spatled/and breathed with turne and halfe turne/and wyth fayst and feyst me not and a thousande feates more of cleane legerdemayne'.
28 Bale 1548a: III.Dd3r, I.B2r, I.Q1r–v; 1550a: A8r; 1545: E4v.
29 Moone 1548: A2r–A4v.
30 Joye 1534: A3v–7v.
31 E.P. 1556: N7v.
32 Frere 1910: II.38–9, II.67, II.115.
33 Bale 1551: I.A5v, II.H6v.
34 Bale 1551: II.G7r. Bale's sources for the miracles of Anselm included Eadmer, Capgrave, Caxton and Polydore Vergil.
35 E.P. 1556: N4r. The same story was repeated in Hoby 1615. The incident, which took place in 1534, was also described by the German historian Sleidan, who provided a detailed narrative of the events in his *Commentaries* (Sleidan 1689: Book 9.170–1). Sleidan alleged that the local Franciscans had clambered onto the roof of the church, and had responded to the questions of the exorcist by banging on the roof, claiming to be a ghost returning from purgatory to request Catholic funeral rights and forgiveness for adherence to the Lutheran heresy. It has been suggested by Alexandra Kess that Sleidan may well have been in Orleans at the time of the incident, although as a convert to the new religion he was unlikely to have attended Mass at the Franciscan church. However, reports of the incident itself do appear to have become familiar of evangelical attacks on the Catholic miraculous. I am grateful to Dr Kess for her advice.
36 Gualther 1556: U4v. The memory of an infamous false miracle exploited in the controversy between Franciscans and Dominicans over the doctrine of the Immaculate Conception would still have been fresh in the mind. In 1507, the Dominicans in Berne had announced the appearance of the Virgin Mary in support of their objections to the Immaculate Conception, and the case had been widely reported.
37 Foxe 1570: I.199. The same miracles were recorded by William of Malmesbury in the *Gesta Pontificum Anglorum* (William of Malmesbury 2002, Book I.c.14), and in the *Nova Legenda Anglie* (Horstmann 1901: 224–8).
38 Foxe 1570: I.167.
39 Foxe 1570: I.168; William of Malmesbury 2002, Book 5. Foxe identified a similar pattern of common miracles in the *lives* of St John of Beverly and St Egwin, recorded in the *Polychronicon*.
40 Foxe 1570: I.182.
41 More 1981: 96, 431.
42 More 1981: 240–1; More 1985: 206–10.
43 More 1981: 85.
44 More 1981: 90.
45 More 1981: 86–7.
46 Tyndale 1849: 297–8.

47 Foxe 1570: I.834, *Henry VI Part 2*.II.i.
48 More 1981: 87–8. The image of the holy fast was common among the *lives* of female saints in the thirteenth century. See Bynum 1987; Goodich 1982. The claim that individuals could survive on the consecrated host alone featured in Lollard criticisms of Catholic piety: Rubin 1991: 337. There were also plenty of examples of the appearance of communion breads in such a manner: see for example the host that was claimed to have flown through the air at the Field of the Cloth of Gold, June 1520 (SP Venice 3.50).
49 E.P. 1556: N8v.
50 E.P. 1556: O2r–v.
51 For a discussion of the Maid of Ipswich, see MacCulloch 1986: 143–6. On Barton see Neame 1971; Rex 1991; Shagan 2001.
52 On the same women, see Bale 1545: E5v; 1550: II.i5r.
53 More 1981: 238, 240.
54 More 1973: 244–7.
55 More 1973: 753. See also 252–7, 341, 669–70, 805–8; More 1990: 112, 239.
56 Tyndale 1848: 287–8.
57 Tyndale 1848: 325–7.
58 Tyndale 1850: 131.
59 E.P. 1556: I3r, I3v, N6r, O4v–5r. For a more general discussion of the problem of 'unwritten verities' see Marshall 1996.
60 Cranmer 1846: 333.
61 Veron 1562: B6v.
62 Gualther 1556: U6r.
63 Anon 1550: C4r. The same debate over miracles and doctrine was still raging in the 1560s: John Jewel argued that 'miracles be not evermore undoubted proofs of true doctrine': Jewel 1845–50: III.197; and in the *Answer to M Harding* claimed that Harding had used 'fables, dreams and visions' to defend the private mass in the absence of any support from scripture and the early church; Jewel 1845–50: III.805–6.
64 Bale 1551: I.A3r–v.
65 Bale 1551: I.F2r, quoting John Harding's *Chronicle*.
66 Bale 1551: I.G5r.
67 Bale 1551: II.M2v.
68 Bale 1550b: C4v.
69 Bale 1551: I.C7v, D8r, I3v, II.C7r; William of Malmesbury 2002, Book II.c.225.
70 Bale 1551: II. D2r; Bale 1557: I.163.The legend did have some basis in truth: Elmer had indeed experimented with aeronautics, and had constructed for himself a pair of wings, which he tested by leaping from the spire of Malmesbury abbey. The twelfth century chronicler William of Malmesbury recorded how Elmer, 'had by some means, I scarcely know what, fastened wings to his hands and feet so that, mistaking fable for truth, he might fly like Daedalus, and, collecting the breeze upon the summit of a tower, flew for more than a furlong. But agitated by the violence of the wind and the swirling of air, as well as by the awareness of his rash attempt, he fell, broke both his legs and was lame ever after' (William of Malmesbury 1887, Book II.225). However, Elmer's career was cut short when his abbot banned any further such experiments.
71 Bale 1551: I.K4r.
72 Napier 1594: K6r, M8r. For a more detailed discussion of the handling of the *life* and miracles of St Dunstan in evangelical literature see Chapter 5 below. The accusations of necromancy levelled against the medieval popes are discussed in Chapter 6.
73 Rubin 1991: 55.
74 Duffy 1992: 93–6.
75 Peacock 1868; Simmons 1879, Appendix V; Rubin 1991: 62–3.

76 James 1983; Duffy 1992: 103.

77 Rubin 1991: 111.

78 Gairdner 1876: 224–5.

79 The representation of the Mass of St Gregory at Stoke Charity Church, Hampshire (Plate 1) is one of the few such images in English churches.

80 Erbe 1905; Dugmore 1958: 75–7; Messenger 1936: 96–105; Rubin 1991: 115–8; Duffy 1992: 102–3.

81 Strype 1822: I.260–1.

82 King 1982: 89; Davies 2002: 19.

83 See for example Punt 1549; Shepherd 1548g; Becon 1550; Crowley 1548a; Moone 1548.

84 Turner 1548: A5r, E5v, E8r. For similar representations of Mistress Missa, see Anon. 1548; Shepherd 1548e; 1548g.

85 Turner 1548: B3r.

86 Veron 1550: A5r–v, F8r–v.

87 Marcourt 1548: A6ɪ–v, B4r; Lancaster 1550: D5r.

88 Cranmer 1846: 260.

89 Hurlestone 1550: A2r.

90 Anon. 1548: A3v–5r.

91 See for example Cranmer 1846: 376–8, for the claim that Satan and his papist supporters had 'feigned a new and false doctrine' of the Mass, 'counterfeiting the church of our Saviour Christ' and leading the people into error.

92 Shepherd 1548e: A4r.

93 Shepherd 2001 cites examples including keeping the host in a chimney to ensure that it remained dry, using an 'honest wafer maker', laying the host 'vpon the leades of the church' to dry out in the sun, and consecrating the host only in fair weather: A2r, A4r–v, A5v, A7r. For a discussion of the orthodox measures that were recommended to preserve the integrity of the consecrated host, see Rubin 1991: 38–45.

94 Shepherd 1548g: A4v.

95 See for example the story recorded in the *Alphabetum Narrationem* (no. 695) of a host that was fed to bees, who built a chapel around the sacrament and venerated it:Rubin 1991: 118.

96 Crowley 1548a: E1r–v.

97 Cranmer 1846: 250, 255. See also Anon. 1550: A4v; Hilarie 1554: A4v–5r. The polemical thrust of the anti-Mass tracts had parallels in contemporary preaching. In September 1549 the Greyfriars Chronicle recorded similar objections levelled against the Mass by the John Cardmaker, in a sermon delivered at Paul's Cross. 'If God were a man he was a vj. or vjj. Foote of lengthe, with the bredth,' Cardmaker had alleged, 'and if it be soo how canne it be that he shulde be in a pesse of brede in a rownde cake on the awter': Nichols 1852: 63.

98 Crowley 1548a: F8r; Punt 1549: A4r.

99 Cranmer 1846: 303.

100 Shepherd 1548c: A2r; Shepherd 2001: A4r.

101 Shepherd 2001: A2r–A4v; cf Punt 1549: A4r; Becon 1637: 93, 256.

102 Bale 1551: I.G6v.

103 E.P. 1556: O3v–4v. The text also included the testimony of a woman who had taken the bread home in her mouth and spat it into a pot, only to find a small child in the container a few days later.

104 Erbe 1905: 170–1. The miracle attributed to Odo is unusual in the respect that such physical appearances of flesh and blood at the Eucharist were less frequently reported before the twelfth century. However, the same incident is recorded among the miracles of Odo in William of Malmesbury's *Gesta Pontificum*, which provided Foxe with his information: William of Malmesbury 2002: 18.

105 Bale 1551: I.G6r–v; Foxe 1570: I.199.
106 Furnivall 1868–72: 167; Gilby 1547: Bb3r; Guest 1548: 3–4; Moone 1548: A2v.
107 Crowley 1548a: D3r, F7v.
108 Bale 1545: F1r, F3r, G7r, H2r; cf. Anon. 1550: A4v, B5v, C4v.
109 Nichols 1859: 172; BL MS Harl 424 fol. 11: 'yf ye will wette of a man that purpowsyth he[m] to haue a benefyce, or go to Relygyo[n], take the letters of hes name and of the benefice & of the daye and depart them be .xxx. and yf there leve eve[n] nowmbre he shall spede & yf there leue odde he shall nott spede, and yf ther leve ix he shall be Relygyous'.
110 Nichols 1859: 334; BL MS Lansdowne 2 art 26.
111 Nichols 1859: 334.
112 Thomas 1991: 36.
113 Rubin 1991: 108–31; Duffy 1992: 102–6.
114 Rubin 1991: 335; Gray 1974; Scribner 1987:10; Thomas 1991, Chapters 2 and 9.
115 Veron 1550: A5r–v; Shepherd 1548h: A4r; Ramsay 1548; Kirchmeyer 1570: L1r; Hilarie 1554: A3r.
116 Turner 1548: A6r, C5v–6r.
117 Foxe 1570: I.168.
118 Calfhill 1846: 317–18.
119 Foxe 1570: I.199.

4 'ENTIQUE GARGLES OF YDOLATRY'

1 Kolb 1987: 3; Thomas 1991: 108–9.
2 Woodward 1996: 74; Duffy 1992: 155. Carlos Eire argues that in the early sixteenth century Europe 'bristled with holy places; life pulsated with the expectation of the miraculous': Eire 1986: 1.
3 Whiting 1999: 49.
4 Harvey 1971; Duffy 1992: 156.
5 Nussbaum 1998: 119–20; Erbe 1905; Ross 1940; Weatherly 1936; Blackie 1924; Wey 1924; White 1963.
6 Nilson 1998: 155.
7 Finucane 1995: 195; Duffy 1992: 195; Whiting 54–5; Brown 1995; Simpson 1874; Carley 1988: 22, LP XII.ii.1325. The miracles associated with William of Norwich included an occasion on which the saint was able to cure a pilgrim who had already attempted to find a cure at the shrine of Becket, indicating the extent to which the fortunes of individual saints could rise and decline even without the pressure of doctrinal challenge: Hart 1865.
8 Sheppard 1877: 29; Woodruff 1932; Finucane 1995: 193.
9 Finucane 1995: 194–5. On the popularity of pilgrimage on the eve of the Reformation, see Sumption 1975; Finucane 1995; Sigal 1974.
10 Duffy 1992: 164; Bokenham 1938.
11 Hutton 2001: 27; McClendon 1999: 4.
12 Duffy 2002: 172; Whiting 1999: 50.
13 Brown 1995: 69.
14 Finucane 1995: 143.
15 Cronin 1907; Hudson 1978.
16 Kolve and Olson 1989: 259, 262.
17 Foxe 1570: 1201, cf. 1172–4, 927; Keeble 2002: 238–40. On destruction in Rickmansworth see Aston 1993b: 263; Haigh 1993: 69.
18 Weiss 1985b; Erasmus 1933, lines 1–125.
19 Erasmus 1965, Appendix I, 623, 631. The text was printed in English in 1536 as 'A

Dialogue or Communication of Two Persons', coinciding with the first official assault on the cult of saints through the Royal Injunctions of the same year. See also White 1963, Chapter 3; Knapp 1972.

20 Erasmus 1965: 311; Knapp 1972.
21 Erasmus 1974: 114–5, 149.
22 Barnes 1573: R5ff.
23 Barnes 1573: R7r. Barnes rejected the traditional understanding of the difference between the honour accorded to the saints (*dulia*), that accorded to the Virgin (*hyperdulia*) and that due to God alone (*latria*). See Aquinas 1947: II–II.103.3. This distinction was also rejected by Joye 1531: C6v–7r.
24 2 Kings 13:14, 20–21; Tyndale 1850: 83.
25 Regius 1537: C3v–4v.
26 Joye 1531: C6r–v. For similar condemnations of Catholic practice see also Veron 1562: A7r, A8r, B6v, L5v; Bale 1548a: Q1r–v, S2r, q6v.
27 More 1981: 54.
28 More 1981: 61.
29 More 1981: 233. More was less convinced by the practice of offering oats to St Uncumber.
30 Barnes 1573: T6r.
31 Tyndale 1850: 84.
32 Bale 1548a: P4r. A similar list was repeated later in the work: 'here were much to be spoken of saynt Germanes euyll, saynt Sytles keye, Saynt Uncombres otes, master Johan shornes bote, Saynte Hertrudes rates, Saynt Job for the pxe, Saynte Fyacre for the aguem, Saynt Apolyne for the tothe ake, Saynt Germayne for lost theyft, Saynt Wolstone for good harvest, Saynt Cornellis for foule euyll, and all other syantes els almost': Bale 1548a: r3v. See also Hurlestone 1550: E4r–5r; Gualther 1556: W6v.
33 Joye 1546: 133r–137v.
34 Geary 1978: 23; Geary 1983; Fichtenau 1952; Little 1993. The practice was prohibited by the papacy in 1274.
35 Owst 1963: 139–40; Aston 1997: 175.
36 Hurlestone 1550: E2r–v.
37 Brigden 1989: 273.
38 LP VI.1311.
39 The tract is printed in Foxe 1846: V. 404–9. The treatise has been identified by Duffy as an 'inside job', drawing upon the reports sent to Cromwell by the monastic Visitors, and revealing the motivation behind the Henrician destruction of images and shrines (Duffy 1992: 408).
40 Foxe 1570: 1172–4.
41 Ellis 1824: II.607.
42 Nichols 1852: 55; Brigden 1989: 433.
43 Aston 1993b: 262; Eire 1986: 151–5.
44 Wilson 1983.
45 Aston 1993b: 266; Wriothesley 1875–7: I.83. By contrast, a woman from Walsingham was placed in the stocks after claiming that the image of the Virgin had worked miracles after its removal from the shrine.
46 Marshall 2003.
47 Cranmer 1846: 460–1; *my italics*.
48 BL Cotton MS Cleop E iv, fol. 21.
49 Duffy 1992: 384. In contrast, the lengthy list of relics discovered by John London at Reading seems to date from the twelfth century, leading Peter Marshall to conclude that few were the object of popular cults in the 1530s. BL Cotton MS Cleop. E.iv, fol. 265r; Marshall 2003: 54; Finucane 1995, Chapter 11; Bethell 1972: 61.
50 BL Cotton MS Cleop E iv fol. 249; Wright 1843: 58. Matilda had been a benefactor at

the time of the foundation of Farley (Wiltshire).

51 Latimer 1845: 33–57.
52 Lloyd 1856: 1–20.
53 Wilkins 1737: III.823–4.
54 Frere and Kennedy 1910: II.1–11.
55 Baddesley 1900: 276–84.
56 See for example the early Tudor *A Little Treatise of Divers Miracles Shown for the Portion of Christ's Blood in Hayles*, Bod dep.d.324; Shagan 2003: 166.
57 Wriothesley 1875–7: I.74–6, LP XIII.i.348; Robinson 1846–7: II.604, 606–9; Marshall 1995; Finucane 1995; Baddesley 1900.
58 LP XIII.i.348. The sentiments of the crowds who participated reflect the same tension between grief and celebration. As Margaret Aston has noted, not all 'miraculous' illusions were necessarily delusions; it was entirely possible that the faithful might respect the miraculous even within the limitations of the physical enactment. Aston 1993b: 270–1; Davidson and Nichols 1989.
59 See Marshall 1995: 694; PRO SP1/143 fol. 198–206; Marshall 2001.
60 Wright 1843: 183–6.
61 Latimer 1845: 393–5.
62 Wright 1843: 219–33.
63 Frere and Kennedy 1910: II.38–9.
64 Wyse 1538; Bullinger 1538.
65 The Reformation Parliament, for example, had exempted from the general pardon those who were found guilty of acts of violence against wayside crosses. Lehmberg 1970: 91.
66 Cranmer 1833: 127; MacCulloch 1999: 61–2; Aston 1993a: 26–36.
67 Duffy 1992: 449.
68 Brigden 1989: 291.
69 Nussbaum 1998: 122; Kettley 1844: 72, 75. Nussbaum 1998: 123 notes that the *Formac ac Ratio* of 1550 omitted all reference to the saints.
70 Hooper 1550; Cranmer 1547, *The Homily on Obedience*; Alford 2002; Bradshaw 1996: 77, 81–2, 87.
71 5–6 Edward VI c.3; Cressy 1989: 6–7.
72 The sermon was reprinted in the reign of Elizabeth: Sermons 1908: 262.
73 BL Cotton MS Galba E.iv; Wright 1843. John London listed the relics that he had found around Reading, including two pieces of the cross, part of the hand of St James, the stole of St Philip, bones of Magdalene and others, a hand of Anastasius, part of the arm of Pancrates, a bone of the arm of David, a bone of the arm of Edward the martyr, a bone of Stephen, Jerome and Osmund, part of the stole of Ursula, a bone of Margaret, a bone of Ethelwold, a bone of Andrew and two parts of his cross, a bone of Frideswide, and a bone of Anne.
74 Geary 1978: 5–6.
75 Finucane 1995, Chapter 11; Marshall 2003: 51–55.
76 Morris 1972; Tanner 1990: I.263.
77 More 1981: 98.
78 LP IX.42 (SP 1/95 fol. 38r–v).
79 Calvin 1854: 218–224, 234.
80 Geary 1978: 7.
81 Geary 1994; Brown 1981, Chapter 3.
82 Anderson 1984: 20; Goodich 1982: 2–4. For a further discussion of these general themes, see Introduction 16–21.
83 Olsen 1980: 410; Heffernan 1988: 6.
84 Burke 1984: 50–2. Burke uses the example of Francis Xavier, Philip Neri, Pope Pius V

and Felice of Cantalice, who all had links with Ignatius Loyola.

85 Ditchfield 1995: 1; Weinstein and Bell 1982; Colgrave 1958: 42.
86 Burke 1984: 48 asks whether saints reflect the age in which they lived or the age in which they were canonised, giving as an example Peter Canisius, whose canonisation occurred 250 years after his death.
87 Kern 1994: 417–26.
88 Vitz 1991: 97–9.
89 On the *Golden Legend* and its publishing history, see White 1963, Chapter 2; Seboldt 1946; Ditchfield 1995.
90 Vitz 1981: 110–112.
91 Bale 1551: I.K4r.
92 Regius 1537: C6r; Bale 1551: K5r.
93 Scot 1584: 498; Holinshed 1587: 84.
94 Bale 1551: A2v.
95 de Valera 1600: 94, 308.
96 Tyndale 1573: I.A4v, H6r.
97 Bale 1551: I.A2v, F8v.
98 Scot 1584: 62–4.
99 Bale 1551: I.A2r.
100 Bale 1551: I.B8r–C1r. Bale referred his readers to the *Nova Legenda Anglie*, and his contentions are supported by Capgrave's text. On Patrick, see Horstman 1901: II.279: 'beatus enim Patricius de genere Britonum ortus est: pater eius Calphurnus, mater vero Conches dicta est'. Gorlach 1994: 40 notes that 'the moder of Seynt Dubryve had no husbonde' and her father had thrown her into the water encased in glass, but she was repeatedly returned safely to the land; cf. Horstman 1901: I.268. For Kentigern see Gorlach 1994: 104 where the mother of the saint was claimed to have fallen with child 'though of trouth it was by company of men': Horstman 1901: I.114–5.
101 Bale 1551: I.C1r, E6v, E5v; Parish 2000b.
102 Bale 1551: I.A3r–v.
103 Bale 1551: I.A3r; Gorlach 1994: 64; Horstman 1901: I.425.
104 Bale 1551: I.A3r; Gorlach 1994: 118; Horstman 1901: II.189–90.
105 Bale 1551: I.A3r; Gorlach 1994: 119; Hortsman 1901: II.193–5.
106 I am indebted to the analysis of the *life* of Wulstan and his cult provided in Duffy 2002.
107 Duffy 2002: 168.
108 Duffy 2002: 169.
109 Bale 1551: II.B8v.
110 Sheingorn and Thiebaux 1996: 6.
111 Ellis 1908: II.62–8.
112 Hardyng 1543: 52r.
113 Bale 1551: I.C4r.
114 Bale avoided comment on the numerical confusion over the 11,000 companions. The origins of the cult may be seen in a fourth- or fifth-century carving in the choir of the church of St Ursula in Cologne, but it was only in the late ninth century that the number of companions had become fixed at 11,000, perhaps the result of a mistranscription of the abbreviation XI. M. V. as *undecim millia virginum* (11,000 Virgins, rather than 11 martyred virgins). Baronius was highly sceptical of the legend, his views perhaps reflecting ongoing uncertainty over the historicity and numerical accuracy of the tale.
115 Bale 1551: II.C4v.
116 Bale 1551: II.G7r.
117 Bale 1551: II.L5v.
118 Bale 1551: I.E5v.

119 Foxe 1570: I.167.
120 Lambarde 1573: 302.
121 BL Cotton MS Cleo E iv.210; Wright 1843: 207–209.

5 'LYING HISTORIES FAYNING FALSE MIRACLES'

 1 Wilkins 1737: III.840.
 2 Wilkins 1737: III.840.
 3 Ward 1982: 89–94; Finucane 1995: 122.
 4 Douglas and Greenaway 1981: 827.
 5 Finucane 1995: 121; Barlow 1986: 2.
 6 Barlow 1986: 2–3.
 7 On the life, death and reputation of Becket, see Barlow 1986; Knowles 1970; Winston 1967; Warren 1973; Passini 1996; Marc'hadour 1994; and most recently Scully 2002.
 8 Caesarius of Heisterbach, 'Dialogues', quoted in Finucane 1995: 210.
 9 Cronin 1907: 300; Shirley 1858: 417–32; Davis 1963: 3–4.
10 Davis 1963: 4–7. For Becket and his prophecies, see Thomas 1991: 464, 468, 486.
11 Davis 1963: 1–15.
12 Furnivall 1866: 62; Wright 1843: 6; Finucane 1995: 211.
13 Ward 1987: 109.
14 MacCulloch 1996: 227.
15 LP XIII ii 133–4. It has been suggested that the trial of the saint was in fact the 'testing' of his relics, and especially the phials of the blood of Becket that were investigated in autumn 1538. Morris 2002: 215; Potter 1931.
16 Lambeth Palace Library MS 157 fol. 4v, discussed in Davis 163: 12.
17 LP XIII ii 257; Butler 1995: 119.
18 LP XIII i 684.
19 LP XIII ii 880.
20 LP XIII ii 974, LP XIV i 11.
21 LP XIV i 200.
22 Pole 1744: I.102; Stapleton 1612: 58.
23 Barlow 1986: 1.
24 Pole 1744: I.102.
25 LP XIII ii 126.
26 LP XII (2) 848.
27 LP XIII ii 281.
28 Williams 1996: 811–4.
29 Wriothesley 1875–7: I.86–7.
30 SP Henry VIII v 245.
31 Knowles 1970: 150; King 1989; Bradshaw 1996.
32 Tyndale 1849: 273.
33 Tyndale 1849: 292.
34 Bale 1560: P7r.
35 Bale 1560: Q4r.
36 Bale 1560: Q1r.
37 Bale 1560: Q3r.
38 Bale 1560: Q5r–v.
39 Bale 1544b: G4r.
40 Bale 1544b: G7r–v.
41 Bale 1544b: G4v.
42 LP XIII 1037.
43 LP VIII 626.

44 LP XIV 76, 444, 1052–4. One of the few surviving medieval images of Thomas Becket is to be found in the parish church of Hauxton, Cambs (Plate 2).

45 LP VIII 480.

46 Butler 1995: 123; BM Harl. 6253.

47 LP IX 868.

48 LP XIII i 1043.

49 LP XIV i 47.

50 Hughes 1952–4: I.240.

51 Ridley 1962: 173.

52 Thomas 1774: 53.

53 Thomas 1774: 55–6.

54 Thomas 1774: 57.

55 Foxe 1570: 263–5, 289; cf. Flacius *et al.* 1559–1574, cent. XII cap. 10 col. 1565.

56 Foxe 1570: II.268.

57 Parker 1572: P1v–P8r.

58 Holinshed 1587: III.85.

59 Godwin 1601: 42–4.

60 Godwin: 45–50; cf. Jewel 1845–50: IV.574.

61 Hastings 1598: 13–14. Hastings misdated the events to the reign of Henry III.

62 Hastings 1600: H3r–I.1v.

63 Hastings 1600: I.2v.

64 Parsons 1599: C3r–4v.

65 Parsons 1602: Cc5v–6v.

66 Baronius 1975: A1r.

67 Baronius 1975: Z5v.

68 Pole 1744: I.102.

69 Parsons 1599: C4r.

70 Dickens 1922: 30–6. I appreciate the assistance of Dr Tom Freeman in bringing this passage to my attention. I am grateful to *Sixteenth Century Journal* for their permission to reproduce here sections of an earlier article: Parish 2001.

71 Farmer 1992: 137–9; Burling 1988; Lewis 1985; Ramsay and Sparks 1988; Dales 1988.

72 Stubbs 1874. The lives were written by 'B' (a Saxon priest), Adelard, Osbern, Eadmer, William of Malmesbury and John Capgrave.

73 Stubbs 1874: ix.

74 Thacker 1992: 223–5; Rollason 1989.

75 Ramsay and Sparks 1988: 31, 26–7. As the patron saint of craftsmen and metalworkers, Dunstan was also honoured by the Goldsmiths Company of London.

76 Ramsay and Sparks 1988: 33; William of Malmesbury 2002: 21.

77 Stubbs 1874: 426–39.

78 Lewis 1985: 58–59; Stubbs 1874: cxvi.

79 Ramsay and Sparks 1988: 33–4.

80 Surtz and Murphy 1988: xxxii.

81 Surtz and Murphy 1988: 260–1; Stubbs 1874: lxvi. The incident was mentioned only briefly by Osbern: Stubbs 1874: 128. Eadmer enlarged upon the account provided by Adelard. The same reference to Dunstan also featured in the *Collectanea* and *The Glasse of Truth*: Surtz and Murphy 1988: xxxiv.

82 Surtz and Murphy 1988: 262.

83 Foxe 1548: l3v, l4r; Foxe 1534: I.1r; Burnet 1865: I.175; Flacius *et al.* 1559–1574: cent. X, 304.

84 Pontifex 1933: 21.

85 'Dubitante vero Dei nullumque ad rogata responsum porrigente, res mira et saeculis, ecce Dominici Corporos forma vexillo crucis infixa in editiore domus parte locata,

humanos exprimens modos, omnium voces compescuit dicens "Absit hoc ut fiat, absit hoc ut fiat". Ad quam vocem rex omnesque majores natu fere usque ad exhalationem perterriti, clamore paritu et Dei laudatione aream complent.' Stubbs 1874: 113; cf. Eadmer: Stubbs 1874: 212–3; William of Malmesbury: Stubbs 1874: 307–8; Capgrave: Stubbs 1874; *Polichronicon* 32, 34.

86 'Ecce vero in mediis altercationibus, vox ex imagine CHRISTI crucifixi palam insonuit. Non fiet, non fiet, iudicastis bene, mutaretis non bene. Attonitis omnium animis, Quid, inquit, de his rebus amplius controuertimus, cum de sublimi Deus ipsi sententiam suam dictauit?' Harpsfield 1622: Bb1v.

87 Vergil 1844–6: I.36, 244–6.

88 For a more detailed examination of the debate over clerical marriage in the sixteenth century see Parish 2000a; Carlson 1994.

89 Bale 1551: I.H5v. I.Tim.4.

90 Bale 1551: I. I5v–6r.

91 Bale 1551: I.I6r; cf. Capgrave's 'Life of Dunstan': Stubbs 1874: 342–3.

92 For a discussion of the promotion of Edward as Josiah, and the employment of Old Testament imagery in reformation polemic see King 1982, 1989; Bradshaw 1996; Aston 1993a.

93 Bale 1551: I.Iir, I6v.

94 Stubbs 1874: 23–4, 91, 181.

95 Bale 1551: I.G7r, quoting Osbern, Malmesbury, Nauclerus, Fabian and Capgrave.

96 Bale 1551: I.G8v.

97 Bale 1551: I.G8v.

98 Bale 1551: I.H1v.

99 Bale 1551: I.H7r; Flacius *et al.* 1559–74: cent. X, col. 303.

100 Bale 1551: I.H7r–v.

101 Foxe 1570: I.207.

102 College of Arms MS Arundel 4, fol. 118r; cf. *Polichronicon*, 32, 34: 'imago crucifixi de pariete locuta est'. I am grateful to Dr Tom Freeman for bringing this note to my attention.

103 Foxe 1570: I.207.

104 'Denique cum a iuuentute cum diabolo habuisset commercia Dunstanus, & magicis artibus nihil non attentaret atque obtineret, ad hasce artes veluti ad asylum sese recipit. Nam cum uideretur sacerdotum causa, exluculento uerbo Dei & observatione primitiua Ecclesiae superior futura: diabolus in auxilium uoccatus uocem edit, non aliter atque ex imagine crucifixi Christi, quae a pariete suspensa erat, ea uox proferretur.' Flacius *et al.* 1559–74: cent. X, col. 453–5.

105 Bale 1551: I.I7v–8r.

106 Flaciuset *et al.* 1559–74: cent. II, col. 454, 635: 'magicis igitur praestigiis & diabolica clementia Dunstanus efficit, ut subito coenaculum illud corruat'; Foxe 1570: I.207. Dickens 1922: 36 suggests to the reader that 'you may be pretty sure that it [the floor] had been weakened under Dunstan's direction, and that it fell at Dunstan's signal'.

107 Bale 1551: I.G6v, G7r.

108 Foxe 1570: I.199, 205v; Flacius *et al.* 1559–74: cent. X, col. 636; Bale 1557: 141; cf. Stubbs 1574: 41–2, 48–9, 117–8, 206–8.

109 Bale 1551: I.K5r.

110 McKisack 1971: 34–44; Levy 1967: 114–5; Robinson 1988: 1061–1083.

111 Parker 1572: 49–64, especially 55.

112 See above, n. 70.

6 'ANTICHRIST, & NOT THE TRUE SUCCESSOUR OF PETER'

1 Foxe 1570: 941.

2 Aston 1993a; King 1989; King 1989.
3 Lynne's work benefited from the patronage and protection of the Edwardian regime. No other printers were permitted to publish the work, and it has been suggested that the initial publication plans were the work of Thomas Cranmer: Alford 2002: 101ff; MacCulloch 1996: 402–3.
4 Lock 1996: 153.
5 Lock 1996; Norton 1570: D3r; Bale 1838: 5.
6 Lock 1996; Levin 1980, 1988. The conflict between Henry II and Thomas Becket emerged as a *locus classicus* for evangelical commentaries on the conflict between church and state in the English past. See Chapter 5.
7 Tyndale 1573: 30, 289, 398.
8 Frith 1529: Vv–Xiv.
9 Frith 1529: XVIv–XVIIr.
10 Frith 1529: XXXv ff.
11 Frith 1529: XLV ff.
12 Frith 1529: LXXXIV ff.
13 Joye 1545: M8v–N4r.
14 Bauckham 1978: 7.
15 Adso 1525.
16 Wycliffe 1548; Wycliffe 1883 *(De Solutione Sathanae)*. For further discussion of the relationship between Lollard and Protestant apocalyptic writings see Bauckham 1978: 28–32.
17 Thomson 1965: 47; Bauckham 1978: 28.
18 See for example Bale 1543: A6v, D6v; Old 1555: F2v; Watt 1534: A4v.
19 Bullinger 1538.
20 The bishop of Norwich, John Parkhurst, recognised the value of Bullinger's *Hundred Sermons*, and instructed his diocesan clergy to obtain a printed copy. Robinson 1842: I.99; Bauckham 1978: 48.
21 Gualter 1556: Bb7r, N3v; cf. K2r.
22 Old 1555.
23 Anon. 1539: A1v–2r.
24 Bale 1543: 37r.
25 Bale 1545, passim.
26 Bale 1545: B2r–v.
27 Bale 1545: B5v, C8r.
28 Bale 1550b: C4v.
29 Bale 1574: C3r.
30 Bale 1574: C3r.
31 Fairfield 1976: 103. Bartolomeo Platina's *Vitae Pontificum* was presented to Pope Sixtus V in 1475. The first full edition was printed in 1479, and the text emerged as the definitive Renaissance study of the medieval papacy. The work was translated into six languages and ran to over 80 editions, adapted and augmented until the eighteenth century. Platina's work was blunt in its criticisms of those popes who failed to live up to the obligations of the office or whose character fell below the high standards that Platina expected of the successors of St Peter. For this reason, the *Vitae* proved popular with evangelical polemicists, who used Platina's histories as a source for evidence of papal corruption. A censored Italian edition appeared in 1592.
32 Tyndale 1573: 406: 'Antichrist disguised himself afetr the fashion of a true Apostle, preached Christ wylyly, bryngyng in now this tradition and now that to darke[n] the doctrine of Christ'; cf. 53–4, 316, 320.
33 Bullinger 1849–52: I.89.
34 Gilby 1547: L5–K2.

35 Ponet 1549: C1r.
36 Material from the *Fasciculi Zizaniorum* was reprinted in the 1563 edition of the *Actes and Monuments*, and Tom Freeman has also established the importance of Bale's *Catalogus* and Matthias Flacius' *Catalogus Testium Veritatis* in providing Foxe with sources and with an interpretative framework for his history. It was Flacius and Bale, for example, who introduced Foxe to German anti-papal histories: see Freeman 2004b for a full discussion. Foxe also drew upon a selection of English chronicles, most notably William of Malmesbury's *Gesta Pontificum Anglorum*, Matthew Paris' *Chronica Majora* and Bede's *Ecclesiastical History of the English People*.
37 Foxe 1579, 1973; Bauckham 1978; Freeman 2004b. The play *Christus Triumphans* identified the papal Antichrist in uncompromising terms: see for example Act 5.1.29–33: 'Europus. Incredibile dictu, Hierologe, Et monstri simile, Pseudamnum te dicere Antichristum esse? Hierologus. Non ficus est ficus magis. Europus. Qui scis? Hierologus. Res, tempus, uita, doctrina arguunt Et locus ipse.'
38 Foxe 1560. Tom Freeman has established the credentials of Foxe as the author of this tracts: Freeman 1994.
39 Foxe 1580: G6r, O7v.
40 For further discussion see Parish 2000a, Chapter 5.
41 Foxe 1580: B3r; Old 1555: A5r: 'he com[m]eth in so disguysed vnder the colour of holynes'; Ponet 1555: 41; Roy 1528: E7r.
42 Tyndale 1573: 115.
43 Bale 1548a: II.a7r.
44 Bale 1548a: 1.B2r.
45 Bale 1550a: D6r.
46 Biographical information may be found in Latouche 1930–7: II.53ff (Richer's biography); Dollinger 1871; Bietenholz 1994.
47 Myths surrounding the pontificate of Silvester II are detailed in Bietenholz 1994, Chapter 2; Oldoni 1977, 1980, 1983; Guyotjeannin and Poulle 1996; Allen 1892; Döllinger 1871.
48 Swinnerton 1534: B5v.
49 Barnes 1535, l2v: 'quam magicis artibus se addiceret & dederet se totum Satane'; l3r: 'diabolus ambigue respondit, non moriturum priusquam in Hierusalem sacra fecerit'.
50 Bale 1545: 16r; 1557: 142; 1558: k8v, l1v–3v: 'In Syluestro secundo, qui suis necromantis Satanam de abysso soluit, ac super habendo Papatu cum eo pactus est ... '.
51 Bale 1543: I6v; 1548: III.Gg3r.
52 Bale 1548a: III.Gg5r.
53 Bale 1545: C8r, I2r; 1548: III.Gg5r.
54 Bale 1557: 142–3; Barnes 1535: l3v.
55 Gualther 1556: L6r.
56 Flacius *et al.* 1559–74: cent. X, col. 547–8; Flacius 1566: 341–2.
57 Foxe 1570: I.217.
58 Napier 1594; Valera 1600.
59 Sacchi 1888: 264–5. The accounts of the pontificate of Silvester provided by Bale in the *Catalogus* and Flacius in his *Catalogus* were the basis for the narrative that appeared in Foxe's *Actes and Monuments*.
60 Stubbs 1887: I.193–203.
61 David Rollo notes that Malmesbury's narrative contained occasional private jokes for an educated readership, intended to demonstrate the difference between the letter of the text and the meaning beyond: Rollo 2000: 5.
62 'Tunc vero papa Romanus Johannes qui est Gerbertus', Stubbs 1887: xciii–iv, lxxiii.
63 Rollo 2000: 12–13 notes that William was an accomplished papal historian, who had

supervised the compilation of the *Liber Pontificalis*, and had clearly engaged in wide research for the *Gesta*. Yet if William was aware of the error, he made no attempt to correct it, leading Rollo to conclude that William had composed his biography of Silvester for a proficient, but small, audience, for whom the error would be clear, and who would joke at the expense of the illiterate majority who could not distinguish fact from fiction.

64 See for example Walter Map 1914: 176–83; Pertz 1848: 288–502. Hugh had backed the anti-pope Clement III, which no doubt coloured his interpretation of the pontificate of Gregory VII: Bietenholz 2000, Chapter 2.

65 Franke 1892: 369ff. I am grateful to Professor Ben Arnold for his help in locating this text.

66 Franke 1892: 376: 'et Gerbertus quidem, Paulo post completum miliarum ascendens de abisso permissionis divinae, quatuor annis sedit mutato nominee dictus Silvester Secundus'.

67 Franke 1892: 376–7.

68 Stubbs 1887: lxix, lxxiii.

69 Baronius 1602: X.926–7.

70 Mabillon 1703–39: IV.163–4; Oldoni 1977: 665–6. The legend of the demon-pope had an enduring history, and at the end of the nineteenth century gained a new interpretation and twist in a short story: Garnett 1944. The story takes a rather different form in Garnett's narrative, in which Silvester at first refused to give his soul to the devil, but later relented and offered to make the devil pope for a day. A group of cardinals were shocked to discover that their pope had a cloven hoof, and one is heard to utter 'Why the devil, if I may so express myself, did your holiness not inform us that you were the devil'. Terrified by his encounter with the college of cardinals, the devil decided to abandon his papal pretensions. I am grateful to Alison Butler for allowing me to read her conference paper on the medieval reputation of Silvester, and for the reference to Garnett's account of the life of the pope.

71 On Gregory VII and the reforming papacy see Robinson 1978, 1990; Ullmann 1962; Blumenthal 2001; Cowdrey 1998, 2000.

72 Plate 4.

73 Barnes 1535: 212; Becon 1564: MMm1v.

74 Bale 1543: K3r.

75 Bale 1551: II.D8r; cf. Pilkington 1842: 564–5 referred to Gregory VII as 'Hell-brand', because he was held to be responsible for the introduction of clerical celibacy.

76 Bale 1545: D1v.

77 Bale 1574: L2v–L3r.

78 Foxe 1570: I.227r; Flacius 1566: 239. Freeman 2004b provides an extremely helpful commentary upon Flacius' sources and his influence on Foxe's account. Foxe's account of the events at Erfurt followed Flacius *Catalogus*, but more especially the chronicle of Lambert of Herzfeld. See Hesse 1845: 217ff.

79 Swinnerton 1534: A1–7v.

80 Swinnerton 1534: A6v.

81 Swinnerton 1534: B6v.

82 Barnes 1535: m5v–6r.

83 Gualther 1556: L6r.

84 Gualther 1556: S4r.

85 Bale 1550b: C5v.

86 Bale 1551: B1ff.

87 Bale 1551: D6v.

88 Bale 1551: D6v. This argument was repeated in Bale 1574: L2v–3r.

89 Foxe 1570: I.225.

90 Foxe 1570: I.228. Freeman 2004b notes that the reference to Antoninus in Foxe's account of the death of Gregory comes straight from Bale's *Catalogus*. Antoninus had expressed his doubts that the pope had repented his evil life at the moment of his death, but Bale chose to ignore this caveat, and Foxe followed suit in repeating the legend.

91 Beard 1625.

92 Beard 1625: D3v.

93 Sheldon 1616: Y2r; Valera 1600: 67–8.

94 Canonisation followed in 1728. Parsons 1603: I.445–68.

95 Flacius 1566: 220–4; Foxe 1570: I.228ff.

96 Franke 1892: 376, 380ff.

97 Franke 1892: 377. See for example the description of the mittens that sent sparks, and false miracles that 'deceived the eyes of the simple', 'qui cum vellet, manicas suas duscutiebat, et in modum scintillarum ignis dissiliebat: et his miraculis oculos simplicium velud signo sanctitatis ludificabat': Foxe 1570: I.228; Flacius 1566: 223; Barnes 1535: M5v; Swinnerton 1534: A6v.

98 Pertz 1844a: 352. There are several variations of the letter of Henry, but the tone of defiance is the same.

99 Bale 1543: K3r; Foxe 1570: I.234; Flacius 1566: 211.

100 Mommsen and Morrison 1962, document 15a.

101 Barnes 1535: n1v. Barnes had also made extensive use of Platina's history of the papacy in his narrative of the career of Gregory VII.

102 Swinnerton 1534: B4r. On this accusation, see also Franke 1892: 376, 'Theophilactus, sacrificiis demoniorum deditus, in silvis et monitbus mulieres post se currere faciebat, quas magicis artibus ad sui amorem coegerat.'

103 Bale 1574: 2v, Z6v, K2v.

104 Bale 1550: Gg5r, 1551, I.A6r.

105 Pertz 1839: 340–6. John XII was deposed by the emperor on charges of devil-worship, but was restored by the people of Rome once imperial forces had left the city, suggesting that the deposition did not enjoy widespread approval outside imperial circles.

106 Beard 1625: D3v.

107 Perkins 1608, Chapter 1, pt III.

108 Napier 1594: D6v, D8v.

109 Coste 1995; Wood 1967.

110 Scot 1584: 91.

111 See for example the inclusion of necromancy in William Turner's diatribe against Stephen Gardiner: Turner 1545: H7–8v.

112 Bale 1552: B5r–v.

113 Summers 1971: I.4; Klaniczay 1997.

114 Kieckhefer 1994a, 2000.

115 Bodley MS e Mus 238.

116 Bale 1548a: I.A3v.

117 Horstmann 1901: II.369; Bale 1551: 44v.

CONCLUSION

1 Macaulay 1910, Chapter 5. Harrison believed that there was still scope for further reform: 'And no great matter were it if the feasts of all our apostles, evangelists, and martyrs, with that of all saints, were brought to the holy days that follow upon Christmas, Easter and Whitsuntide, and those of the Virgin Mary, with the rest, utterly removed from the calendars, as neither necessary nor commendable in a reformed church.'

2 Pythian Adams 1975: 10. In his survey of the labours of Matthew Parker and his circle,

Benedict Robinson concludes that one of the challenges faced by the Elizabethan church was the creation of a new past which would replace the history that had been 'cast off' in 1559: Robinson 1998.

3 Hutton 2001, Chapter 1.
4 Cressy 1989: 13.
5 Aston 1993b: 283–305.
6 Machyn 1848: 130; Davidson and Nichols 1989: 93; Wall 1905: 26; Sacks 1986.
7 See for example, Duffy 1992, Chapter 5; Rubin 1991, Chapters 3 and 4; McClendon 1999; Sacks 1986.
8 Marsh 1988; Ingram 1995; Walsham 1999; Watt 1991.
9 Strype 1824: II.181; Thomas 1991: 78.
10 Scot 1584: 4–6.
11 James VI & I 1597.
12 Clark 1997: 53.
13 Scribner 1997; Walsham 1999; Parish and Naphy 2003.
14 Latimer 1845: 248.
15 May Day celebrations were often referred to as 'Robin Hood Games': Schmidt 1978: 5.395–6; Aston 1993b: 285.
16 Cressy 1989: 9; Duffy 1992: 576; Haigh 1993: 245.
17 Thomas 1991: 80.
18 Spufford 1981, especially Chapter 9.
19 Purvis 1948: 164. For the destruction of the cult of Becket, see Chapter 5.
20 Legend maintained that the culprit was blinded by a splinter in the process of cutting down the tree.
21 Stow 1592: 972; Aston 1984: 316–7.
22 Fuller 1845: I.351–2; Walsham 1994.
23 Scot 1584, bk 15, cap. 33; bk 8, cap. 1.
24 Scot 1584, bk 9, cap. 6; *my italics*.
25 Lambarde 1576: 81–2.
26 Lambarde 1576: 247.
27 Lambarde 1576: 182–5.
28 Lambarde 1576: 286–8.
29 Fox 2000: 232–4; Foxe 1996; Defoe 1724–6.
30 BL Lansdowne MS 231 fol. 110.
31 See for example Greenblatt's suggestion that it took 50 years for memory to die out, until a generation was born which had no first-hand experience of the traditions that could be passed on to successive generations: Greenblatt 2002: 248.
32 See Chapter 5, 206–211.
33 Beard 1625: D3v.
34 See Chapter 5.
35 Watt 1991: 213.
36 McClendon 1999.
37 Bruhn 2002.
38 See Chapter 5.
39 Heal 2003.
40 Keeble 2002.
41 For an exploration of these themes, see especially Buell 1950; Walsham 1999.
42 Walsham 1994, 1999.
43 Freeman 2000; see also Scribner 1987: 84–5.
44 Walker 1988.
45 Floyd 1613; Sheldon 1616; Tynley 1609; Lipsius 1604.
46 Numan 1606: A6v, B4v, F5v, J8r–v.

47 Floyd 1613: preface, 127–140.
48 Hoby 1615, Chapter 5. Hoby described the false claims of a beggar to have been cured at St Albans, and the attempts of the clergy of Orleans to fake the appearance of the ghost of the wife of the Provost. For the discussion of these miracles by earlier writers, see Chapter 3.
49 For the response to Floyd, see Sheldon 1616: Y3v.
50 Sheldon 1616: F1r, I3v.
51 Sheldon 1616: Y1v ff; Ff3v.
52 Waterworth 1848: 234–6.
53 Ditchfield 1993, 1995; Klauser 1969; Burke 1984; Dunn Lardeau 1995; Eilington 2001.
54 Johnson 1996: 279–80. Johnson notes that the relics of St Ursula and the 11,000 virgins provided another fruitful source for relic hunters, although the cult itself had been the subject of some controversy during the Reformation. See Chapter 3.
55 Burke 1984: 45–6.
56 Kern 1994; Palmieri 1923.
57 Ryan 1936; Ditchfield 1995: 45ff.
58 See for example Gentilcore 1994; and in the English context, Walsham 2004.
59 Eilington 2001; Bossy 1985: 95–6.
60 Cameron 1993.
61 For a discussion of attitudes to saints and martyrs in the German Reformation, see Kolb 1987.
62 Bale 1546, 1547; Betteridge 1997; Freeman and Wall 2001.
63 Foxe 1570: II.1937ff., 2066.
64 Nussbaum 1998: 113–4.
65 Huggarde 1556: G6v–8v.
66 Harpsfield 1573: 602–25; Parsons 1603, pt II.
67 Stapleton 1565a; Parsons 1603: especially pt II. In a controversial volume, Wooden suggests that the marvellous signs that Foxe attributed to the Protestant martyrs were a 'palpable substitute' for the miracles of the saints recounted in the *Golden Legend*. Wooden 1983: 45–6.
68 Parsons 1602: Ee4r–v.
69 Parsons 1603, pt II.
70 Aston 1993b: 295–99.
71 Shagan 2003, Chapter 5.
72 Lyly 1580: 14–15.
73 Capp 1979.
74 Frere and Kennedy 1910: II.126, *my italics*; Duffy 1992: 480.

BIBLIOGRAPHY

Manuscript sources

British Library

BL Cotton MS Vitellius E xiv.
BL Cotton MS Cleo E iv.
BL Cotton MS Galba E iv.
BL Cotton MS Nero C iii.
BL MS Harl 424.
BL MS Harl 6253.
BL Lansdowne MS 231.

Bodleian Library

Bod MS e Mus 238.
Bod dep.d.324: *A Little Treatise of Divers Miracles Shown for the Portion of Christ's Blood in Hayles*.

College of Arms

College of Arms MS Arundel 4.

Corpus Christi College, Cambridge

CCCC MSS 5, 9, 16, 26, 41, 42, 43, 45, 96, 100, 111, 145, 161, 162, 164, 167, 173, 174, 178, 182, 183, 195, 198, 200, 295, 298, 302, 303, 307, 308, 312, 318, 338, 375, 389, 400, 408, 419, 420, 421.

Printed primary sources

Acta Sanctorum (1643–1867) *Quotquot Toto Orbe Coluntur Vel a Catholicis Scriptoribus Celebrantur* ... , 58 vols, Antwerp: Societe des Bollandistes.

Adso (1525) *Here begynneth the byrthe and lyfe of the moost false and deceytfull Antechryst*, London: W. de Worde.

Aelfric (1566) *A testimonie of antiquitie shewing the auncient fayth in the Church of England* ... , London: John Day.

Anon. (1538) *The Sum of the Actes and Decrees Made by Divers Bishops of Rome*, London: Thomas Gibson.

Anon. (1539) *The sum of the actes and decrees made by dyuerse bysshops of Rome*, London: Thomas Gybson.

Anon. (1548) *A Breife Recantation of Maystres Missa*, London: R. Wyer.

Anon. (1549?) *The Olde Faythe of Greate Brittaynge*, n.p.

Anon. (1550) *Here begynneth a booke called the fal of the Romish church* ... , London: W. Copland [?].

Anon. (1555) *A Plaine and Godlye Treatise Concernynge the Masse* ... , London: J. Wayland [?].

Aquinas, T. (1947) *Summa Theologia*, trans. Fathers of the English Dominican Province, 3 vols, London: Burns, Oates & Washbourne Ltd.

——(1928) *Summa Contra Gentiles*, trans. Fathers of the English Domincan Province, 4 vols, London: Burns, Oates & Washbourne Ltd.

Augustine of Hippo (1990) *St Augustine's Confessions and City of God*, M. Versfeld (ed.), Cape Town: Carrefour.

Bacon, F. (1892) *The Works of Francis Bacon*, J. Spedding, R.L. Ellis and D.D. Heath (eds), London: Longmans.

—— (1927) *The Philosophical Works of Francis Bacon*, J. Spedding, R.L. Ellis and J.M. Robertson (eds), London: Routledge.

Bale, J. (1543) *Yet a course at the Romyshe foxe* ... , Zurich [Antwerp]: Olyuer Iacobson [A. Goinus].

—— (1544a) *The epistle exhortatorye of an Englyshe Christiane* ... , Antwerp: A. Goinus.

—— (1544b) *A brefe chronycle concerning the examination and death of ... Sir John Oldecastell* ... , Antwerp: n.p.

—— (1545) *A mysterye of inyquyte contayned within the heretycall genealogye of Ponce Pantolabus* ... , Geneua [Antwerp]: M. Wood [A. Goinus].

—— (1546) *The first examinacyon of Anne Askewe lately martyred in Smythfelde* ... , Wesel: D. van der Straten.

—— (1547) *The lattre examinacyon of Anne Askewe latelye martyred in Smythfelde* ... , Wesel: D. van der Straten.

—— (1548a) *The image of bothe churches after the moste wonderfull and heauenly Reuelacion of Sainct John* ... , London: Richard Iugge.

—— (1548b) *An answere to a papystycall exhortacyon* ... , Antwerp: S. Mierdman.

—— (1548c) *Illustrium Maioris Britanniae scriptorum, hoc est, Angliae, Cambriae, ac Scotiae summariu[m]* ... , Gippeswici in Anglia [Wesel]: Per [D. van der Straten for] Ioannem Ouerton.

—— (1550a) *The image of both churches after the moste wonderful and heauenly Reuelacion of Sainct John* ... , London: John Day & William Seres.

—— (1550b) *The apology of Iohan Bale agaynste a ranke papist* ... , London: S. Mierdman for John Day.

—— (1551) *The first two partes of the Actes, or vnchast examples of the Englysh votaryes* … , London: S. Mierdman.

—— (1552) *An expostulation or complaynte agaynste the blasphemyes of a franticke papyst of Hamshyre*, London: S. Mierdman for John Day.

—— (1553) *The vocacyon of Ioha[n] Bale to the bishiprick of Ossorie in Irela[n]de* … , Rome [Wesel?]: J. Lambrecht[?] for Hugh Singleton.

—— (1557) *Scriptorum illustriu[m] maioris Brytannie quam nunc Angliam & Scotiam uocant catalogues* … , Basle: J. Oporinus.

—— (1558) *Acta Romanorum Pontificum a Dispersione Discipulorum Christi* ... , Basle: J. Oporinus.

—— (1560) *The first two partes of the Actes or vnchaste examples of the Englyshe votaryes*, London: John Tysdale.

—— (1574) *The pageant of popes contayninge the lyues of all the bishops of Rome*, London: Thomas Marsh.

—— (1838) *King Johan*, J.P. Collier (ed.), London: Camden Society.

Barclay, A. and Nelson, W. (eds) (1955) *The Life of St George*, London: Early English Texts Society.

Barnes, R. (1534) *A supplicacion vnto the most gracyous prynce H. the viij*, London: John Byddell.

—— (1535) *Vitae Romanorum Pontificum quod papas uocamus*, Basle: [s.n.].

—— (1573) *The vvhole workes of W. Tyndall, John Frith, and Doct. Barnes* … , London: Iohn Daye.

Baronius, C. (1593–1607) *Annales Ecclesiastici*, Rome: Congregation of the Oratory.

—— (1975) *The Life or the Ecclesiasticall Historie of St Thomas Archbishope of Canterbury, 1639*, Aldershot: Scolar Press.

Beard, T. (1625) *Antichrist. The Pope of Rome*, London: I Jaggard for I Bellamie.

Becon, T. (1549) *The castell of comforte in the whiche it is euidently proued, [that] God alone absolueth* … , London: John Daye.

—— (1564) *The worckes of Thomas Becon whiche he hath hitherto made and published* … , London: John Day.

—— (1637) *The displaying of the Popish masse* … , London: A. G[riffin].

—— (1844) *Prayer and other Pieces*, J. Ayre (ed.), Cambridge: Parker Society.

Bede (1907) *The Ecclesiastical History of England*, trans. A.M. Sellar, London: G. Bell and Sons.

—— (1940) *Vita Sancti Cuthberti* in *Two Lives of Saint Cuthbert*, B. Colgrave (ed.), Cambridge: Cambridge University Press.

Blackie, E.M. (ed.) (1924) *The Pilgrimage of Robert Langton*, Cambridge, MA: Harvard University Press.

Bokenham, O. (1938) *Legendys of Hooly Wummen. By Osbern Bokenham*, M.S. Serjeantson (ed.), London: Early English Texts Society.

Brie, F.W.D. (1906) *The Brut, or the Chronicles of England* … , London: Kegan Paul.

Brooks, J. (1553) *A sermon very notable, fruictefull, and godlie made at Paules crosse* … , London: Roberte Caly.

Bruce, J. and Perowne, T.T. (eds) (1853) *Correspondence of Matthew Parker*, Cambridge: Parker Society.

Bullinger, H. (1538) *A commentary vpon the seconde epistle of S Paul to the Thessalonia[n]s*, Southwark: Iames Nicolson.

—— (1849–52) *The Decades of Henry Bullinger*, 4 vols, T. Harding (ed.), Cambridge: Parker Society.

Burnet, G. (1865) *The History of the Reformation of the Church of England*, N. Pocock (ed.), Oxford: Clarendon Press.

Caesarius (1851) *Dialogus miraculorum*, 2 vols, J. Strange (ed.), 1851, repr 1966, Ridgewood, NJ: Gregg Press.

Calendar of State Papers, Domestic Series, of the Reigns of Edward V., Mary, Elizabeth, (James I) 1547–1580 (1581–1625), Preserved in the State Paper Department of Her Majesty's Public Record Office (1547–1590), 12 vols, R. Lemon (ed.), with addenda 1547–1579, by M.A.E. Green, London: HMSO, 1856–72.

Calendar of the State Papers Relating to Ireland, of the Reigns of Henry VIII, Edward VI, Mary, and Elizabeth, 1509–1573 (–1586, June) Preserved in the State Paper Department of Her Majesty's Public Record Office, 5 vols, H.C. Hamilton (ed.), London: Longman & Co., 1860–1890.

Calfhill, J. (1846) *An Answer to John Martialls Treatise of the Cross*, R. Gibbings (ed.), Cambridge: Parker Society.

Calvin, J. (1854) *A Treatise on Relics*, V. Krasinksi (ed.), Edinburgh: Johnston and Hunter.

Carion, J. (1550) *The thre bokes of cronicles, whyche John Carion … gathered wyth great diligence of the beste authours …* , London: [By S. Mierdman] for G. Lynne.

Cheke J. (1821) 'A treatise of superstition', in J. Strype (ed.), *The Life of the Learned Sir John Cheke*, Oxford: Clarendon Press.

Cheney, C.R. and Semple, W.H. (eds) (1953) *Selected Letters of Pope Innocent III Concerning England, 1198–1216*, London: Thomas Nelson and Sons.

Colgan, J. (ed.) (1645–7) *De sacris Hiberniæ antiquitatibus*, Louvain: C. Coenestenium, E. de Witte.

Cooper, T. (1617) *The Mystery of Witchcraft …* , London: Nicholas Okes.

Coverdale, M. (1564) *Certain most godly, fruitful, and comfortable letters of such true saintes and holy martyrs of God …* , London: John Day.

Cranmer, T. (1547) *Certayne sermons, or homelies appoynted by the kynges Maiestie …* , London: Rychard Grafton.

—— (1833) *The Remains of Thomas Cranmer …* , 4 vols, H. Jenkyns (ed.), Oxford: OUP.

—— (1844) *Miscellaneous Writings and Letters of Thomas Cranmer, Archbishop of Canterbury*, J.E. Cox (ed.), Cambridge: Parker Society.

—— (1846) *The Writings and Disputations of Thomas Cranmer*, J.E. Cox (ed.), Cambridge: Parker Society.

Crowley, R. (1548a) *The confutation of the mishapen aunswer to the misnamed, wicked ballade …* , London: John Day and William Seres.

—— (1548b) *The confutation of the xiii. articles, wherunto Nicolas Shaxton, late byshop of Salilburye …* , London: By [S. Mierdman? for] John Day and William Seres.

Daneau, L. (1589) *A treatise touching Antichrist … plainly laid open out of the word of God …* , London: Thomas Orwin, for John Porter, and Thomas Gubbin.

Defoe, D. (1724–6) *A Tour thro' the Whole Island of Great Britain, divided into circuits or journeys …* , 2 vols, London: G. Strahan.

Douglas, D.C. and Greenaway, G.W. (eds) (1981) *English Historical Documents, vol. II, 1042–1189*, London: Eyre Methuen.

E.P. (1556) *A confutatio[n] of vnwritte[n] verities … made up by Thomas Cranmer … translated and set forth, by E.P.*, Wesel[?]: J. Lambrecht[?].

Ellis, F.S. (ed.) (1908) *The Golden Legend or the Lives of the Saints*, London: Dent, Temple Classics.

Ellis, H. (ed.) (1824) *Original Letters Illustrative of English History*, 3 vols, London: Triphook and Lepard.

Erasmus, D. (1933) 'Stridowensis Vita', in W.K. Ferguson (ed.), *Erasmi opuscula. A Supplement to the Opera Omnia*, The Hague: Martinus Nijhoff.

—— (1965) 'A pilgrimage for religion's sake', in *The Colloquies of Erasmus*, trans. C.R. Thompson, Chicago & London: University of Chicago Press.

—— (1974) 'In praise of folly', in *The Collected Works of Erasmus*, vol. 27, Toronto: University of Toronto Press.

Erbe, T. (ed.) (1905) *Mirks Festial. A Collection of Homilies by Joahnnes Mirkus*, London: Early English Texts Society.

Esquillus, P. (1552) *Wonderfull newes of the death of Paule the. iii. last byshop of Rome …* , London: Thomas Gaultier.

Fish, S. (1529) *A supplicacyon for the beggers*, Antwerp[?]: J. Grapheus[?].

Flacius, M. (1566) *Catalogus testium veritatis locupletissimus, omnium orthodoxæ Matris Ecclesiæ Doctorum …* , Basle: J. Oporinus.

Flacius, M., Judex, M. and Wigand, J. (1559–1574) *Ecclesiastica Historia, Integram Ecclesiae Christi Ideam …* , Basle: J. Oporinus.

Floyd. J. (1613) *Purgatories triumph ouer hell maugre the barking of Cerberus*, Saint-Omer: English College Press.

Forester, T. (ed.) (1863) *The Historical Works of Giraldus Cambrensis*, London: H.G. Bohn.

Foxe, E. (1534) *Opus Eximivm. De vera differentia Regiae potestatis et Ecclesiasticae et quae sit ipsa veritas ac virtus vtrivsque*, London: Thomas Berthelet.

—— (1548) *The true dyffere[n]s betwen ye regall power and the ecclesiasticall power …* , London: W. Copland.

Foxe, J. (1560) *A solemne contestation of diuerse popes, for the aduaunsing of theyr supremacie …* , London: John Daye.

—— (1563) *Actes and monuments of these latter and perilous daies …* , London: Iohn Day, Cum priuilegio Regi[a]e Maiestatis.

—— (1570) *The first volume of the ecclesiasticall history contaynyng the actes and monumentes of thynges passed in euery kynges tyme in this realme …* , London: John Daye.

—— (1579) *Christ Iesus triumphant A fruitefull treatise, wherin is described the most glorious triumph, and conquest of Christ Iesus our sauiour …* , London: John Day.

—— (1580) *The Pope Confuted. The Holy and Apostolique Church Confuting the Pope*, trans. J. Bell, London: Thomas Dawson.

—— (1583) *Actes and monuments of matters most speciall and memorable, happenyng in the Church with an vniuersall history of the same …* , London: John Day.

—— (1846) *The Acts and Monuments of John Foxe*, 8 vols, G. Townsend (ed.), London: Oates and Seeley.

—— (1973) *Two Latin Comedies by John Foxe the Martyrologist*, J.H. Smith (ed.), London: Cornell University Press.

Franke, K. (ed.) (1892) 'Benonis Aliorumque Cardinalium Schismaticorum Contra Gregorium VII et Urbanum II', *Monumenta Germaniae Historica Libelli de Lite vol. II*, Hanover: Impensis Bibliopolii Hahniani.

Frere, W.H. and Kennedy, W.M. (eds) (1910) *Visitation Articles and Injunctions of the Period of the Reformation*, 3 vols, London: Alcuin Club.

Frith, J. (1529) *A pistle to the Christen reader The revelation of Antichrist*, Malborow in the lande of Hesse [Antwerp]: Hans Luft [Johannes Hoochstraten].

Fuller, T. (1845) *The Church History of Britain from the Birth of Jesus Christ Until the Year MDCXLVIII*, 6 vols, J.S. Brewer (ed.), Oxford: Clarendon Press.

Furnivall, F.J. (ed.) (1868–72) *Ballads from Manuscripts*, 2 vols, London: Ballad Society.

—— (ed.) (1866) *Political, Religious and Love Poems*, London: Early English Texts Society.

Gairdner, J. (ed.) (1876) *The Historical Collections of a Citizen of London [viz. William Gregory]* … , London: Camden Society.

Galbraith, V.H. (ed.) (1937) *The St Albans Chronicle 1406–1420 edited from Bodley 462*, Oxford: Clarendon Press.

Gibson, T. (1548) *A breve cronycle of the Bysshope of Romes blessynge* … , London: [R. Wyer for] John Daye.

Gilby, A. (1547) *An ansvver to the deuillish detection of Stephane Gardiner* … London[?]: S. Mierdman for John Day.

—— (1551) *A commentarye vpon the prophet Mycha. Wrytten by Antony Gilby. Anno Domi. M.D.LI.*, London: John Day.

Giles, J.A. (1848) *Six Old English Chronicles*, London: Henry G. Bohn.

Godwin, F. (1601) *A Catalogue of the Bishops of England, Since the first Planting of Christian Religion in this Island* … , London: Eliot's Court Press.

Golden Legend (1527) *Thus endeth the legende, named in latyn Lege[n]da aurea that is to saye in englysshe the golden legende* … , London: Wynkyn de Worde.

—— (1978) *The Golden legend. A Reproduction from a Copy in the Manchester Free Library*, London: Holbein Society.

Gorlach, M. (1994) *The Kalendre of the Newe Legende of England*, Heidelberg: Winter.

Grafton, R. (ed.) (1809) *A Chronicle at Large and meere History of the affayres of England* … , H. Ellis (ed.), London: Camden Society.

Gregory the Great (1959) *Dialogues*, trans. O. Zimmerman, Washington, DC: Catholic University of America Press.

Gualther, R. (1556) *Antichrist, that is to saye: A true reporte, that Antichriste is come* … , Southwarke [Emden]: Christophor Trutheall [Egidius van der Erve].

Guest, E. (1548) *Treatise againste the preuee Masse* … , London: T. Raynald.

Hall, E. (1548) *The vnion of the two noble and illustrate famelies of Lancastre [and] Yorke* … , London: Richard Grafton.

Hardyng, J. (1543) *The chronicle of Ihon Hardyng from the firste begynnyng of Englande, vnto the reigne of kyng Edward the fourth* … , London: Richard Grafton.

Harpsfield, N. (1573) *Dialogi Sex Contra Summi Pontificatus, Monasticae Vitae, Sanctorum, Sacrarum Imaginum Oppugnatores, et Pseudomartyres*, Antwerp: Christopher Plantin.

—— (1622) *Historia Anglicana ecclesiastica a primis gentis susceptæ fidei incunabulis ad nostra fere tempora deducta* … , Douai: M. Wyon.

Hastings, F. (1598) *A watch-word to all religious, and true hearted English-men. By Sir Francis Hastings, knight*, London: Felix Kingston for Ralph Jackson.

—— (1600) *An apologie or defence of the watch-vvord, against the virulent and seditious ward-vvord published by an English-Spaniard* … , London: Felix Kyngston, for Ralph Jacson.

Hilarie, H. (1554) *The resurreccion of the masse with the wonderful vertues of the same* … , Strasburgh [Wesel?] in Elsas: [by J. Lambrecht? for H. Singleton].

Hilton, W. (1516) *Here begynneth the kalendre of the newe legende of Englande*, London: Richard Pynson.

Hoby, E. (1615) *A curry-combe for a coxe-combe. Or Purgatories knell* … , London: William Stansby for Nathaniel Butter.

Holland, H. (1590) *A treatise against vvitchcraft: or A dialogue, wherein the greatest doubts concerning that sinne, are briefly answered* … , Cambridge: John Legatt.

Hollinshed, R. (1587) *The first and second volumes of Chronicles comprising 1 The description and historie of England, 2 The description and historie of Ireland, 3 The description and historie of Scotland* … , London: Henry Denham.

Holmes, T.S. (ed.) (1915–16) 'Reg. John Stafford', *Somerset Record Society*, 31–2.

Homer, R. (ed.) (1978) *Three Lives from the Gilte Legende*, Heidelberg: Carl Winter.

Hooper, J. (1550) *An ouersight, and deliberacion vpon the holy prophete Ionas* … , London: John Day.

—— (1843) *Early Writings of Bishop Hooper*, S. Carr (ed.), Cambridge: Parker Society.

—— (1852) *Later Writings of Bishop Hooper, Together with his Letters and Other Pieces*, C. Nevinson (ed.), Cambridge: Parker Society.

Horstmann, C. (ed.) (1901) *Nova legenda Anglie, as collected by John of Tynemouth, John Capgrave, and Others* … , Oxford: Clarendon Press.

Huggarde, M. (1554) *The assault of the sacrame[n]t of the altar containyng aswell six seuerall assaultes made from tyme to tyme against the sayd blessed sacrament* … , London: Robert Caly.

—— (1556) *The displaying of the Protestantes, [and] sondry their practises* … , London: Robert Caly.

Hurlestone, R. (1550) *Newes from Rome concerning the blasphemous sacrifice of the papisticall Masse* … , Canterbury: I. Mychell for E. Campion.

James VI & I (1597) *Daemonologie in forme of a dialogue, diuided into three bookes*, Edinburgh: Robert Walde-graue.

James, M.R. (1917) 'Lives of St Walstan', *Norfolk Archaeology*, 19: 238–67.

Jewel, J. (1845–50) *The Works of John Jewel, Bishop of Salisbury*, 4 vols, J. Ayre (ed.), Cambridge: Parker Society.

John of Salisbury (1909) *Policraticus*, 2 vols, C.J. Webb (ed.), Oxford: Clarendon Press.

Joye, G. (1531) *The letters which Iohan Ashwel priour of Newnham Abbey … sente secretely to the Bishope of Lyncolne* … , Antwerp: M. de Keyser.

—— (1534) *The subuersio[n] of Moris false foundacion* … , Antwerp: Jacob Aurick [G. von der Haghen].

—— (1541) *The defence of the mariage of preistes agenst Steuen Gardiner bisshop of Wynchester* … , Antwerp: Widow of C. Ruremond.

—— (1543a) *George Ioye confuteth, Vvinchesters false articles*, Wesill in Cliefe lande [Antwerp]: By the Widow of C. Ruremond.

—— (1543b) *The vnitie and scisme of the olde chirche*, Antwerp: Widow of C. Ruremond.

—— (1545) *The exposicion of Daniel the prophete gathered oute of Philip Melanchton, Iohan Ecolampadius, Chonrade Pellicane [and] out of Iohan Draconite* … , Geneue [Antwerp]: Successor of A. Goinus.

—— (1546) *The refutation of the byshop of Winchesters derke declaratio[n]* … , London: J. Herford.

—— (1550) *The exposicio[n] of Daniell the prophete* … , London: John Day.

Kettley, J. (ed.) (1844) *The Two Liturgies of Edward VI*, Cambridge: Parker Society.

Kirchmeyer, T. (1570) *The popish kingdome, or reigne of Antichrist* … , London: Henrie Denham, for Richarde Watkins.

Kolve, V.A. and Olson, G. (eds) (1989) *The Canterbury Tales by Geoffrey Chaucer*, New York: W.W. Norton & Co.

Lambarde, W. (1576) *A perambulation of Kent conteining the description, hystorie, and customes of that shyre* … , London: [By Henrie Middleton] for Ralphe Newberie.

Lancaster, T. (1550) *The ryght and trew vndersta[n]dynge of the Supper of the Lord and the vse therof* … , London: [By E. Whitechurch?] for Iohan Turke.

Latimer, H. (1845) *Sermons and Remains of Hugh Latimer, Sometime Bishop of Worcester*, G.E. Corrie (ed.), Cambridge: Parker Society.

Latouche, R. (ed.) (1930–7) *Richer: Histoire de France*, Paris: Librairie Ancienne.

Leland, J. (1549) *The laboryouse iourney [and] serche of Iohan Leylande …* , London: S. Mierdman.

—— (1964) *The Itinerary of John Leland, in or about the Years 1535–1543*, L.T. Smith (ed.), London: Centaur Press.

Letters and Papers, Foreign and Domestic of the reign of Henry VIII, 21 vols, J.S. Brewer and R.H. Brodie (eds), London: HMSO, 1862–1932.

Lipsius, J. (1604) *De Virgo Hallensis*, Antwerp: Plantin Moretus.

Lloyd, C. (1856) *Formularies of Faith put forth by Authority during the Reign of Henry VIII …* , Oxford: OUP.

Lyly, J. (1580) *Euphues and his England Containing his voyage and his aduentures …* , London: [By T. East] for Gabriell Cawood.

Lynne, W. (1548) *The beginning and endynge of all popery, or popishe kyngedome*, London: John Herforde.

Mabillon, J. (ed.) (1703–39) *Annales ordinis sancti Benedicti …* , 6 vols, Paris: Luteciae Parisiorum.

Macaulay, G.C. (ed.) (1910) *Chronicle and Romance: Froissart, Malory, Holinshed With Introductions and Notes*, New York: P.F. Collier.

Machyn, H. (1848) *The Diary of Henry Machyn*, J.G. Nichols (ed.), London: Camden Society.

Marcourt, A. (1548) *A declaration of the masse the fruyte therof …* , Ipswich: John Oswen.

Martin, T. (1554) *A Treatise Declaryng and Plainly Provyng that the pretensed marriage of priestes … is no marriage*, London: Robert Caly.

Mason, J. (1612) *The anatomie of sorcerie VVherein the wicked impietie of charmers, inchanters, and such like, is discouered and confuted*, London: John Legatte.

Matthew, P. (1570) *Flores historiarum per Matthaeum Westmonasteriensem collecti*, London: Thomas March.

—— (1571) *Matthaei Paris, monachi Albanensis, Angli, historia maior à Guilielmo Conquaestore, ad vltimum annum Henrici tertij*, London: R. Wolfe.

Mirk, J. (1905) *Mirk's Festial: A Collection of Homilies*, T. Erbe (ed.), London: Early English Texts Society.

Moone, P. (1548) *A short treatise of certayne thinges abused in the Popysh Church long vsed …* , London: Wyllyam Copland.

More, T. (1963) *Utopia*, E. Surtz, S.J. and J.H. Hexter (eds), *The Complete Works of St. Thomas More*, vol. 4, New Haven and London: Yale University Press.

—— (1969) *Responsio ad Lutherum*, J.M. Headley (ed.), *The Complete Works of St. Thomas More*, vol. 5, New Haven and London: Yale University Press.

—— (1973) *The Confutation of Tyndale', Answer*, L.A. Schuster, R.C. Marius, J.P. Lusardi and R.J. Schoek (eds), *The Complete Works of St. Thomas More*, vol. 8, New Haven and London: Yale University Press.

—— (1976) *De Tristitia Christi*, C.H. Miller (ed.), *The Complete Works of St. Thomas More*, vol. 14, New Haven and London: Yale University Press.

—— (1979) *The Apology*, J.B. Trapp (ed.), *The Complete Works of St. Thomas More*, vol. 9, New Haven and London: Yale University Press.

—— (1981) *A Dialogue Concerning Heresies*, T.M.C. Lawler, G. Marc'hadour and R.C. Marius (eds), *The Complete Works of St. Thomas More*, vol. 6, New Haven and London: Yale University Press.

—— (1985) *The Answer to a Poisoned Book*, C.H. Miller and S. Foley (eds), *The Complete Works of St. Thomas More*, vol. 11, New Haven and London: Yale University Press.

—— (1990) *Letter to Bugenhagen, Supplication of Souls, Letter against Frith*, F. Manley, G. Marc'hadour, R. Marius and C.H. Miller (eds), *The Complete Works of St. Thomas More*, vol. 7, New Haven and London: Yale University Press.

Morse, R. (1975) *St Erkenwald*, Cambridge: D.S. Brewer.

Munday, A. (1584) *A vvatch-vvoord to Englande to beware of traytours and tretcherous practises* … , London: Thomas Hacket.

Napier, J. (1594) *A plaine discoverie of the whole Revelation of Saint John set down in two treatises* … , Edinburgh: Robert Waldegrave.

Nichols, J.G. (ed.) (1852) *Chronicle of the Greyfriars of London*, London: Camden Society.

—— (ed.) (1859) *Narratives of the Days of the Reformation*, London: Camden Society.

—— (ed.) (1875) *Erasmus' Pilgrimages to Saint Mary of Walsingham and Saint Thomas of Canterbury*, London: Camden Society.

Norton, T. (1570) *A warning agaynst the dangerous practises of papistes and specially the parteners of the late rebellion* … , London: Iohn Daye.

Numan, P. (1606) *Miracles lately vvrought by the intercession of the glorious Virgin Marie, at Mont-aigu* … , Antwerp: Arnold Conings.

Ochino, B. (1549) trans. J. Ponet, *A tragoedie or dialoge of the vniuste vsurped primacie of the Bishop of Rome* … , London: By N. Hill for Gwalter Lynne.

Old, J. (1555) *A short description of Antichrist vnto the nobilitie of Englande* … , Emden: E. van der Erve.

Origen (1953) *Contra Celsum*, H. Chadwick (ed.), Cambridge: Cambridge University Press.

Parker, H. (1493) *Here endith a compendiouse treetise dyalogue of Diues [and] paup[er] … that is to say. The riche [and] the pore fructuously tretyng vpon the x. co[m]mandmentes* … , London: Richard Pynson.

Parker, M. (1567) *Defence of priestes mariages stablysshed by the imperiall lawes of the realme of Englande* … , London: Richarde Iugge.

—— (1570) *Flores historiarum per Matthaeum Westmonasteriensem collecti*, London: Thomas Marsh.

—— (1572) *De antiquitate Britannicae ecclesiae & priuilegiis ecclesiae Cantuariensis, cum Archiepiscopis eiusdem 70*, London: John Day.

Parsons, R. (1581) *The copie of a double letter sent by an English gentilman from beyond the seas, to his frende in London*, Rheims: J. Foigny.

—— (1599) *A temperate vvard-vvord, to the turbulent and seditious VVach-word of Sir Francis Hastings knight* … , Antwerp: A. Conincx.

—— (1602) *The vvarn-vvord to Sir Francis Hastinges wast-word conteyning the issue of three former treatises* … , Antwerp: A. Conincx.

—— (1603) *A treatise of three conuersions of England from paganisme to Christian religion* … , Saint-Omer: François Bellet.

Patrologia Latina (1844–64) *Patrologiae cursus completus: seu bibliotheca universalis, integra, uniformis, commoda, oeconomica, omnium SS. Patrum, doctorum scriptorumque ecclesiasticorum* … , 221 vols, J.P. Migne (ed.), Paris: Excudebatur apud Migne.

Peacock, E. (ed.) (1868) *Instructions for Parish Priests*, London: Early English Texts Society.

Perkins, W. (1608) *A Discourse of the Damned Art of Witchcraft* … , Cambridge: Cantrel Legge.

Pertz, H. (ed.) (1839) 'Liutprand, *De Rebus Gestis Ottonis*', in *Monumenta Germaniae Historica Scriptorum*, vol. III, Hanover: Impensis Bibliopolii Hahniani.

—— (1844a) 'Bruno, *De bello Saxonice*', in *Monumenta Germaniae Historica Scriptorum*, vol. V, Hanover: Impensis Bibliopolii Hahniani, 327–84.

—— (1844b) 'Lambert of Herzfeld, *Chronicon*', in *Monumenta Germaniae Historica Scriptorum*, vol. V, Hanover: Impensis Bibliopolii Hahniani, 131–41.

—— (1848) 'Hugo of Flavigny, *Chronicon Virdunense seu Flaviniacense*', in *Monumenta Germaniae Historica Scriptorum*, vol. VIII, Hanover: Impensis Bibliopolii Hahniani, 280–502.

Pilkington, J. (1842) *The Works of James Pilkington, D.D., Lord Bishop of Durham*, J. Scholefield (ed.), Cambridge: Parker Society.

Plummer, C. (ed.) (1968) *Vitae Sanctorum Hiberniae*, 2 vols, Oxford: Clarendon Press.

Pole, R. (1744) *Epistolarum Reginaldi Poli S.R.E. Cardinalis et Aliorum ad Ipsum* … , 5 vols, A.M. Quirini (ed.), Brixiae: J-M Rizzari.

Ponet, J. (1549) *A defence for mariage of priestes by Scripture and aunciente writers* … , London: Reynold Wolff.

—— (1555) *An apologie fully ansvveringe by scriptures and auncea[n]t doctors, a blasphemose book gathered by D. Steph. Gardiner* … , Strasbourg: Heirs of W. Köpfel [?].

Punt, W. (1549) *A new dialoge called the endightment against mother Messe*, London: William Hill and William Seres.

Purvis, J. (ed.) (1948) *Tudor Parish Documents of the Diocese of York*, Cambridge: Cambridge University Press.

R.M. (1867) *A Newe Ballad*, in *Ancient Ballads and Broadsides published in England in the Sixteenth Century*, London: Philobiblon Society.

Ramsay, J. (1548) *A plaister for a galled horse* … , London: Thomas Raynalde.

Rhegius, U. (1537) *A co[m]parison betwene the olde learnynge [and] the newe* … , Sowthwarke: James Nicolso[n].

—— (1548) *The olde learnyng and the new, compared together* … , London: Robert Stoughton.

Robinson, H. (ed.) (1842) *The Zurich Letters Comprising the Correspondence of Several English Bishops and Others with Some of the Helvetian Reformers*, Cambridge: Parker Society.

—— (1846–7) *Original Letters Relative to the English Reformation*, 2 vols, Cambridge: Parker Society.

Rogers, T. (1589) *An historical dialogue touching antichrist and poperie* … , London: Andrew Maunsell.

Ross, W. (ed.) (1940) *Middle English Sermons*, London: Early English Texts Society.

Roy, W. (1528) *Rede me and be nott wrothe for I saye no thynge but trothe* … , Strasbourg: Johann Schott.

Sacchi, B. (1505) *Platinae Historici liber de Vita Christi: ac Pontificum omnium qui hactenus ducenti et viginti duo fuere*, Paris.

—— (1888) trans. W. Benham, *The Lives of the Popes from the Time of our Saviour Jesus Christ to the Accession of Gregory VII*, London: Griffith, Farran, Okeden and Welsh.

Sanders, N. (1585) *De Origine ac progressue schismatic Anglicai* … , Rheims: C. Agrippinae.

Schmidt, A.V.C. (ed.) (1978) *William Langland The Vision of Piers Plowman*, London and New York: Dent & Dutton.

Scot, R. (1584) *The discouerie of witchcraft vvherein the lewde dealing of witches and witchmongers is notablie detected* … , London: William Brome.

Sermons (1908) *Certain Sermons or Homilies Appointed to be Read in the Churches in the Time of Queen Elizabeth*, London: SPCK.

Sheldon, R. (1616) *A suruey of the miracles of the Church of Rome, prouing them to be antichristian* … , London: Nathaniel Butter.

Shepherd, L. (1548a) *Philogamus*, London: W. Hill.

—— (1548b) *Antipus To heare of such thinges ye be not wont nam horum contraria verissima sunt*, London: John Day.

—— (1548c) *The comparison betwene the Antipus and the Antigraphe or answere therunto with* … , London: John Day.

—— (1548d) *Doctour doubble ale*, London: A. Scoloker?

—— (1548e) *John Bon and Mast Person*, London: J. Daye and W. Seres.

—— (1548f) *Pathose, or an inward passion of the pope for the losse of hys daughter the masse*, London: John Daye and William Seres.

—— (1548g) *A pore helpe The buklar [and] defence of mother holy kyrke and weape[n] to driue he[n]ce al the against here wircke*, London: J. Day and W. Seres.

—— (1548h) *The vpcheringe of the messe*, London: Iohn Daye Willyam Seres.

—— (2001a) 'Caueteles Preseruatory Concerning the Preservation of the Gods which are Kept in the Pixe', in J. Devereux (ed.), *An Edition of Luke Shepherd's Satires*, Tempe, AZ: Arizona Centre for Medieval and Renaissance Studies, 97–102.

—— (2001b) 'The comparison between the antipus and the antigraphe or answere thereunto', in J. Devereux (ed.), *An Edition of Luke Shepherd's Satires*, Tempe, AZ: Arizona Centre for Medieval and Renaissance Studies, 60–8.

Sheingorn, P. and Thiebaux, T. (eds) (1996) *The Passion of St Ursula and the Sermon on the Birthday of St Ursula*, Toronto: Peregrina.

Shirley, W.W. (ed.) (1858) *Fasciculi Zizaniorum*, London: Rolls Series.

Simmons, T. (ed.) (1879) *The Lay Folks Mass Book*, London: Early English Texts Society.

Sleidan, J. (1689) *The General History of the Reformation of the Church from the Errors and Corruptions of the Church of Rome* … , trans. E. Bohun, London.

Stapleton, T. (1565a) *A fortresse of the faith first planted amonge vs Englishmen* … , Antwerp: John Laet.

—— (1565b) *The history of the church of Englande. Compiled by venerable Bede, Englishman*, Antwerp: John Laet.

—— (1612) *Tres Thomae seu de S Thomae Apostoli rebus gestis*, Coloniae Aggrippinae: B. Gualteri.

Stow, J. (1565) *A summarie of Englyshe chronicles conteynyng the true accompt of yeres* … , London: Thomas Marshe.

—— (1580) *The chronicles of England from Brute vnto this present yeare of Christ*, London: Henry Bynneman for Ralphe Newberie.

—— (1592) *The annales of England faithfully collected out of the most autenticall authors, records, and other monuments of antiquitie*, London: Ralfe Newbery.

Strype, J. (1812) *Memorials of the Most Reverend Father in God Thomas Cranmer, sometime Lord Archbishop of Canterbury*, Oxford: Clarendon Press.

—— (1821) *The Life and Acts of Matthew Parker. The First Archbishop of Canterbury in the Reign of Queen Elizabeth*, Oxford: Clarendon Press.

—— (1822) *Ecclesiastical Memorials Relating Chiefly to Religion and the Reformation of it* … , 3 vols, Oxford: Clarendon Press.

—— (1824) *Annals of the Reformation and the Establishment of Religion and Various other Occurrences During Queen Elizabeth's Happy Reign*, Oxford: Clarendon Press.

Stubbes, J. (1574) *The life off the 70. Archbishopp off Canterbury presentlye sittinge Englished, and to be added to the 69. lately sett forth in Latin*, Zurich: Christoph Froschauer[?].

Stubbs, W. (ed.) (1874) *The Memorials of St Dunstan, Archbishop of Canterbury, Edited from Various Manuscripts*, London: Rolls Series.

Summers, M. (ed.) (1971) *The Malleus Maleficarum of Heinrich Kramer and James Sprenger*, New York: Dover.

Surtz, E. and Murphy, V. (eds) (1988) *The Divorce Tracts of Henry VIII*, Angers: Moreana.

Swinburn, L. (ed.) (1917) *The Lanterne of Light*, London: Early English Texts Society.

Swinnerton, T. (1534) *A mustre of scismatyke bysshopes of Rome otherwyse naming them selues popes …* , London: Johan Byddell.

Tanner, N.P. (ed.) (1990) *The Decrees of the Ecumenical Councils*, 2 vols, London and Washington: Sheed and Ward.

Thomas, W. (1774) 'Il Peregrino Inglese', in A. D'Aubant (ed.), *The Works of William Thomas*, London: J. Almon.

Thomas Walsingham, (1574) *Historia breuis Thomae VValsingham, ab Edwardo primo, ad Henricum quantum*, London: Henricum Binneman.

—— (1574) *Ypodigma Neustriae vel Normanniae …* , London: John Day.

—— (1866–9) *Historia Anglorum sive historia minor (1067–1253)*, 3 vols, F. Madden (ed.), London: Rolls Society.

Tjernagel, N.S. (ed.) (1963) *The Reformation Essays of Dr Barnes*, London: Concordia.

Turner, W. (1543) *The huntyng & fyndyng out of the Romishe fox …* , Basyl [Bonn]: L. Mylius.

—— (1545) *The rescuynge of the romishe fox other vvyse called the examination of the hunter deuised by steuen gardiner …* , Winchester [Bonn]: Laurenz von der Meulen.

—— (1548) *A newe dialogue vvherin is conteyned the examinatio[n] of the messe …* , London: John Day and William Seres.

—— (1555) *The huntyng of the romyshe vuolfe …* , Emden: Egidius van der Erve.

Tyndale, W. (1573) *The vvhole workes of W. Tyndall, John Frith, and Doct. Barnes …* , London: Iohn Daye.

—— (1848) *Doctrinal Treatises and Introductions to Different Portions of the Holy Scriptures*, H. Walter (ed.), Cambridge: Parker Society.

—— (1849) *Expositions and Notes on … the Holy Scriptures … Together with the Practice of Prelates*, H. Walter (ed.), Cambridge: Parker Society.

—— (1850) *An Answer to Sir Thomas More's Dialogue*, H. Walter (ed.), Cambridge: Parker Society.

Tynley, R. (1609) *Tvvo learned sermons The one, of the mischieuous subtiltie, and barbarous crueltie, the other of the false doctrines, and refined haeresis of the romish synagogue …* , London: W. Hall for Thomas Adams.

Vadian, J. (1534) *A worke entytled of ye olde god [and] the newe of the olde faythe [and] the newe …* , London: William Marshall.

Valera, C. (1600) *Two treatises the first, of the liues of the popes, and their doctrine. The second, of the masse …* , London: John Harison.

Vergil, P. (1528) *De Inventoribus Rerum …* , Paris: Roberti Stephani.

—— (1844–6) *Polydore Vergil's English History from an Early Translation*, H. Ellis (ed.), London: Camden Society.

—— (1972) *Anglia Historia*, Menston: Scolar Press.

—— (1997) *Beginnings and Discoveries. Polydore Vergil's De Inventoribus Rerum*, B. Weiss and L.C. Perez (eds), Nieuwkoop: De Graaf.

Veron, J. (1548) *The V. abhominable blasphemies co[n]teined in the Masse …* , London: Humfrey Powell.

—— (1550) *The godly saiyngs of the old auncient faithful fathers vp on the Sacrament of the bodye and bloude of Chryste …* , Worrcester: John Oswen.

—— (1562) *A Stronge Battery against the Idolatrous Inuocation of the Dead Saintes …* , London: Henry Sutton for Thomas Hacket.

Verstegan, R. (1605) *A Restitution of Decayed Intelligence: in Antiquities …* , Antwerp: Robert Bruney.

Walter Map (1914) *De Nugis Curialium*, M.R. James (ed.), Oxford: Clarendon Press.

Waterworth, J. (ed. and trans.) (1848) *The Canons and Decrees of the Sacred and Oecumenical Council of Trent*, London: Dolman.

von Watt, J. (1534) *A worke entytled of ye olde god & the newe, of the olde faythe & the newe, of the olde doctryne and ye newe*, trans. W. Turner, London: J. Bydell.

Weatherly, E. (1936) *Speculum Sacerdotale*, London: Early English Texts Society.

Wey, W. (1924) 'The best mode of proceeding on a pilgrimage', in E.L. Guilford (ed.), *Travellers and Travelling in the Middle Ages*, London: The Sheldon Press.

Wilkins, D. (1737) *Concilia Magnae Britanniae et Hiberniae*, 4 vols, London: R. Gosling.

William of Malmesbury (1887) *De Gesta Regum Anglorum*, W.W. Stubbs (ed.), London: Rolls Series.

—— (2002) *Gesta Pontificum Anglorum. The Deeds of the Bishops of England*, D. Preest (ed.), Woodbridge: Boydell.

Williams, C.H. (ed.) (1996) *English Historical Documents, vol. 5, 1485–1555*, London: Routledge.

Wright, T. (ed.) (1843) *Letters Relating to the Suppression of the Monasteries*, London: Camden Society.

Wriothesley, C. (1875–7) *A Chronicle of England During the Reigns of the Tudors from A.D. 1485–1559*, W.D. Hamilton (ed.), London: Camden Society.

Wycliffe, J. (1548) *Vvicklieffes Wicket. Faythfully Ouerseene and Corrected after the Originall and First Copie …* , London: John Day[?].

—— (1883) *J. Wiclif's Polemical Works in Latin, for the First Time Edited from the Manuscripts, with Critical and Historical Notes*, 2 vols, R. Buddensieg (ed.), London and Leipzig: Trubner & Co.

—— (1922) *De Mandatis Divinis … with an Appendix De Differentia inter Peccatum Morale et Veniale*, J. Loserth (ed.), London: Wyclif Society.

Wyse, N. (1538) *A consolacyon for chrysten people to repayre agayn the lordes temple …* , London: John Waylande.

Secondary sources

Abou-el-Haj, B. (1994) *The Medieval Cult of the Saints. Formation and Transformation*, Cambridge: Cambridge University Press.

Alford, S. (2002) *Kingship and Politics in the Reign of Edward VI*, Cambridge: Cambridge University Press.

Allen, R. (1892) 'Gerbert, Pope Silvester', *English Historical Review*, 7: 625–68.

Anderson, J. (1984) *Biographical Truth. The Representation of Historical Persons in Tudor-Stuart Writing*, New Haven and London: Yale University Press.

Ankarloo, B. and Henningsen, G. (eds) (1993) *Early Modern European Witchcraft. Centres and Peripheries*, Oxford: Clarendon Press.

Ashley, K. (1982) 'The Guiler beguiled. Christ and Satan as theological tricksters in medieval religious literature', *Criticism*, 24: 126–37.

Ashworth, W. (1986) 'Catholicism and early modern science', in D.C. Lindberg and R.L. Numbers (eds), *God and Nature. Historical Essays on the Encounter Between Christianity and Science*, Berkeley: University of California Press, 136–66.

Aston, M. (1984) *Lollards and Reformers. Images and Literacy in Late Medieval Religion*, London: Hambledon.

—— (1988) *England's Iconoclasts*, Oxford: Clarendon Press.

—— (1993a) *The King's Bedpost: Reformation and Iconography in a Tudor Group Portrait*, Cambridge: Cambridge University Press.

—— (1993b) *Faith and Fire: Popular and Unpopular Religion 1350–1600*, London and Rio Grande: Hambledon.

—— (1997) 'Iconoclasm in England. Official and clandestine', in P. Marshall (ed.), *The Impact of the English Reformation 1500–1640*, London: Arnold, 167–92.

Attwater, D. (1959) *A Dictionary of the Popes from Peter to Pius XII*, London: Burns, Oats and Washbourne.

Aurner, N.S. (1926) *Caxton: Mirror of Fifteenth Century Letters*, London: Philip Allan.

Baddesley, S.C. (1900) 'The holy blood of Hayles', *Transactions of the Bristol and Gloucester Archaeological Society*, 23: 276–85.

Bagchi, D. (1993) 'Luther and the problem of martyrdom', in D. Wood (ed.), *Martyrs and Martyrologies: Studies in Church History*, Oxford: Blackwell, 30: 209–20.

Barb, A. (1963) 'The survival of magical arts', in A. Momigliano (ed.), *Conflict Between Paganism and Christianity in the Fourth Century*, Oxford: Clarendon Press.

Baring-Gould, S. and Fisher, J. (1990) *The Lives of the British Saints*, Felinfach: Llanerch.

Barlow, F. (1986) *Thomas Becket*, London: Weidenfeld & Nicolson.

Barnes, R.B. (1988) *Prophecy and Gnosis. Apocalypticism in the Wake of the Lutheran Reformation*, Stanford, California: University of Stanford Press.

Baroja, J.C. (1993) 'Witchcraft and Catholic theology', in B. Ankarloo and G. Henningsen (eds), *Early Modern European Witchcraft. Centres and Peripheries*, Oxford: Clarendon Press, 19–43.

Barry, J. (1995) 'Literacy and literature in popular culture: reading and writing in historical perspective', in T. Harris (ed.), *Popular Culture in England c. 1500–1850*, Basingstoke: Macmillan, 69–94.

Bartlett, R. (1986) *Trial by Fire and Water: The Medieval Judicial Ordeal*, Oxford: Clarendon Press.

Baskerville, E. (1979) *A Chronological Bibliography of Propaganda and Polemic Published in England Between 1553 and 1558: From the Death of Edward VI to the Death of Mary*, Philadelphia: American Philosophical Society.

Bauckham, R. (1978) *Tudor Apocalypse. Sixteenth Century Apocalypticism, Millennarianism, and the English Reformation: From John Bale to John Foxe and Thomas Brightman*, Sutton Courtenay: Courtenay Library of Reformation Classics.

Beer, B. (1985) 'John Stow and the English Reformation 1547–1559', *Sixteenth Century Journal*, 16: 257–71.

Benson, R.G. and Naylor, E.W. (eds) (1991) *Essays in Honour of Edward B. King*, Sewanee, Tennessee: The University of the South.

Bernard, G. (1990) 'The church of England c. 1529–1642', *History*, 75: 183–206.

—— (1998) 'Vitality and vulnerability in the late medieval church: pilgrimage on the eve of the break with Rome', in J.L. Watts (ed.), *The End of the Middle Ages? England in the Fifteenth and Sixteenth Centuries*, Stroud: Sutton.

Bethell, D. (1972) 'The making of a twelfth century relic collection', in G.J. Cuming and D. Baker (eds), *Popular Belief and Practice Papers: Read at the Ninth Summer Meeting and the Tenth Winter Meeting of the Ecclesiastical History Society* (Studies in Church History, vol. 8), Cambridge: Cambridge University Press, 61–72.

Betteridge, T. (1997) 'Anne Askew, John Bale, and Protestant history', *Journal of Medieval and Early Modern Studies*, 27: 265–84.

—— (1999) *Tudor Histories of the English Reformations 1530–1583*, Aldershot: Ashgate.

Bietenholz, P. (1994) *Historia and Fabula. Myths and Legends in Historical Thought from Antiquity to the Middle Ages*, Leiden: Brill.

Blaher, D.J. (1949) *The Ordinary Processes in Causes of Beatification and Canonisation*, Washington, DC: Catholic University of America, Canon Law Studies.

Blake, N.F. (1965) 'William Caxton, his choice of texts', *Anglia*, 83: 289–307.

Blumenfeld-Kosinksi, B. and Szell, T. (eds) (1991) *Images of Sainthood in Medieval Europe*, Ithaca and London: Cornell University Press.

Blumenthal, U. (2001) *Gregor VII: Papst Zwischen Canossa und Kirchenreform*, Darmstadt: Wissenschaftliche Buchgesellschaft.

Booty, J. (1963) *An Apology of the Church of England*, Ithaca: Cornell University Press.

Bossy, J. (1970) 'The counter-Reformation and the people of Catholic Europe', *Past and Present*, 47: 51–70.

—— (1985) *Christianity in the West*, Oxford: OUP.

Bouwsma, W. (1990) *A Useable Past. Essays in European Cultural History*, Berkeley: University of California Press.

Bowd, S. (2002) *Reform Before the Reformation. Vincenzo Querini and the Religious Renaissance in Italy*, Leiden: Brill.

Bradshaw, C.J. (1996) 'David or Josiah? Old Testament kings as exemplars in Edwardian religious polemic', in B. Gordon (ed.), *Protestant History and Identity in Sixteenth-Century Europe*, 2 vols, Aldershot: Ashgate, 77–90.

—— (1999) 'The exile literature of the early Reformation: obedience to God and the king', in N. Scott Amos, A.D.M. Pettegree and H. van Nierop (eds), *The Education of a Christian Society. Humanism and the Reformation in Britain and the Netherlands*, Aldershot: Ashgate, 112–30.

Brann, N.L. (1984) 'Pre-Reformation humanism in Germany and the papal monarchy: a study in ambivalence', *Journal of Medieval and Renaissance Studies*, 14: 159–85.

Brigden, S. (1989) *London and the Reformation*, Oxford: Clarendon Press.

Bromwich, J. (1962) 'The first book printed in Anglo-Saxon type', *Transactions of the Cambridge Bibliographical Society*, 4: 265–91.

Brooke, C. (1991) 'Reflections on late medieval cults and devotions', in R.G. Benson and E.W. Naylor (eds), *Essays in Honour of Edward B. King*, Sewanee, Tennessee: the University of the South.

Brown, A. (1995) *Popular Piety in Late Medieval England. The Diocese of Salisbury 1250–1550*, Oxford: Clarendon Press.

Brown, P. (1967) *Augustine of Hippo*, Berkeley: University of California Press.

—— (1970) 'Sorcery, demons and the rise of Christianity from late antiquity into the middle ages', in M. Douglas (ed.), *Witchcraft Confessions and Accusations*, London: Tavistock Publications.

—— (1975) 'Society and the supernatural. A medieval change', *Daedalus*, 104: 133–52.

—— (1977) *Relics and Social Status in the Age of Gregory of Tours*, Reading: Stenton Lecture.

—— (1981) *The Cult of the Saints: Its Rise and Function in Latin Christianity*, Chicago: University of Chicago Press.

Brownhill, J. (1883) 'Boxley Abbey and the Rood of Grace', *The Antiquary*, 7: 162–5.

Bruhn, K. (2002) 'Reforming St Peter. Protestant constructions of St Peter the apostle in early modern England', *Sixteenth Century Journal*, 33: 33–50.

Buell, L.M. (1950) 'Elizabethan portents: superstition or doctrine?', in Members of the Department of English (eds), University of California, *Essays Critical and Historical Dedicated to Lily B. Campbell*, Berkeley: University of California Press, 27–41.

Burke, P. (1978) *Popular Culture in Early Modern Europe*, New York: New York University Press.

—— (1984) 'How to be a counter-Reformation saint', in K. von Greyerz (ed.), *Religion and Society in Early Modern Europe 1500–1800*, London: Allen and Unwin, 45–56.

—— (ed.) (1987) 'Rituals of healing in early modern Italy', in *The Historical Anthropology of Early Modern Italy. Essays on Perception and Communication*, Cambridge: Cambridge University Press.

Burling, P. (1988) *The Life of St Dunstan*, King's Heath: St Dunstan's Church.

Burns, R.M. (1981) *The Great Debate on Miracles*, Lewisburg: Bucknell University Press.

Butler, J. (1995) *The Quest for Becket's Bones. The Mystery of the Relics of St Thomas Becket of Canterbury*, New Haven and London: Yale University Press.

Butterworth, C.C. and Chester, A.G. (1962) *George Joye, 1495–1553. A Chapter in the History of the English Bible and the English Reformation*, Philadelphia: University of Philadelphia Press.

Byles, A.T.P. (1934) 'William Caxton as a man of letters', *The Library*, 4th series, 15: 1–25.

Bynum, C.W. (1987) *Holy Feast and Holy Fast. The Religious Significance of Food to Medieval Women*, London and Berkeley: University of California Press.

Bynum, S. (1978) 'Ritualistic acts and compulsive behaviour: the pattern of Tudor martyrdom', *American Historical Review*, 83: 623–43.

Cameron, E. (1993) 'Medieval heretics as Protestant martyrs', in D. Wood (ed.), *Studies in Church History*, Oxford: Blackwell, 30: 185–207.

—— (1998) 'For reasoned faith or embattled creed? Religion for the people in early modern Europe', *Transactions of the Royal Historical Society*, 6th series, 8: 165–87.

Campbell, J. (1984) 'Some twelfth century views of the Anglo-Saxon past', *Peritia*, 3: 131–50.

Campbell, L. (1947) *Shakespeare's Histories*, San Marino, CA: The Huntingdon Library.

Capp, B. (1979) *Astrology and the Popular Press. English Almanacs 1500–1800*, London: Faber.

Carley, J.P. (1988) *Glastonbury Abbey: The Holy House at the Head of the Moors Adventurous*, New York: St Martins.

Carlson, E.J. (1994) *Marriage and the English Reformation*, Oxford: Blackwell.

—— (ed.) (1998) *Religion and the English People, 1500–1640. New Voices, New Perspectives*, Kirksville, MO: Thomas Jefferson University Press.

Cavendish, R. (1977) *A History of Magic*, London: Weidenfeld and Nicholson.

Cazelles, B. (1991) 'Introduction', in R. Blumenfeld Kosinksi and T. Szell (eds), *Images of Sainthood in Medieval Europe*, 1–17.

Clark, S. (1993) 'Protestant demonology: sin, superstition and society c. 1520–1630', in B. Ankarloo and G. Henningsen (eds), *Early Modern European Witchcraft. Centres and Peripheries*, Oxford: Clarendon Press, 45–81.

—— (1997) *Thinking with Demons. The Idea of Witchcraft in Early Modern Europe*, Oxford: Clarendon Press.

Clark, S. and Morgan, P.T.J. (1976) 'Religion and magic in Elizabethan Wales. Robert Holland's *Dialogue on Witchcraft*', *Journal of Ecclesiastical History*, 27: 31–46.

Clebsch, W.A. (1980) *England's Earliest Protestants 1520–1535*, Westport: Greenwood Press.

Clogan, M. (1975) 'Medieval hagiography and romance', *Medievalia at Humanistica*, ns. 6: 189–98.

Cochrane, E.W. (1981) *Historians and Historiography in the Italian Renaissance*, Chicago: University of Chicago Press.

Cohn, N. (1993a) *The Pursuit of the Millennium*, London: Pimlico.

—— (1993b) *Europe's Inner Demons. The Demonisation of Christians in Medieval Christendom*, London: Pimlico.

Colgrave, B. (1935) 'Bede's miracle stories', in A.H. Thompson (ed.), *Bede, his Life, Times and Writings*, Oxford: Clarendon Press.

—— (1958) 'The earliest saints' lives written in English', *Proceedings of the British Academy*, 44: 35–60.

Collinson, P. (1983) *Godly People. Essays on English Protestantism and Puritanism*, London: Hambledon.

—— (1997) 'Truth, lies and fiction in sixteenth-century Protestant historiography', in D. Kelley and D. Sachs (eds), *The Historical Imagination in Early Modern Britain*, Cambridge: Cambridge University Press, 37–68.

—— (2004) *John Foxe as Historian*. Available online at www.hrionline.ac.uk/foxe/apparatus/collinsonessay.html (accessed February 2004).

Collinson, P., Ramsay, N. and Sparks, M. (eds) (1995) *A History of Canterbury Cathedral*, Oxford: OUP.

Congar, Y.-M. (1966) *Tradition and Traditions. An Historical and a Theological Essay*, London: Burns and Oates.

Coste, J. (1995) *Boniface VIII en Procès. Articles d'Accusation et Dépositions des Témoins (1303–1311)*, Rome: L'Erma di Bretschneider.

Cowdrey, H.E.J. (1998) *Pope Gregory VII 1073–1085*, Oxford: Clarendon Press.

—— (2000) *Popes and Church Reform in the Eleventh Century*, Aldershot: Ashgate.

Cressy, D. (1977) 'Levels of literacy in England 1539–1730', *Historical Journal*, 20: 1–23.

—— (1989) *Bonfires and Bells. National Memory and the Protestant Calendar in Elizabethan and Stuart England*, London: Weidenfeld and Nicolson.

Cronin, H.S. (1907) 'The twelve conclusions of the Lollards', *English Historical Review*, 22: 292–304.

Cummings, B. (2002) 'Iconoclasm and bibliophobia in the English Reformations 1521–1558', in J. Dimmick, J. Simpson and N. Zeeman (eds), *Images, Idolatry and Iconoclasm in Late Medieval England*, Oxford: OUP, 185–206.

Dales, D. (1988) *Dunstan: Saint and Statesman*, Cambridge: Lutterworth.

Daniell, D. (1994) *William Tyndale. A Biography*, New Haven and London: Yale University Press.

Daston, L. (1999) 'Marvelous facts and miraculous evidence in early modern Europe', in P.G. Platt (ed.), *Wonders, Marvels and Monsters in Early Modern Culture*, Newark and London: University of Delaware Press, 76–104.

Davidson, C. and Nichols, A.E. (1989) *Iconoclasm vs Art and Drama*, Kalamazoo: Early Drama, Art and Music Monograph Series.

Davies, C.F. (1987) '"Poor persecuted little flock" or commonwealth of Christians: Edwardian Protestant concepts of the church', in P. Lake and M. Dowling (eds), *Protestantism and the National Church in Sixteenth Century England*, London: Croom Helm, 36–77.

—— (2002) *A Religion of the Word. The Defence of the Reformation in the Reign of Edward VI*, Manchester and New York: Manchester University Press.

Davies, R.T. (1947) *Four Centuries of Witch Beliefs with Special Reference to the Great Rebellion*, London: Methuen.

Davis, J.F. (1963) 'Lollards, reformers, and St Thomas of Canterbury', *Birmingham Historical Journal*, 9: 1–15.

—— (1981) 'The trials of Thomas Bylney and the English Reformation', *Historical Journal*, 24: 775–90.

—— (1983) *Heresy and Reformation in the South East of England, 1520–1529*, London: Royal Historical Society.

Davis, W.T. (1940) 'A bibliography of John Bale', *Oxford Bibliographic Society Proceedings and Papers*, 5: 201–79.

Dawson, J.E.A. (1994) 'The apocalyptic thinking of the Marian Exiles', *Studies in Church History* (Subsidia), 10: 75–92.

Delehaye, H. (1922) *Oeuvres des Bollandistes à travers trois siècles*, Princeton: Princeton University Press.

—— (1962) *The Legends of the Saints*, trans. D. Attwater, London: Geoffrey Chapman.

Delooz, P. (1969) *Sociologie et Canonisations*, Liege: Martinus Nijhoff.

—— (1983) 'Towards a sociological study of canonized sainthood in the Catholic Church', in S. Wilson (ed.), *Saints and their Cults, Studies in Relgious Sociology, Folklore and History*, Cambridge: Cambridge University Press, 189–216.

Devereux, E.J. (1990) 'Empty turns and unfruitfull grafts: Richard Grafton's historical publications', *Sixteenth Century Journal*, 21: 48–52.

Dick, J.A.R. (1991) '"To trye his true frendes": imagery as argument in Tyndale's *The Parable of the Wicked Mammon*', *Moreana*, 49: 69–82.

Dickens, A.G. (1978) *Contemporary Historians of the German Reformation*, London: Blithell Memorial Lecture.

—— (1989) *The English Reformation*, 2nd edn, London: Batsford.

Dickens, A.G. and Tonkin, J.M. (eds) (1985) *The Reformation in Historical Thought*, Oxford: Blackwell.

Dickens, C. (1922) *A Child's History of England*, London: British Books.

Dickinson, J. (1956) *The Shrine of Our Lady of Walsingham*, Cambridge: Cambridge University Press.

Dinzelbacher, P. (1990) 'Heilige oder Hexen', in D. Simon (ed.), *Religiose Devianz: Untersuchungen zu socialzen rechtlichen und theologischen Reaktionen auf religiose Abweichung in westlichen und oslichen Mittelalter*, Frankfurt am Main: Klostermann.

Ditchfield, S. (1993) 'Martyrs on the move. Relics as vindications of local diversity in the Tridentine Church', *Studies in Church History*, 30: 283–94.

—— (1995) *Liturgy, Sanctity and History in Tridentine Italy*, Cambridge: Cambridge University Press.

Dobson, B. (1995) 'The monks of Canterbury', in P. Collinson, N. Ramsay and M. Sparks (eds), *A History of Canterbury Cathedral*, Oxford: OUP.

Dollinger, J. (1871) *Fables Respecting the Popes of the Middle Ages*, trans. A. Plummer, London: Rivingtons.

Dugmore, C.W. (1958) *The Mass and the English Reformers*, London: Macmillan.

Duffy, E. (1992) *The Stripping of the Altars. Traditional Religion in England 1400–1580*, New Haven and London: Yale University Press.

—— (2002) 'The dynamics of pilgrimage in late medieval England', in C. Morris and P. Roberts (eds), *Pilgrimage: The English Experience from Becket to Bunyan*, Cambridge: Cambridge University Press, 164–77.

Dunn-Lardeau, B. (1995) 'From the *Legend Doree* to the *Fleurs des Vies de saints*. A new image of the saint and sainthood?', *History of European Ideas*, 20: 299–304.

Eamon, W. (1983) 'Technology as magic in the late middle ages and the Renaissance', *Janus*, 70: 171–212.

—— (1994) *Science and the Secrets of Nature. Books of Secrets in Medieval and Early Modern Culture*, Princeton: Princeton University Press.

Eilington, D.S. (2001) *From Sacred Body to Angelic Soul. Understanding Mary in Late Medieval and Early Modern Culture*, Washington, DC: Catholic University of America Press.

Eire, C.M.N. (1986) *War Against the Idols. The Reformation of Worship from Erasmus to Calvin*, Cambridge and New York: Cambridge University Press.

Ellis, J.T. (1969) 'The ecclesiastical historian in the service of Clio', *Church History*, 38: 106–20.

Evans, G.R. (1992) *Problems of Authority in the Reformation Debates*, Cambridge: Cambridge University Press.

Fairfield, L.P. (1971) 'The vocation of John Bale: an early English autobiography', *Renaissance Quarterly*, 24: 327–40.

—— (1976) *John Bale. Mythmaker for the English Reformation*, West Lafayette, Indiana: Purdue University Press.

Farmer, D. (1992) *The Oxford Dictionary of the Saints*, Oxford: OUP.

Farmer, S. and Rosenwein, B.H. (eds) (2000) *Monks and Nuns, Saints and Outasts*, Ithaca and London: Cornell University Press.

Farrar, R. (1973) 'Structure and fiction in representative Old English Saints' *Lives*', *Neophilogus*, 57: 83–93.

Ferguson, A.B. (1979) *Clio Unbound: Perceptions of the Social and Cultural Past in Renaissance England*, Durham, NC: Duke University Press.

Ferguson, W.K. (1948) *The Renaissance in Historical Thought. Five Centuries of Interpretation*, Cambridge, MA: Houghton Mifflin.

Fichtenau, H. (1952) 'Zum Reliquienwesen im früheren Mittelalter', *Mitteilungen des Institutes für österreichische Geschichtsforschung*, 60: 60–89.

Finucane, R.C. (1995) *Miracles and Pilgrims. Popular Beliefs in Medieval England*, Basingstoke: Macmillan.

Firth, K.R. (1979) *The Apocalyptic Tradition in Reformation Britain 1530–1645*, Oxford: OUP.

Flesseman-van Leer, E. (1960) 'The controversy about ecclesiology between Thomas More and William Tyndale', *Nederlands Archief Voor Kerkesgeschiedenis*, 44: 65–86.

Flint, V. (1991) *The Rise of Magic in Early Medieval Europe*, Oxford: OUP.

Flower, R. (1935) 'Laurence Nowell and the discovery of England in Tudor times', *Proceedings of the British Academy*, 21: 47–73.

Forster, R. and Ranum, O. (1982) *Ritual, Religion and the Sacred. Selections from the Annales*, Baltimore and London: Johns Hopkins University Press.

Fox, A. (1986) 'Prophecies and politics in the reign of Henry VIII', in A. Fox and J. Guy (eds), *Reassessing the Henrician Age. Humanism, Politics and Reform, 1500–1550*, Oxford: Blackwell.

—— (1993) *Thomas More: History and Providence*, Oxford: OUP.

—— (1996) 'Custom, memory and the authority of writing', in P. Griffiths, A. Fox and S. Hindle (eds), *The Experience of Authority in Early Modern England*, Basingstoke: Macmillan.

—— (2000) *Oral and Literate Culture in England 1500–1700*, Oxford: OUP.

Franz, A. (1909) *Die kirchlichen Benediktionen im Mittelalter*, Freiburg: Herder.

Frazer, J. (1993) *The Golden Bough*, Ware: Wordsworth.

Freeman, T.S. (1994) 'A solemne contestation of Divers Popes: a work by John Foxe?', *English Language Notes*, 31: 35–42.

—— (1997) 'The importance of dying earnestly: the metamorphosis of the account of James Bainham in Foxe's *Book of Martyrs*', in R.N. Swanson (ed.), *The Church Retrospective*, Woodbridge: Boydell, 267–88.

—— (2000) 'Fate, faction and fiction in Foxe's *Book of Martyrs*', *Historical Journal*, 43: 601–23.

—— (2004a) *John Foxe, a Biography*. Available online at www.hrionline.ac.uk/foxe/apparatus/freemanessay.html (accessed February 2004).

—— (2004b) '"St Peter did not do thus": papal history in the *Actes and Monuments*'. Available online at www.hrionline.ac.uk/foxe/apparatus/freemanStPeterpart1.html (accessed February 2004).

Freeman, T.S. and Wall, S.E. (2001) 'Racking the body, shaping the text: the account of Anne Askew in Foxe's *Book of Martyrs*', *Renaissance Quarterly*, 54: 1165–96.

Fueter, E. (1968) *Geschichte der Neueren Historiographie*, repr. NY: Johnson Reprint Co.

Fussner, F.S. (1962) *The Historical Revolution, English Historical Writing and Thought 1580–1640*, Westport: Connecticut.

Galbraith, V.H. (1970) *Roger of Wendover and Matthew Paris*, Glasgow: Jackson.

Garnett, R. (1994) 'The Demon Pope', in T. Shippey (ed.), *The Oxford Book of Fantasy Stories*, Oxford and New York: OUP, 1–9.

Geary, P. (1978) *Furta Sacra. Thefts of Relics in the Central Middle Ages*, Princeton: Princeton University Press.

—— (1983) 'Humiliation of saints', in S. Wilson (ed.), *Saints and their Cults: Studies in Religious Sociology, Folklore and History*, Cambridge: Cambridge University Press, 123–40.

—— (1984) 'The saint and the shrine: the pilgrim's God in the middle ages', in L. Kriss-Retterbeck and G. Mohler (eds), *Wallfahrt Kennt Keine Grenzen*, Munich: Das National Museum.

—— (1994a) *Living with the Dead in the Middle Ages*, Ithaca: Cornell University Press.

—— (1994b) *Phantoms of Remembrance. Memory and Oblivion at the End of the First Millennium*, Princeton: Princeton University Press.

Geertz, H. (1975) 'An anthropology of religion and magic', *Journal of Interdisciplinary History*, 6: 71–89.

van Gennep, A. (1960) *Rites of Passage*, trans. M.B. Vizedom and G.L. Caffre, London: Routledge and Kegan Paul.

Gentilcore, D. (1992) *From Bishop to Witch: The System of the Sacred in Early Modern Terra d'Otranto*, Manchester: Manchester University Press.

—— (1994) 'Adapt yourself to the people's capabilities: missionary strategies, methods and impact in the Kingdom of Naples', *Journal of Ecclesiastical History*, 45: 269–96.

—— (1998) *Healers and Healing in Early Modern Italy*, Manchester: Manchester University Press.

Gibbon, E. (1952) *The Decline and Fall of the Roman Empire*, New York: Viking.

Gijswijt-Hofstra, M. and Frijhoff, W. (eds) (1991) *Witchcraft in the Netherlands from the Fourteenth to the Twentieth Century*, Rotterdam: Universitaire Presse.

Gillett, C.R. (1932) *Burned Books: Neglected Chapters in British History and Literature*, New York: Columbia University Press.

Ginzburg, C. (1976) 'High and low. The theme of forbidden knowledge in the 16th and 17th centuries', *Past and Present*, 73: 28–41.

Gogan, B. (1982) *The Common Corps of Christendom. Ecclesiological Themes in the Writings of Sir Thomas More*, Leiden: Brill.

Goodich, M. (1982) *Vita Perfecta. The Ideal of Sainthood in the Thirteenth Century*, Stuttgart: Anton Hiersemann.

Gordon, B. (ed.) (1996) *Protestant History and Identity in Sixteenth Century Europe*, 2 vols, Aldershot: Ashgate.

Graham T. and Watson, A.G. (1998) *The Recovery of the Past in Early Elizabethan England: Documents by John Bale and John Joscelyn from the Circle of Matthew Parker*, Cambridge: Cambridge Bibliographical Society.

Gransden, A. (1992) *Legends, Traditions and History in Medieval England*, London: Hambledon.

Graus, F. (1965) *Volk, Herrscher und Heiliger im Reich der Merowingen. Studien zur Hagiographie der Merowingerzeit*, Prague: Nakladatelstvy Ceskoslovensku Akademie Ved.

Gray, D. (1974) 'Notes on Middle English charms', in B. Rowland (ed.), *Chaucer and Middle English Studies in Honour of Russell Hope Robbins*, London: Allen and Unwin, 56–71.

Greenblatt, S. (1980) *Renaissance Self-Fashioning from More to Shakespeare*, Chicago: University of Chicago.

—— (2002) *Hamlet in Purgatory*, Princeton and Oxford: Princeton University Press.

Greenslade, S. (1960) *The English Reformers and the Fathers of the Church*, Oxford: Clarendon Press.

—— (1971–2) 'The authority of the tradition of the early Church in early Anglican thought', *Oecumenica*: 9–33.

Greg, W.W. (1935) 'Books and bookmen in the correspondence of Matthew Parker', *The Library*, 4th series, 16: 243–79.

Gregory, G. (1998) 'The making of a Protestant nation: success and failure in England's long Reformation', in N. Tyacke (ed.), *England's Long Reformation, 1500–1800*, London: UCL Press.

Gurevich, A. (1988) *Medieval Popular Culture. Problems of Belief and Perception*, trans. J.M. Bak and P.A. Hollingsworth, Cambridge: Cambridge University Press.

Guyotkeannin, O. and Poulle, E. (eds) (1996) *Autour de Gerbert d'Aurillac: le Pape l'an mil*, Paris: Ecole des Chartes.

Hadfield, A. (1994) *Literature, Politics and National Identity, Reformation to Renaissance*, Cambridge: Cambridge University Press.

Haigh, C. (1993) *English Reformations. Religion, Politics and Society under the Tudors*, Oxford: Clarendon Press.

Haller, W. (1963) *Foxe's Book of Martyrs and the Elect Nation*, London: Jonathan Cape.

de Hamel, C. (2000) *The Parker Library*, Cambridge: Corpus Christi College.

Hamilton, D. (2003) 'Catholic use of Anglo-Saxon precedents, 1565–1625: Thomas Stapleton, Nicholas Harpsfield, Robert Person, and others', *Recusant History*, 26 (4): 537–55.

Hanson, E. (1991) 'Torture and truth in Renaissance England', *Representations*, 34: 53–84.

Harris, J. (1940) *John Bale. A Study in the Minor Literature of the Reformation*, Urbana: University of Illinois Press.

Harris, T. (ed.) (1995) *Popular Culture in England c. 1500–1850*, Basingstoke: Macmillan.

Harrison, P. (1999) 'Prophecy, early modern apologetics and Hume's argument against miracles', *Journal of the History of Ideas*, 60: 241–56.

Hart, R. (1865) 'The shrines and pilgrimages of the county of Norfolk', *Norfolk Archaeology*, 6: 277–94.

Harvey, B. (1971) 'Work and *Festa Ferianda* in medieval England', *Journal of Ecclesiastical History*, 23: 289–308.

Hay, D. (1952) *Polydore Vergil. Renaissance Historian and Man of Letters*, Oxford: Clarendon Press.

Head, T. (2000) 'Saints, heretics and fire: finding meaning through the ordeal', in S. Farmer and B.H. Rosenwein (eds), *Monks and Nuns, Saints and Outasts*, Ithaca and London: Cornell University Press, 220–38.

Headley, J.M. (1963) *Luther's View of Church History*, New Haven and London: Yale University Press.

—— (1967) 'Thomas Murner, Thomas More, and the first expression of More's ecclesiology', *Studies in the Renaissance*, 14: 73–92.

—— (1987) 'The Reformation as a crisis in the understanding of tradition', *Archiv fur Reformationsgeschichte*, 78: 5–22.

Heal, B. (2003) 'Images of the Virgin Mary and Marian devotion in Protestant Nuremberg', in H. Parish and W.G. Naphy (eds), *Religion and Superstition in Reformation Europe*, Manchester: MUP, 25–46.

Heal, F.M. (2003) *Reformation in Britain and Ireland*, Oxford: OUP.

Heffernan, T. (1988) *Sacred Biography. Saints and their Biographers in the Middle Ages*, Oxford: OUP.

Helgerson, R. (1992) *Forms of Nationhood. The Elizabethan Writing of England*, Chicago and London: University of Chicago Press.

Heming, C.P. (2003) *Protestants and the Cult of the Saints in German-Speaking Europe, 1517–1531*, Kirksville, MO: Truman State University Press.

Hertling, L. (1933) 'Der Mittelalterliche Heiligentypus nach den Tugendkatalogen', *Zeitschreift fur Aszese und Mystik*, 8: 260–88.

Herzog, R. (1931) 'Die Wunderheilungen von Epidauros', *Philologus*, Suppl. XXII.3.

Hill, J. and Swan, M. (eds) (1998) *The Community, the Family and the Saint. Patterns of Power in Early Medieval Europe*, Turnhout: Brepols.

Hillerbrand, H. (1973) 'The historicity of miracles: the early eighteenth century debate among Woolston, Annet, Sherlock and West', *Studies in Religion*, 3: 132–51.

Hobsbawm, E. and Ranger, T. (eds) (1992) *The Invention of Tradition*, Cambridge: Cambridge University Press.

Hogarth, P. (1980) 'St George: The evolution of a saint and his dragon', *History Today*, 30: 17–22.

Holt, J.C. (1963) *King John*, London: Historical Association.

Hudson, A. (1978) *Selections from English Wycliffite Writings*, Cambridge: Cambridge University Press.

—— (1988) *The Premature Reformation. Wycliffite Texts and Lollard History*, Oxford: Clarendon Press.

Hughes, P. (1952–4) *The Reformation in England*, 3 vols, London: Hollis & Carter.

Huizinga, J. (1954) *The Waning of the Middle Ages: A Study of the Forms of Life, Thought and Art in France and the Netherlands in the Dawn of the Renaissance*, New York: Doubleday Anchor.

Hutton, R. (1990) 'The local impact of the Tudor Reformations', in C. Haigh (ed.), *The English Reformation Revised*, Cambridge: Cambridge University Press, 114–38.

—— (2001) *The Rise and Fall of Merry England. The Ritual Year 1400–1700*, Oxford: OUP.

Ingram, M. (1995) 'From Reformation to toleration. Popular religious cultures in England 1540–1690', in T. Harris (ed.), *Popular Culture in England c. 1500–1850*, Basingstoke: Macmillan.

Jaech, S.J. (1985) 'The prophisies of Rymour, Beid and Marlyng: Henry VIII and a sixteenth century political prophecy', *Sixteenth Century Journal*, 16: 291–300.

James, M. (1983) 'Ritual, drama and social body in the late medieval town', *Past and Present*, 98: 3–29.

—— (1986) *Society, Politics, and Culture: Studies in Early Modern England*, Cambridge: Cambridge University Press.

James, M.R. (1912) *A Descriptive Catalogue of the Manuscripts in the Library of Corpus Christi College, Cambridge*, 2 vols, Cambridge: Cambridge University Press.

Jansen, S. (1991) *Political Protest Under Henry VIII*, Woodbridge: Boydell.

Johnson, T. (1996) 'Holy fabrications. The Catacomb Saints and the Counter-Reformation in Bavaria', *Journal of Ecclesiastical History*, 47: 274–96.

Jolly, K., Raudvere, C. and Peters, E. (eds) (2002) *Witchcraft and Magic in Europe*, vol. 3, London: Athlone.

Jones, A.E. (1980) *The Trial of Joan of Arc*, Chichester and London: Barry Rose.

Jones, N. (1981) 'Matthew Parker, John Bale, and the Magdeburg centuriators', *Sixteenth Century Journal*, 12: 35–48.

Jones, T. (1970) *The Becket Controversy*, London and New York: Wiley.

Jones, W.R. (1973) 'Lollards and images: The defence of religious art in later medieval England', *Journal of the History of Ideas*, 34: 27–50.

Jones, W.R.D. (1988) *William Turner. Tudor Naturalist, Physician and Divine*, London and New York: Routledge.

Kamen, H. (1993) *The Phoenix and the Flame. Catalonia and the Counter-Reformation*, New Haven and London: Yale University Press.

Kay, D. (1999) 'Who says miracles are past? Some Jacobean marvels and the margins of the unknown', in P.G. Platt (ed.), *Wonders, Marvels and Monsters in Early Modern Culture*, Newark and London: University of Delaware Press, 76–104.

Kee, H. (1983) *Miracle in the Early Christian World. A Study in Sociohistorical Method*, New Haven: Yale University Press.

Keeble, N.H. (2002) 'To be a pilgrim: constructing the Protestant life in early modern England', in C. Morris and P. Roberts (eds), *Pilgrimage: The English Experience from Becket to Bunyan*, Cambridge: Cambridge University Press, 238–56.

Kelley, D. and Sachs, D. (eds) (1997) *The Historical Imagination in Early Modern Britain*, Cambridge: Cambridge University Press.

Kern, E. (1994) 'Counter Reformation sanctity: the Bollandists 'Vita' of Blessed Hemma of Gurk', *Journal of Ecclesiastical History*, 45: 412–34.

Kieckhefer, R. (1994a) 'The holy and the unholy: sainthood, witchcraft and magic in late medieval Europe', *Journal of Medieval and Renaissance Studies*, 24: 355–85.

—— (1994b) 'The specific rationality of medieval magic', *American Historical Review*, 99: 813–36.

—— (2000) *Magic in the Middle Ages*, Cambridge: Canto.

King, J.N. (1966–67) 'Freedom of the press, Protestant propaganda and Protector Somerset', *Huntingdon Library Quarterly*, 40: 1–10.

—— (1982) *English Reformation Literature. The Tudor Origins of the Protestant Tradition*, Princeton: Princeton University Press.

—— (1989) *Tudor Royal Iconography: Literature and Art in an Age of Religious Crisis*, Princeton: Princeton University Press.

Kingsford, C. (1962) *English Historical Literature in the Fifteenth Century*, New York: Burt Franklin.

Klaniczay, G. (1990a) *The Uses of Supernatural Power: The Transformation of Popular Religion in Medieval and Early-Modern Europe*, trans. S. Singerman, Cambridge: Polity.

—— (1990b) 'Hungary: The accusations and the universe of popular magic', in B. Ankarloo and G. Hennigsen (eds), *Early Modern European Witchcraft. Centres and Peripheries*, Oxford: Clarendon Press, 219–56.

—— (1997) 'Miraculum und Maleficium: Reflections concerning late medieval female sainthood', in R. Po Chia Hsia and R.W. Scribner (eds), *Problems in the Historical Anthropology of Early Modern Europe*, Wiesbaden: Harrassowitz, 49–74.

Klauser, T. (1969) *A Short History of the Western Liturgy: An Account and Some Reflections*, London: OUP.

Kleinberg, A.M. (1989) 'Proving sanctity: selection and authentication of saints in the later middle ages', *Viator*, 20: 183–206.

—— (1992) *Prophets in their Own Country. Living Saints and the Making of Sainthood in the later Middle Ages*, Chicago and London: University of Chicago Press.

Knapp, D. (1972) 'The Relyk of A Seint: a gloss on Chaucer's Pilgrimage', *Journal of English Literary History*, 39: 1–26.

Knott, J.R. (1993) *Discourses of Martyrdom in English Literature 1563–1694*, Cambridge: Cambridge University Press.

Knowles, D. (1940) *The Monastic Order in England*, Cambridge: Cambridge University Press.

—— (1970) *Thomas Becket*, London: A & C Black.

Knox, R. and Leslie, S. (eds) (1923) *The Miracles of Henry VI*, Cambridge: Cambridge University Press.

Koebner, R. (1953) '"The imperial crown of this realm": Henry VIII, Constantine the Great and Polydore Vergil', *Bulletin of the Institute of Historical Research*, 26: 29–52.

Kolb, R. (1987) *For All the Saints: Changing Perceptions of Martyrdom and Sainthood in the Lutheran Reformation*, Macon, GA: Mercer.

Kumin, B. (1996) *The Shaping of a Community: The Rise and Reformation of the English Parish*, c. 1400–1650, Aldershot: Scolar Press.

Lehmberg, S. (1970) *The Reformation Parliament 1529–1536*, Cambridge: Cambridge University Press.

Levin, C. (1980) 'A good prince. King John and early Tudor propaganda', *Sixteenth Century Journal*, 11: 23–32.

—— (1988) *Propaganda in the English Reformation. Heroic and Villainous Images of King John*, Lewiston & Queenston: Edwin Mellon.

Levine, J.M. (1987a) *Humanism and History. Origins of Modern English Historiography*, Ithaca and London: Cornell University Press.

—— (1987b) *Caxton's Histories. Fact and Fiction at the Close of the Middle Ages in Humanism and History*, Ithaca: Cornell University Press.

—— (1997) 'Thomas More and the English Renaissance: history and fiction in *Utopia*', in D. Kelley and D. Sachs (eds), *The Historical Imagination in Early Modern Britain*, Cambridge: Cambridge University Press, 69–92.

Levy, F.J. (1961) 'The Elizabethan historiographical revolution', *History*, 4: 25–52.

—— (1967) *Tudor Historical Thought*, San Marino: Huntingdon Library.

Lewis, L.S. (1985) *Glastonbury, the Mother of Saints: Her saints AD37–1539*, Wellingborough.

Lifshitz, F. (1994) 'Beyond positivism and genre: "hagiographical" texts as historical narrative', *Viator*, 25: 95–113.

Little, L. (1993) *Benedictine Maledictions. Liturgical Cursing in Romanesque France*, Ithaca and London: Cornell University Press.

Litzenberger, C. (1997) *The English Reformation and the Laity: Gloucestershire 1540–1580*, Cambridge: Cambridge University Press.

Lloyd, C.H. (1825) *Formularies of Faith Put Forth by Authority During the Reign of Henry VIII*, Oxford: Clarendon Press.

Loach, J. (1975) 'Pamphlets and politics 1553–1558', *Bulletin of the Institute of Historical Research*, 48: 31–44.

Loades, D.M. (1964) 'The press under the Tudors. A study in censorship and sedition', *Transactions of the Cambridge Bibliographical Society*, 4: 29–50.

—— (1997) *John Foxe and the English Reformation*, Aldershot: Scolar Press.

Lock, J. (1996) 'Plantagenets against the papacy: Protestant England's search for royal heroes', in B. Gordon (ed.), *Protestant History and Identity in Sixteenth Century Europe*, vol. 1, Aldershot: Ashgate, 153–73.

Luard, H.R. (1879) 'A letter from Bale to Archbishop Parker', *Cambridge Antiquarian Communications*, 3: 157–73.

McClendon, M. (1999) 'A moveable feast: Saint George's Day celebrations and religious change in early modern England', *Journal of British Studies*, 38: 1–27.

McCready, W.D. (1994) *Miracles and the Venerable Bede*, Toronto: Pontifical Institute of Medieval Studies.

MacCulloch, D. (1986) *Suffolk and the Tudors. Politics and Religion in an English County 1500–1600*, Oxford: Clarendon Press.

—— (1991) 'The myth of the English Reformation', *Journal of British Studies*, 30: 1–19.

—— (1996) *Thomas Cranmer*, New Haven and London: Yale University Press.

—— (1999) *The Tudor Church Militant. Edward VI and the Protestant Reformation*, London: Allen Lane.

McCulloh, J.M. (1975) 'The cult of relics in the letters and dialogues of Pope Gregory the Great, a lexicographical study', *Traditio*, 32: 145–84.

McCusker, H. (1936) 'Books and manuscripts formerly in the possession of John Bale', *The Library*, 4th series, 19: 144–65.

—— (1942) *John Bale: Dramatist and Antiquary*, Pennsylvania: Bryn Mawr.

McCutcheon, R.R. (1991) 'The *Responsio ad Lutherum:* Thomas More's inchoate Dialogue with Heresy', *Sixteenth Century Journal*, 22: 77–90.

McHardy, A.K. (1972) 'Bishop Buckingham and the Lollards of the Lincoln Diocese', in *Studies in Church History*, London: Cambridge University Press, 9: 131–46.

McKenna, J.W. (1974) 'Piety and propaganda: The cult of Henry VI', in B. Rowland (ed.), *Chaucer and Middle English Studies*, London: Allen and Unwin, 72–88.

McKisack, M. (1971) *Medieval History in the Tudor Age*, Oxford: Clarendon Press.

MacLure, P. (1958) *The Paul's Cross Sermon 1534–1642*, Oxford: OUP.

—— (1989) *Register of Sermons Preached at Pauls' Cross 1534–1642*, revised and expanded by P. Pauls and J.C. Boswel, Ottawa: Centre for Reformation and Renaissance Studies.

MacMullen, R. (1983) 'Two types of conversion to Christianity', *Vigiliae Christianae*, 37: 174–92.

MacNeill, J.T. and Gamer, H.M. (1990) *Medieval Handbooks of Penance. A Translation of the Principal "libri poenitentiales" and Selections from Related Documents*, New York: Columbia.

Malowinski, B. (1948) *Magic, Science and Religion and Other Essays*, Boston, MA: Beacon Press

Marc'hadour, G. (1994) 'The confrontation between Thomas Becket and Henry II as a historical paradigm', *Cahier civilis mediéval*, 37: 101–10.

Marsh, C. (1998) *Popular Religion in Sixteenth Century England: Holding Their Peace*, Basingstoke: Macmillan.

Marshall, P. (1995) 'The rood of Boxley, the blood of Hailes, and the defence of the Henrician Settlement', *Journal of Ecclesiastical History*, 46: 689–96.

—— (1996) 'The debate over "unwritten verities" in early Reformation England', in B. Gordon (ed.), *Protestant History and Identity in Sixteenth Century Europe*, 2 vols, Aldershot: Scolar Press, 60–77.

—— (1997) *The Impact of the English Reformation 1500–1640*, London: Arnold.

—— (2001) 'The other black legend: the Henrician Reformation and the Spanish people', *English Historical Review*, 116: 31–49.

—— (2003) 'Forgery and miracles in the reign of Henry VIII', *Past and Present*, 178: 39–73.

Mason, A.J. (1920) *What Became of the Bones of Thomas Becket?* Cambridge: Cambridge University Press.

Mason, R. (1997) '"Useable pasts": history and identity in Reformation Scotland', *Scottish Historical Review*, 76: 54–68.

Mecklin, J.M. (1941) *The Passing of the Saint: A Study of a Cultural Type*, Chicago: University of Chicago Press.

Merkel, I. and Debus, A.G. (1988) *Hermeticism and the Renaissance. Intellectual History and the Occult in Early Modern Europe*, Washington: Folger Shakespeare Library.

Messenger, E. (1936) *The Reformation, the Mass and the Priesthood. A Documented History with Special Reference to the Questions of Anglican Orders*, 2 vols, London: Longmans.

Milman, H.H. (1867) *History of Latin Christianity Including that of the Popes to the Pontificate of Nicholas I*, 9 vols, London: John Murray.

Mommsen, T.E. and Morrison, K.F. (eds) (1962) *Imperial Lives and Letters of the Eleventh Century*, New York: Columbia University Press.

Morris, C. (1972) 'A criticism of popular religion: Guibert of Nogent on *The Relics of the Saints*', in G.J. Cuming and D. Baker (eds), *Popular Belief and Practice: Papers read at the Ninth Summer Meeting and the Tenth Winter Meeting of the Ecclesiastical History Society* (Studies in Church History, vol. 8), Cambridge: Cambridge University Press.

Morris, C. and Roberts, P. (eds) (2002) *Pilgrimage: The English Experience from Becket to Bunyan*, Cambridge: Cambridge University Press.

Mozley, J.F. (1940) *John Foxe and His Book*, London: SPCK.

Moyes, J. (1894) 'Warham: An English primate on the eve of the Reformation, *Dublin Review*, 114: 390–420.

Muchembled, R. (1982) 'Witchcraft, popular culture and Christianity in the sixteenth century, with an emphasis on Flanders and Artois', in R. Forster and O. Ranum (eds), *Ritual, Religion and the Sacred. Selections from the Annales*, Baltimore and London: Johns Hopkins University Press, 213–36.

Muller, J.A. (1933) *Letters of Stephen Gardiner*, Cambridge: Cambridge University Press.

Mullin, R. (1979) *Miracles and Magic. The Miracles and Spells of Saints and Witches*, London and Oxford: Mowbrays.

Murray, A. (1992) 'Missionaries and magic in dark age Europe', *Past and Present*, 136: 186–205.

Myers, R. and Harris, M. (eds) (1990) *Spreading the Word: The Distribution Networks of Print, 1550–1850*, Winchester: St Paul's.

Neame, A. (1971) *The Holy Maid of Kent. The Life of Elizabeth Barton, 1506–1534*, London: Hodder and Stoughton.

Nelson, W. (1973) *Fact or Fiction: The Dilemma of the Renaissance Storyteller*, Cambridge, MA: Harvard University Press.

Nilson, B. (1998) *The Cathedral Shrines of Medieval England*, Woodbridge: Boydell.

Northeast, P. (1993) 'Superstition and belief: a Suffolk case of the fifteenth century', *Suffolk Review*, 20: 43–6.

Nussbaum, D. (1998) '"Reviling the saints or reforming the calendar?": John Foxe and his "kalendar" of marytrs', in S. Wabuda and C. Litzenberger (eds), *Belief and Practice in Reformation England. A Tribute to Patrick Collinson from his Students*, Aldershot: Ashgate, 113–36.

Oates, J.C. (1958) 'Robert Pynson and the Holy Blood of Hayles', *The Library*, 5th series, 13: 269–77.

Oldoni, M. (1977) 'Gerberto e la sua Storia', *Studi Medievali*, 3rd series, 18: 629–704.

—— (1980) 'A fantasia dicitur fantasma (Gerberto e la sua storia, II), parte prima', *Studi medievali*, 21: 493–622.

—— (1983) 'A fantasia dicitur fantasma (Gerberto e la sua storia, II), parte seconda', *Studi medievali*, 24: 167–245.

Olsen, A. (1980) 'De Historiis Sanctorum: A generic study of hagiography', *Genre*, 13: 407–29.

Omar, C.W.C. (1921) 'Some medieval conceptions of ancient history', *Transactions of the Royal Historical Society*, 4th series 4: 1–22.

Otter, M. (1996) *Inventiones. Fiction and Referentiality in Twelfth Century English Historical Writing*, Chapel Hill: University of North Carolina Press.

Owst, G. (1965) *Literature and Pulpit in Medieval England*, 2nd edn, Cambridge: Cambridge University Press.

Page, W. (ed.) (1973) *The Victoria County History of the County of Sussex*, vol. II, Woodbridge: Boydell.

Palmieri, A. (1923) 'The Bollandists', *Catholic Historical Review*, 3: 341–57.

Parish, H.L. (2000a) *Clerical Marriage and the English Reformation. Precedent Policy and Practice*, Aldershot: Ashgate.

—— (2000b) '"Then May the Deuyls of Hell be Sayntes Also": the medieval Church in sixteenth-century England', *Reformation*, 4: 71–92.

—— (2001) 'Impudent and abhominable fictions: rewriting saints' lives in the English Reformation', *Sixteenth Century Journal*, 32: 45–65.

—— (2002) 'Lying histories fayning false miracles: magic, miracles and medieval history in Reformation polemic', *Reformation and Renaissance Review*, 4: 230–40.

—— (2003) 'Monks, miracles and magic: the medieval Church in English Reformation polemic', *Reformation*, 8: 117–42.

Parish, H.L. and Naphy, W.G. (eds) (2003) *Religion and Superstition in Reformation Europe*, Manchester: MUP.

Parry, G. (1997) 'John Foxe, "Father of Lyes", and the Papists', in J. Loades (ed.), *John Foxe and the English Reformation*, Aldershot: Scolar Press, 295–305.

Passini, F. (1996) 'Did Henry II order the murder of Thomas Becket?', *Historia*, 592.

Patrides, C.A. and Wittreich, J. (eds) (1984) *The Apocalypse in English Renaissance Thought and Literature. Patterns, Antecedents and Reprecussions*, Manchester: MUP.

Pelikan, J. (1964) *Obedient Rebels: Catholic Substance and Protestant Principle in Luther's Reformation*, London: SCM Press.

—— (1984) 'Some uses of the Apocalypse in the magisterial reformers', in C.A. Patrides and J. Wittreich (eds), *The Apocalypse in English Renaissance Thought and Literature. Patterns, Antecedents and Repercussions*, Manchester: MUP.

Pearce, E.C. (1925) 'Matthew Parker', *The Library*, 4th series, 6: 209–28.

Pettegree, A. (1992) 'Rewriting the English Reformation', *Nederlands Archief voor Kerkgeschiedenis*, 72: 37–58.

Phillips, J. (1973) *The Reformation of Images. The Destruction of Art in England, 1535–1660*, Berkeley: University of California Press.

Pineas, R. (1962a) 'William Tyndale's use of history as a weapon of religious controversy', *Harvard Theological Review*, 55: 121–41.

—— (1962b) 'William Tyndale's influence on John Bale's polemical use of history', *Archiv fur Reformationsgeschichte*, 53: 79–96.

—— (1962c) 'William Tyndale's polemical use of the scriptures', *Nederlands Archief voor Kerkesgeschiedenis*, 45: 65–78.

—— (1962d) 'John Bale's nondramatic works of religious controversy', *Studies in the Renaissance*, 9: 218–33.

—— (1962e) 'Thomas Becon as a religious controversialist', *Nederlands Archief voor Kerkesgeschiedenis*, 45: 206–20.

—— (1964) 'Robert Barnes' polemical use of history', *Bibliothèque d' Humanisme et Renaissance*, 26: 55–69.

—— (1968) *Thomas More and Tudor Polemics*, Bloomington and London: Indiana University Press.

—— (1972) 'George Joye's polemical use of history in his controversy with Stephen Gardiner', *Nederlands Archief voor Kerkesgeschiedenis*, 55: 21–31.

—— (1975a) 'George Joye's *Exposicion of Daniel*', *Renaissance Quarterly*, 28: 332–43.

—— (1975b) 'William Turner and Reformation politics', *Bibliothèque d'Humanisme et Renaissance*, 37: 193–200.

—— (1980) 'William Turner's polemical use of ecclesiastical history and his controversy with Stephen Gardiner', *Renaissance Quarterly*, 33: 599–608.

Platelle, H. (1979) 'Le receuil des miracles de Thomas de Cantimpre et la vie religieuse dans le pays-bas et le nord de la France au xiii siècle', *Actes du 97e Congrès des Sociétés Savantes, Nantes, 1992*, Paris: Bibliothèque National, 469–98.

Platt, P.G. (1977) *Reason Diminished. Shakespeare and the Marvelous*, Lincoln and London: University of Nebraska Press.

—— (ed.) (1999) *Wonders, Marvels and Monsters in Early Modern Culture*, Newark and London: University of Delaware Press, 76–104.

Po Chia Hsia, R. and Scribner, R.W. (eds) (1997) *Problems in the Historical Anthropology of Early Modern Europe*, Wiesbaden: Harrassowitz.

Pocock, J.G.A. (1985) 'The sense of history in Renaissance England', in J. Andrews (ed.), *William Shakespeare: His World*, New York: Scribner, 143–57.

Pollen, J.H. (1921) 'Henry VIII and St Thomas Becket', *The Month*, 137: 119–28, 324–33.

Polman, P.L. (1932) *L'élément historique dans la controverse religieuse du XVIe siècle*, Gembloux: J. Duculot.

Pontifex, Dom D. (1933) 'St Dunstan in his first biography', *Downside Review*, 51: 20–40, 309–25.

Potter, J. (1984) *Good King Richard? An Account of Richard III and his Reputation*, London: Constable.

Potter, J.H. (1931) 'Henry VIII and St Thomas Becket', *The Month*, 137: 119–28; 324–33.

Power, P. (1914) *Life of St. Declan of Ardmore … and of St. Mochuda of Lismore*, London: Irish Texts Society.

Preston, J.H. (1971) 'English ecclesiastical historians and the problem of bias, 1559–1742', *Journal of the History of Ideas*, 32: 203–19.

Pythian Adams, C.V. (1972) 'Ceremony and the citizen: The communal year at Coventry, 1450–1550', in P. Clark and P. Slack (eds), *Crisis and Order in English Towns 1500–1700. Essays in Urban History*, London.

—— (1975) *Local History and Folklore. A New Framework*, London: Bedford Square Press.

Ramsay, N. and Sparks, M. (1988) *The Image of St Dunstan*, Canterbury: Dunstan Millennium Committee.

Ramsay, N., Sparks, M. and Tatton-Brown, T. (eds) (1992) *St Dunstan, his Life, Times and Cult*, Woobridge: Boydell.

Reeves, M. (1984) 'The development of apocalyptic thought: medieval attitudes', in C.A. Patrides and J. Wittreich (eds), *The Apocalypse in English Renaissance Thought and Literature. Patterns, Antecedents and Reprecussions*, Manchester: MUP.

Remus, H. (1983) *Pagan Christian Conflict in the Second Century*, Cambridge, MA: Philadelphia Patristic Foundation.

Rex, R. (1989) 'The English campaign against Luther in the 1520s', *TRHS*, 5th series, 39: 85–106.

—— (1991) 'The execution of the Holy Maid of Kent', *Bulletin of the Institute of Historical Research*, 64: 216–20.

—— (1993) *Henry VIII and the English Reformation*, Basingstoke: Macmillan.

Ridley, J. (1962) *Thomas Cranmer*, Oxford: Clarendon Press.

Ridyard, S.J. (1987) '*Condigna Veneratio*: post-conquest attitudes to the saints of the Anglo-Saxons', *Anglo-Norman Studies*, 9: 179–206.

—— (1988) *The Royal Saints of Anglo Saxon England. A Study of West Saxon and East Anglian Cults*, Cambridge: Cambridge University Press.

Robinson, B.S. (1988) '"Darke speech": Matthew Parker and the reforming of history', *Sixteenth Century Journal*, 29: 1061–83.

Robinson, I.S. (1978) *Authority and Resistance in the Investiture Contest: The Polemical Literature of the Late Eleventh Century*, Manchester and New York: MUP.

—— (1990) *The Papacy, 1073–1198. Continuity and Innovation*, Cambridge: Cambridge University Press.

Rollason, D. (1982) *The Mildreth Legend. A Study in Early Medieval Hagiography*, Leicester: Leicester University Press.

—— (1989) *Saints and Relics in Anglo-Saxon England*, Oxford: Blackwell.

Rollo, D. (2000) *Glamorous Sorcery. Magic and Literacy in the High Middle Ages*, University of Minnesota Press.

Rubin, M. (1991) *Corpus Christi. The Eucharist in Medieval Culture*, Cambridge: Cambridge University Press.

Ryan, E.A. (1936) *The Historical Scholarship of Saint Bellarmine*, Louvain: Bureau de Recueil.

Rydberg, V. (1879) *The Magic of the Middle Ages*, trans. A.H. Edgren, New York: H. Holt & Co.

Sabean, D. (1984) *Power in the Blood. Popular Culture and Village Discourse in Early Modern Germany*, Cambridge: Cambridge University Press.

Sacks, D.H. (1986) 'The demise of the martyrs: the feasts of St Clement and St Katherine in Britsol, 1400–1600', *Social History*, 11: 141–69.

Sargent, S.D. (1986) 'Miracle books and pilgrimage shrines in late medieval Bavaria', *Historical Reflections / Reflexions historiques*, 15. 455–71.

Scarisbrick, J.J. (1984) *The Reformation and the English People*, Oxford: Clarendon Press.

Schoedel, W.R. and Malina, B.J. (1986) 'Miracle or magic?', *Religious Studies Review*, 12: 31–42.

Scribner, R.W. (1987) *Popular Culture and Popular Movement in Reformation Germany*, London and Ronceverte: Hambledon.

—— (1990) 'Witchcraft and judgement in Reformation Germany', *History Today*, 40: 12–19.

—— (1997) 'Reformation and desacralisation: from sacramental world to moralised universe', in R.W. Scribner and R. Po Chia Hsia (eds), *Problems in the Historical Anthropology of Early Modern Europe*: 75–92.

Scully, R.E. (2002) 'The unmaking of a saint: Thomas Becket and the English Reformation', *Catholic Historical Review*, 86: 579–602.

Seboldt, R.F. (1946) 'A fifteenth century edition of the *Legenda Aurea*', *Speculum*, 21: 327–38.

Shagan, E. (2001) 'Print, orality and communications in the Maid of Kent affair', *Journal of Ecclesiastical History*, 52: 21–33.

—— (2003) *Popular Politics and the English Reformation*, Cambridge: Cambridge University Press.

Sheppard, J.B. (ed.) (1877) *Christ Church Letters. A Volume of Medieval Letters Relating to the Affairs of the Priory of Christ Church, Canterbury*, London: Camden Society.

Sigal, P. (1974) *Les marcheurs de Dieu. Pélerinage et pélerins au moyen age*, Paris: Armand Colin.

Simpson, W. (1874) 'On pilgrimage to Bromholm in Norfolk', *Journal of the British Archaeological Association*, 30: 52–9.

Sluhovsky, M. (1995) 'Calvinist miracles and the concept of the miraculous in sixteenth-century Huguenot thought', *Renaissance and Reformation*, 19: 5–25.

Smallwood, T.M. (1985) 'The prophecy of the six kings', *Speculum*, 60: 571–92.

Soergel, P.M. (1993) *Wondrous in his Saints. Counter-Reformation Propaganda in Bavaria*, Berkeley, LA and London: University of California Press.

Sorokin, P. (1950) *Altruistic Love*, Boston: Beacon Press.

Southern, R.W. (1962) *The Life of St Anselm, Archbishop of Canterbury by Eadmer*, Oxford: Clarendon Press.

—— (1963) *Saint Anselm and his Biographer. A Study of Monastic Life and Thought c. 1059–1130*, Cambridge: Cambridge University Press.

Southgate, W.M. (1962) *John Jewel and the Problem of Doctrinal Authority*, Cambridge, MA: Harvard University Press.

Sox, D. (1985) *Relics and Shrines*, London: Allen and Unwin.

Spencer, B. (1978) 'King Henry of Windsor and the London pilgrim', in J. Bird, H. Clapman and J. Clark (eds), *Collectanea Londoniensa*, London: London and Middlesex Archaeological Society Special Papers.

Spufford, M. (1981) *Small Books and Pleasant Histories, Popular Fiction and its Readership in Seventeenth-Century England*, London: Methuen.

Stancliffe, C. (1990) *St. Martin and his Hagiographer: History and Miracle in Sulpicius Severus*, Oxford: Clarendon Press.

Stanley, D. (1928) *Thomas Becket*, London and Edinburgh: Thomas Nelson.

Sumption, J. (1975) *Pilgrimage. An Image of Medieval Religion*, London: Faber.

Talbot, C.H. (1954) *The Anglo-Saxon Missionaries in Germany being the lives of SS. Willibrord, Boniface, Sturm, Leoba and Lebuin, together with the Hodeporicon of St. Willibald and a Selection from the Correspondence of St. Boniface*, London: Sheed and Ward.

Tanner, N.P. (1977) *Heresy Trials in the Diocese of Norwich*, London: Camden Society.

Tavard, C.H. (1959) *Holy Writ or Holy Church. The Crisis of the Protestant Reformation*, London: Burns and Oates.

Thacker, A. (1992) 'Cults at Canterbury: relics and reform under Dunstan and his successors', in N. Ramsay, M. Sparks and T. Tatton-Brown (eds), *St Dunstan, His Life, Times, and Cult*, Woodbridge: Boydell.

Thomas, K. (1975) 'An anthropology of religion and magic, II', *Journal of Interdisciplinary History*, 6: 91–109.

—— (1984) *The Perception of the Past in Early Modern England*, London: Creighton Trust Lecture, University of London.

—— (1991) *Religion and the Decline of Magic*, London: Penguin.

Thomson, J. (1965) *The Later Lollards, 1414–1520*, Oxford: OUP.

Thomson, R. (1987) *William of Malmesbury*, Woodbridge: Boydell.

Thorndike, L. (1923–58) *A History of Magic and Experimental Science*, 8 vols, New York.

Tyacke, N. (ed.) (1998) *England's Long Reformation, 1500–1800*, London: UCL Press.

Ullmann, W. (1962) *The Growth of Papal Government in the Middle Ages*, London: Methuen.

Urlin, E.L. (1915) *Festivals, Holy Days and Saints days. A Study in the Origins and Survivals in Church Ceremonies and Secular Customs*, London: Simpkin, Marshall, Hamilton, Kent & Co.

Van Engen, J.A. (1986) 'The Christian Middle Ages as an historiographical problem', *American Historical Review*, 91: 519–52.

Vauchez, A. (1997) *Sainthood in the Later Middle Ages*, trans. J. Birrell, Cambridge: Cambridge University Press.

Vitz, E.B. (1991) 'From the oral to the written in Medieval and Renaissance saints lives', in R. Blumenfeld-Kosinksi and T. Szell (eds), *Images of Sainthood in Medieval Europe*, Ithaca and London: Cornell University Press.

Vogler, B. (1972) 'La réforme et le concept de miracle au XVIeme siècle', *Revue de l'histoire de la spiritualité*, 48.

Wabuda, S. (1993) 'Equivocation and recantation during the English Reformation: the "subtle shadows" of Dr Edward Crome', *Journal of Ecclesiastical History*, 44: 224–42.

Walker, D.P. (1988) 'The cessation of miracles', in I. Merkel and A.G. Debus (eds), *Hermeticism and the Renaissance. Intellectual History and the Occult in Early Modern Europe*, Washington: Folger Shakespeare Library, 111–24.

Walker, G. (1989) 'Saint or schemer? The 1527 heresy trial of Thomas Bilney reconsidered', *Journal of Ecclesiastical History*, 40: 219–48.

Walker, S. (1995) 'Political saints in later medieval England', in R.H. Britnell and A.J. Pollard (eds), *The Macfarlane Legacy. Studies in Late Medieval Politics and Society*, Stroud: Alan Sutton.

Walker Bynum, C. (1987) *Holy Feast and Holy Fast. The Religious Significance of Food to Medieval Women*, Berkeley and London: University of California Press.

Wall, J.C. (1905) *The Shrines of British Saints*, London: Methuen.

Walsham, A. (1993) *Church Papists: Catholicism, Conformity and Confessional Polemic in Early Modern England*, Woodbridge: Boydell.

—— (1994) 'The "Fatall vesper": providentialism and anti-popery in late Jacobean London', *Past and Present*, 144: 36–87.

—— (1999) *Providence in Early Modern England*, Oxford: OUP.

—— (2004) 'Miracles and the counter-Reformation mission to England', *Historical Journal*, 46: 779–816.

Ward, B. (1987) *Miracles and the Medieval Mind. Theory, Record and Event, 1000–1215*, Aldershot: Scolar Press.

Warren, W.L. (1973) *Henry II*, London: Eyre Methuen.

Watt, D. (1996) 'The posthumous reputation of the Holy Maid of Kent', *Recusant History*, 23: 148–58.

Watt, T. (1991) *Cheap Print and Popular Piety, 1550–1640*, Cambridge: Cambridge University Press.

Watts, J.L. (ed.) (1998) *The End of the Middle Ages? England in the Fifteenth and Sixteenth Centuries*, Stroud: Sutton.

Webb, D. (2002) *Medieval European Pilgrimage, c. 700–1500*, Basingstoke: Palgrave.

Webster, C. (1995) 'Paracelsus confronts the saints: miracles, healing and the secularization of magic', *Social History of Medicine*, 8: 403–21.

Weinstein, D. and Bell, R. (1982) *Saints and Society. The Two Worlds of Western Christendom 1000–1700*, Chicago and London.

Weiss, J.M. (1985a) 'Luther and his colleagues on the lives of the saints', *Harvard Library Bulletin*, 33: 174–95.

—— (1985b) 'Historiography by German humanists, 1483–1516', *Journal of Medieval and Renaissance Studies*, 15: 299–316.

White, H. (1963) *Tudor Books of Saints and Martyrs*, Madison: University of Wisconsin Press.

Whiting, R. (1982) 'Abominable idols. Images and image breaking under Henry VIII', *Journal of Ecclesiastical History*, 33: 30–47.

—— (1998a) *Local Responses to the English Reformation*, Basingstoke: Macmillan.

—— (1998b) *Reformation*, Cambridge: Cambridge University Press.

Wilken, R. (1971) *The Myth of Christian Beginnings*, Notre Dame, Indiana: University of Notre Dame Press.

Williams, G. (1970) *Reformation Views of Church History*, London: Lutterworth.

—— (1976) *The Welsh Church from Conquest to Reformation*, Cardiff: University of Wales Press.

Wills, G. (1985) *Witches and Jesuits. Shakespeare's Macbeth*, Oxford: OUP.

Wilson, S. (1983) *Saints and their Cults, Studies in Religious Sociology, Folklore and History,* Cambridge: Cambridge University Press.

—— (2000) *The Magical Universe. Everyday Ritual and Magic in Pre-Modern Europe,* London: Hambledon.

Winstead, K.A. (1997) *Virgin Martyrs. Legends of Sainthood in Late Medieval England,* Ithaca and London: Cornell University Press.

Winston, R. (1967) *Thomas Becket,* London: Constable.

Wood, C.T. (ed.) (1967) *Philip the Fair and Boniface VIII: State vs Papacy,* London and New York: Holt, Rinehart and Winston.

Wooden, W.W. (1983) *John Foxe,* Boston: Twayne Publishers.

Wooding, L.E.C. (2000) *Rethinking Catholicism in Reformation England,* Oxford: OUP.

Woodruff, C.E. (1932) 'The financial aspect of the cult of St Thomas of Canterbury', *Archaeologia Cantiana,* xliv: 13–22.

Woodward, K.L. (1996) *Making Saints,* New York: Simon and Schuster.

Woolf, D. (1990) *The Idea of History in Early Stuart England. Erudition, Ideology and 'The Light of Truth' from the Accession of James I to the Civil War,* Toronto and London: University of Toronto Press.

—— (2000) *Reading History in Early Modern England,* Cambridge: Cambridge University Press.

—— (2003) *The Social Circulation of the Past: English Historical Culture, 1500–1730,* Oxford: OUP.

Wright, A.D. (1975) 'The people of Catholic Europe and the people of Anglican England', *Historical Journal,* 18: 451–66.

Wright, C.E. (1951) 'The dispersal of the monastic libraries and the beginnings of Anglo-Saxon studies. Matthew Parker and his circle', *Transactions of the Cambridge Bibliographical Society,* 1: 208–37.

INDEX

Page numbers in *italics* indicate illustrations